HERODOTUS

Born about 484 B.C. at Halicarnassus. Travelled
extensively throughout the known world. Went
to Athens about 447. Assisted in the foundation
of Thurii, of which he became a citizen, and
died there about 424 B.C.

The Histories of Herodotus

IN TWO VOLUMES   VOLUME TWO

TRANSLATED BY
GEORGE RAWLINSON

EDITED BY
E. H. BLAKENEY, M.A.

INTRODUCTION BY
JOHN WARRINGTON

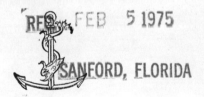

DENT: LONDON
EVERYMAN'S LIBRARY
DUTTON: NEW YORK

© Introduction, J. M. Dent & Sons Ltd, 1964
Made in Great Britain
at the
Aldine Press · Letchworth · Herts
for
J. M. DENT & SONS LTD
Aldine House · Bedford Street · London
First included in Everyman's Library 1910
Last reprinted 1970

NO. 406

ISBN: 0 460 00406 9

CONTENTS

THE FIFTH BOOK, ENTITLED TERPSICHORE

THE SIXTH BOOK, ENTITLED ERATO

THE SEVENTH BOOK, ENTITLED POLYMNIA

Contents

THE EIGHTH BOOK, ENTITLED URANIA

THE NINTH BOOK, ENTITLED CALLIOPÉ

Contents

THE FIFTH BOOK, ENTITLED TERPSICHORE

1. THE Persians left behind by King Darius in Europe, who had Megabazus for their general,[1] reduced, before any other Hellespontine state, the people of Perinthus,[2] who had no mind to become subjects of the king. Now the Perinthians had ere this been roughly handled by another nation, the Pæonians. For the Pæonians from about the Strymon were once bidden by an oracle to make war upon the Perinthians, and if these latter, when the camps faced one another, challenged them by name to fight, then to venture on a battle, but if otherwise, not to make the hazard. The Pæonians followed the advice. Now the men of Perinthus drew out to meet them in the skirts of their city; and a threefold single combat was fought on challenge given. Man to man, and horse to horse, and dog to dog, was the strife waged; and the Perinthians, winners of two combats out of the three, in their joy had raised the pæan; when the Pæonians, struck by the thought that this was what the oracle had meant, passed the word one to another, saying, "Now of a surety has the oracle been fulfilled for us; now our work begins." Then the Pæonians set upon the Perinthians in the midst of their pæan, and defeated them utterly, leaving but few of them alive.

2. Such was the affair of the Pæonians, which happened a long time previously. At this time the Perinthians, after a brave struggle for freedom, were overcome by numbers, and yielded to Megabazus and his Persians. After Perinthus had been brought under, Megabazus led his host through Thrace, subduing to the dominion of the king all the towns and all the nations of those parts.[3] For the king's command to him was, that he should conquer Thrace.

[1] Vide supra, iv. 143.

[2] The modern *Erekli*, a place of some consequence on the sea of Marmora.

[3] The conquests of Megabazus were confined to the tracts along the coast.

3. The Thracians are the most powerful people in the world, except, of course, the Indians;[1] and if they had one head, or were agreed among themselves, it is my belief that their match could not be found anywhere, and that they would very far surpass all other nations. But such union is impossible for them, and there are no means of ever bringing it about. Herein therefore consists their weakness. The Thracians bear many names in the different regions of their country, but all of them have like usages in every respect, excepting only the Getæ,[2] the Trausi, and those who dwell above the people of Creston.[3]

4. Now the manners and customs of the Getæ, who believe in their immortality, I have already spoken of.[4] The Trausi in all else resemble the other Thracians, but have customs at births and deaths which I will now describe. When a child is born all its kindred sit round about it in a circle and weep for the woes it will have to undergo now that it is come into the world, making mention of every ill that falls to the lot of humankind; when, on the other hand, a man has died, they bury him with laughter and rejoicings, and say that now he is free from a host of sufferings, and enjoys the completest happiness.

5. The Thracians who live above the Crestonæans observe the following customs. Each man among them has several wives; and no sooner does a man die than a sharp contest ensues among the wives upon the question, which of them all the husband loved most tenderly; the friends of each eagerly plead on her behalf, and she to whom the honour is adjudged, after receiving the praises both of men and women, is slain over the grave by the hand of her next of kin, and then buried with her husband. The others are sorely grieved, for nothing is considered such a disgrace.[5]

6. The Thracians who do not belong to these tribes have the customs which follow. They sell their children to traders. On their maidens they keep no watch, but leave them altogether free, while on the conduct of their wives they keep a most strict watch. Brides are purchased of their parents for large sums of money. Tattooing among them marks noble birth, and the want of it low birth. To be idle is accounted the most honourable thing, and to be a tiller of the ground the most dishonourable.

[1] Alluding to what he had said before (Bk. iii. ch. 94).
[2] Concerning the Getæ, vide supra, Bk. iv. ch. 93.
[3] Concerning Creston, vide supra, i. 57.
[4] Supra, iv. 94.
[5] [Analogous to this custom is the Indian *Suttee*, in which two distinct motives were combined: Lyall, *Asiatic Studies*, vol. ii. p. 313.—E. H. B.]

To live by war and plunder is of all things the most glorious.
These are the most remarkable of their customs.

7. The gods which they worship are but three, Mars, Bacchus,
and Dian.[1] Their kings, however, unlike the rest of the citizens,
worship Mercury more than any other god, always swearing
by his name, and declaring that they are themselves sprung
from him.

8. Their wealthy ones are buried in the following fashion.
The body is laid out for three days; and during this time they
kill victims of all kinds, and feast upon them, after first bewail-
ing the departed. Then they either burn the body [2] or else bury
it in the ground. Lastly, they raise a mound over the grave,
and hold games of all sorts, wherein the single combat is awarded
the highest prize. Such is the mode of burial among the
Thracians.

9. As regards the region lying north of this country no one
can say with any certainty what men inhabit it. It appears
that you no sooner cross the Ister than you enter on an inter-
minable wilderness.[3] The only people of whom I can hear as
dwelling beyond the Ister are the race named Sigynnæ, who
wear, they say, a dress like the Medes, and have horses which
are covered entirely with a coat of shaggy hair, five fingers in
length. They are a small breed, flat-nosed, and not strong
enough to bear men on their backs; but when yoked to chariots,
they are among the swiftest known, which is the reason why
the people of that country use chariots. Their borders reach
down almost to the Eneti upon the Adriatic Sea, and they call
themselves colonists of the Medes; but how they can be colonists
of the Medes I for my part cannot imagine. Still nothing is
impossible in the long lapse of ages. Sigynnæ is the name
which the Ligurians who dwell above Massilia [4] give to traders,
while among the Cyprians the word means spears.

10. According to the account which the Thracians give, the
country beyond the Ister is possessed by bees, on account of
which it is impossible to penetrate farther.[5] But in this they
seem to me to say what has no likelihood; for it is certain that

[1] War, drinking, and the chase—the principal delights of a nation in the
condition of the Thracians—had, it would seem, their respective deities,
which the Greeks identified with their Ares, Dionysus, and Artemis.

[2] Cremation was the mode in which the Indo-European nations most
usually disposed of their dead. [So in Homer; but inhumation was normal
in the Mycenæan age in Greece.—E. H. B.]

[3] Hungary and Austria.

[4] The modern Marseilles.   [5] Mosquitoes.

those creatures are very impatient of cold. I rather believe
that it is on account of the cold that the regions which lie under
the Bear are without inhabitants. Such then are the accounts
given of this country, the sea-coast whereof Megabazus was now
employed in subjecting to the Persians.

11. King Darius had no sooner crossed the Hellespont and
reached Sardis, than he bethought himself of the good deed of
Histiæus the Milesian,[1] and the good counsel of the Mytilenean
Coës.[2] He therefore sent for both of them to Sardis, and bade
them each crave a boon at his hands. Now Histiæus, as he was
already king of Miletus, did not make request for any government besides, but asked Darius to give him Myrcinus of the
Edonians, where he wished to build him a city. Such was the
choice that Histiæus made. Coës, on the other hand, as he was
a mere burgher, and not a king, requested the sovereignty of
Mytilênê. Both alike obtained their requests, and straightway
betook themselves to the places which they had chosen.

12. It chanced in the meantime that King Darius saw a sight
which determined him to bid Megabazus remove the Pæonians
from their seats in Europe and transport them to Asia. There
were two Pæonians, Pigres and Mantyes, whose ambition it was
to obtain the sovereignty over their countrymen. As soon
therefore as ever Darius crossed into Asia, these men came to
Sardis, and brought with them their sister, who was a tall and
beautiful woman. Having so done, they waited till a day came
when the king sat in state in the suburb of the Lydians; and
then dressing their sister in the richest gear they could, sent her
to draw water for them. She bore a pitcher upon her head, and
with one arm led a horse, while all the way as she went she span
flax. Now as she passed by where the king was, Darius took
notice of her; for it was neither like the Persians nor the Lydians,
nor any of the dwellers in Asia, to do as she did. Darius accordingly noted her, and ordered some of his guard to follow her
steps, and watch to see what she would do with the horse. So
the spearmen went; and the woman, when she came to the
river, first watered the horse, and then filling the pitcher, came
back the same way she had gone, with the pitcher of water upon
her head, and the horse dragging upon her arm, while she still
kept twirling the spindle.

13. King Darius was full of wonder both at what they who
had watched the woman told him, and at what he had himself

[1] Supra, iv. 137.   [2] Supra, iv. 97.

seen. So he commanded that she should be brought before him.
And the woman came; and with her appeared her brothers, who
had been watching everything a little way off. Then Darius
asked them of what nation the woman was; and the young
men replied that they were Pæonians, and she was their sister.
Darius rejoined by asking, " Who the Pæonians were, and in
what part of the world they lived? and, further, what business
had brought the young men to Sardis? " Then the brothers
told him they had come to put themselves under his power, and
Pæonia was a country upon the river Strymon, and the Strymon
was at no great distance from the Hellespont. The Pæonians,
they said, were colonists of the Teucrians from Troy. When
they had thus answered his questions, Darius asked if all the
women of their country worked so hard? Then the brothers
eagerly answered, Yes; for this was the very object with which
the whole thing had been done.

14. So Darius wrote letters to Megabazus, the commander
whom he had left behind in Thrace,[1] and ordered him to remove
the Pæonians from their own land, and bring them into his
presence, men, women, and children. And straightway a horseman took the message, and rode at speed to the Hellespont;
and, crossing it, gave the paper to Megabazus. Then Megabazus, as soon as he had read it, and procured guides from
Thrace, made war upon Pæonia.

15. Now when the Pæonians heard that the Persians were
marching against them, they gathered themselves together, and
marched down to the sea-coast, since they thought the Persians
would endeavour to enter their country on that side. Here then
they stood in readiness to oppose the army of Megabazus. But
the Persians, who knew that they had collected, and were gone
to keep guard at the pass near the sea, got guides, and taking
the inland route before the Pæonians were aware, poured down
upon their cities, from which the men had all marched out; and
finding them empty, easily got possession of them. Then the
men, when they heard that all their towns were taken, scattered
this way and that to their homes, and gave themselves up to
the Persians. And so these tribes of the Pæonians, to wit, the
Siropæonians, the Pæoplians, and all the others as far as Lake
Prasias, were torn from their seats and led away into Asia.

16. They on the other hand who dwelt about Mount Pangæum [2]

---

[1] Supra, iv. 143; and v. 1.
[2] The range which runs parallel to the coast between the valley of the
Anghista and the high road from *Orfano to Pravista*.

and in the country of the Dobêres, the Agrianians, and the Odomantians, and they likewise who inhabited Lake Prasias, were not conquered by Megabazus. He sought indeed to subdue the dwellers upon the lake, but could not effect his purpose. Their manner of living is the following. Platforms supported upon tall piles stand in the middle of the lake, which are approached from the land by a single narrow bridge.[1] At the first the piles which bear up the platforms were fixed in their places by the whole body of the citizens, but since that time the custom which has prevailed about fixing them is this:—they are brought from a hill called Orbêlus, and every man drives in three for each wife that he marries. Now the men have all many wives apiece; and this is the way in which they live. Each has his own hut, wherein he dwells, upon one of the platforms, and each has also a trap-door giving access to the lake beneath; and their wont is to tie their baby children by the foot with a string, to save them from rolling into the water. They feed their horses and their other beasts upon fish, which abound in the lake to such a degree that a man has only to open his trap-door and to let down a basket by a rope into the water, and then to wait a very short time, when he draws it up quite full of them. The fish are of two kinds, which they call the paprax and the tilon.

17. The Pæonians [2] therefore—at least such of them as had been conquered—were led away into Asia. As for Megabazus, he no sooner brought the Pæonians under, than he sent into Macedonia an embassy of Persians, choosing for the purpose the seven men of most note in all the army after himself. These persons were to go to Amyntas, and require him to give earth and water to King Darius. Now there is a very short cut from the lake Prasias across to Macedonia. Quite close to the lake is the mine which yielded afterwards a talent of silver a day to Alexander; and from this mine you have only to cross the mountain called Dysôrum to find yourself in the Macedonian territory.

18. So the Persians sent upon this errand, when they reached the court, and were brought into the presence of Amyntas,

[1] Discoveries in the lakes of central Europe, particularly those of Switzerland, have confirmed in the most remarkable way this whole description of Herodotus. A similar mode of life to that here described, and apparently practised by the early inhabitants of Switzerland, is found among the natives of New Guinea [Borneo, Celebes, and among the Ainus of Japan. —E. H. B.]

[2] Pæonia in ancient times appears to have consisted of two distinct tracts. Herodotus seems to have known only of the Strymonic Pæonia.

required him to give earth and water to King Darius. And Amyntas not only gave them what they asked, but also invited them to come and feast with him; after which he made ready the board with great magnificence, and entertained the Persians in right friendly fashion. Now when the meal was over, and they were all set to the drinking, the Persians said—

" Dear Macedonian, we Persians have a custom when we make a great feast to bring with us to the board our wives and concubines, and make them sit beside us.[1] Now then, as thou hast received us so kindly, and feasted us so handsomely, and givest moreover earth and water to King Darius, do also after our custom in this matter."

Then Amyntas answered—" O, Persians! we have no such custom as this; but with us men and women are kept apart. Nevertheless, since you, who are our lords, wish it, this also shall be granted to you."

When Amyntas had thus spoken, he bade some go and fetch the women. And the women came at his call and took their seats in a row over against the Persians. Then, when the Persians saw that the women were fair and comely, they spoke again to Amyntas and said, that " what had been done was not wise; for it had been better for the women not to have come at all, than to come in this way, and not sit by their sides, but remain over against them, the torment of their eyes." So Amyntas was forced to bid the women sit side by side with the Persians. The women did as he ordered; and then the Persians, who had drunk more than they ought, began to put their hands on them, and one even tried to give the woman next him a kiss.

19. King Amyntas saw, but he kept silence, although sorely grieved, for he greatly feared the power of the Persians. Alexander, however, Amyntas' son, who was likewise there and witnessed the whole, being a young man and unacquainted with suffering, could not any longer restrain himself. He therefore, full of wrath, spake thus to Amyntas:—" Dear father, thou art old and shouldest spare thyself. Rise up from table and go take thy rest; do not stay out the drinking. I will remain with the guests and give them all that is fitting."

Amyntas, who guessed that Alexander would play some wild prank, made answer:—" Dear son, thy words sound to me as those of one who is well nigh on fire, and I perceive thou sendest

---

[1] The seclusion of the women was as much practised by the Persians as by any other Orientals.

me away that thou mayest do some wild deed. I beseech thee make no commotion about these men, lest thou bring us all to ruin, but bear to look calmly on what they do. For myself, I will e'en withdraw as thou biddest me."

20. Amyntas, when he had thus besought his son, went out; and Alexander said to the Persians, "Look on these ladies as your own, dear strangers, all or any of them—only tell us your wishes. But now, as the evening wears, and I see you have all had wine enough, let them, if you please, retire, and when they have bathed they shall come back again." To this the Persians agreed, and Alexander, having got the women away, sent them off to the harem, and made ready in their room an equal number of beardless youths, whom he dressed in the garments of the women, and then, arming them with daggers, brought them in to the Persians, saying as he introduced them, "Methinks, dear Persians, that your entertainment has fallen short in nothing. We have set before you all that we had ourselves in store, and all that we could anywhere find to give you—and now, to crown the whole, we make over to you our sisters and our mothers, that you may perceive yourselves to be entirely honoured by us, even as you deserve to be—and also that you may take back word to the king who sent you here, that there was one man, a Greek, the satrap of Macedonia, by whom you were both feasted and lodged handsomely." So speaking, Alexander set by the side of each Persian one of those whom he had called Macedonian women, but who were in truth men. And these men, when the Persians began to be rude, despatched them with their daggers.

21. So the ambassadors perished by this death, both they and also their followers. For the Persians had brought a great train with them, carriages, and attendants, and baggage of every kind —all of which disappeared at the same time as the men themselves. Not very long afterwards the Persians made strict search for their lost embassy; but Alexander, with much wisdom, hushed up the business, bribing those sent on the errand, partly with money, and partly with the gift of his own sister Gygæa,[1] whom he gave in marriage to Bubares,[2] a Persian, the chief leader of the expedition which came in search of the lost men. Thus the death of these Persians was hushed up, and no more was said of it.

[1] Vide infra, viii. 136.
[2] Bubares was the son of Megabazus. He was afterwards overseer of the workmen at Athos (infra, vii. 22).

22. Now that the men of this family are Greeks, sprung from Perdiccas, as they themselves affirm, is a thing which I can declare of my own knowledge, and which I will hereafter make plainly evident.[1] That they are so has been already adjudged by those who manage the Pan-Hellenic contest at Olympia. For when Alexander wished to contend in the games, and had come to Olympia with no other view, the Greeks who were about to run against him would have excluded him from the contest— saying that Greeks only were allowed to contend, and not barbarians. But Alexander proved himself to be an Argive, and was distinctly adjudged a Greek; after which he entered the lists for the foot-race, and was drawn to run in the first pair. Thus was this matter settled.

23. Megabazus, having reached the Hellespont with the Pæonians, crossed it, and went up to Sardis. He had become aware while in Europe that Histiæus the Milesian was raising a wall at Myrcinus—the town upon the Strymon which he had obtained from King Darius as his guerdon for keeping the bridge. No sooner therefore did he reach Sardis with the Pæonians than he said to Darius, " What mad thing is this that thou hast done, sire, to let a Greek, a wise man and a shrewd, get hold of a town in Thrace, a place too where there is abundance of timber fit for shipbuilding, and oars in plenty, and mines of silver,[2] and about which are many dwellers both Greek and barbarian, ready enough to take him for their chief, and by day and night to do his bidding! I pray thee make this man cease his work, if thou wouldest not be entangled in a war with thine own followers. Stop him, but with a gentle message, only bidding him to come to thee. Then when thou once hast him in thy power, be sure thou take good care that he never get back to Greece again."

24. With these words Megabazus easily persuaded Darius, who thought he had shown true foresight in this matter. Darius therefore sent a messenger to Myrcinus, who said, " These be the words of the king to thee, O Histiæus! I have looked to find a man well affectioned towards me and towards my greatness; and I have found none whom I can trust like thee. Thy deeds, and not thy words only, have proved thy love for me.

[1] Vide infra, viii. 137.
[2] Histiæus showed excellent judgment in selecting this site. The vicinity of the rich and extensive Strymonic plain, the abundance of timber, the neighbourhood of gold and silver mines, the ready access to the sea, were all points of the utmost importance to a new settlement.

Now then, since I have a mighty enterprise in hand, I pray thee come to me, that I may show thee what I purpose!"

Histiæus, when he heard this, put faith in the words of the messenger; and, as it seemed to him a grand thing to be the king's counsellor, he straightway went up to Sardis. Then Darius, when he was come, said to him, " Dear Histiæus, hear why I have sent for thee. No sooner did I return from Scythia, and lose thee out of my sight, than I longed, as I have never longed for aught else, to behold thee once more, and to interchange speech with thee. Right sure I am there is nothing in all the world so precious as a friend who is at once wise and true: both which thou art, as I have had good proof in what thou hast already done for me. Now then 'tis well thou art come; for look, I have an offer to make to thee. Let go Miletus and thy newly-founded town in Thrace, and come with me up to Susa; share all that I have; live with me, and be my counsellor.[1]

25. When Darius had thus spoken he made Artaphernes, his brother by the father's side, governor of Sardis, and taking Histiæus with him, went up to Susa. He left as general of all the troops upon the sea-coast Otanes, son of Sisamnes,[2] whose father King Cambyses slew and flayed,[3] because that he, being of the number of the royal judges, had taken money to give an unrighteous sentence. Therefore Cambyses slew and flayed Sisamnes, and cutting his skin into strips, stretched them across the seat of the throne whereon he had been wont to sit when he heard causes. Having so done Cambyses appointed the son of Sisamnes to be judge in his father's room, and bade him never forget in what way his seat was cushioned.

26. Accordingly this Otanes, who had occupied so strange a throne, became the successor of Megabazus in his command, and took first of all Byzantium and Chalcêdon,[4] then Antandrus[5] in the Troas, and next Lampônium. This done, he borrowed ships of the Lesbians, and took Lemnos and Imbrus, which were still inhabited by Pelasgians.[6]

[1] Compare, for this Oriental practice, 2 Sam. ix. 7, 11; xix. 33; 1 Kings ii. 7.
[2] *Not* the conspirator, who was Otanes, son of *Pharnaspes* (iii. 68).
[3] In later times the Persians seem to have flayed their criminals *alive*
[4] Vide supra, iv. 144.
[5] Antandrus lay on the sea-coast of the gulf of *Adramyti*, a short distance west of Adramyttium. The name remains in the *Antandro* of the present day.
[6] Vide supra, iv. 145.

27. Now the Lemnians stood on their defence, and fought gallantly; but they were brought low in course of time. Such as outlived the struggle were placed by the Persians under the government of Lycarêtus, the brother of that Mæandrius [1] who was tyrant of Samos. (This Lycarêtus died afterwards in his government.) The cause which Otanes alleged for conquering and enslaving all these nations was, that some had refused to join the king's army against Scythia, while others had molested the host on its return. Such were the exploits which Otanes performed in his command.

28. Afterwards, but for no long time,[2] there was a respite from suffering. Then from Nazos and Miletus troubles gathered anew about Ionia. Now Naxos at this time surpassed all the other islands in prosperity;[3] and Miletus had reached the height of her power, and was the glory of Ionia. But previously for two generations the Milesians had suffered grievously from civil disorders, which were composed by the Parians, whom the Milesians chose before all the rest of the Greeks to rearrange their government.[4]

29. Now the way in which the Parians healed their differences was the following. A number of the chief Parians came to Miletus, and when they saw in how ruined a condition the Milesians were, they said that they would like first to go over their country. So they went through all Milesia, and on their way, whenever they saw in the waste and desolate country any land that was well farmed, they took down the names of the owners in their tablets; and having thus gone through the whole region, and obtained after all but few names, they called the people together on their return to Miletus, and made proclamation that they gave the government into the hands of those persons whose lands they had found well farmed; for they thought it likely (they said) that the same persons who had managed their own affairs well would likewise conduct aright the business of the state. The other Milesians, who in time past had been at variance, they placed under the rule of these men. Thus was the Milesian government set in order by the Parians.

30. It was, however, from the two cities above mentioned that

[1] Supra, iii. 142-148.
[2] Perhaps Clinton is not far wrong in reckoning it " a tranquillity of two years."
[3] The fertility of Naxos was proverbial in ancient times.
[4] Concerning the practice of calling in foreigners to settle the domestic differences of a state, vide supra, iv. 161.

troubles began now to gather again about Ionia; and this is the way in which they arose. Certain of the rich men had been banished from Naxos by the commonalty, and, upon their banishment, had fled to Miletus. Aristagoras, son of Molpagoras, the nephew and likewise the son-in-law of Histiæus, son of Lysagoras, who was still kept by Darius at Susa, happened to be regent of Miletus at the time of their coming. For the kingly power belonged to Histiæus; but he was at Susa when the Naxians came. Now these Naxians had in times past been bond-friends of Histiæus; and so on their arrival at Miletus they addressed themselves to Aristagoras and begged him to lend them such aid as his ability allowed, in hopes thereby to recover their country. Then Aristagoras, considering with himself that, if the Naxians should be restored by his help, he would be lord of Naxos, put forward the friendship with Histiæus to cloak his views, and spoke as follows:—

"I cannot engage to furnish you with such a power as were needful to force you, against their will, upon the Naxians who hold the city; for I know they can bring into the field eight thousand bucklers, and have also a vast number of ships of war. But I will do all that lies in my power to get you some aid, and I think I can manage it in this way. Artaphernes happens to be my friend. Now he is a son of Hystaspes, and brother to King Darius. All the sea-coast of Asia is under him,[1] and he has a numerous army and numerous ships. I think I can prevail on him to do what we require."

When the Naxians heard this, they empowered Aristagoras to manage the matter for them as well as he could, and told him to promise gifts and pay for the soldiers, which (they said) they would readily furnish, since they had great hope that the Naxians, so soon as they saw them returned, would render them obedience, and likewise the other islanders.[2] For at that time not one of the Cyclades was subject to King Darius.

31. So Aristagoras went to Sardis and told Artaphernes that Naxos was an island of no great size, but a fair land and fertile,[3] lying near Ionia,[4] and containing much treasure and a vast

[1] This is evidently an exaggeration.

[2] Naxos would appear by this to have exercised a species of sovereignty over some of the other Cyclades.

[3] Naxos is considerably larger than Jersey, but not more than half the size of the Isle of Wight.

[4] Naxos is distant from the Ionian coast at least 80 miles. From Samos, however, which was now in the possession of the Persians, it is not more than 65 miles, and in clear weather is *visible*.

number of slaves. "Make war then upon this land (he said) and reinstate the exiles; for if thou wilt do this, first of all, I have very rich gifts in store for thee (besides the cost of the armament, which it is fair that we who are the authors of the war should pay); and, secondly, thou wilt bring under the power of the king not only Naxos but the other islands which depend on it, as Paros, Andros, and all the rest of the Cyclades. And when thou hast gained these, thou mayest easily go on against Euboea, which is a large and wealthy island not less in size than Cyprus,[1] and very easy to bring under. A hundred ships were quite enough to subdue the whole." The other answered—"Truly thou art the author of a plan which may much advantage the house of the king, and thy counsel is good in all points except the number of the ships. Instead of a hundred, two hundred shall be at thy disposal when the spring comes. But the king himself must first approve the undertaking."

32. When Aristagoras heard this he was greatly rejoiced, and went home in good heart to Miletus. And Artaphernes, after he had sent a messenger to Susa to lay the plans of Aristagoras before the king, and received his approval of the undertaking, made ready a fleet of two hundred triremes and a vast army of Persians and their confederates. The command of these he gave to a Persian named Megabates, who belonged to the house of the Achæmenids, being nephew both to himself and to King Darius. It was to a daughter of this man that Pausanias the Lacedæmonian, the son of Cleombrotus (if at least there be any truth in the tale [2]), was affianced many years afterwards, when he conceived the desire of becoming tyrant of Greece. Artaphernes now, having named Megabates to the command, sent forward the armament to Aristagoras.

33. Megabates set sail, and, touching at Miletus, took on board Aristagoras with the Ionian troops and the Naxians; after which he steered, as he gave out, for the Hellespont; and when he reached Chios, he brought the fleet to anchor off Caucasa, being minded to wait there for a north wind, and then sail straight to Naxos. The Naxians however were not to perish at this time; and so the following events were brought about. As Megabates went his rounds to visit the watches on board the ships, he found a Myndian vessel upon which there was none

---

[1] Cyprus is really more than twice the size of Euboea (*Negropont*).

[2] For the true account of these proceedings of Pausanias, cf. Thucyd. i. 128-130.

set. Full of anger at such carelessness, he bade his guards to seek out the captain, one Scylax by name, and thrusting him through one of the holes in the ship's side,[1] to fasten him there in such a way that his head might show outside the vessel, while his body remained within. When Scylax was thus fastened, one went and informed Aristagoras that Megabates had bound his Myndian friend and was entreating him shamefully. So he came and asked Megabates to let the man off; but the Persian refused him; whereupon Aristagoras went himself and set Scylax free. When Megabates heard this he was still more angry than before, and spoke hotly to Aristagoras. Then the latter said to him—

"What hast thou to do with these matters? Wert thou not sent here by Artaphernes to obey me, and to sail whithersoever I ordered? Why dost meddle so?"

Thus spake Aristagoras. The other, in high dudgeon at such language, waited till the night, and then despatched a boat to Naxos, to warn the Naxians of the coming danger.

34. Now the Naxians up to this time had not had any suspicion that the armament was directed against them; as soon, therefore, as the message reached them, forthwith they brought within their walls all that they had in the open field, and made themselves ready against a siege by provisioning their town both with food and drink. Thus was Naxos placed in a posture of defence; and the Persians, when they crossed the sea from Chios, found the Naxians fully prepared for them. However they sat down before the place, and besieged it for four whole months. When at length all the stores which they had brought with them were exhausted, and Aristogoras had likewise spent upon the siege no small sum from his private means, and more was still needed to insure success, the Persians gave up the attempt, and first building certain forts, wherein they left the banished Naxians, withdrew to the mainland, having utterly failed in their undertaking.

35. And now Aristagoras found himself quite unable to make good his promises to Artaphernes; nay, he was even hard pressed to meet the claims whereto he was liable for the pay of the troops; and at the same time his fear was great, lest, owing to the failure of the expedition and his own quarrel with Megabates, he should be ousted from the government of Miletus. These manifold alarms had already caused him to contemplate raising

[1] The "holes in the side" of a Greek vessel were, of course, for the oars.

a rebellion, when the man with the marked head came from Susa, bringing him instructions on the part of Histiæus to revolt from the king. For Histiæus, when he was anxious to give Aristagoras orders to revolt, could find but one safe way, as the roads were guarded, of making his wishes known; which was by taking the trustiest of his slaves, shaving all the hair from off his head, and then pricking letters upon the skin, and waiting till the hair grew again. Thus accordingly he did; and as soon as ever the hair was grown, he despatched the man to Miletus, giving him no other message than this—" When thou art come to Miletus, bid Aristagoras shave thy head, and look thereon." Now the marks on the head, as I have already mentioned, were a command to revolt. All this Histiæus did because it irked him greatly to be kept at Susa, and because he had strong hopes that, if troubles broke out, he would be sent down to the coast to quell them, whereas, if Miletus made no movement, he did not see a chance of his ever again returning thither.

36. Such, then, were the views which led Histiæus to despatch his messenger; and it so chanced that all these several motives to revolt were brought to bear upon Aristagoras at one and the same time.

Accordingly, at this conjuncture Aristagoras held a council of his trusty friends, and laid the business before them, telling them both what he had himself purposed, and what message had been sent him by Histiæus. At this council all his friends were of the same way of thinking, and recommended revolt, except only Hecatæus the historian. He, first of all, advised them by all means to avoid engaging in war with the king of the Persians, whose might he set forth, and whose subject nations he enumerated. As however he could not induce them to listen to this counsel, he next advised that they should do all that lay in their power to make themselves masters of the sea. " There was one only way," he said, " so far as he could see, of their succeeding in this. Miletus was, he knew, a weak state—but if the treasures in the temple at Branchidæ,[1] which Crœsus the Lydian gave to it, were seized, he had strong hopes that the mastery of the sea might be thereby gained; at least it would give them money to begin the war, and would save the treasures from falling into the hands of the enemy." Now these treasures were of very great value, as I showed in the first part of my

---

[1] [For a note on the Temple of Apollo at Branchidæ (near Miletus), see Frazer's *Pausanias*, vol. iv. pp. 125, 126.—E. H. B.]

History.[1] The assembly, however, rejected the counsel of Hecatæus, while, nevertheless, they resolved upon a revolt. One of their number, it was agreed, should sail to Myus,[2] where the fleet had been lying since its return from Naxos, and endeavour to seize the captains who had gone there with the vessels.

37. Iatragoras accordingly was despatched on this errand, and he took with guile Oliatus the son of Ibanôlis the Mylassian,[3] and Histiæus the son of Tymnes[4] the Termerean,—Coës likewise, the son of Erxander, to whom Darius gave Mytilêné,[5] and Aristagoras the son of Heraclides the Cymæan, and also many others. Thus Aristagoras revolted openly from Darius; and now he set to work to scheme against him in every possible way. First of all, in order to induce the Milesians to join heartily in the revolt, he gave out, that he laid down his own lordship over Miletus, and in lieu thereof established a commonwealth: after which, throughout all Ionia he did the like; for from some of the cities he drove out their tyrants, and to others, whose goodwill he hoped thereby to gain, he handed theirs over, thus giving up all the men whom he had seized at the Naxian fleet, each to the city whereto he belonged.

38. Now the Mytileneans had no sooner got Coës into their power, than they led him forth from the city and stoned him; the Cymæans, on the other hand, allowed their tyrant to go free; as likewise did most of the others. And so this form of government ceased throughout all the cities. Aristagoras the Milesian, after he had in this way put down the tyrants, and bidden the cities choose themselves captains in their room, sailed away himself on board a trireme to Lacedæmon; for he had great need of obtaining the aid of some powerful ally.

39. At Sparta, Anaxandridas the son of Leo was no longer king: he had died, and his son Cleomenes had mounted the throne, not however by right of merit, but of birth. Anaxandridas took to wife his own sister's daughter,[6] and was tenderly attached to her; but no children came from the marriage. Hereupon the Ephors[7] called him before them, and said—" If

---

[1] Supra, i. 92.
[2] Myus was one of the twelve cities of Ionia (supra, i. 142).
[3] Mylasa or Mylassa was, like Termera, a town of Caria.
[4] This Histiæus afterwards accompanied the expedition of Xerxes (infra, vii. 98).   [5] Supra, ch. 11.
[6] Marriages of this kind were common at Sparta. Leonidas married his niece, Gorgo (infra, vii. 239); Archidamus his aunt, Lampito (infra, vi. 71).
[7] Concerning the Ephors at Sparta, vide supra, i. 65. This passage is very important, as marking their power over the kings.

thou hast no care for thine own self, nevertheless *we* cannot allow this, nor suffer the race of Eurysthenes to die out from among us. Come then, as thy present wife bears thee no children, put her away, and wed another. So wilt thou do what is well-pleasing to the Spartans." Anaxandridas however refused to do as they required, and said it was no good advice the Ephors gave, to bid him put away his wife when she had done no wrong, and take to himself another. He therefore declined to obey them.

40. Then the Ephors and Elders[1] took counsel together, and laid this proposal before the king:—" Since thou art so fond, as we see thee to be, of thy present wife, do what we now advise, and gainsay us not, lest the Spartans make some unwonted decree concerning thee. We ask thee not now to put away thy wife to whom thou art married—give her still the same love and honour as ever,—but take thee another wife beside, who may bear thee children."

When he heard this offer, Anaxandridas gave way—and henceforth he lived with two wives in two separate houses, quite against all Spartan custom.

41. In a short time, the wife whom he had last married bore him a son, who received the name of Cleomenes; and so the heir to the throne was brought into the world by her. After this, the first wife also, who in time past had been barren, by some strange chance conceived, and came to be with child. Then the friends of the second wife, when they heard a rumour of the truth, made a great stir, and said it was a false boast, and she meant, they were sure, to bring forward as her own a supposititious child. So they raised an outcry against her; and therefore, when her full time was come, the Ephors, who were themselves incredulous, sat round her bed, and kept a strict watch on the labour.[2] At this time then she bore Dorieus, and after him, quickly, Leonidas, and after him, again quickly, Cleombrotus. Some even say that Leonidas and Cleombrotus were twins. On the

[1] The council of twenty-eight, mentioned, with the Ephors, in Book i. ch. 65, and again spoken of in Book vi. ch. 57. It seems that, when the Ephors and the Elders agreed together, the king had no power to withstand them.

[2] Compare with this, the practice in our own country of summoning the great officers of state to the queen's apartments at the birth of a prince or princess. With the Spartans there was a religious motive at work, in addition to the political one which alone obtains with ourselves. It was necessary for them, in a religious point of view, to preserve the purity of the blood of Hercules.

other hand, the second wife, the mother of Cleomenes (who was a daughter of Prinetadas, the son of Demarmenus), never gave birth to a second child.

42. Now Cleomenes, it is said, was not right in his mind; indeed he verged upon madness; while Dorieus surpassed all his co-mates, and looked confidently to receiving the kingdom on the score of merit. When, therefore, after the death of Anaxandridas, the Spartans kept to the law, and made Cleomenes, his eldest son, king in his room, Dorieus, who had imagined that he should be chosen, and who could not bear the thought of having such a man as Cleomenes to rule over him, asked the Spartans to give him a body of men, and left Sparta with them in order to found a colony. However, he neither took counsel of the oracle at Delphi as to the place whereto he should go,[1] nor observed any of the customary usages; but left Sparta in dudgeon, and sailed away to Libya, under the guidance of certain men who were Theræans.[2] These men brought him to Cinyps, where he colonised a spot, which has not its equal in all Libya, on the banks of a river:[3] but from this place he was driven in the third year by the Macians, the Libyans, and the Carthaginians.

43. Dorieus returned to the Peloponnese; whereupon Antichares the Eleônian gave him a counsel (which he got from the oracles of Laïus[4]), to "found the city of Heraclea in Sicily; the whole country of Eryx[5] belonged," he said, "to the Heracleids, since Hercules himself conquered it." On receiving this advice, Dorieus went to Delphi to inquire of the oracle whether he would take the place to which he was about to go. The Pythoness prophesied that he would; whereupon Dorieus went back to Libya, took up the men who had sailed with him at the first, and proceeded upon his way along the shores of Italy.

44. Just at this time, the Sybarites[6] say, they and their king Têlys were about to make war upon Crotôna, and the Crotoniats,

---

[1] The sanction of some oracle or other was required for every colony; the sanction of the oracle at Delphi, when the colony was Dorian.

[2] The connection of Thera with Cyrênê (iv. 150-159) would explain the choice of Cinyps as a settlement.

[3] This place, which Herodotus regarded as the most fertile spot in Africa, has been already described (iv. 198; compare ch. 175).

[4] We may understand " oracles given to Laïus."

[5] It lay at the western point of the island, a little to the north of Drepanum, the modern Trapani.

[6] Sybaris was one of the most important towns of Magna Græcia. Its luxury is proverbial (cf. vi. 127). It was taken (B.C. 510) after a siege of 70 days by the Crotoniats; who turned the river upon the town, and so destroyed it—[an event which preluded the decadence of Magna Græcia.—E. H. B.]

greatly alarmed, besought Dorieus to lend them aid. Dorieus was prevailed upon, bore part in the war against Sybaris, and had a share in taking the town. Such is the account which the Sybarites give of what was done by Dorieus and his companions. The Crotoniats, on the other hand, maintain that no foreigner lent them aid in their war against the Sybarites, save and except Callias the Elean, a soothsayer of the race of the Iamidæ; and he only forsook Têlys the Sybaritic king, and deserted to their side, when he found on sacrificing that the victims were not favourable to an attack on Crotôna. Such is the account which each party gives of these matters.

45. Both parties likewise adduce testimonies to the truth of what they say. The Sybarites show a temple and sacred precinct near the dry stream of the Crastis, which they declare that Dorieus, after taking their city, dedicated to Minerva Crastias. And further, they bring forward the death of Dorieus as the surest proof; since he fell, they say, because he disobeyed the oracle. For had he in nothing varied from the directions given him, but confined himself to the business on which he was sent, he would assuredly have conquered the Erycian territory, and kept possession of it, instead of perishing with all his followers. The Crotoniats, on the other hand, point to the numerous allotments within their borders which were assigned to Callias the Elean by their countrymen, and which to my day remained in the possession of his family; while Dorieus and his descendants (they remark) possess nothing. Yet if Dorieus had really helped them in the Sybaritic war, he would have received very much more than Callias. Such are the testimonies which are adduced on either side; it is open to every man to adopt whichever view he deems the best.

46. Certain Spartans accompanied Dorieus on his voyage as co-founders, to wit, Thessalus, Paræbates, Celeas, and Euryleon. These men and all the troops under their command reached Sicily; but there they fell in a battle wherein they were defeated by the Egesteans and Phœnicians, only one, Euryleon, surviving the disaster. He then, collecting the remnants of the beaten army, made himself master of Minôa, the Selinusian colony, and helped the Selinusians to throw off the yoke of their tyrant Peithagoras. Having upset Peithagoras, he sought to become tyrant in his room, and he even reigned at Selinus for a brief space—but after a while the Selinusians rose up in revolt against

him, and though he fled to the altar of Jupiter Agoræus,[1] they notwithstanding put him to death.

47. Another man who accompanied Dorieus, and died with him, was Philip the son of Butacidas, a man of Crotôna; who, after he had been betrothed to a daughter of Têlys the Sybarite, was banished from Crotôna, whereupon his marriage came to nought; and he in his disappointment took ship and sailed to Cyrêné. From thence he became a follower of Dorieus, furnishing to the fleet a trireme of his own, the crew of which he supported at his own charge. This Philip was an Olympian victor, and the handsomest Greek of his day. His beauty gained him honours at the hands of the Egestæans which they never accorded to any one else; for they raised a hero-temple over his grave, and they still worship him with sacrifices.

48. Such then was the end of Dorieus, who if he had brooked the rule of Cleomenes, and remained in Sparta, would have been king of Lacedæmon; since Cleomenes, after reigning no great length of time, died without male offspring, leaving behind him an only daughter, by name Gorgo.[2]

49. Cleomenes, however, was still king when Aristagoras, tyrant of Miletus, reached Sparta. At their interview, Aristagoras, according to the report of the Lacedæmonians, produced a bronze tablet, whereupon the whole circuit of the earth was engraved, with all its seas and rivers. Discourse began between the two; and Aristagoras addressed the Spartan king in these words following:—" Think it not strange, O King Cleomenes, that I have been at the pains to sail hither; for the posture of affairs, which I will now recount unto thee, made it fitting. Shame and grief is it indeed to none so much as to us, that the sons of the Ionians should have lost their freedom, and come to be the slaves of others; but yet it touches you likewise, O Spartans, beyond the rest of the Greeks, inasmuch as the pre-eminence over all Greece appertains to you. We beseech you, therefore, by the common gods of the Grecians, deliver the Ionians, who are your own kinsmen, from slavery. Truly the task is not difficult; for the barbarians are an unwarlike people; and you are the best and bravest warriors in the whole world. Their mode of fighting is the following:—they use bows and

---

[1] That is, " Protector of the Forum " (ἀγορά). It probably stood in the market-place.

[2] She became the wife of Leonidas, her uncle, according to a usual Spartan custom (infra, vii. 239).

arrows and a short spear; they wear trousers in the field, and cover their heads with turbans.[1] So easy are they to vanquish! Know too that the dwellers in these parts have more good things than all the rest of the world put together—gold, and silver, and brass, and embroidered garments, beasts of burthen, and bond-servants—all which, if you only wish it, you may soon have for your own. The nations border on one another, in the order which I will now explain. Next to these Ionians " (here he pointed with his finger to the map of the world which was engraved upon the tablet that he had brought with him) " these Lydians dwell; their soil is fertile, and few people are so rich in silver. Next to them," he continued, " come these Phrygians, who have more flocks and herds than any race that I know,[2] and more plentiful harvests. On them border the Cappadocians, whom we Greeks know by the name of Syrians: they are neighbours to the Cilicians, who extend all the way to this sea, where Cyprus (the island which you see here) lies. The Cilicians pay the king a yearly tribute of five hundred talents.[3] Next to them come the Armenians, who live here—they too have numerous flocks and herds. After them come the Matiêni, in-habiting this country; then Cissia, this province, where you see the river Choaspes marked, and likewise the town Susa upon its banks, where the Great King holds his court,[4] and where the treasuries are in which his wealth is stored.[5] Once masters of this city, you may be bold to vie with Jove himself for riches. In the wars which ye wage with your rivals of Messenia, with them of Argos likewise and of Arcadia, about paltry boundaries and strips of land not so remarkably good,[6] ye contend with those who have no gold, nor silver even, which often give men heart to fight and die. Must ye wage such wars, and when ye might so easily be lords of Asia, will ye decide otherwise? " Thus spoke Aristagoras; and Cleomenes replied to him,— " Milesian stranger, three days hence I will give thee an answer."

---

[1] Vide infra, vii. 61.
[2] The high table-land of Phrygia is especially adapted for pasturage.
[3] Supra, iii. 90.
[4] Susa had by this time certainly become the Persian capital. The Choaspes is at present a mile and a half to the west of the town. The magnificent palace of Susa had a great fame in antiquity (infra, ch. 53). [See A. H. Sayce in Hastings' *Dict. of Bible*, vol. iv. p. 511.—E. H. B.]
[5] When Susa was entered by Alexander the Great, the silver captured amounted to 50,000 talents, or more than twelve millions sterling.
[6] Cf. i. 66-68, and 82.

50. So they proceeded no further at that time. When, however, the day appointed for the answer came, and the two once more met, Cleomenes asked Aristagoras, "how many days' journey it was from the sea of the Ionians to the king's residence?" Hereupon Aristagoras, who had managed the rest so cleverly, and succeeded in deceiving the king, tripped in his speech and blundered; for instead of concealing the truth, as he ought to have done if he wanted to induce the Spartans to cross into Asia, he said plainly that it was a journey of three months. Cleomenes caught at the words, and, preventing Aristagoras from finishing what he had begun to say concerning the road, addressed him thus:—" Milesian stranger, quit Sparta before sunset. This is no good proposal that thou makest to the Lacedæmonians, to conduct them a distance of three months' journey from the sea." When he had thus spoken, Cleomenes went to his home.

51. But Aristagoras took an olive-bough in his hand, and hastened to the king's house, where he was admitted by reason of his suppliant's guise. Gorgo, the daughter of Cleomenes, and his only child, a girl of about eight or nine years of age, happened to be there, standing by her father's side. Aristagoras, seeing her, requested Cleomenes to send her out of the room before he began to speak with him; but Cleomenes told him to say on, and not mind the child. So Aristagoras began with a promise of ten talents if the king would grant him his request, and when Cleomenes shook his head, continued to raise his offer till it reached fifty talents; whereupon the child spoke:— " Father," she said, " get up and go, or the stranger will certainly corrupt thee." Then Cleomenes, pleased at the warning of his child, withdrew and went into another room. Aristagoras quitted Sparta for good, not being able to discourse any more concerning the road which led up to the king.

52. Now the true account of the road in question is the following:—Royal stations[1] exist along its whole length, and excellent caravanserais; and throughout, it traverses an inhabited tract, and is free from danger. In Lydia and Phrygia there are twenty stations within a distance of 94½ parasangs. On leaving Phrygia the Halys has to be crossed; and here are gates through which you must needs pass ere you can traverse

---

[1] By " royal stations " are to be understood the abodes of the king's " couriers," who conveyed despatches from their own station to the next, and then returned (infra, viii. 98).

the stream. A strong force guards this post. When you have made the passage, and are come into Cappadocia, 28 stations and 104 parasangs bring you to the borders of Cilicia, where the road passes through two sets of gates, at each of which there is a guard posted. Leaving these behind, you go on through Cilicia, where you find three stations in a distance of 15½ parasangs. The boundary between Cilicia and Armenia is the river Euphrates, which it is necessary to cross in boats. In Armenia the resting-places are 15 in number, and the distance is 56½ parasangs. There is one place where a guard is posted. Four large streams intersect this district, all of which have to be crossed by means of boats. The first of these is the Tigris; the second and the third have both of them the same name,[1] though they are not only different rivers, but do not even run from the same place.[2] For the one which I have called the first of the two has its source in Armenia, while the other flows afterwards out of the country of the Matienians. The fourth of the streams is called the Gyndes, and this is the river which Cyrus dispersed by digging for it three hundred and sixty channels. Leaving Armenia and entering the Matienian country, you have four stations; these passed you find yourself in Cissia, where eleven stations and 42½ parasangs bring you to another navigable stream, the Choaspes, on the banks of which the city of Susa is built. Thus the entire number of the stations is raised to one hundred and eleven; and so many are in fact the resting-places that one finds between Sardis and Susa.

53. If then the royal road be measured aright, and the parasang equals, as it does, thirty furlongs,[3] the whole distance from Sardis to the palace of Memnon (as it is called), amounting thus to 450 parasangs, would be 13,500 furlongs. Travelling then at the rate of 150 furlongs a day,[4] one will take exactly ninety days to perform the journey.

54. Thus when Aristagoras the Milesian told Cleomenes the

[1] Undoubtedly the two Zabs, the Greater and the Lesser.

[2] What Herodotus here states is exactly true of the two Zabs.

[3] Supra, ii. 6. This was the ordinary estimate of the Greeks. Strabo, however, tells us that it was not universally agreed upon, since there were some who considered the parasang to equal 40, and others 60 stades. The truth is, that the ancient parasang, like the modern farsakh, was originally a measure of time (an hour), not a measure of distance. In passing from the one meaning to the other, it came to mark a different length in different places, according to the nature of the country traversed.

[4] Herodotus takes here the rate at which an army would be likely to move. Elsewhere (iv. 101) he reckons the journey of the ordinary pedestrian at 200 stades (about 23 miles).

Lacedæmonian that it was a three months' journey from the sea up to the king, he said no more than the truth. The exact distance (if any one desires still greater accuracy) is somewhat more; for the journey from Ephesus to Sardis must be added to the foregoing account; and this will make the whole distance between the Greek Sea and Susa (or the city of Memnon, as it is called [1]) 14,040 furlongs; since Ephesus is distant from Sardis 540 furlongs. This would add three days to the three months' journey.

55. When Aristagoras left Sparta he hastened to Athens, which had got quit of its tyrants in the way that I will now describe. After the death of Hipparchus (the son of Pisistratus, and brother of the tyrant Hippias), who, in spite of the clear warning he had received concerning his fate in a dream, was slain by Harmodius and Aristogeiton (men both of the race of the Gephyræans), the oppression of the Athenians continued by the space of four years; [2] and they gained nothing, but were worse used than before.

56. Now the dream of Hipparchus was the following:—The night before the Panathenaic festival, he thought he saw in his sleep a tall and beautiful man, who stood over him, and read him the following riddle:—

" Bear thou unbearable woes with the all-bearing heart of a lion;
    Never, be sure, shall wrong-doer escape the reward of wrong-doing."

As soon as day dawned he sent and submitted his dream to the interpreters, after which he offered the averting sacrifices, and then went and led the procession in which he perished.

57. The family of the Gephyræans, to which the murderers of Hipparchus belonged, according to their own account, came originally from Eretria. My inquiries, however, have made it clear to me that they are in reality Phœnicians, descendants of those who came with Cadmus into the country now called Bœotia. Here they received for their portion the district of Tanagra, in which they afterwards dwelt. On their expulsion from this country by the Bœotians (which happened some time

[1] The fable of Memnon is one of those in which it is difficult to discover any germs of truth. The earliest author who is *known* to have connected Memnon with Susa is Æschylus, who made his mother a Cissian woman. It is clear, however, that by the time of Herodotus, the story that he built Susa, or its great palace, was generally accepted in Greece. Perhaps the adoption of this account may be regarded as indicating some knowledge of the *ethnic* connection which really existed between Ethiopia and Susiana.
[2] From B.C. 514 to B.C. 510.

after that of the Cadmeians from the same parts by the Argives[1]) they took refuge at Athens. The Athenians received them among their citizens upon set terms, whereby they were excluded from a number of privileges which are not worth mentioning.

58. Now the Phœnicians who came with Cadmus, and to whom the Gephyræi belonged, introduced into Greece upon their arrival a great variety of arts, among the rest that of writing,[2] whereof the Greeks till then had, as I think, been ignorant. And originally they shaped their letters exactly like all the other Phœnicians, but afterwards, in course of time, they changed by degrees their language, and together with it the form likewise of their characters. Now the Greeks who dwelt about those parts at that time were chiefly the Ionians. The Phœnician letters were accordingly adopted by them, but with some variation in the shape of a few, and so they arrived at the present use, still calling the letters Phœnician, as justice required, after the name of those who were the first to introduce them into Greece. Paper rolls also were called from of old " parchments " by the Ionians, because formerly when paper was scarce they used, instead, the skins of sheep and goats—on which material many of the barbarians are even now wont to write.[3]

59. I myself saw Cadmeian characters[4] engraved upon some tripods in the temple of Apollo Ismenias[5] in Bœotian[6] Thebes, most of them shaped like the Ionian. One of the tripods has the inscription following:—

" Me did Amphitryon place, from the far Teleboans coming."

This would be about the age of Laïus, the son of Labdacus, the son of Polydorus, the son of Cadmus.

[1] Herodotus alludes here to the legend of the Epigoni.

[2] Homer (Il. vi. 168) shows that in his time the Greeks wrote on folding wooden tablets. [See *n.* on that passage, in my ed. of Homer, vol. i.—E. H. B.]

[3] This is a remarkable statement. Among the " barbarians " alluded to, we may assume the Persians to be included. Stone and clay seem to have been the common material in Assyria and Babylonia; wood, leather, and paper in Egypt; the bark of trees and linen in Italy; stone, wood, and metal among the Jews. Parchment seems never to have been much used, even by the Greeks, till the time of Eumenes II. (B.C. 197-159).

[4] The old Greek letters, like the Phœnician, were written from right to left. They continued to be so written till a late time on vases; but this appears to have been then merely the imitation of an old fashion; for already, in the age of Psammetichus, the seventh century B.C., inscriptions were written from left to right.   [5] Cf. i. 52.

[6] *Bœotian* Thebes is here distinguished from *Egyptian*.

60. Another of the tripods has this legend in the hexameter measure:—

> " I to far-shooting Phœbus was offered by Scæus the boxer,
> When he had won at the games—a wondrous beautiful offering."

This might be Scæus, the son of Hippocoön;[1] and the tripod, if dedicated by him, and not by another of the same name, would belong to the time of Œdipus, the son of Laïus.

61. The third tripod has also an inscription in hexameters, which runs thus:—

> " King Laodamas gave this tripod to far-seeing Phœbus,
> When he was set on the throne—a wondrous beautiful offering."

It was in the reign of this Laodamas, the son of Eteocles, that the Cadmeians were driven by the Argives out of their country,[2] and found a shelter with the Encheleans.[3] The Gephyræans at that time remained in the country, but afterwards they retired before the Bœotians, and took refuge at Athens, where they have a number of temples for their separate use, which the other Athenians are not allowed to enter—among the rest, one of Achæan Ceres, in whose honour they likewise celebrate special orgies.

62. Having thus related the dream which Hipparchus saw, and traced the descent of the Gephyræans, the family whereto his murderers belonged, I must proceed with the matter whereof I was intending before to speak; to wit, the way in which the Athenians got quit of their tyrants. Upon the death of Hipparchus, Hippias, who was king, grew harsh towards the Athenians; and the Alcmæonidæ,[4] an Athenian family which had been banished by the Pisistratidæ,[5] joined the other exiles, and endeavoured to procure their own return, and to free Athens, by force. They seized and fortified Leipsydrium above Pæonia, and tried to gain their object by arms; but great disasters befell them, and their purpose remained unaccomplished. They therefore resolved to shrink from no contrivance that might bring them success; and accordingly they contracted with the

---

[1] Hippocoön was the brother of Tyndareus and Icarion. Assisted by his twelve sons, he drove his two biothers from Lacedæmon. Afterwards Hercules slew him and his sons, and restored Tyndareus.

[2] Laödamas succeeded his father Eteocles upon the throne of Thebes.

[3] The Encheleans were an Illyrian tribe.

[4] Vide infra, vi. 125-131, where the earlier history of the Alcmæonidæ s given.

[5] That is by Pisistratus himself, who is included among the Pisistratidæ (vide supra, i. 64).

Amphictyons to build the temple which now stands at Delphi, but which in those days did not exist.[1] Having done this, they proceeded, being men of great wealth and members of an ancient and distinguished family, to build the temple much more magnificently than the plan obliged them. Besides other improvements, instead of the coarse stone whereof by the contract the temple was to have been constructed, they made the facings of Parian marble.

63. These same men, if we may believe the Athenians, during their stay at Delphi persuaded the Pythoness by a bribe [2] to tell the Spartans, whenever any of them came to consult the oracle, either on their own private affairs or on the business of the state, that they must free Athens. So the Lacedæmonians, when they found no answer ever returned to them but this, sent at last Anchimolius, the son of Aster—a man of note among their citizens—at the head of an army against Athens, with orders to drive out the Pisistratidæ, albeit they were bound to them by the closest ties of friendship. For they esteemed the things of heaven more highly than the things of men. The troops went by sea and were conveyed in transports. Anchimolius brought them to an anchorage at Phalerum; [3] and there the men disembarked. But the Pisistratidæ, who had previous knowledge of their intentions, had sent to Thessaly, between which country and Athens there was an alliance,[4] with a request for aid. The Thessalians, in reply to their entreaties, sent them by a public vote 1000 horsemen,[5] under the command of their king, Cineas, who was a Coniæan. When this help came, the Pisistratidæ laid their plan accordingly: they cleared the whole plain about Phalerum so as to make it fit for the movements of cavalry, and then charged the enemy's camp with their horse, which fell with such fury upon the Lacedæmonians as to kill numbers, among the rest Anchimolius, the general, and to drive the remainder to their ships. Such was the fate of the first army sent from Lacedæmon, and the tomb of Anchi-

[1] The old temple had been burnt (vide supra, ii. 180).
[2] The Delphic oracle is again bribed by Cleomenes, infra, vi. 66.
[3] Phalerum is the most ancient, as it is the most natural, harbour of Athens. It is nearer than Piræus to the city. The Piræus seems not to have been used as a port until the time of Pericles.
[4] As Bœotia is found generally on the Spartan, so Thessaly appears on the Athenian side. Mutual jealousy of Bœotia would appear to be the chief ground of the alliance.
[5] The country was favourable for pasturage; and Thessalian horses were of special excellency (vide infra, vii. 196).

molius may be seen to this day in Attica; it is at Alopecæ (Foxtown), near the temple of Hercules in Cynosargos.[1]

64. Afterwards, the Lacedæmonians despatched a larger force against Athens, which they put under the command of Cleomenes, son of Anaxandridas, one of their kings. These troops were not sent by sea, but marched by the mainland. When they were come into Attica, their first encounter was with the Thessalian horse, which they shortly put to flight, killing above forty men; the remainder made good their escape, and fled straight to Thessaly. Cleomenes proceeded to the city, and, with the aid of such of the Athenians as wished for freedom, besieged the tyrants, who had shut themselves up in the Pelasgic fortress.[2]

65. And now there had been small chance of the Pisistratidæ falling into the hands of the Spartans, who did not even design to sit down before the place,[3] which had moreover been well provisioned beforehand with stores both of meat and drink,— nay, it is likely that after a few days' blockade the Lacedæmonians would have quitted Attica altogether, and gone back to Sparta,—had not an event occurred most unlucky for the besieged, and most advantageous for the besiegers. The children of the Pisistratidæ were made prisoners, as they were being removed out of the country. By this calamity all their plans were deranged, and—as the ransom of their children—they consented to the demands of the Athenians, and agreed within five days' time to quit Attica. Accordingly they soon afterwards left the country, and withdrew to Sigeum on the Scamander,[4] after reigning thirty-six years over the Athenians. By descent they were Pylians, of the family of the Neleids,[5] to which Codrus and Melanthus likewise belonged, men who in former times from foreign settlers became kings of Athens. And hence it was that Hippocrates [6] came to think of calling his son Pisis-

---

[1] Vide infra, vi. 116.   [2] That is, the Acropolis.

[3] Aware, apparently, of their inability to conduct sieges (vide infra, ix. 70). That the acropolis was not at this time very strong appears from the account of its siege by Xerxes (viii. 52, 53). It was afterwards fortified by Cimon.

[4] Vide infra, ch. 94, 95.

[5] The tale went, that Melanthus (the fifth in descent from the Homeric Nestor, son of Neleus, and king of Pylos), was king of Messenia at the time of the return of the Heraclidæ. Being expelled, he sought a refuge in Attica, where he was kindly received, and even placed upon the throne— Thymœtes, the existing monarch, being forced to abdicate in his favour. This will explain the terms " Pylians " and " Neleids."

[6] Supra, i. 59.

tratus: he named him after the Pisistratus who was a son of Nestor. Such then was the mode in which the Athenians got quit of their tyrants. What they did and suffered worthy of note from the time when they gained their freedom until the revolt of Ionia from King Darius, and the coming of Aristagoras to Athens with a request that the Athenians would lend the Ionians aid, I shall now proceed to relate.

66. The power of Athens had been great before; but, now that the tyrants were gone, it became greater than ever. The chief authority was lodged with two persons, Clisthenes, of the family of the Alcmæonids, who is said to have been the persuader of the Pythoness,[1] and Isagoras, the son of Tisander, who belonged to a noble house, but whose pedigree I am not able to trace further. Howbeit his kinsmen offer sacrifice to the Carian Jupiter. These two men strove together for the mastery; and Clisthenes, finding himself the weaker, called to his aid the common people. Hereupon, instead of the four tribes [2] among which the Athenians had been divided hitherto, Clisthenes made ten tribes, and parcelled out the Athenians among them. He likewise changed the names of the tribes; for whereas they had till now been called after Geleon, Ægicores, Argades, and Hoples, the four sons of Ion, Clisthenes set these names aside, and called his tribes after certain other heroes, all of whom were native, except Ajax. Ajax was associated because, although a foreigner, he was a neighbour and an ally of Athens.[3]

67. My belief is that in acting thus he did but imitate his maternal grandfather, Clisthenes, king of Sicyon.[4] This king, when he was at war with Argos, put an end to the contests of the rhapsodists at Sicyon, because in the Homeric poems Argos and the Argives were so constantly the theme of song. He likewise conceived the wish to drive Adrastus, the son of Talaüs, out of his country,[5] seeing that he was an Argive hero. For Adrastus had a shrine at Sicyon, which yet stands in the market-place of the town. Clisthenes therefore went to Delphi, and asked the oracle if he might expel Adrastus. To this the Pythoness is reported to have answered—"Adrastus is the Sicyonians' king, but thou art only a robber." So when the

---

[1] Supra, ch. 62.
[2] That is, the ancient *hereditary* tribes of Attica.
[3] Ajax was the tutelary hero of Salamis (vide infra, viii. 64 and 121).
[4] Concerning this king, see below, vi. 126.
[5] Adrastus, king of Argos, and leader of the first (mythic) attack upon Thebes, was worshipped as a hero in several places.

god would not grant his request, he went home and began to
think how he might contrive to make Adrastus withdraw of his
own accord. After a while he hit upon a plan which he thought
would succeed. He sent envoys to Thebes in Bœotia, and informed the Thebans that he wished to bring Melanippus,[1] the
son of Astacus, to Sicyon. The Thebans consenting, Clisthenes
carried Melanippus back with him, assigned him a precinct
within the government-house, and built him a shrine there in
the safest and strongest part. The reason for his so doing
(which I must not forbear to mention) was, because Melanippus
was Adrastus' great enemy, having slain both his brother
Mecistes and his son-in-law Tydeus.[2] Clisthenes, after assigning
the precinct to Melanippus, took away from Adrastus the sacrifices and festivals wherewith he had till then been honoured,
and transferred them to his adversary. Hitherto the Sicyonians
had paid extraordinary honours to Adrastus, because the country
had belonged to Polybus,[3] and Adrastus was Polybus' daughter's
son; whence it came to pass that Polybus, dying childless, left
Adrastus his kingdom. Besides other ceremonies, it had been
their wont to honour Adrastus with tragic choruses, which they
assigned to him rather than Bacchus, on account of his calamities.
Clisthenes now gave the choruses to Bacchus, transferring to
Melanippus the rest of the sacred rites.

68. Such were his doings in the matter of Adrastus. With
respect to the Dorian tribes, not choosing the Sicyonians to
have the same tribes as the Argives, he changed all the old
names for new ones; and here he took special occasion to mock
the Sicyonians, for he drew his new names from the words
" pig," and " ass," adding thereto the usual tribe-endings; only
in the case of his own tribe he did nothing of the sort, but gave
them a name drawn from his own kingly office. For he called
his own tribe the Archelaï, or Rulers, while the others he named
Hyatæ, or Pig-folk, Oneatæ, or Ass-folk, and Chœreatæ, or
Swine-folk. The Sicyonians kept these names, not only during
the reign of Clisthenes, but even after his death, by the space
of sixty years: then, however, they took counsel together, and
changed to the well-known names of Hyllæans, Pamphylians,

---

[1] A *statue* of Melanippus is probably intended. See below, ch. 80.
[2] Melanippus, the son of Astacus, is mentioned among the defenders of
Thebes by Pherecydes (Fr. 51) and Apollodorus. He is said to have lost
his own life at the siege, being slain by Amphiaraus.
[3] Polybus was king of Corinth, and Sicyon was included in his dominions.

and Dymanatæ, taking at the same time, as a fourth name, the
title of Ægialeans, from Ægialeus the son of Adrastus.[1]

69. Thus had Clisthenes the Sicyonian done.[2] The Athenian
Clisthenes, who was grandson by the mother's side of the other,
and had been named after him, resolved, from contempt (as I
believe) of the Ionians, that his tribes should not be the same
as theirs; and so followed the pattern set him by his namesake
of Sicyon. Having brought entirely over to his own side the
common people of Athens, whom he had before disdained, he
gave all the tribes new names, and made the number greater
than formerly; instead of the four phylarchs he established ten;
he likewise placed ten demes in each of the tribes; and he was,
now that the common people took his part, very much more
powerful than his adversaries.

70. Isagoras in his turn lost ground; and therefore, to counter-
plot his enemy, he called in Cleomenes the Lacedæmonian, who
had already, at the time when he was besieging the Pisistratidæ,
made a contract of friendship with him. A charge is even
brought against Cleomenes that he was on terms of too great
familiarity with Isagoras's wife. At this time the first thing that
he did, was to send a herald and require that Clisthenes, and a
large number of Athenians besides, whom he called "The
Accursed," should leave Athens. This message he sent at the
suggestion of Isagoras: for in the affair referred to, the blood-
guiltiness lay on the Alcmæonidæ and their partisans, while he
and his friends were quite clear of it.

71. The way in which "The Accursed" at Athens got their
name, was the following. There was a certain Athenian called
Cylon, a victor at the Olympic games, who aspired to the
sovereignty, and aided by a number of his companions, who were
of the same age with himself, made an attempt to seize the
citadel. But the attack failed; and Cylon became a suppliant
at the image. Hereupon the Heads of the Naucraries, who at
that time bore rule in Athens, induced the fugitives to remove

---

[1] Ægialeans was the ancient name of the primitive Ionians of this tract.
[2] Clisthenes was the youngest of three brothers, and had therefore, in
the natural course of things, little hope of the succession. Myron, however,
his eldest brother, having been guilty of adultery with the wife of Isodemus
the second brother, Clisthenes persuaded the latter to revenge himself
by slaying the adulterer. He then represented to him that he could not
reign alone, as it was impossible for him to offer the sacrifices; and was
admitted as joint king on this account. Finally, he had Isodemus persuaded
to go into voluntary exile for a year, in order to purge his pollution; and
during his absence made himself sole king.

by a promise to spare their lives. Nevertheless they were all slain; and the blame was laid on the Alcmæonidæ. All this happened before the time of Pisistratus.

72. When the message of Cleomenes arrived, requiring Clisthenes and " The Accursed " to quit the city, Clisthenes departed of his own accord. Cleomenes, however, notwithstanding his departure, came to Athens, with a small band of followers; and on his arrival sent into banishment seven hundred Athenian families, which were pointed out to him by Isagoras. Succeeding here, he next endeavoured to dissolve the council, and to put the government into the hands of three hundred of the partisans of that leader. But the council resisted, and refused to obey his orders; whereupon Cleomenes, Isagoras, and their followers took possession of the citadel. Here they were attacked by the rest of the Athenians, who took the side of the council, and were besieged for the space of two days: on the third day they accepted terms, being allowed—at least such of them as were Lacedæmonians—to quit the country. And so the word which came to Cleomenes received its fulfilment. For when he first went up into the citadel, meaning to seize it, just as he was entering the sanctuary of the goddess, in order to question her, the priestess arose from her throne, before he had passed the doors, and said—" Stranger from Lacedæmon, depart hence, and presume not to enter the holy place—it is not lawful for a Dorian to set foot there." But he answered, " Oh! woman, I am not a Dorian, but an Achæan." [1] Slighting this warning, Cleomenes made his attempt, and so he was forced to retire, together with his Lacedæmonians.[2] The rest were cast into prison by the Athenians, and condemned to die,—among them Timasitheüs the Delphian, of whose prowess and courage I have great things which I could tell.

73. So these men died in prison. The Athenians directly afterwards recalled Clisthenes, and the seven hundred families which Cleomenes had driven out; and, further, they sent envoys to Sardis, to make an alliance with the Persians, for they knew that war would follow with Cleomenes and the Lacedæmonians. When the ambassadors reached Sardis and delivered their message, Artaphernes, son of Hystaspes, who was at that time governor of the place, inquired of them " who they were, and in

---

[1] The Heraclidæ were. according to the unanimous tradition, the old royal family of the Peloponnese.

[2] The Athenians always cherished a lively recollection of this triumph over their great rivals.   [Cf. Aristoph. *Lysist.* 271 sqq.—E. H. B.]

what part of the world they dwelt,[1] that they wanted to become allies of the Persians?" The messengers told him; upon which he answered them shortly—that " if the Athenians chose to give earth and water to King Darius, he would conclude an alliance with them; but if not, they might go home again." After consulting together, the envoys, anxious to form the alliance, accepted the terms; but on their return to Athens, they fell into deep disgrace on account of their compliance.

74. Meanwhile Cleomenes, who considered himself to have been insulted by the Athenians both in word and deed, was drawing a force together from all parts of the Peloponnese, without informing any one of his object; which was to revenge himself on the Athenians, and to establish Isagoras, who had escaped with him from the citadel,[2] as despot of Athens. Accordingly, with a large army, he invaded the district of Eleusis,[3] while the Bœotians, who had concerted measures with him, took Œnoë and Hysiæ,[4] two country towns upon the frontier; and at the same time the Chalcideans,[5] on another side, plundered divers places in Attica. The Athenians, notwithstanding that danger threatened them from every quarter, put off all thought of the Bœotians and Chalcideans till a future time, and marched against the Peloponnesians, who were at Eleusis.

75. As the two hosts were about to engage, first of all the Corinthians, bethinking themselves that they were perpetrating a wrong, changed their minds, and drew off from the main army. Then Demaratus, son of Ariston, who was himself king of Sparta and joint-leader of the expedition, and who till now had had no sort of quarrel with Cleomenes, followed their example. On account of this rupture between the kings, a law was passed at Sparta, forbidding both monarchs to go out together with the army, as had been the custom hitherto. The law also provided, that, as one of the kings was to be left behind, one of the Tyndaridæ should also remain at home; whereas hitherto both had accompanied the expeditions, as auxiliaries. So when the rest of the allies saw that the Lacedæmonian kings were not of one mind, and that the Corinthian troops had quitted their post, they likewise drew off and departed.

[1] Vide supra, i. 153, and infra, ch. 105.
[2] Disguised, probably as a Spartan.
[3] Eleusis was the key to Attica on the south.
[4] Hysiæ lay on the north side of Cithæron, in the plain of the Asopus.
[5] Chalcis had been one of the most important cities in Greece. It was said to have been originally a colony from Athens. It is the modern Egripo, or Negropont.

76. This was the fourth time that the Dorians had invaded Attica: twice they came as enemies, and twice they came to do good service to the Athenian people. Their first invasion took place at the period when they founded Megara, and is rightly placed in the reign of Codrus at Athens; the second and third occasions were when they came from Sparta to drive out the Pisistratidæ; the fourth was the present attack, when Cleomenes, at the head of a Peloponnesian army, entered at Eleusis. Thus the Dorians had now four times invaded Attica.

77. So when the Spartan army had broken up from its quarters thus ingloriously, the Athenians, wishing to revenge themselves, marched first against the Chalcideans. The Bœotians, however, advancing to the aid of the latter as far as the Euripus, the Athenians thought it best to attack them first. A battle was fought accordingly; and the Athenians gained a very complete victory, killing a vast number of the enemy, and taking seven hundred of them alive. After this, on the very same day, they crossed into Eubœa, and engaged the Chalcideans with the like success; whereupon they left four thousand settlers[1] upon the lands of the Hippobotæ,[2]—which is the name the Chalcideans give to their rich men. All the Chalcidean prisoners whom they took were put in irons, and kept for a long time in close confinement, as likewise were the Bœotians, until the ransom asked for them was paid; and this the Athenians fixed at two minæ the man. The chains wherewith they were fettered the Athenians suspended in their citadel; where they were still to be seen in my day, hanging against the wall scorched by the Median flames,[3] opposite the chapel which faces the west. The Athenians made an offering of the tenth part of the ransom-money: and expended it on the brazen chariot drawn by four steeds, which stands on the left hand

---

[1] Literally, " allotment-holders " (κληροῦχοι). These allotment-holders are to be carefully distinguished from the ordinary colonists (ἄποικοι), who went out to find themselves a home wherever they might be able to settle, and who retained but a very slight connection with the mother-country. The cleruchs were a military garrison planted in a conquered territory, the best portions of which were given to them. They continued Athenian subjects, and retained their full rights as Athenian citizens, occupying a position closely analogous to that of the Roman *coloni* in the earlier times.

[2] The Chalcidean Hippobotæ, or " horse-keepers," were a wealthy aristocracy and correspond to the knights (ἱππεῖς) of most Grecian states, and the " equites," or " celeres," of the Romans. In early times wealth is measured by the ability to maintain a horse, or horses.

[3] Infra, viii. 53.

immediately that one enters the gateway [1] of the citadel. The inscription runs as follows:—

> " When Chalcis and Bœotia dared her might,
> Athens subdued their pride in valorous fight;
> Gave bonds for insults; and, the ransom paid,
> From the full tenths these steeds for Pallas made."

78. Thus did the Athenians increase in strength. And it is plain enough, not from this instance only, but from many everywhere, that freedom is an excellent thing; since even the Athenians, who, while they continued under the rule of tyrants, were not a whit more valiant than any of their neighbours, no sooner shook off the yoke than they became decidedly the first of all. These things show that, while undergoing oppression, they let themselves be beaten, since then they worked for a master; but so soon as they got their freedom, each man was eager to do the best he could for himself. So fared it now with the Athenians.

79. Meanwhile the Thebans, who longed to be revenged on the Athenians, had sent to the oracle, and been told by the Pythoness that of their own strength they would be unable to accomplish their wish: " they must lay the matter," she said, " before the many-voiced, and ask the aid of those nearest them." The messengers, therefore, on their return, called a meeting, and laid the answer of the oracle before the people, who no sooner heard the advice to " ask the aid of those nearest them " than they exclaimed,—" What! are not they who dwell the nearest to us the men of Tanagra, of Coronæa, and Thespiæ? Yet these men always fight on our side, and have aided us with a good heart all through the war. Of what use is it to ask them? But maybe this is not the true meaning of the oracle."

80. As they were thus discoursing one with another, a certain man, informed of the debate, cried out,—" Methinks that I understand what course the oracle would recommend to us. Asôpus, they say, had two daughters, Thêbé and Egina. The god means that, as these two were sisters, we ought to ask the Eginetans to lend us aid." As no one was able to hit on any better explanation, the Thebans forthwith sent messengers to Egina, and, according to the advice of the oracle, asked their aid, as the people " nearest to them." In answer to this petition the Eginetans said, that they would give them the Æacidæ for helpers.

---

[1] The great *Propylæa*, the most magnificent of the works of Pericles.

81. The Thebans now, relying on the assistance of the Æacidæ, ventured to renew the war; but they met with so rough a reception, that they resolved to send to the Eginetans again, returning the Æacidæ, and beseeching them to send some men instead. The Eginetans, who were at that time a most flourishing people, elated with their greatness, and at the same time calling to mind their ancient feud with Athens,[1] agreed to lend the Thebans aid, and forthwith went to war with the Athenians, without even giving them notice by a herald. The attention of these latter being engaged by the struggle with the Bœotians, the Eginetans in their ships of war made descents upon Attica, plundered Phalerum,[2] and ravaged a vast number of the townships upon the sea-board, whereby the Athenians suffered very grievous damage.

82. The ancient feud between the Eginetans and Athenians arose out of the following circumstances. Once upon a time the land of Epidaurus would bear no crops; and the Epidaurians sent to consult the oracle of Delphi concerning their affliction. The answer bade them set up the images of Damia and Auxesia, and promised them better fortune when that should be done. " Shall the images be made of bronze or stone? " the Epidaurians asked; but the Pythoness replied, " Of neither: but let them be made of the garden olive." [3] Then the Epidaurians sent to Athens and asked leave to cut olive wood in Attica, believing the Athenian olives to be the holiest; or, according to others, because there were no olives at that time anywhere else in all the world but at Athens.[4] The Athenians answered that they would give them leave, but on condition of their bringing offerings year by year to Minerva Polias and to Erechtheus.[5] The Epidaurians agreed, and having obtained what they wanted, made the images of olive wood, and set them up in their own

---

[1] Related in the next chapter.

[2] The port of Athens at the time.

[3] Statues in wood preceded those in stone and bronze. The materia suited a ruder state of the arts.

[4] This is, of course, not true, for the olive had been cultivated in the east from a very remote antiquity. (Deuteronomy vi. 11; viii. 8, etc.) It is, however, very likely that the olive may have been introduced into Attica from Asia, before it was known to the rest of Greece.

[5] By " Minerva Polias " we are to understand the Minerva who presided over the city (πόλις). Her temple in later times was a portion of the building known to the Athenians by the general name of Erechtheium, which stood on the north side of the Acropolis, nearly opposite the spot afterwards occupied by the Parthenon.

country. Henceforth their land bore its crops; and they duly paid the Athenians what had been agreed upon.

83. Anciently, and even down to the time when this took place, the Eginetans were in all things subject to the Epidaurians, and had to cross over to Epidaurus for the trial of all suits in which they were engaged one with another. After this, however, the Eginetans built themselves ships, and, growing proud, revolted from the Epidaurians. Having thus come to be at enmity with them, the Eginetans, who were masters of the sea, ravaged Epidaurus, and even carried off these very images of Damia and Auxesia, which they set up in their own country, in the interior, at a place called Œa, about twenty furlongs from their city. This done, they fixed a worship for the images, which consisted in part of sacrifices, in part of female satiric choruses; while at the same time they appointed certain men to furnish the choruses, ten for each goddess. These choruses did not abuse men, but only the women of the country. Holy orgies of a similar kind were in use also among the Epidaurians, and likewise another sort of holy orgies, whereof it is not lawful to speak.

84. After the robbery of the images the Epidaurians ceased to make the stipulated payments to the Athenians, wherefore the Athenians sent to Epidaurus to remonstrate. But the Epidaurians proved to them that they were not guilty of any wrong:—" While the images continued in their country," they said, " they had duly paid the offerings according to the agreement; now that the images had been taken from them, they were no longer under any obligation to pay: the Athenians should make their demand of the Eginetans, in whose possession the figures now were." Upon this the Athenians sent to Egina, and demanded the images back; but the Eginetans answered that the Athenians had nothing whatever to do with them.

85. After this the Athenians relate that they sent a trireme to Egina with certain citizens on board, and that these men, who bore commission from the state, landed in Egina, and sought to take the images away, considering them to be their own, inasmuch as they were made of their wood. And first they endeavoured to wrench them from their pedestals, and so carry them off; but failing herein, they in the next place tied ropes to them, and set to work to try if they could haul them down. In the midst of their hauling suddenly there was a thunderclap, and with the thunderclap an earthquake; and the

crew of the trireme were forthwith seized with madness, and, like enemies, began to kill one another; until at last there was but one left, who returned alone to Phalerum.

86. Such is the account given by the Athenians. The Eginetans deny that there was only a single vessel:—" Had there been only one," they say, " or no more than a few, they would easily have repulsed the attack, even if they had had no fleet at all; but the Athenians came against them with a large number of ships, wherefore they gave way, and did not hazard a battle." They do not however explain clearly whether it was from a conviction of their own inferiority at sea that they yielded, or whether it was for the purpose of doing that which in fact they did. Their account is that the Athenians, disembarking from their ships, when they found that no resistance was offered, made for the statues, and failing to wrench them from their pedestals, tied ropes to them and began to haul. Then, they say,—and some people will perhaps believe them, though I for my part do not,—the two statues, as they were being dragged and hauled, fell down both upon their knees; in which attitude they still remain. Such, according to them, was the conduct of the Athenians; they meanwhile, having learnt beforehand what was intended, had prevailed on the Argives to hold themselves in readiness; and the Athenians accordingly were but just landed on their coasts when the Argives came to their aid. Secretly and silently they crossed over from Epidaurus, and, before the Athenians were aware, cut off their retreat to their ships, and fell upon them; and the thunder came exactly at that moment, and the earthquake with it.

87. The Argives and the Eginetans both agree in giving this account; and the Athenians themselves acknowledge that but one of their men returned alive to Attica. According to the Argives, he escaped from the battle in which the rest of the Athenian troops were destroyed by them. According to the Athenians, it was the god who destroyed their troops; and even this one man did not escape, for he perished in the following manner. When he came back to Athens, bringing word of the calamity, the wives of those who had been sent out on the expedition took it sorely to heart, that he alone should have survived the slaughter of all the rest;—they therefore crowded round the man, and struck him with the brooches by which their dresses were fastened—each, as she struck, asking him, where he had left her husband. And the man died in this way.

The Athenians thought the deed of the women more horrible even than the fate of the troops; as however they did not know how else to punish them, they changed their dress and compelled them to wear the costume of the Ionians. Till this time the Athenian women had worn a Dorian dress, shaped nearly like that which prevails at Corinth. Henceforth they were made to wear the linen tunic, which does not require brooches.[1]

88. In very truth, however, this dress is not originally Ionian, but Carian; for anciently the Greek women all wore the costume which is now called the Dorian. It is said further that the Argives and Eginetans made it a custom, on this same account, for their women to wear brooches half as large again as formerly, and to offer brooches rather than anything else in the temple of these goddesses. They also forbade the bringing of anything Attic into the temple, were it even a jar of earthenware,[2] and made a law that none but native drinking vessels should be used there in time to come. From this early age to my own day the Argive and Eginetan women have always continued to wear their brooches larger than formerly, through hatred of the Athenians.

89. Such then was the origin of the feud which existed between the Eginetans and the Athenians. Hence, when the Thebans made their application for succour, the Eginetans, calling to mind the matter of images, gladly lent their aid to the Bœotians. They ravaged all the sea-coast of Attica; and the Athenians were about to attack them in return, when they were stopped by the oracle of Delphi, which bade them wait till thirty years had passed from the time that the Eginetans did the wrong, and in the thirty-first year, having first set apart a precinct for Æacus, then to begin the war. " So should they succeed to their wish," the oracle said; " but if they went to war at once, though they would still conquer the island in the end, yet they must go through much suffering and much exertion before taking it." On receiving this warning the Athenians

---

[1] The large horseshoe brooch with which ladies in our times occasionally fasten their shawls, closely resembles the ancient περόνη, which was not a buckle, but " a brooch, consisting of a pin, and a curved portion, furnished with a hook." The Dorian tunic was of woollen; it had no sleeves, and was fastened over both the shoulders by brooches. It was scanty and short, sometimes scarcely reaching the knee. The Ionic tunic was of linen: it had short loose sleeves, as we see in statues of the Muses, and so did not need brooches; it was a long and full dress hiding the form, and reaching down generally to the feet.

[2] The pottery of Athens was the most celebrated in ancient Greece.

set apart a precinct for Æacus—the same which still remains dedicated to him in their market-place—but they could not hear with any patience of waiting thirty years, after they had suffered such grievous wrong at the hands of the Eginetans.

90. Accordingly they were making ready to take their revenge when a fresh stir on the part of the Lacedæmonians hindered their projects. These last had become aware of the truth—how that the Alcmæonidæ had practised on the Pythoness, and the Pythoness had schemed against themselves, and against the Pisistratidæ; and the discovery was a double grief to them, for while they had driven their own sworn friends into exile, they found that they had not gained thereby a particle of good will from Athens. They were also moved by certain prophecies, which declared that many dire calamities should befall them at the hands of the Athenians. Of these in times past they had been ignorant; but now they had become acquainted with them by means of Cleomenes, who had brought them with him to Sparta, having found them in the Athenian citadel, where they had been left by the Pisistratidæ when they were driven from Athens: they were in the temple,[1] and Cleomenes having discovered them, carried them off.

91. So when the Lacedæmonians obtained possession of the prophecies, and saw that the Athenians were growing in strength, and had no mind to acknowledge any subjection to their control, it occurred to them that, if the people of Attica were free, they would be likely to be as powerful as themselves, but if they were oppressed by a tyranny, they would be weak and submissive. Under this feeling they sent and recalled Hippias, the son of Pisistratus, from Sigeum upon the Hellespont, where the Pisistratidæ had taken shelter.[2] Hippias came at their bidding, and the Spartans on his arrival summoned deputies from all their other allies, and thus addressed the assembly:—

" Friends and brothers in arms, we are free to confess that we did lately a thing which was not right. Misled by counterfeit oracles, we drove from their country those who were our sworn and true friends, and who had, moreover, engaged to keep Athens in dependence upon us; and we delivered the government into the hands of an unthankful people—a people who no sooner got their freedom by our means, and grew in power, than they turned us and our king, with every token of insult, out of their city.

---

[1] The temple of Minerva Polias (vide supra, chs. 72 and 82).
[2] Vide supra, ch. 65 [and Bury's *Hist. of Greece*, ch. v.—E. H. B.].

Since then they have gone on continually raising their thoughts higher, as their neighbours of Bœotia and Chalcis have already discovered to their cost, and as others too will presently discover if they shall offend them.   Having thus erred, we will endeavour now, with your help, to remedy the evils we have caused, and to obtain vengeance on the Athenians.   For this cause we have sent for Hippias to come here, and have summoned you likewise from your several states, that we may all now with heart and hand unite to restore him to Athens, and thereby give him back that which we took from him formerly."

92. (§ 1.) Such was the address of the Spartans.   The greater number of the allies listened without being persuaded.   None however broke silence, but Sosicles the Corinthian, who exclaimed—

" Surely the heaven will soon be below, and the earth above, and men will henceforth live in the sea, and fish take their place upon the dry land, since you, Lacedæmonians, propose to put down free governments in the cities of Greece, and to set up tyrannies in their room.   There is nothing in the whole world so unjust, nothing so bloody, as a tyranny.   If, however, it seems to you a desirable thing to have the cities under despotic rule, begin by putting a tyrant over yourselves, and then establish despots in the other states.   While you continue yourselves, as you have always been, unacquainted with tyranny, and take such excellent care that Sparta may not suffer from it, to act as you are now doing is to treat your allies unworthily.   If you knew what tyranny was as well as ourselves, you would be better advised than you now are in regard to it.   (§ 2.) The government at Corinth was once an oligarchy a single race, called Bacchiadæ, who intermarried only among themselves, held the management of affairs.   Now it happened that Amphion, one of these, had a daughter, named Labda, who was lame, and whom therefore none of the Bacchiadæ would consent to marry; so she was taken to wife by Aëtion, son of Echecrates, a man of the township of Petra, who was, however, by descent of the race of the Lapithæ, and of the house of Cæneus.   Aëtion, as he had no child, either by this wife or by any other, went to Delphi to consult the oracle concerning the matter.   Scarcely had he entered the temple when the Pythoness saluted him in these words—

' No one honours thee now, Aëtion, worthy of honour;—
Labda shall soon be a mother—her offspring a rock, that will one day
Fall on the kingly race, and right the city of Corinth.'

By some chance this address of the oracle to Aëtion came to the ears of the Bacchiadæ, who till then had been unable to perceive the meaning of another earlier prophecy which likewise bore upon Corinth, and pointed to the same event as Aëtion's prediction. It was the following:—

> 'When mid the rocks an eagle shall bear a carnivorous lion,
> Mighty and fierce, he shall loosen the limbs of many beneath them—
> Brood ye well upon this, all ye Corinthian people,
> Ye who dwell by fair Peirênê, and beetling Corinth.'

(§ 3.) The Bacchiadæ had possessed this oracle for some time; but they were quite at a loss to know what it meant until they heard the response given to Aëtion; then however they at once perceived its meaning, since the two agreed so well together. Nevertheless, though the bearing of the first prophecy was now clear to them, they remained quiet, being minded to put to death the child which Aëtion was expecting. As soon, therefore, as his wife was delivered, they sent ten of their number to the township where Aëtion lived, with orders to make away with the baby. So the men came to Petra, and went into Aëtion's house, and there asked if they might see the child; and Labda, who knew nothing of their purpose, but thought their inquiries arose from a kindly feeling towards her husband, brought the child, and laid him in the arms of one of them. Now they had agreed by the way that whoever first got hold of the child should dash it against the ground. It happened, however, by a providential chance, that the babe, just as Labda put him into the man's arms, smiled in his face. The man saw the smile, and was touched with pity, so that he could not kill it; he therefore passed it on to his next neighbour, who gave it to a third; and so it went through all the ten without any one choosing to be the murderer. The mother received her child back; and the men went out of the house, and stood near the door, and there blamed and reproached one another; chiefly however accusing the man who had first had the child in his arms, because he had not done as had been agreed upon. At last, after much time had been thus spent, they resolved to go into the house again and all take part in the murder. (§ 4.) But it was fated that evil should come upon Corinth from the progeny of Aëtion; and so it chanced that Labda, as she stood near the door, heard all that the men said to one another, and fearful of their changing their mind, and returning to destroy her baby, she carried him off and hid him in what seemed to her the most unlikely place to be

suspected, viz., a ' cypsel ' or corn-bin. She knew that if they
came back to look for the child, they would search all her house;
and so indeed they did, but not finding the child after looking
everywhere, they thought it best to go away, and declare to
those by whom they had been sent that they had done their
bidding. And thus they reported on their return home. (§ 5.)
Aëtion's son grew up, and, in remembrance of the danger from
which he had escaped, was named Cypselus, after the corn-bin.
When he reached to man's estate, he went to Delphi, and on
consulting the oracle, received a response which was two-sided.
It was the following:—

> ' See there comes to my dwelling a man much favour'd of fortune,
> Cypselus, son of Aëtion, and king of the glorious Corinth,—
> He and his children too, but not his children's children.'

Such was the oracle; and Cypselus put so much faith in it that
he forthwith made his attempt, and thereby became master of
Corinth. Having thus got the tyranny, he showed himself a
harsh ruler—many of the Corinthians he drove into banishment,
many he deprived of their fortunes, and a still greater number
of their lives. (§ 6.) His reign lasted thirty years, and was prosperous to its close; insomuch that he left the government to
Periander, his son. This prince at the beginning of his reign was
of a milder temper than his father; but after he corresponded
by means of messengers with Thrasybulus, tyrant of Miletus,
he became even more sanguinary. On one occasion he sent a
herald to ask Thrasybulus what mode of government it was
safest to set up in order to rule with honour. Thrasybulus led
the messenger without the city, and took him into a field of
corn, through which he began to walk, while he asked him again
and again concerning his coming from Corinth, ever as he went
breaking off and throwing away all such ears of corn as over-
topped the rest. In this way he went through the whole field,
and destroyed all the best and richest part of the crop; then,
without a word, he sent the messenger back. On the return of
the man to Corinth, Periander was eager to know what Thrasybulus had counselled, but the messenger reported that he had
said nothing; and he wondered that Periander had sent him to
so strange a man, who seemed to have lost his senses, since he
did nothing but destroy his own property. And upon this he
told how Thrasybulus had behaved at the interview. (§ 7.)
Periander, perceiving what the action meant, and knowing that
Thrasybulus advised the destruction of all the leading citizens,

treated his subjects from this time forward with the very greatest cruelty. Where Cypselus had spared any, and had neither put them to death nor banished them, Periander completed what his father had left unfinished.[1] One day he stripped all the women of Corinth stark naked, for the sake of his own wife Melissa. He had sent messengers into Thesprotia to consult the oracle of the dead upon the Acheron[2] concerning a pledge which had been given into his charge by a stranger, and Melissa appeared, but refused to speak or tell where the pledge was,—' she was chill,' she said, ' having no clothes; the garments buried with her were of no manner of use, since they had not been burnt. And this should be her token to Periander, that what she said was true— the oven was cold when he baked his loaves in it.' When this message was brought him, Periander knew the token; wherefore he straightway made proclamation, that all the wives of the Corinthians should go forth to the temple of Juno. So the women apparelled themselves in their bravest, and went forth, as if to a festival. Then, with the help of his guards, whom he had placed for the purpose, he stripped them one and all, making no difference between the free women and the slaves; and, taking their clothes to a pit, he called on the name of Melissa, and burnt the whole heap. This done, he sent a second time to the oracle; and Melissa's ghost told him where he would find the stranger's pledge. Such, O Lacedæmonians! is tyranny, and such are the deeds which spring from it. We Corinthians marvelled greatly when we first knew of your having sent for Hippias; and now it surprises us still more to hear you speak as you do. We adjure you, by the common gods of Greece, plant not despots in her cities. If however you are determined, if you persist, against all justice, in seeking to restore Hippias,—know, at least, that the Corinthians will not approve your conduct."

93. When Sosicles, the deputy from Corinth, had thus spoken, Hippias replied, and, invoking the same gods, he said,—" Of a surety the Corinthians will, beyond all others, regret the Pisistratidæ, when the fated days come for them to be distressed by the Athenians." Hippias spoke thus because he knew the prophecies better than any man living. But the rest of the allies, who till Sosicles spoke had remained quiet, when they heard him utter his thoughts thus boldly, all together broke silence, and

---

[1] The cruel tyranny of Periander is agreed on by all writers.

[2] [A river of Epirus; now known as the *Suliotiko* or *Phanariotiko* : see Frazer's *n.* on *Pausanias*, I. xvii. 5.—E. H. B.]

declared themselves of the same mind; and withal, they con-
jured the Lacedæmonians " not to revolutionise a Grecian city."
And in this way the enterprise came to nought.

94. Hippias hereupon withdrew; and Amyntas the Macedonian offered him the city of Anthemûs, while the Thessalians
were willing to give him Iolcôs: [1] but he would accept neither the
one nor the other, preferring to go back to Sigêum,[2] which city
Pisistratus had taken by force of arms from the Mytilenæans.
Pisistratus, when he became master of the place, established
there as tyrant his own natural son, Hegesistratus, whose mother
was an Argive woman.   But this prince was not allowed to enjoy
peaceably what his father had made over to him; for during
very many years there had been war between the Athenians of
Sigêum and the Mytilenæans of the city called Achillêum.[3]
They of Mytilêné insisted on having the place restored to them:
but the Athenians refused, since they argued that the Æolians
had no better claim to the Trojan territory than themselves, or
than any of the other Greeks who helped Menelaüs on occasion
of the rape of Helen.

95. War accordingly continued, with many and various in-
cidents, whereof the following was one.   In a battle which was
gained by the Athenians, the poet Alcæus took to flight, and
saved himself, but lost his arms, which fell into the hands of the
conquerors.   They hung them up in the temple of Minerva at
Sigêum; and Alcæus made a poem, describing his misadventure
to his friend Melanippus, and sent it to him at Mytilêné.   The
Mytilenæans and Athenians were reconciled by Periander, the
son of Cypselus, who was chosen by both parties as arbiter—he
decided that they should each retain that of which they were at
the time possessed; and Sigêum passed in this way under the
dominion of Athens.

96. On the return of Hippias to Asia from Lacedæmon,
he moved heaven and earth to set Artaphernes against the
Athenians, and did all that lay in his power to bring Athens
into subjection to himself and Darius.   So when the Athenians
learnt what he was about, they sent envoys to Sardis, and exhorted the Persians not to lend an ear to the Athenian exiles.
Artaphernes told them in reply, " that if they wished to remain
safe, they must receive back Hippias."   The Athenians, when

[1] Iolcos, the port from which the Argonauts were said to have sailed,
lay at the bottom of the Pagasean gulf in the district called Magnesia.
[2] Supra, ch. 65.
[3] So called because it was supposed to contain the tomb of Achilles.

this answer was reported to them, determined not to consent, and therefore made up their minds to be at open enmity with the Persians.

97. The Athenians had come to this decision, and were already in bad odour with the Persians, when Aristagoras the Milesian, dismissed from Sparta by Cleomenes the Lacedæmonian, arrived at Athens. He knew that, after Sparta, Athens was the most powerful of the Grecian states.[1] Accordingly he appeared before the people, and, as he had done at Sparta,[2] spoke to them of the good things which there were in Asia, and of the Persian mode of fight—how they used neither shield nor spear, and were very easy to conquer. All this he urged, and reminded them also, that Miletus was a colony from Athens,[3] and therefore ought to receive their succour, since they were so powerful—and in the earnestness of his entreaties, he cared little what he promised —till, at the last, he prevailed and won them over. It seems indeed to be easier to deceive a multitude than one man—for Aristagoras, though he failed to impose on Cleomenes the Lacedæmonian, succeeded with the Athenians, who were thirty thousand. Won by his persuasions, they voted that twenty ships should be sent to the aid of the Ionians, under the command of Melanthius, one of the citizens, a man of mark in every way. These ships were the beginning of mischief both to the Greeks and to the barbarians.

98. Aristagoras sailed away in advance, and when he reached Miletus, devised a plan, from which no manner of advantage could possibly accrue to the Ionians;—indeed, in forming it, he did not aim at their benefit, but his sole wish was to annoy King Darius. He sent a messenger into Phrygia to those Pæonians who had been led away captive by Megabazus from the river Strymon,[4] and who now dwelt by themselves in Phrygia, having a tract of land and a hamlet of their own. This man, when he reached the Pæonians, spoke thus to them:—

" Men of Pæonia, Aristagoras, king of Miletus, has sent me to you, to inform you that you may now escape, if you choose to follow the advice he proffers. All Ionia has revolted from the king; and the way is open to you to return to your own land. You have only to contrive to reach the sea-coast; the rest shall be our business."

When the Pæonians heard this, they were exceedingly re-

---

[1] Compare, i. 56.

[2] Supra, ch. 49.

[3] Supra, i. 147, and infra, ix. 97.

[4] Vide supra, chs. 15-17.

joiced, and, taking with them their wives and children, they made all speed to the coast; a few only remaining in Phrygia through fear. The rest, having reached the sea, crossed over to Chios, where they had just landed, when a great troop of Persian horse came following upon their heels, and seeking to overtake them. Not succeeding, however, they sent a message across to Chios, and begged the Pæonians to come back again. These last refused, and were conveyed by the Chians from Chios to Lesbos, and by the Lesbians thence to Doriscus; [1] from which place they made their way on foot to Pæonia.

99. The Athenians now arrived with a fleet of twenty sail, and brought also in their company five triremes of the Eretrians; [2] which had joined the expedition, not so much out of goodwill towards Athens, as to pay a debt which they already owed to the people of Miletus. For in the old war between the Chalcideans and Eretrians, the Milesians fought on the Eretrian side throughout, while the Chalcideans had the help of the Samian people. Aristagoras, on their arrival, assembled the rest of his allies, and proceeded to attack Sardis, not however leading the army in person, but appointing to the command his own brother Charopinus, and Hermophantus, one of the citizens, while he himself remained behind in Miletus.

100. The Ionians sailed with this fleet to Ephesus, and, leaving their ships at Coressus in the Ephesian territory, took guides from the city, and went up the country, with a great host. They marched along the course of the river Caÿster,[3] and, crossing over the ridge of Tmôlus, came down upon Sardis and took it, no man opposing them;—the whole city fell into their hands, except only the citadel, which Artaphernes defended in person, having with him no contemptible force.

101. Though, however, they took the city, they did not succeed in plundering it; for, as the houses in Sardis were most of them built of reeds, and even the few which were of brick had a reed thatching for their roof, one of them was no sooner fired by a soldier than the flames ran speedily from house to house, and spread over the whole place.[4] As the fire raged, the Lydians,

---

[1] Herodotus gives the name of Doriscus to the great alluvial plain through which the river Hebrus (*Maritza*) empties itself into the sea.

[2] Eretria lay upon the coast of Eubœa, 12 or 13 miles below Chalcis.

[3] The Caÿster, now the Little Mendere, washed Ephesus on the north. and formed its harbour.

[4] In Eastern capitals the houses are still rarely of brick or stone. Reeds and wood constitute the chief building materials. Hence the terrible conflagrations which from time to time devastate them.

and such Persians as were in the city, inclosed on every side
by the flames, which had seized all the skirts of the town, and
finding themselves unable to get out, came in crowds into the
market-place, and gathered themselves upon the banks of the
Pactôlus. This stream, which comes down from Mount Tmôlus,
and brings the Sardians a quantity of gold-dust, runs directly
through the market place of Sardis, and joins the Hermus, before
that river reaches the sea. So the Lydians and Persians, brought
together in this way in the market-place and about the Pactôlus,
were forced to stand on their defence; and the Ionians, when
they saw the enemy in part resisting, in part pouring towards
them in dense crowds, took fright, and drawing off to the ridge
which is called Tmôlus, when night came, went back to their
ships.

102. Sardis however was burnt, and, among other buildings, a
temple of the native goddess Cybelé was destroyed; [1] which was
the reason afterwards alleged by the Persians for setting on fire
the temples of the Greeks. As soon as what had happened was
known, all the Persians who were stationed on this side the Halys
drew together, and brought help to the Lydians. Finding
however, when they arrived, that the Ionians had already withdrawn from Sardis, they set off, and, following close upon their
track, came up with them at Ephesus. The Ionians drew out
against them in battle array; and a fight ensued, wherein the
Greeks had very greatly the worse. Vast numbers were slain
by the Persians: among other men of note, they killed the
captain of the Eretrians, a certain Eualcidas, a man who had
gained crowns at the games, and received much praise from
Simonides the Cean. [2] Such as made their escape from the battle,
dispersed among the several cities.

103. So ended this encounter. Afterwards the Athenians
quite forsook the Ionians, and, though Aristagoras besought
them much by his ambassadors, refused to give him any further
help. Still the Ionians, notwithstanding this desertion, continued unceasingly their preparations to carry on the war against
the Persian king, which their late conduct towards him had
rendered unavoidable. Sailing into the Hellespont, they brought

[1] Cybêbé, Cybelé, or Rhea, was the Magna Mater, or Mother of the Gods,
a principal object of worship among all the Oriental nations. Her temple
at Sardis was a magnificent structure, of the Ionic order, formed of blocks
of white marble of an enormous size.

[2] Simonides the Cean, like Pindar, wrote odes in praise of those who
carried off prizes in the games.

Byzantium, and all the other cities in that quarter, under their sway. Again, quitting the Hellespont, they went to Caria, and won the greater part of the Carians to their side; while Caunus, which had formerly refused to join with them, after the burning of Sardis, came over likewise.

104. All the Cyprians too, excepting those of Amathûs, of their own proper motion espoused the Ionian cause. The occasion of their revolting from the Medes was the following. There was a certain Onesilus, younger brother of Gorgus, king of Salamis, and son of Chersis, who was son of Siromus, and grandson of Evelthon. This man had often in former times entreated Gorgus to rebel against the king; but, when he heard of the revolt of the Ionians, he left him no peace with his importunity. As, however, Gorgus would not hearken to him, he watched his occasion, and when his brother had gone outside the town, he with his partisans closed the gates upon him. Gorgus, thus deprived of his city, fled to the Medes; and Onesilus, being now king of Salamis, sought to bring about a revolt of the whole of Cyprus. All were prevailed on except the Amathusians, who refused to listen to him; whereupon Onesilus sate down before Amathûs,[1] and laid siege to it.

105. While Onesilus was engaged in the siege of Amathûs, King Darius received tidings of the taking and burning of Sardis by the Athenians and Ionians; and at the same time he learnt that the author of the league, the man by whom the whole matter had been planned and contrived, was Aristagoras the Milesian. It is said that he no sooner understood what had happened, than, laying aside all thought concerning the Ionians, who would, he was sure, pay dear for their rebellion, he asked, "Who the Athenians were?"[2] and, being informed, called for his bow, and placing an arrow on the string, shot upward into the sky,[3] saying, as he let fly the shaft—"Grant me, Jupiter,[4] to revenge myself on the Athenians!" After this speech, he bade one of his servants every day, when his dinner was spread, three times repeat these words to him—"Master, remember the Athenians."

106. Then he summoned into his presence Histiæus of Miletus,

---

[1] Amathus, one of the most ancient Phœnician settlements in Cyprus.
[2] Compare i. 153, and supra, ch. 73.
[3] Compare with this what is said of the Thracians (supra, iv. 94). The notion here seems to be, to send the message to heaven on the arrow.
[4] That is, "Ormuzd." The Greeks identify the *supreme* God of each nation with their own Zeus (vide supra, i. 131; ii. 55, etc.).

whom he had kept at his court for so long a time; and on his appearance addressed him thus—" I am told, O Histiæus, that thy lieutenant, to whom thou hast given Miletus in charge, has raised a rebellion against me. He has brought men from the other continent to contend with me, and, prevailing on the Ionians—whose conduct I shall know how to recompense—to join with this force, he has robbed me of Sardis! Is this as it should be, thinkest thou? Or can it have been done without thy knowledge and advice? Beware lest it be found hereafter that the blame of these acts is thine."

Histiæus answered—" What words are these, O king, to which thou hast given utterance? I advise aught from which unpleasantness of any kind, little or great, should come to thee! What could I gain by so doing? Or what is there that I lack now? Have I not all that thou hast, and am I not thought worthy to partake all thy counsels? If my lieutenant has indeed done as thou sayest, be sure he has done it all of his own head. For my part, I do not think it can really be that the Milesians and my lieutenant have raised a rebellion against thee. But if they have indeed committed aught to thy hurt, and the tidings are true which have come to thee, judge thou how ill-advised thou wert to remove me from the sea-coast. The Ionians, it seems, have waited till I was no longer in sight, and then sought to execute that which they long ago desired; whereas, if I had been there, not a single city would have stirred. Suffer me then to hasten at my best speed to Ionia, that I may place matters there upon their former footing, and deliver up to thee the deputy of Miletus, who has caused all the troubles. Having managed this business to thy heart's content, I swear by all the gods of thy royal house, I will not put off the clothes in which I reach Ionia till I have made Sardinia, the biggest island in the world, thy tributary."

107. Histiæus spoke thus, wishing to deceive the king; and Darius, persuaded by his words, let him go; only bidding him be sure to do as he had promised, and afterwards come back to Susa.

108. In the meantime—while the tidings of the burning of Sardis were reaching the king, and Darius was shooting the arrow and having the conference with Histiæus, and the latter, by permission of Darius, was hastening down to the sea—in Cyprus the following events took place. Tidings came to Onesilus, the Salaminian, who was still besieging Amathûs, that a

certain Artybius, a Persian, was looked for to arrive in Cyprus with a great Persian armament.   So Onesilus, when the news reached him, sent off heralds to all parts of Ionia, and besought the Ionians to give him aid.   After brief deliberation, these last in full force passed over into the island; and the Persians about the same time crossed in their ships from Cilicia, and proceeded by land to attack Salamis; while the Phœnicians, with the fleet, sailed round the promontory which goes by the name of " the Keys of Cyprus."

109. In this posture of affairs the princes of Cyprus called together the captains of the Ionians, and thus addressed them:—

" Men of Ionia, we Cyprians leave it to you to choose whether you will fight with the Persians or with the Phœnicians.   If it be your pleasure to try your strength on land against the Persians, come on shore at once, and array yourselves for the battle; we will then embark aboard your ships and engage the Phœnicians by sea.   If, on the other hand, ye prefer to encounter the Phœnicians, let that be your task: only be sure, whichever part you choose, to acquit yourselves so that Ionia and Cyprus, so far as depends on you, may preserve their freedom."

The Ionians made answer—" The commonwealth of Ionia sent us here to guard the sea, not to make over our ships to you, and engage with the Persians on shore.   We will therefore keep the post which has been assigned to us, and seek therein to be of some service.   Do you, remembering what you suffered when you were the slaves of the Medes, behave like brave warriors."

110. Such was the reply of the Ionians.   Not long afterwards the Persians advanced into the plain before Salamis,[1] and the Cyprian kings[2] ranged their troops in order of battle against them, placing them so that while the rest of the Cyprians were drawn up against the auxiliaries of the enemy, the choicest troops of the Salaminians and the Solians[3] were set to oppose the Persians.   At the same time Onesilus, of his own accord, took post opposite to Artybius, the Persian general.

111. Now Artybius rode a horse which had been trained to rear up against a foot-soldier.   Onesilus, informed of this, called

---

[1] Salamis was situated on the eastern coast of Cyprus.
[2] Cyprus, like Phœnicia, seems to have been at all times governed by a number of petty kings.
[3] Soli lay on the north coast of Cyprus.

to him his shieldbearer, who was a Carian by nation, a man well
skilled in war, and of daring courage; and thus addressed him:—
" I hear," he said, " that the horse which Artybius rides, rears
up and attacks with his fore legs and teeth the man against
whom his rider urges him. Consider quickly therefore and tell
me which wilt thou undertake to encounter, the steed or the
rider? " Then the squire answered him, " Both, my liege, or
either, am I ready to undertake, and there is nothing that I will
shrink from at thy bidding. But I will tell thee what seems to
me to make most for thy interests. As thou art a prince and a
general, I think thou shouldest engage with one who is himself
both a prince and also a general. For then, if thou slayest thine
adversary, 'twill redound to thine honour, and if he slays thee
(which may Heaven forefend!), yet to fall by the hand of a
worthy foe makes death lose half its horror. To us, thy followers,
leave his war-horse and his retinue. And have thou no fear of
the horse's tricks. I warrant that this is the last time he will
stand up against any one."

112. Thus spake the Carian; and shortly after, the two hosts
joined battle both by sea and land. And here it chanced that
by sea the Ionians, who that day fought as they have never done
either before or since, defeated the Phœnicians, the Samians
especially distinguishing themselves. Meanwhile the combat
had begun on land, and the two armies were engaged in a sharp
struggle, when thus it fell out in the matter of the generals.
Artybius, astride upon his horse, charged down upon Onesilus,
who, as he had agreed with his shieldbearer, aimed his blow at
the rider; the horse reared and placed his fore feet upon the
shield of Onesilus, when the Carian cut at him with a reaping-
hook, and severed the two legs from the body. The horse fell
upon the spot, and Artybius, the Persian general, with him.

113. In the thick of the fight, Stesanor, tyrant of Curium,[1]
who commanded no inconsiderable body of troops, went over
with them to the enemy. On this desertion of the Curians—
Argive colonists, if report says true—forthwith the war-chariots
of the Salaminians followed the example set them, and went
over likewise; whereupon victory declared in favour of the
Persians; and the army of the Cyprians being routed, vast
numbers were slain, and among them Onesilus, the son of
Chersis, who was the author of the revolt, and Aristocyprus,
king of the Solians. This Aristocyprus was son of Philocyprus,

[1] Curium lay upon the southern coast, between Paphos and Amathûs.

whom Solon the Athenian, when he visited Cyprus, praised in his poems [1] beyond all other sovereigns.

114. The Amathusians, because Onesilus had laid siege to their town, cut the head off his corpse, and took it with them to Amathûs, where it was set up over the gates. Here it hung till it became hollow; whereupon a swarm of bees took possession of it, and filled it with a honeycomb. On seeing this the Amathusians consulted the oracle, and were commanded " to take down the head and bury it, and thenceforth to regard Onesilus as a hero, and offer sacrifice to him year by year; so it would go the better with them." And to this day the Amathusians do as they were then bidden.

115. As for the Ionians who had gained the sea-fight, when they found that the affairs of Onesilus were utterly lost and ruined, and that siege was laid to all the cities of Cyprus excepting Salamis, which the inhabitants had surrendered to Gorgus,[2] the former king—forthwith they left Cyprus, and sailed away home. Of the cities which were besieged, Soli held out the longest: the Persians took it by undermining the wall in the fifth month from the beginning of the siege.

116. Thus, after enjoying a year of freedom, the Cyprians were enslaved for the second time. Meanwhile Daurises, who was married to one of the daughters of Darius, together with Hymeas, Otanes, and other Persian captains, who were likewise married to daughters of the king,[3] after pursuing the Ionians who had fought at Sardis, defeating them, and driving them to their ships, divided their efforts against the different cities, and proceeded in succession to take and sack each one of them.

117. Daurises attacked the towns upon the Hellespont, and took in as many days the five cities of Dardanus, Abydos, Percôté, Lampsacus, and Pæsus. From Pæsus he marched against Parium; but on his way receiving intelligence that the Carians had made common cause with the Ionians, and thrown off the Persian yoke, he turned round, and, leaving the Hellespont, marched away towards Caria.

118. The Carians by some chance got information of this

[1] The poems of Solon were written chiefly in the elegiac metre, and were hortatory or gnomic.

[2] Gorgus is still king at the time of the expedition of Xerxes (infra, vii. 98).

[3] The practice of marrying the king's daughters to the most distinguished of the Persian nobles had in view the consolidation of the empire and the strengthening of the royal power, by attaching to the throne those who would have been most likely to stir up revolts.

movement before Daurises arrived, and drew together their
strength to a place called "the White Columns," which is on
the river Marsyas, a stream running from the Idrian country,
and emptying itself into the Mæander. Here when they were
met, many plans were put forth; but the best, in my judgment, was that of Pixodarus, the son of Mausôlus, a Cindyan,
who was married to a daughter of Syennesis, the Cilician king.
His advice was, that the Carians should cross the Mæander, and
fight with the river at their back; that so, all chance of flight
being cut off, they might be forced to stand their ground, and
have their natural courage raised to a still higher pitch. His
opinion, however, did not prevail; it was thought best to make
the enemy have the Mæander behind them; that so, if they
were defeated in the battle and put to flight, they might have
no retreat open, but be driven headlong into the river.

119. The Persians soon afterwards approached, and, crossing
the Mæander, engaged the Carians upon the banks of the Marsyas; where for a long time the battle was stoutly contested,
but at last the Carians were defeated, being overpowered by
numbers. On the side of the Persians there fell 2000, while the
Carians had not fewer than 10,000 slain. Such as escaped from
the field of battle collected together at Labranda, in the vast
precinct of Jupiter Stratius—a deity worshipped only by the
Carians—and in the sacred grove of plane-trees. Here they
deliberated as to the best means of saving themselves, doubting
whether they would fare better if they gave themselves up to
the Persians, or if they abandoned Asia for ever.

120. As they were debating these matters a body of Milesians
and allies came to their assistance; whereupon the Carians, dismissing their former thoughts, prepared themselves afresh for
war, and on the approach of the Persians gave them battle a
second time. They were defeated, however, with still greater
loss than before; and while all the troops engaged suffered
severely, the blow fell with most force on the Milesians.

121. The Carians, some while after, repaired their ill fortune
in another action. Understanding that the Persians were about
to attack their cities, they laid an ambush for them on the road
which leads to Pedasus; the Persians, who were making a
night-march, fell into the trap, and the whole army was destroyed, together with the generals, Daurises, Amorges, and
Sisimaces: Myrsus too, the son of Gyges, was killed at the same
time. The leader of the ambush was Heraclides, the son of

Ibanôlis, a man of Mylasa. Such was the way in which these Persians perished.

122. In the meantime Hymeas, who was likewise one of those by whom the Ionians were pursued after their attack on Sardis, directing his course towards the Propontis, took Cius,[1] a city of Mysia. Learning, however, that Daurises had left the Hellespont, and was gone into Caria, he in his turn quitted the Propontis, and marching with the army under his command to the Hellespont, reduced all the Æolians of the Troad, and likewise conquered the Gergithæ, a remnant of the ancient Teucrians. He did not, however, quit the Troad, but, after gaining these successes, was himself carried off by disease.

123. After his death, which happened as I have related, Artaphernes, the satrap of Sardis, and Otanes, the third general,[2] were directed to undertake the conduct of the war against Ionia and the neighbouring Æolis. By them Clazomenæ in the former,[3] and Cymé in the latter,[4] were recovered.

124. As the cities fell one after another, Aristagoras the Milesian (who was in truth, as he now plainly showed, a man of but little courage), notwithstanding that it was he who had caused the disturbances in Ionia and made so great a commotion, began, seeing his danger, to look about for means of escape. Being convinced that it was in vain to endeavour to overcome King Darius, he called his brothers-in-arms together, and laid before them the following project:—" 'Twould be well," he said, " to have some place of refuge, in case they were driven out of Miletus. Should he go out at the head of a colony to Sardinia,[5] or should he sail to Myrcinus in Edonia, which Histiæus had received as a gift from King Darius, and had begun to fortify? "

125. To this question of Aristagoras, Hecatæus, the historian, son of Hegesander, made answer, that in his judgment neither place was suitable. " Aristagoras should build a fort," he said, " in the island of Leros,[6] and, if driven from Miletus, should go there and bide his time; from Leros attacks might readily be made, and he might re-establish himself in Miletus." Such was the advice given by Hecatæus.

126. Aristagoras, however, was bent on retiring to Myrcinus.

[1] Cius, like most other towns upon this coast, was a colony of the Milesians.
[2] Supra, ch. 116.   [3] Supra, i. 142.   [4] Supra, i. 149.
[5] Sardinia seems to have been viewed by the Greeks of this time as a sort of El Dorado.
[6] Lĕros, one of the Sporades, retains its ancient name almost unchanged.

Accordingly, he put the government of Miletus into the hands of one of the chief citizens, named Pythagoras, and, taking with him all who liked to go, sailed to Thrace, and there made himself master of the place in question. From thence he proceeded to attack the Thracians; but here he was cut off with his whole army, while besieging a city whose defenders were anxious to accept terms of surrender.

———

ADDED NOTE BY THE EDITOR

" The theme of Herodotus—the struggle of Greece with the Orient—possessed for him a deeper meaning than the political result of the Persian War. It was the contact and collision of two different types of civilisation; of peoples of two different characters and different political institutions. In the last division of his work, where the final struggle of Persia and Greece is narrated, this contest between the slavery of the barbarian and the liberty of the Greek, between Oriental autocracy and Hellenic constitutionalism, is ever present and is forcibly brought out. But the contrast of Hellenic with Oriental culture pervades the whole work; it informs the unity of the external theme with the deeper unity of an inner meaning. It is the keynote of the History of Herodotus."

" Herodotus was the Homer of the Persian War; and that war originally inspired him. His work presents a picture of sixth century civilisation; and it is also a universal history in so far as it gathers the greater part of the known world into a narrative which is concentrated on a single issue. It is fortunate for literature that he was not too critical; if his criticism had been more penetrating and less naïve, he could not have been a second Homer."—From J. B. Bury's *Ancient Greek Historians* (1909), lecture ii.

THE SIXTH BOOK, ENTITLED ERATO

1. ARISTAGORAS, the author of the Ionian revolt, perished in the way which I have described. Meanwhile Histiæus, tyrant of Miletus, who had been allowed by Darius to leave Susa, came down to Sardis. On his arrival, being asked by Artaphernes, the Sardian satrap, what he thought was the reason that the Ionians had rebelled, he made answer that he could not conceive, and it had astonished him greatly, pretending to be quite unconscious of the whole business. Artaphernes, however, who perceived that he was dealing dishonestly, and who had in fact full knowledge of the whole history of the outbreak, said to him, " I will tell thee how the case stands, Histiæus: this shoe is of thy stitching; Aristagoras has but put it on."

2. Such was the remark made by Artaphernes concerning the rebellion. Histiæus, alarmed at the knowledge which he displayed, so soon as night fell, fled away to the coast. Thus he forfeited his word to Darius; for though he had pledged himself to bring Sardinia, the biggest island in the whole world, under the Persian yoke,[1] he in reality sought to obtain the direction of the war against the king. Crossing over to Chios, he was there laid in bonds by the inhabitants, who accused him of intending some mischief against them in the interest of Darius. Howuvor, when the whole truth was laid before them, and they found that Histiæus was in reality a foe to the king, they forthwith set him at large again.

3. After this the Ionians inquired of him for what reason he had so strongly urged Aristagoras to revolt from the king, thereby doing their nation so ill a service. In reply, he took good care not to disclose to them the real cause, but told them that King Darius had intended to remove the Phœnicians from their own country, and place them in Ionia, while he planted the Ionians in Phœnicia, and that it was for this reason he sent Aristagoras the order. Now it was not true that the king had

---

[1] Vide supra, v. 106. " An expedition against Sardinia," as Grote observes, " seems to have been among the favourite fancies of the Ionic Greeks of that day."

entertained any such intention, but Histiæus succeeded hereby in arousing the fears of the Ionians.[1]

4. After this, Histiæus, by means of a certain Hermippus, a native of Atarneus, sent letters to many of the Persians in Sardis, who had before held some discourse with him concerning a revolt. Hermippus, however, instead of conveying them to the persons to whom they were addressed, delivered them into the hands of Artaphernes, who, perceiving what was on foot, commanded Hermippus to deliver the letters according to their addresses, and then bring him back the answers which were sent to Histiæus. The traitors being in this way discovered, Artaphernes put a number of Persians to death, and caused a commotion in Sardis.

5. As for Histiæus, when his hopes in this matter were disappointed, he persuaded the Chians to carry him back to Miletus; but the Milesians were too well pleased at having got quit of Aristagoras to be anxious to receive another tyrant into their country; besides which they had now tasted liberty. They therefore opposed his return; and when he endeavoured to force an entrance during the night, one of the inhabitants even wounded him in the thigh. Having been thus rejected from his country, he went back to Chios; whence, after failing in an attempt to induce the Chians to give him ships, he crossed over to Mytilêné, where he succeeded in obtaining vessels from the Lesbians. They fitted out a squadron of eight triremes, and sailed with him to the Hellespont, where they took up their station, and proceeded to seize all the vessels which passed out from the Euxine, unless the crews declared themselves ready to obey his orders.

6. While Histiæus and the Mytilenæans were thus employed, Miletus was expecting an attack from a vast armament, which comprised both a fleet and also a land force. The Persian captains had drawn their several detachments together, and formed them into a single army; and had resolved to pass over all the other cities, which they regarded as of lesser account, and to march straight on Miletus. Of the naval states, Phœnicia showed the greatest zeal; but the fleet was composed likewise of the Cyprians (who had so lately been brought under),[2] the Cilicians, and also the Egyptians.

[1] The readiness with which this was believed proves, even better than historical instances, how frequent such transfers of population were in the great oriental empires.
[2] Supra, v. 115, 116.

7. While the Persians were thus making preparations against Miletus and Ionia, the Ionians, informed of their intent, sent their deputies to the Panionium,[1] and held a council upon the posture of their affairs. Hereat it was determined that no land force should be collected to oppose the Persians, but that the Milesians should be left to defend their own walls as they could; at the same time they agreed that the whole naval force of the states, not excepting a single ship, should be equipped, and should muster at Ladé,[2] a small island lying off Miletus—to give battle on behalf of the place.

8. Presently the Ionians began to assemble in their ships, and with them came the Æolians of Lesbos; and in this way they marshalled their line:—The wing towards the east was formed of the Milesians themselves, who furnished eighty ships; next to them came the Prienians with twelve, and the Myusians with three ships; after the Myusians were stationed the Teians, whose ships were seventeen; then the Chians, who furnished a hundred. The Erythræans and Phocæans followed, the former with eight, the latter with three ships; beyond the Phocæans were the Lesbians, furnishing seventy; last of all came the Samians, forming the western wing, and furnishing sixty vessels. The fleet amounted in all to three hundred and fifty-three triremes. Such was the number on the Ionian side.

9. On the side of the barbarians the number of vessels was six hundred. These assembled off the coast of Milesia, while the land army collected upon the shore; but the leaders, learning the strength of the Ionian fleet, began to fear lest they might fail to defeat them, in which case, not having the mastery at sea, they would be unable to reduce Miletus, and might in consequence receive rough treatment at the hands of Darius. So when they thought of all these things, they resolved on the following course:—Calling together the Ionian tyrants, who had fled to the Medes for refuge when Aristagoras deposed them from their governments, and who were now in camp, having joined in the expedition against Miletus, the Persians addressed them thus: " Men of Ionia, now is the fit time to show your zeal for the house of the king. Use your best efforts, every one of you, to detach your fellow-countrymen from the general body. Hold forth to them the promise that, if they submit, no harm shall happen to them on account of their rebellion; their temples

---

[1] Supra, i. 141 and 148.
[2] Ladé is now a hillock in the plain of the Mæander.

shall not be burnt, nor any of their private buildings; neither shall they be treated with greater harshness than before the outbreak. But if they refuse to yield, and determine to try the chance of a battle, threaten them with the fate which shall assuredly overtake them in that case. Tell them, when they are vanquished in fight, they shall be enslaved; their boys shall be made eunuchs, and their maidens transported to Bactra; while their country shall be delivered into the hands of foreigners.

10. Thus spake the Persians. The Ionian tyrants sent accordingly by night to their respective citizens, and reported the words of the Persians; but the people were all staunch, and refused to betray their countrymen, those of each state thinking that they alone had had overtures made to them. Now these events happened on the first appearance of the Persians before Miletus.

11. Afterwards, while the Ionian fleet was still assembled at Ladé, councils were held, and speeches made by divers persons—among the rest by Dionysius, the Phocæan captain, who thus expressed himself:—" Our affairs hang on the razor's edge, men of Ionia, either to be free or to be slaves; and slaves, too, who have shown themselves runaways. Now then you have to choose whether you will endure hardships, and so for the present lead a life of toil, but thereby gain ability to overcome your enemies and establish your own freedom; or whether you will persist in this slothfulness and disorder, in which case I see no hope of your escaping the king's vengeance for your rebellion. I beseech you, be persuaded by me, and trust yourselves to my guidance. Then, if the gods only hold the balance fairly between us, I undertake to say that our foes will either decline a battle, or, if they fight, suffer complete discomfiture."

12. These words prevailed with the Ionians, and forthwith they committed themselves to Dionysius; whereupon he proceeded every day to make the ships move in column, and the rowers ply their oars, and exercise themselves in breaking the line;[1] while the marines were held under arms, and the vessels were kept, till evening fell, upon their anchors,[2] so that the men had nothing but toil from morning even to night. Seven days

[1] This was the most important naval manœuvre with which the Greeks were acquainted. It is supposed to have had two objects; one, the breaking of the oars of the two vessels between which the ship using the manœuvre passed, and the other, the cutting off of a portion of the enemy's fleet from the rest.

[2] Instead of being drawn up on shore, as was the usual practice.

did the Ionians continue obedient, and do whatsoever he bade them; but on the eighth day, worn out by the hardness of the work and the heat of the sun, and quite unaccustomed to such fatigues, they began to confer together, and to say one to another, " What god have we offended to bring upon ourselves such a punishment as this? Fools and distracted that we were, to put ourselves into the hands of this Phocæan braggart, who does but furnish three ships to the fleet! He, now that he has got us, plagues us in the most desperate fashion; many of us, in consequence, have fallen sick already—many more expect to follow. We had better suffer anything rather than these hardships; even the slavery with which we are threatened, however harsh, can be no worse than our present thraldom. Come, let us refuse him obedience." So saying, they forthwith ceased to obey his orders, and pitched their tents, as if they had been soldiers, upon the island, where they reposed under the shade all day, and refused to go aboard the ships and train themselves.

13. Now when the Samian captains perceived what was taking place, they were more inclined than before to accept the terms which Æaces, the son of Syloson, had been authorised by the Persians to offer them, on condition of their deserting from the confederacy. For they saw that all was disorder among the Ionians, and they felt also that it was hopeless to contend with the power of the king; since if they defeated the fleet which had been sent against them, they knew that another would come five times as great. So they took advantage of the occasion which now offered, and as soon as ever they saw the Ionians refuse to work, hastened gladly to provide for the safety of their temples and their properties. This Æaces, who made the overtures to the Samians, was the son of Syloson, and grandson of the earlier Æaces. He had formerly been tyrant of Samos, but was ousted from his government by Aristagoras the Milesian, at the same time with the other tyrants of the Ionians.

14. The Phœnicians soon afterwards sailed to the attack; and the Ionians likewise put themselves in line, and went out to meet them. When they had now neared one another, and joined battle, which of the Ionians fought like brave men and which like cowards, I cannot declare with any certainty, for charges are brought on all sides; but the tale goes that the Samians, according to the agreement which they had made with Æaces, hoisted sail, and quitting their post bore away for Samos, except eleven ships, whose captains gave no heed to the orders

of the commanders, but remained and took part in the battle. The state of Samos, in consideration of this action, granted to these men, as an acknowledgment of their bravery, the honour of having their names, and the names of their fathers, inscribed upon a pillar, which still stands in the market-place. The Lesbians also, when they saw the Samians, who were drawn up next them, begin to flee, themselves did the like; and the example, once set, was followed by the greater number of the Ionians.

15. Of those who remained and fought, none were so rudely handled as the Chians, who displayed prodigies of valour, and disdained to play the part of cowards. They furnished to the common fleet, as I mentioned above, one hundred ships, having each of them forty armed citizens, and those picked men, on board; and when they saw the greater portion of the allies betraying the common cause, they for their part, scorning to imitate the base conduct of these traitors, although they were left almost alone and unsupported, a very few friends continuing to stand by them, notwithstanding went on with the fight, and ofttimes cut the line of the enemy, until at last, after they had taken very many of their adversaries' ships, they ended by losing more than half of their own. Hereupon, with the remainder of their vessels, the Chians fled away to their own country.

16. As for such of their ships as were damaged and disabled, these, being pursued by the enemy, made straight for Mycalé,[1] where the crews ran them ashore, and abandoning them began their march along the continent. Happening in their way upon the territory of Ephesus, they essayed to cross it; but here a dire misfortune befell them. It was night, and the Ephesian women chanced to be engaged in celebrating the Thesmophoria —the previous calamity of the Chians had not been heard of [2]— so when the Ephesians saw their country invaded by an armed band, they made no question of the new-comers being robbers who purposed to carry off their women;[3] and accordingly they marched out against them in full force, and slew them all. Such were the misfortunes which befell them of Chios.

17. Dionysius, the Phocæan, when he perceived that all was lost, having first captured three ships from the enemy, himself

[1] For a description of Mycalé, vide supra, i. 148. It was the name given to the mountainous headland which runs out from the coast in the direction of Samos.

[2] In this fact we seem to have another indication that Ephesus kept aloof from the revolt.

[3] For the frequency of such outrages, vide infra, ch. 138.

took to flight. He would not, however, return to Phocæa, which he well knew must fall again, like the rest of Ionia, under the Persian yoke; but straightway, as he was, he set sail for Phœnicia, and there sunk a number of merchantmen, and gained a great booty; after which he directed his course to Sicily, where he established himself as a corsair, and plundered the Carthaginians and Tyrrhenians, but did no harm to the Greeks.

18. The Persians, when they had vanquished the Ionians in the sea-fight, besieged Miletus both by land and sea, driving mines under the walls, and making use of every known device, until at length they took both the citadel and the town, six years from the time when the revolt first broke out under Aristagoras. All the inhabitants of the city they reduced to slavery, and thus the event tallied with the announcement which had been made by the oracle.

19. For once upon a time, when the Argives had sent to Delphi to consult the god about the safety of their own city, a prophecy was given them, in which others besides themselves were interested; for while it bore in part upon the fortunes of Argos, it touched in a by-clause the fate of the men of Miletus. I shall set down the portion which concerned the Argives when I come to that part of my History,[1] mentioning at present only the passage in which the absent Milesians were spoken of. This passage was as follows:—

> " Then shalt thou, Miletus, so oft the contriver of evil,
> Be, thyself, to many a feast and an excellent booty:
> Then shall thy matrons wash the feet of long-haired masters;—
> Others shall then possess our lov'd Didymian temple."

Such a fate now befell the Milesians; for the Persians, who wore their hair long, after killing most of the men, made the women and children slaves; and the sanctuary at Didyma,[2] the oracle no less than the temple was plundered and burnt; of the riches whereof I have made frequent mention in other parts of my History.

20. Those of the Milesians whose lives were spared, being carried prisoners to Susa, received no ill treatment at the hands of King Darius, but were established by him in Ampé, a city on the shores of the Erythræan sea, near the spot where the Tigris flows into it. Miletus itself, and the plain about the city, were

---

[1] Vide infra, ch. 77.
[2] Didyma was the name of the place called also Branchidæ, in the territory of Miletus, where the famous temple of Apollo stood.

kept by the Persians for themselves, while the hill-country was assigned to the Carians of Pedasus.[1]

21. And now the Sybarites, who after the loss of their city occupied Laüs and Scidrus, failed duly to return the former kindness of the Milesians. For these last, when Sybaris was taken by the Crotoniats,[2] made a great mourning, all of them, youths as well as men, shaving their heads; since Miletus and Sybaris were, of all the cities whereof we have any knowledge, the two most closely united to one another. The Athenians, on the other hand, showed themselves beyond measure afflicted at the fall of Miletus, in many ways expressing their sympathy, and especially by their treatment of Phrynichus.[3] For when this poet brought out upon the stage his drama of the Capture of Miletus, the whole theatre burst into tears; and the people sentenced him to pay a fine of a thousand drachms, for recalling to them their own misfortunes. They likewise made a law, that no one should ever again exhibit that piece.

22. Thus was Miletus bereft of its inhabitants. In Samos the people of the richer sort were much displeased with the doings of the captains, and the dealings they had had with the Medes; they therefore held a council, very shortly after the sea-fight, and resolved that they would not remain to become the slaves of Æaces and the Persians, but before the tyrant set foot in their country, would sail away and found a colony in another land. Now it chanced that about this time the Zanclæans of Sicily had sent ambassadors to the Ionians, and invited them to Kalé-Acté, where they wished an Ionian city to be founded. This place, Kalé-Acté (or the Fair Strand) as it is called, is in the country of the Sicilians,[4] and is situated in the part of Sicily which looks towards Tyrrhenia.[5] The offer thus made to all the Ionians was embraced only by the Samians, and by such of the Milesians as had contrived to effect their escape.

23. Hereupon this is what ensued. The Samians on their voyage reached the country of the Epizephyrian Locrians,[6] at a time when the Zanclæans and their king Scythas were engaged in the siege of a Sicilian town which they hoped to take,

---

[1] Supra, i. 175.　　　　　　　　[2] Supra, v. 44.

[3] Phrynichus, the disciple of Thespis, began to exhibit tragedies about the year B.C. 511.

[4] [The Sicels (Σικελοί) (Σικελιῶται, Sicilian Greeks) were part of the pre-Hellenic population of Sicily.—E. H. B.]

[5] That is, on the north coast.

[6] The Epizephyrian or Western Locrians are the Locrians of Italy, who possessed a city, Locri, and a tract of country, near the extreme south of the modern Calabria.

Anaxilaüs, tyrant of Rhegium,[1] who was on ill terms with the Zanclæans, knowing how matters stood, made application to the Samians, and persuaded them to give up the thought of Calé-Acté, the place to which they were bound, and to seize Zanclé itself, which was left without men. The Samians followed this counsel and possessed themselves of the town; which the Zanclæans no sooner heard than they hurried to the rescue, calling to their aid Hippocrates, tyrant of Gela,[2] who was one of their allies. Hippocrates came with his army to their assistance; but on his arrival he seized Scythas, the Zanclæan king, who had just lost his city, and sent him away in chains, together with his brother Pythogenes, to the town of Inycus; after which he came to an understanding with the Samians, exchanged oaths with them, and agreed to betray the people of Zanclé. The reward of his treachery was to be one-half of the goods and chattels, including slaves, which the town contained, and all that he could find in the open country. Upon this Hippocrates seized and bound the greater number of the Zanclæans as slaves; delivering, however, into the hands of the Samians three hundred of the principal citizens, to be slaughtered; but the Samians spared the lives of these persons.

24. Scythas, the king of the Zanclæans, made his escape from Inycus, and fled to Himera;[3] whence he passed into Asia, and went up to the court of Darius. Darius thought him the most upright of all the Greeks to whom he afforded a refuge; for with the king's leave he paid a visit to Sicily, and thence returned back to Persia, where he lived in great comfort, and died by a natural death at an advanced age.

25. Thus did the Samians escape the yoke of the Medes, and possess themselves without any trouble of Zanclé,[4] a most beautiful city. At Samos itself the Phœnicians, after the fight which had Miletus for its prize was over, re-established Æaces, the son of Syloson, upon his throne. This they did by the command of the Persians, who looked upon Æaces as one who had rendered them a high service and therefore deserved well at their hands. They likewise spared the Samians, on account of the desertion of their vessels, and did not burn either their

[1] Rhegium retains its name almost unchanged. It is the modern *Reggio*.
[2] Infra, vii. 153, 154.
[3] Himera was an important place, and the only Greek colony on the north coast of Sicily.
[4] Zanclé, the modern *Messina*.

city or their temples, as they did those of the other rebels. Immediately after the fall of Miletus the Persians recovered Caria, bringing some of the cities over by force, while others submitted of their own accord.

26. Meanwhile tidings of what had befallen Miletus reached Histiæus the Milesian, who was still at Byzantium, employed in intercepting the Ionian merchantmen as they issued from the Euxine.[1] Histiæus had no sooner heard the news than he gave the Hellespont in charge to Bisaltes, son of Apollophanes, a native of Abydos, and himself, at the head of his Lesbians, set sail for Chios. One of the Chian garrisons which opposed him he engaged at a place called " The Hollows," situated in the Chian territory, and of these he slaughtered a vast number; afterwards, by the help of his Lesbians, he reduced all the rest of the Chians, who were weakened by their losses in the sea-fight, Polichné, a city of Chios, serving him as head-quarters.

27. It mostly happens that there is some warning when great misfortunes are about to befall a state or nation; and so it was in this instance, for the Chians had previously had some strange tokens sent to them. A choir of a hundred of their youths had been despatched to Delphi; and of these only two had returned; the remaining ninety-eight having been carried off by a pestilence. Likewise, about the same time, and very shortly before the sea-fight, the roof of a school-house had fallen in upon a number of their boys, who were at lessons; and out of a hundred and twenty children there was but one left alive. Such were the signs which God sent to warn them. It was very shortly afterwards that the sea-fight happened, which brought the city down upon its knees; and after the sea-fight came the attack of Histiæus and his Lesbians, to whom the Chians, weakened as they were, furnished an easy conquest.

28. Histiæus now led a numerous army, composed of Ionians and Æolians, against Thasos, and had laid siege to the place when news arrived that the Phœnicians were about to quit Miletus and attack the other cities of Ionia. On hearing this, Histiæus raised the siege of Thasos, and hastened to Lesbos with all his forces. There his army was in great straits for want of food; whereupon Histiæus left Lesbos and went across to the mainland, intending to cut the crops which were growing in the Atarnean territory, and likewise in the plain of the Caïcus, which belonged to Mysia. Now it chanced that a certain Persian

[1] Supra, ch. 5.

named Harpagus was in these regions at the head of an army
of no little strength. He, when Histiæus landed, marched out
to meet him, and engaging with his forces destroyed the greater
number of them, and took Histiæus himself prisoner.

29. Histiæus fell into the hands of the Persians in the following manner. The Greeks and Persians engaged at Malêna,
in the region of Atarneus; and the battle was for a long time
stoutly contested, till at length the cavalry came up, and,
charging the Greeks, decided the conflict. The Greeks fled;
and Histiæus, who thought that Darius would not punish his
fault with death, showed how he loved his life by the following
conduct. Overtaken in his flight by one of the Persians, who
was about to run him through, he cried aloud in the Persian
tongue that he was Histiæus the Milesian.

30. Now, had he been taken straightway before King Darius,
I verily believe that he would have received no hurt, but the king
would have freely forgiven him. Artaphernes, however, satrap
of Sardis, and his captor Harpagus, on this very account,—
because they were afraid that, if he escaped, he would be again
received into high favour by the king,—put him to death as
soon as he arrived at Sardis. His body they impaled at that
place,[1] while they embalmed his head and sent it up to Susa to
the king. Darius, when he learnt what had taken place, found
great fault with the men engaged in this business for not bringing Histiæus alive into his presence, and commanded his servants
to wash and dress the head with all care, and then bury it, as
the head of a man who had been a great benefactor to himself
and the Persians.[2] Such was the sequel of the history of
Histiæus.

31. The naval armament of the Persians wintered at Miletus,
and in the following year proceeded to attack the islands off the
coast, Chios, Lesbos, and Tenedos,[3] which were reduced without difficulty. Whenever they became masters of an island, the
barbarians, in every single instance, netted the inhabitants.
Now the mode in which they practise this netting is the following. Men join hands, so as to form a line across from the north
coast to the south, and then march through the island from end
to end and hunt out the inhabitants.[4] In like manner the

---

[1] According to the Persian custom with rebels.
[2] Compare Cæsar's conduct on receiving the head of Pompey.
[3] Tenedos retains its name absolutely unchanged to the present day. It
is a small but fertile island, producing an excellent wine.
[4] Supra, iii. 149.

Persians took also the Ionian towns upon the mainland, not however netting the inhabitants, as it was not possible.

32. And now their generals made good all the threats wherewith they had menaced the Ionians before the battle.[1] For no sooner did they get possession of the towns than they choose out all the best favoured boys and made them eunuchs, while the most beautiful of the girls they tore from their homes and sent as presents to the king, at the same time burning the cities themselves, with their temples. Thus were the Ionians for the third time reduced to slavery; once by the Lydians, and a second, and now a third time, by the Persians.

33. The sea force, after quitting Ionia, proceeded to the Hellespont, and took all the towns which lie on the left shore as one sails into the straits. For the cities on the right bank had already been reduced by the land force of the Persians. Now these are the places which border the Hellespont on the European side; the Chersonese, which contains a number of cities, Perinthus,[2] the forts in Thrace, Selybria,[3] and Byzantium.[4] The Byzantines at this time, and their opposite neighbours, the Chalcedonians, instead of awaiting the coming of the Phœnicians, quitted their country, and sailing into the Euxine, took up their abode at the city of Mesêmbria. The Phœnicians, after burning all the places above mentioned, proceeded to Proconnêsus[5] and Artaca, which they likewise delivered to the flames; this done, they returned to the Chersonese, being minded to reduce those cities which they had not ravaged in their former cruise. Upon Cyzicus they made no attack at all, as before their coming the inhabitants had made terms with Œbares, the son of Megabazus, and satrap of Dascyleium, and had submitted themselves to the king. In the Chersonese the Phœnicians subdued all the cities, excepting Cardia.[6]

34. Up to this time the cities of the Chersonese had been under the government of Miltiades, the son of Cimon, and grandson of Stesagoras, to whom they had descended from Miltiades, the son of Cypselus, who obtained possession of them in the following manner. The Dolonci, a Thracian tribe, to whom the Chersonese at that time belonged, being harassed by a war in

---

[1] Supra, ch. 9.   [2] Supra, v. 1.
[3] A small town upon the Sea of Marmora, about 40 miles from Constantinople.
[4] Supra, iv. 144.   [5] Supra, iv. 13.
[6] It was situated on the western side of the Thracian Chersonese.

which they were engaged with the Apsinthians,[1] sent their princes to Delphi to consult the oracle about the matter. The reply of the Pythoness bade them " take back with them as a colonist into their country the man who should first offer them hospitality after they quitted the temple." The Dolonci, following the Sacred Road,[2] passed through the regions of Phocis and Bœotia; after which, as still no one invited them in, they turned aside, and travelled to Athens.

35. Now Pisistratus was at this time sole lord of Athens; but Miltiades, the son of Cypselus, was likewise a person of much distinction. He belonged to a family which was wont to contend in the four horse-chariot races,[3] and traced its descent to Æacus and Egina, but which, from the time of Philæas, the son of Ajax, who was the first Athenian citizen of the house, had been naturalised at Athens. It happened that as the Dolonci passed his door Miltiades was sitting in his vestibule, which caused him to remark them, dressed as they were in outlandish garments, and armed moreover with lances.[4] He therefore called to them, and, on their approach, invited them in, offering them lodging and entertainment. The strangers accepted his hospitality, and, after the banquet was over, they laid before him in full the directions of the oracle, and besought him on their own part to yield obedience to the god. Miltiades was persuaded ere they had done speaking; for the government of Pisistratus was irksome to him, and he wanted to be beyond the tyrant's reach. He therefore went straightway to Delphi, and inquired of the oracle whether he should do as the Dolonci desired.

36. As the Pythoness backed their request, Miltiades, son of Cypselus, who had already won the four-horse chariot-race at Olympia, left Athens, taking with him as many of the Athenians as liked to join in the enterprise, and sailed away with the Dolonci. On his arrival at the Chersonese, he was made king by those who had invited him. After this his first act was to build a wall across the neck of the Chersonese from the city of

[1] A Thracian people who occupied the tract immediately north of the Chersonese.

[2] By " the sacred road " is meant apparently the road which led from Delphi *eastward*.

[3] The maintenance of such a stud as could entitle a man to contend with any chance of success in the great games, mark the owner as a person of ample fortune.

[4] The wearing of arms had gone out of fashion in Greece some little time before.

Cardia to Pactya, to protect the country from the incursions and ravages of the Apsinthians. The breadth of the isthmus at this part is thirty-six furlongs, the whole length of the peninsula within the isthmus being four hundred and twenty furlongs.

37. When he had finished carrying the wall across the isthmus, and had thus secured the Chersonese against the Apsinthians, Miltiades proceeded to engage in other wars, and first of all attacked the Lampsacenians; but falling into an ambush which they had laid he had the misfortune to be taken prisoner. Now it happened that Miltiades stood high in the favour of Crœsus, king of Lydia. When Crœsus therefore heard of his calamity, he sent and commanded the men of Lampsacus to give Miltiades his freedom; "if they refused," he said, "he would destroy them like a fir." Then the Lampsacenians were somewhile in doubt about this speech of Crœsus, and could not tell how to construe his threat "that he would destroy them like a fir;" but at last one of their elders divined the true sense, and told them that the fir is the only tree which, when cut down, makes no fresh shoots, but forthwith dies outright. So the Lampsacenians, being greatly afraid of Crœsus, released Miltiades, and let him go free.

38. Thus did Miltiades, by the help of Crœsus, escape this danger. Some time afterwards he died childless, leaving his kingdom and his riches to Stesagoras, who was the son of Cimon, his half-brother.[1] Ever since his death the people of the Chersonese have offered him the customary sacrifices of a founder; and they have further established in his honour a gymnic contest and a chariot-race, in neither of which is it lawful for any Lampsacenian to contend. Before the war with Lampsacus was ended Stesagoras too died childless: he was sitting in the hall of justice when he was struck upon the head with a hatchet by a man who pretended to be a deserter, but was in good sooth an enemy, and a bitter one.

39. Thus died Stesagoras; and upon his death the Pisistratidæ fitted out a trireme, and sent Miltiades, the son of Cimon, and brother of the deceased, to the Chersonese, that he might undertake the management of affairs in that quarter. They had already shown him much favour at Athens, as if, forsooth, they had been no parties to the death of his father Cimon—a matter whereof I will give an account in another place.[2] He upon his

[1] Literally, "his brother on the mother's side."   [2] Infra, ch. 103.

arrival remained shut up within the house, pretending to do honour to the memory of his dead brother; whereupon the chief people of the Chersonese gathered themselves together from all the cities of the land, and came in a procession to the place where Miltiades was, to condole with him upon his misfortune. Miltiades commanded them to be seized and thrown into prison; after which he made himself master of the Chersonese, maintained a body of five hundred mercenaries, and married Hegesipyla, daughter of the Thracian king Olorus.

40. This Miltiades, the son of Cimon, had not been long in the country when a calamity befell him yet more grievous than those in which he was now involved: for three years earlier he had had to fly before an incursion of the Scyths. These nomads, angered by the attack of Darius, collected in a body and marched as far as the Chersonese.[1] Miltiades did not await their coming, but fled, and remained away until the Scyths retired, when the Dolonci sent and fetched him back. All this happened three years before the events which befell Miltiades at the present time.

41. He now no sooner heard that the Phœnicians were attacking Tenedos [2] than he loaded five triremes with his goods and chattels, and set sail for Athens. Cardia was the point from which he took his departure; and as he sailed down the gulf of Melas, along the shore of the Chersonese, he came suddenly upon the whole Phœnician fleet. However he himself escaped, with four of his vessels, and got into Imbrus, one trireme only falling into the hands of his pursuers. This vessel was under the command of his eldest son Metiochus, whose mother was not the daughter of the Thracian king Olorus, but a different woman. Metiochus and his ship were taken; and when the Phœnicians found out that he was a son of Miltiades they resolved to convey him to the king, expecting thereby to rise high in the royal favour. For they remembered that it was Miltiades who counselled the Ionians to hearken when the Scyths prayed them to break up the bridge and return home.[3] Darius, however, when the Phœnicians brought Metiochus into his presence, was so far from doing him any hurt, that he loaded him with benefits. He gave him a house and estate, and also a Persian wife, by whom there were children born to him who were accounted

---

[1] This appears to have been a marauding expedition, to which the Scythians were encouraged by the success of the Ionian revolt up to that time.

[2] Supra, ch. 31.   [3] Supra, iv. 137.

Persians. As for Miltiades himself, from Imbrus he made his way in safety to Athens.

42. At this time the Persians did no more hurt to the Ionians; but on the contrary, before the year was out, they carried into effect the following measures, which were greatly to their advantage. Artaphernes, satrap of Sardis, summoned deputies from all the Ionian cities, and forced them to enter into agreements with one another, not to harass each other by force of arms, but to settle their disputes by reference.[1] He likewise took the measurement of their whole country in parasangs— such is the name which the Persians give to a distance of thirty furlongs [2]—and settled the tributes which the several cities were to pay, at a rate that has continued unaltered from the time when Artaphernes fixed it down to the present day. The rate was very nearly the same as that which had been paid before the revolt.[3] Such were the peaceful dealings of the Persians with the Ionians.

43. The next spring Darius superseded all the other generals, and sent down Mardonius, the son of Gobryas,[4] to the coast, and with him a vast body of men, some fit for sea, others for land service. Mardonius was a youth at this time, and had only lately married Artazôstra, the king's daughter. When Mardonius, accompanied by this numerous host, reached Cilicia, he took ship and proceeded along shore with his fleet, while the land army marched under other leaders towards the Hellespont. In the course of his voyage along the coast of Asia he came to Ionia; and here I have a marvel to relate which will greatly surprise those Greeks who cannot believe that Otanes advised the seven conspirators to make Persia a commonwealth. Mardonius put down all the despots throughout Ionia, and in lieu of them established democracies. Having so done, he hastened to the Hellespont, and when a vast multitude of ships had been brought together, and likewise a powerful land force, he conveyed his troops across the strait by means of his vessels, and proceeded through Europe against Eretria and Athens.[5]

[1] These provisoes were common in the Greek treaties.
[2] Supra, ii. 6, and v. 53.
[3] Supra, iii. 90. What necessitated the new rating and measurement was the alteration of territory which had taken place in consequence of the revolt.
[4] This is another instance of the alternation of names among the Persians. (Compare iii. 160, etc.) Gobryas was the son of a Mardonius.
[5] The aggressors in the late war (supra, v. 99).

44. At least these towns served as a pretext for the expedition, the real purpose of which was to subjugate as great a number as possible of the Grecian cities; and this became plain when the Thasians, who did not even lift a hand in their defence, were reduced by the sea force, while the land army added the Macedonians to the former slaves of the king. All the tribes on the hither side of Macedonia had been reduced previously.[1] From Thasos the fleet stood across to the mainland, and sailed along shore to Acanthus, whence an attempt was made to double Mount Athos. But here a violent north wind sprang up, against which nothing could contend, and handled a large number of the ships with much rudeness, shattering them and driving them aground upon Athos. 'Tis said the number of the ships destroyed was little short of three hundred; and the men who perished were more than twenty thousand.[2] For the sea about Athos abounds in monsters beyond all others; and so a portion were seized and devoured by these animals, while others were dashed violently against the rocks; some, who did not know how to swim, were engulfed; and some died of the cold.

45. While thus it fared with the fleet, on land Mardonius and his army were attacked in their camp during the night by the Brygi, a tribe of Thracians; and here vast numbers of the Persians were slain, and even Mardonius himself received a wound. The Brygi, nevertheless, did not succeed in maintaining their own freedom: for Mardonius would not leave the country till he had subdued them and made them subjects of Persia. Still, though he brought them under the yoke, the blow which his land force had received at their hands, and the great damage done to his fleet off Athos, induced him to set out upon his retreat; and so this armament, having failed disgracefully, returned to Asia.

46. The year after these events, Darius received information from certain neighbours of the Thasians that those islanders were making preparations for revolt; he therefore sent a herald, and bade them dismantle their walls, and bring all their ships to Abdêra.[3] The Thasians, at the time when Histiæus the Milesian made his attack upon them,[4] had resolved that, as their income was very great, they would apply their wealth to building ships of war, and surrounding their city with another and a stronger

[1] Supra, v. 18.
[2] The navigation of this coast is still full of danger.
[3] On its site, vide infra, vii. 109.   [4] Supra, ch. 28.

wall. Their revenue was derived partly from their possessions upon the mainland, partly from the mines which they owned. They were masters of the gold-mines at Scapté-Hylé, the yearly produce of which amounted in all to eighty talents. Their mines in Thasos yielded less, but still were so far prolific that, besides being entirely free from land-tax, they had a surplus income, derived from the two sources of their territory on the main and their mines, in common years of two hundred, and in the best years of three hundred talents.

47. I myself have seen the mines in question: by far the most curious of them are those which the Phœnicians discovered at the time when they went with Thasus and colonised the island, which afterwards took its name from him. These Phœnician workings are in Thasos itself, between Cœnyra and a place called Ænyra, over against Samothrace:[1] a huge mountain has been turned upside down in the search for ores. Such then was the source of their wealth. On this occasion no sooner did the Great King issue his commands than straightway the Thasians dismantled their wall, and took their whole fleet to Abdêra.

48. After this Darius resolved to prove the Greeks, and try the bent of their minds, whether they were inclined to resist him in arms or prepared to make their submission. He therefore sent out heralds in divers directions round about Greece, with orders to demand everywhere earth and water for the king. At the same time he sent other heralds to the various seaport towns which paid him tribute, and required them to provide a number of ships of war and horse-transports.

49. These towns accordingly began their preparations; and the heralds who had been sent into Greece obtained what the king had bid them ask from a large number of the states upon the mainland, and likewise from all the islanders whom they visited. Among these last were included the Eginetans, who, equally with the rest, consented to give earth and water to the Persian king.

When the Athenians heard what the Eginetans had done, believing that it was from enmity to themselves that they had given consent, and that the Eginetans intended to join the Persian in his attack upon Athens, they straightway took the matter in hand. In good truth it greatly rejoiced them to have so fair a pretext; and accordingly they sent frequent embassies

[1] That is, on the south-east side of the island.

to Sparta,[1] and made it a charge against the Eginetans that their conduct in this matter proved them to be traitors to Greece.

50. Hereupon Cleomenes, the son of Anaxandridas, who was then king of the Spartans, went in person to Egina, intending to seize those whose guilt was the greatest. As soon however as he tried to arrest them, a number of the Eginetans made resistance, a certain Crius, son of Polycritus, being the foremost in violence. This person told him " he should not carry off a single Eginetan without it costing him dear—the Athenians had bribed him to make this attack, for which he had no warrant from his own government—otherwise *both* the kings would have come together to make the seizure." This he said in consequence of instructions which he had received from Demaratus.[2] Hereupon Cleomenes, finding that he must quit Egina, asked Crius his name; and when Crius told him, " Get thy horns tipped with brass with all speed, O Crius! "[3] he said, "for thou wilt have to struggle with a great danger."

51. Meanwhile Demaratus, son of Ariston, was bringing charges against Cleomenes at Sparta. He too, like Cleomenes, was king of the Spartans, but he belonged to the lower house— not indeed that his house was of any lower origin than the other, for both houses are of one blood—but the house of Eurysthenes is the more honoured of the two, inasmuch as it is the elder branch.

52. The Lacedæmonians declare, contradicting therein all the poets,[4] that it was king Aristodemus himself, son of Aristo- machus, grandson of Cleodæus, and great-grandson of Hyllus, who conducted them to the land which they now possess, and not the sons of Aristodemus. The wife of Aristodemus, whose name (they say) was Argeia, and who was daughter of Autesion,[5]

---

[1] The great importance of this appeal is that it raised Sparta to the general protectorate of Greece. Hitherto she had been a leading power, frequently called in to aid the weaker against the stronger, but with no definite *hegemony*, excepting over the states of the Peloponnese (supra, v. 91). Now she was acknowledged to have a paramount authority over the whole of Greece, as the proper guardian of the Grecian liberties. It gave additional weight to the appeal that it was made by Athens, the second city of Greece.

[2] This was the *second* time that Demaratus had thwarted Cleomenes (vide supra, v. 75).

[3] Cleomenes puns upon the name Crius, which signifies " a ram " in Greek.

[4] These poets are not those of the Epic cycle, which concluded with the adventures of Telegonus, the son of Ulysses.

[5] Sister therefore, according to the myth, of Theras, the coloniser of Thera (supra, iv. 147).

son of Tisamenus, grandson of Thersander, and great-grandson
of Polynices, wtihin a little while after their coming into the
country, gave birth to twins. Aristodemus just lived to see his
children, but died soon afterwards of a disease. The Lacedæmonians of that day determined, according to custom, to take
for their king the elder of the two children; but they were so
alike, and so exactly of one size, that they could not possibly
tell which of the two to choose: so when they found themselves
unable to make a choice, or haply even earlier, they went to the
mother and asked her to tell them which was the elder, whereupon she declared that " she herself did not know the children
apart; " although in good truth she knew them very well, and
only feigned ignorance in order that, if it were possible, both
of them might be made kings of Sparta. The Lacedæmonians
were now in a great strait; so they sent to Delphi and inquired
of the oracle how they should deal with the matter. The
Pythoness made answer, " Let both be taken to be kings; but
let the elder have the greater honour." So the Lacedæmonians
were in as great a strait as before, and could not conceive how
they were to discover which was the first-born, till at length a
certain Messenian, by name Panites, suggested to them to watch
and see which of the two the mother washed and fed first; if
they found she always gave one the preference, that fact would
tell them all they wanted to know; if, on the contrary, she herself varied, and sometimes took the one first, sometimes the
other, it would be plain that she knew as little as they; in
which case they must try some other plan. The Lacedæmonians did according to the advice of the Messenian, and,
without letting her know why, kept a watch upon the mother;
by which means they discovered that, whenever she either
washed or fed her children, she always gave the same child the
preference. So they took the boy whom the mother honoured
the most, and regarding him as the first-born, brought him up
in the palace; and the name which they gave to the elder boy
was Eurysthenes, while his brother they called Procles. When
the brothers grew up, there was always, so long as they lived,
enmity between them; and the houses sprung from their loins
have continued the feud to this day.

53. Thus much is related by the Lacedæmonians, but not by
any of the other Greeks; in what follows I give the tradition of
the Greeks generally. The kings of the Dorians (they say)—
counting up to Perseus, son of Danaë, and so omitting the god—

are rightly given in the common Greek lists, and rightly considered to have been Greeks themselves; for even at this early time they ranked among that people. I say " up to Perseus," and not further, because Perseus has no mortal father by whose name he is called, as Hercules has in Amphitryon; whereby it appears that I have reason on my side, and am right in saying, "up to Perseus." If we follow the line of Danaë, daughter of Acrisius, and trace her progenitors, we shall find that the chiefs of the Dorians are really genuine Egyptians.[1] In the genealogies here given I have followed the common Greek accounts.

54. According to the Persian story, Perseus was an Assyrian who became a Greek;[2] his ancestors, therefore, according to them, were not Greeks. They do not admit that the forefathers of Acrisius were in any way related to Perseus, but say they were Egyptians, as the Greeks likewise testify.

55. Enough however of this subject. How it came to pass that Egyptians obtained the kingdoms of the Dorians,[3] and what they did to raise themselves to such a position, these are questions concerning which, as they have been treated by others, I shall say nothing. I proceed to speak of points on which no other writer has touched.

56. The prerogatives which the Spartans have allowed their kings are the following. In the first place, two priesthoods, those (namely) of Lacedæmonian and of Celestial Jupiter;[4] also the right of making war on what country soever they please, without hindrance from any of the other Spartans, under pain of outlawry; on service the privilege of marching first in the advance and last in the retreat, and of having a hundred[5] picked men for their body-guard while with the army; likewise the liberty of sacrificing as many cattle in their expeditions as it seems them good, and the right of having the skins and the chines of the slaughtered animals for their own use.

---

[1] Supra. ii. 91. Herodotus believes in the tale which brings Danaüs from Egypt.

[2] This is an entirely distinct story from that related below (vii. 150)—that Perseus, son of Danaë, had a son Perses, the progenitor of the Achæmenian kings—which latter the Greeks generally adopted. Both stories seem to me pure inventions.

[3] That is to say, the kingdoms of the Peloponnese, afterwards conquered by the Dorians.

[4] I.e. of king Zeus in the heavenly realm, and of the divine king from whom the royal line in Sparta was derived.—[E. H. B.] The necessary union of the priestly with the kingly office was an idea almost universal in early times.

[5] The number of the knights who formed the king's body-guard is always elsewhere declared to be 300.

57. Such are their privileges in war; in peace their rights are as follows. When a citizen makes a public sacrifice the kings are given the first seats at the banquet; they are served before any of the other guests, and have a double portion of everything; they take the lead in the libations; and the hides of the sacrificed beasts belong to them. Every month, on the first day, and again on the seventh of the first decade,[1] each king receives a beast without blemish at the public cost, which he offers up to Apollo; likewise a medimnus of meal,[2] and of wine a Laconian quart. In the contests of the games they have always the seat of honour; they appoint the citizens who have to entertain foreigners; they also nominate, each of them, two of the Pythians, officers whose business it is to consult the oracle at Delphi, who eat with the kings, and, like them, live at the public charge. If the kings do not come to the public supper, each of them must have two chœnixes of meal and a cotylè of wine sent home to him at his house; if they come, they are given a double quantity of each, and the same when any private man invites them to his table. They have the custody of all the oracles which are pronounced; but the Pythians must likewise have knowledge of them. They have the whole decision of certain causes, which are these, and these only:—When a maiden is left the heiress of her father's estate, and has not been betrothed by him to any one, they decide who is to marry her; in all matters concerning the public highways they judge; and if a person wants to adopt a child, he must do it before the kings. They likewise have the right of sitting in council with the eight-and-twenty senators; and if they are not present, then the senators nearest of kin to them have their privileges, and give two votes as the royal proxies, besides a third vote, which is their own.

58. Such are the honours which the Spartan people have allowed their kings during their lifetime; after they are dead other honours await them. Horsemen carry the news of their death through all Laconia, while in the city the women go hither and thither drumming upon a kettle. At this signal, in every house two free persons, a man and a woman, must put on mourning, or else be subject to a heavy fine. The Lacedæmo-

---

[1] The division of the Greek month was into decades. The seventh day of each month was sacred to Apollo, who was believed to have been born on the seventh of Thargelion (May).

[2] [The *medimnus* was about 12 gallons, the *chœnix* rather less than a quart, and a *cotylè* half a pint.—E. H. B.]

nians have likewise a custom at the demise of their kings which is common to them with the barbarians of Asia—indeed with the greater number of the barbarians everywhere—namely, that when one of their kings dies, not only the Spartans, but a certain number of the country people from every part of Laconia are forced, whether they will or no, to attend the funeral. So these persons and the Helots, and likewise the Spartans themselves,[1] flock together to the number of several thousands, men and women intermingled; and all of them smite their foreheads violently, and weep and wail without stint, saying always that their last king was the best. If a king dies in battle, then they make a statue of him, and placing it upon a couch right bravely decked, so carry it to the grave. After the burial, by the space of ten days there is no assembly, nor do they elect magistrates, but continue mourning the whole time.

59. They hold with the Persians also in another custom. When a king dies, and another comes to the throne, the newly-made monarch forgives all the Spartans the debts which they owe either to the king or to the public treasury. And in like manner among the Persians each king when he begins to reign remits the tribute due from the provinces.

60. In one respect the Lacedæmonians resemble the Egyptians. Their heralds and flute-players, and likewise their cooks, take their trades by succession from their fathers. A flute-player must be the son of a flute-player, a cook of a cook, a herald of a herald; and other people cannot take advantage of the loudness of their voice to come into the profession and shut out the heralds' sons; but each follows his father's business. Such are the customs of the Lacedæmonians.

61. At the time of which we are speaking, while Cleomenes in Egina was labouring for the general good of Greece, Demaratus at Sparta continued to bring charges against him, moved not so much by love of the Eginetans as by jealousy and hatred of his colleague. Cleomenes therefore was no sooner returned from Egina than he considered with himself how he might deprive Demaratus of his kingly office; and here the following circumstance furnished a ground for him to proceed upon. Ariston, king of Sparta, had been married to two wives, but neither of

[1] The three classes of which the Lacedæmonian population consisted are here very clearly distinguished from one another:—1. The Periœci, or free inhabitants of the country districts; 2. The Helots, or serfs who tilled the soil; and 3. The Spartans, or Dorian conquerors, who were the only *citizens*, and who lived almost exclusively in the capital.

them had borne him any children; as however he still thought it was possible he might have offspring, he resolved to wed a third; and this was how the wedding was brought about. He had a certain friend, a Spartan, with whom he was more intimate than with any other citizen. This friend was married to a wife whose beauty far surpassed that of all the other women in Sparta; and what was still more strange, she had once been as ugly as she now was beautiful. For her nurse, seeing how ill-favoured she was, and how sadly her parents, who were wealthy people, took her bad looks to heart, bethought herself of a plan, which was to carry the child every day to the temple of Helen at Therapna,[1] which stands above the Phœbeum,[2] and there to place her before the image, and beseech the goddess to take away the child's ugliness. One day, as she left the temple, a woman appeared to her, and begged to know what it was she held in her arms. The nurse told her it was a child, on which she asked to see it; but the nurse refused; the parents, she said, had forbidden her to show the child to any one. However the woman would not take a denial; and the nurse, seeing how highly she prized a look, at last let her see the child. Then the woman gently stroked its head, and said, " One day this child shall be the fairest dame in Sparta." And her looks began to change from that very day. When she was of marriageable age, Agêtus, son of Alcides, the same whom I have mentioned above as the friend of Ariston, made her his wife.

62. Now it chanced that Ariston fell in love with this person; and his love so preyed upon his mind that at last he devised as follows. He went to his friend, the lady's husband, and proposed to him, that they should exchange gifts, each taking that which pleased him best out of all the possessions of the other. His friend, who felt no alarm about his wife, since Ariston was also married, consented readily; and so the matter was confirmed between them by an oath. Then Ariston gave Agêtus the present, whatever it was, of which he had made choice, and when it came to his turn to name the present which he was to receive in exchange, required to be allowed to carry home with him Agêtus's wife. But the other demurred, and said, " except his wife, he might have anything else: " however, as he could not resist the oath which he had sworn, or the

---

[1] Therapna was a place of some importance on the left bank of the Eurotas, nearly opposite Sparta, from which it was distant probably about two miles.

[2] A precinct sacred to Apollo, at a little distance from the town itself.

trickery which had been practised on him, at last he suffered Ariston to carry her away to his house.

63. Ariston hereupon put away his second wife and took for his third this woman; and she, in less than the due time—when she had not yet reached her full term of ten months,—gave birth to a child, the Demaratus of whom we have spoken. Then one of his servants came and told him the news, as he sat in council with the Ephors; whereat, remembering when it was that the woman became his wife, he counted the months upon his fingers, and having so done, cried out with an oath, "The boy cannot be mine." This was said in the hearing of the Ephors; but they made no account of it at the time. The boy grew up; and Ariston repented of what he had said; for he became altogether convinced that Demaratus was truly his son. The reason why he named him Demaratus was the following. Some time before these events the whole Spartan people, looking upon Ariston as a man of mark beyond all the kings that had reigned at Sparta before him, had offered up a prayer that he might have a son. On this account, therefore, the name Demaratus [1] was given.

64. In course of time Ariston died; and Demaratus received the kingdom: but it was fated, as it seems, that these words, when bruited abroad, should strip him of his sovereignty. This was brought about by means of Cleomenes, whom he had twice sorely vexed, once when he led the army home from Eleusis,[2] and a second time when Cleomenes was gone across to Egina against such as had espoused the side of the Medes.[3]

65. Cleomenes now, being resolved to have his revenge upon Demaratus, went to Leotychides, the son of Menares, and grandson of Agis, who was of the same family as Demaratus, and made agreement with him to this tenor following. Cleomenes was to lend his aid to make Leotychides king in the room of Demaratus; and then Leotychides was to take part with Cleomenes against the Eginetans. Now Leotychides hated Demaratus chiefly on account of Percalus, the daughter of Chilon, son of Demarmenus: this lady had been betrothed to Leotychides; but Demaratus laid a plot, and robbed him of his bride, forestalling him in carrying her off,[4] and marrying her. Such was the origin of the enmity. At the time of which we speak, Leotychides was pre-

---

[1] Dem-aratus (ὅτῳ δήμῳ ἀρατός) is the "People-prayed-for" king. Compare the Louis le Désiré of French history.

[2] Supra, v. 75.

[3] Supra, chs. 50 and 51.

[4] The seizure of the bride was a necessary part of a Spartan marriage.

vailed upon by the earnest desire of Cleomenes to come forward against Demaratus and make oath " that Demaratus was not rightful king of Sparta, since he was not the true son of Ariston." After he had thus sworn, Leotychides sued Demaratus, and brought up against him the phrase which Ariston had let drop when, on the coming of his servant to announce to him the birth of his son, he counted the months, and cried out with an oath that the child was not his. It was on this speech of Ariston's that Leotychides relied to prove that Demaratus was not his son, and therefore not rightful king of Sparta; and he produced as witnesses the Ephors who were sitting with Ariston at the time and heard what he said.

66. At last, as there came to be much strife concerning this matter, the Spartans made a decree that the Delphic oracle should be asked to say whether Demaratus were Ariston's son or no. Cleomenes set them upon this plan; and no sooner was the decree passed than he made a friend of Cobon, the son of Aristophantus, a man of the greatest weight among the Delphians; and this Cobon prevailed upon Perialla, the prophetess, to give the answer which Cleomenes wished.[1] Accordingly, when the sacred messengers came and put their question, the Pythoness returned for answer, " that Demaratus was not Ariston's son." Some time afterwards all this became known; and Cobon was forced to fly from Delphi; while Perialla the prophetess was deprived of her office.

67. Such were the means whereby the deposition of Demaratus was brought about; but his flying from Sparta to the Medes was by reason of an affront which was put upon him. On losing his kingdom he had been made a magistrate; and in that office soon afterwards, when the feast of the Gymnopædiæ[2] came round, he took his station among the lookers-on; whereupon Leotychides, who was now king in his room, sent a servant to him and asked him, by way of insult and mockery, " how it felt to be a magistrate after one had been a king?"[3] Demaratus, who was hurt at the question, made answer—" Tell him I have tried them both, but he has not. Howbeit this speech will be the cause to Sparta of infinite blessings or else of infinite woes." Having thus spoken

---

[1] The venality of the Delphic oracle appears both by this instance, and by the former one of the Alcmæonidæ (v. 63). Such cases, however, appear to have been rare.

[2] The feast of the Gymnopædiæ, or *naked youths*, was one of the most important at Sparta. [Warlike songs were sung by choruses.—E. H. B.]

[3] Compare i. 129.

he wrapped his head in his robe, and, leaving the theatre, went home to his own house, where he prepared an ox for sacrifice, and offered it to Jupiter, after which he called for his mother.

68. When she appeared, he took of the entrails, and placing them in her hand, besought her in these words following:—

" Dear mother, I beseech you, by all the gods, and chiefly by our own hearth-god Jupiter, tell me the very truth, who was really my father. For Leotychides, in the suit which we had together, declared, that when thou becamest Ariston's wife thou didst already bear in thy womb a child by thy former husband; and others repeat a yet more disgraceful tale, that our groom found favour in thine eyes, and that I am his son. I entreat thee therefore by the gods to tell me the truth. For if thou hast gone astray, thou hast done no more than many a woman; and the Spartans remark it as strange, if I am Ariston's son, that he had no children by his other wives."

69. Thus spake Demaratus; and his mother replied as follows: " Dear son, since thou entreatest so earnestly for the truth, it shall indeed be fully told to thee. When Ariston brought me to his house, on the third night after my coming, there appeared to me one like to Ariston, who, after staying with me a while, rose, and taking the garlands from his own brows placed them upon my head, and so went away. Presently after Ariston entered, and when he saw the garlands which I still wore, asked me who gave them to me. I said, 'twas he; but this he stoutly denied; whereupon I solemnly swore that it was none other, and told him he did not do well to dissemble when he had so lately risen from my side and left the garlands with me. Then Ariston, when he heard my oath, understood that there was something beyond nature in what had taken place. And indeed it appeared that the garlands had come from the hero-temple which stands by our court gates—the temple of him they call Astrabacus— and the soothsayers, moreover, declared that the apparition was that very person. And now, my son, I have told thee all thou wouldest fain know. Either thou art the son of that hero— either thou mayest call Astrabacus sire; or else Ariston was thy father. As for that matter which they who hate thee urge the most, the words of Ariston, who, when the messenger told him of thy birth, declared before many witnesses that ' thou wert not his son, forasmuch as the ten months were not fully out,' it was a random speech, uttered from mere ignorance. The truth is, children are born not only at ten months, but at nine, and

even at seven.[1] Thou wert thyself, my son, a seven months'
child. Ariston acknowledged, no long time afterwards, that his
speech sprang from thoughtlessness. Hearken not then to other
tales concerning thy birth, my son: for be assured thou hast
the whole truth. As for grooms, pray Heaven Leotychides and
all who speak as he does may suffer wrong from them!" Such
was the mother's answer.

70. Demaratus, having learnt all that he wished to know,
took with him provision for the journey, and went into Elis,
pretending that he purposed to proceed to Delphi, and there
consult the oracle. The Lacedæmonians, however, suspecting
that he meant to fly his country, sent men in pursuit of him;
but Demaratus hastened, and leaving Elis before they arrived,
sailed across to Zacynthus.[2] The Lacedæmonians followed, and
sought to lay hands upon him, and to separate him from his
retinue; but the Zacynthians would not give him up to them:
so he escaping, made his way afterwards by sea to Asia,[3] and
presented himself before King Darius, who received him gener-
ously, and gave him both lands and cities. Such was the chance
which drove Demaratus to Asia, a man distinguished among the
Lacedæmonians for many noble deeds and wise counsels, and who
alone of all the Spartan kings [4] brought honour to his country
by winning at Olympia the prize in the four-house chariot-race.

71. After Demaratus was deposed, Leotychides, the son of
Menares, received the kingdom. He had a son, Zeuxidamus,
called Cyniscus [5] by many of the Spartans. This Zeuxidamus
did not reign at Sparta, but died before his father, leaving a
son, Archidamus. Leotychides, when Zeuxidamus was taken
from him, married a second wife, named Eurydamé, the sister of
Menius and daughter of Diactorides. By her he had no male
offspring, but only a daughter called Lampito, whom he gave in
marriage to Archidamus, Zeuxidamus' son.

72. Even Leotychides, however, did not spend his old age in
Sparta, but suffered a punishment whereby Demaratus was fully
avenged. He commanded the Lacedæmonians when they made
war against Thessaly, and might have conquered the whole of
it, but was bribed by a large sum of money. It chanced that
he was caught in the fact, being found sitting in his tent on a

---

[1] Supra, ch. 63.
[2] Zacynthus is the modern *Zante*.
[3] In B.C. 486 (infra, vii. 3).
[4] Wealth was the chief requisite for success in this contest.
[5] Or " the Whelp."

gauntlet, quite full of silver. Upon this he was brought to trial and banished from Sparta; his house was razed to the ground; and he himself fled to Tegea, where he ended his days. But these events took place long afterwards.

73. At the time of which we are speaking, Cleomenes, having carried his proceedings in the matter of Demaratus to a prosperous issue, forthwith took Leotychides with him, and crossed over to attack the Eginetans; for his anger was hot against them on account of the affront which they had formerly put upon him. Hereupon the Eginetans, seeing that both the kings were come against them, thought it best to make no further resistance. So the two kings picked out from all Egina the ten men who for wealth and birth stood the highest, among whom were Crius,[1] son of Polycritus, and Casambus, son of Aristocrates, who wielded the chief power; and these men they carried with them to Attica, and there deposited them in the hands of the Athenians, the great enemies of the Eginetans.

74. Afterwards, when it came to be known what evil arts had been used against Demaratus, Cleomenes was seized with fear of his own countrymen, and fled into Thessaly. From thence he passed into Arcadia, where he began to stir up troubles, and endeavoured to unite the Arcadians against Sparta. He bound them by various oaths to follow him whithersoever he should lead, and was even desirous of taking their chief leaders with him to the city of Nonacris, that he might swear them to his cause by the waters of the Styx. For the waters of Styx, as the Arcadians say, are in that city, and this is the appearance they present: you see a little water, dripping from a rock into a basin, which is fenced round by a low wall.[2] Nonacris, where this fountain is to be seen, is a city of Arcadia near Pheneus.

75. When the Lacedæmonians heard how Cleomenes was engaged, they were afraid, and agreed with him that he should come back to Sparta and be king as before. So Cleomenes came back; but had no sooner returned than he, who had never been altogether of sound mind,[3] was smitten with downright madness. This he showed by striking every Spartan he met upon the face with his sceptre. On his behaving thus, and showing that he was gone quite out of his mind, his kindred imprisoned him, and even put his feet in the stocks. While so

[1] Supra, ch. 50.
[2] Superstitious feelings of dread still attach to the water, which is considered to be of a peculiarly noxious character.
[3] Supra, v. 42.

bound, finding himself left alone with a single keeper, he asked the man for a knife. The keeper at first refused, whereupon Cleomenes began to threaten him, until at last he was afraid, being only a helot, and gave him what he required. Cleomenes had no sooner got the steel than, beginning at his legs, he horribly disfigured himself, cutting gashes in his flesh, along his legs, thighs, hips, and loins, until at last he reached his belly, which he likewise began to gash, whereupon in a little time he died. The Greeks generally think that this fate came upon him because he induced the Pythoness to pronounce against Demaratus; the Athenians differ from all others in saying that it was because he cut down the sacred grove of the goddesses [1] when he made his invasion by Eleusis; while the Argives ascribe it to his having taken from their refuge and cut to pieces certain Argives who had fled from battle into a precinct sacred to Argus, where Cleomenes slew them, burning likewise at the same time, through irreverence, the grove itself.

76. For once, when Cleomenes had sent to Delphi to consult the oracle, it was prophesied to him that he should take Argos; upon which he went out at the head of the Spartans, and led them to the river Erasinus. This stream is reported to flow from the Stymphalian [2] lake, the waters of which empty themselves into a pitch-dark chasm, and then (as they say) reappear in Argos, where the Argives call them the Erasinus. Cleomenes, having arrived upon the banks of this river, proceeded to offer sacrifice to it, but, in spite of all that he could do, the victims were not favourable to his crossing. So he said that he admired the god for refusing to betray his countrymen, but still the Argives should not escape him for all that. He then withdrew his troops, and led them down to Thyrea, where he sacrificed a bull to the sea, and conveyed his men on shipboard to Nauplia [3] in the Tirynthian territory.[4]

77. The Argives, when they heard of this, marched down to the sea, to defend their country; and arriving in the neighbourhood of Tiryns, at the place which bears the name of Sêpeia, they pitched their camp opposite to the Lacedæmonians, leaving

[1] The great goddesses, Ceres and Proserpine.
[2] The lake Stymphalia, or Stymphâlis, was in Northern Arcadia.
[3] Nauplia, called in our maps by its Turkish name *Anapli*, is still known by its ancient appellation among the Greeks.
[4] Tiryns was situated at a short distance from Argos. [For a description of the ruins of Tiryns, consult Frazer's *Pausanias*, vol. iii. pp. 217 sqq.— E. H. B.]

no great space between the hosts. And now their fear was not
so much lest they should be worsted in open fight as lest some
trick should be practised on them; for such was the danger
which the oracle given to them in common with the Milesians [1]
seemed to intimate. The oracle ran as follows:—

" Time shall be when the female shall conquer the male, and shall chase him
    Far away,—gaining so great praise and honour in Argos;
    Then full many an Argive woman her cheeks shall mangle;—
    Hence, in the times to come 'twill be said by the men who are unborn,
    ' Tamed by the spear expired the coilèd terrible serpent.' " [2]

At the coincidence of all these things the Argives were greatly
cast down; and so they resolved that they would follow the
signals of the enemy's herald. Having made this resolve, they
proceeded to act as follows: whenever the herald of the Lacedæmonians gave any order to the soldiers of his own army, the
Argives did the like on their side.

78. Now when Cleomenes heard that the Argives were acting
thus, he commanded his troops that, so soon as the herald gave
the word for the soldiers to go to dinner, they should instantly
seize their arms and charge the host of the enemy. Which the
Lacedæmonians did accordingly, and fell upon the Argives just
as, following the signal, they had begun their repast; whereby
it came to pass that vast numbers of the Argives were slain,
while the rest, who were more than they which died in the fight,
were driven to take refuge in the grove of Argus hard by, where
they were surrounded, and watch kept upon them.

79. When things were at this pass Cleomenes acted as follows:
Having learnt the names of the Argives who were shut up in the
sacred precinct from certain deserters who had come over to
him, he sent a herald to summon them one by one, on pretence
of having received their ransoms. Now the ransom of prisoners
among the Peloponnesians is fixed at two minæ the man. So
Cleomenes had these persons called forth severally, to the
number of fifty, or thereabouts, and massacred him. All this
while they who remained in the enclosure knew nothing of what
was happening; for the grove was so thick that the people
inside were unable to see what was taking place without. But
at last one of their number climbed up into a tree and spied the

---

[1] Vide supra, ch. 19.
[2] It is hopeless to attempt a rational explanation of this oracle, the
obscurity of which gives it a special claim to be regarded as a genuine
Pythian response. [Query: is it prophetic of Sparta's victory over
Argos?—E. H. B.]

treachery; after which none of those who were summoned would go forth.

80. Then Cleomenes ordered all the helots to bring brushwood, and heap it around the grove; which was done accordingly; and Cleomenes set the grove on fire. As the flames spread he asked a deserter " Who was the god of the grove? " whereto the other made answer, " Argus." So he, when he heard that, uttered a loud groan, and said—

" Greatly hast thou deceived me, Apollo, god of prophecy, in saying that I should take Argos. I fear me thy oracle has now got its accomplishment."

81. Cleomenes now sent home the greater part of his army, while with a thousand of his best troops he proceeded to the temple of Juno,[1] to offer sacrifice. When however he would have slain the victim on the altar himself, the priest forbade him, as it was not lawful (he said) for a foreigner to sacrifice in that temple. At this Cleomenes ordered his helots to drag the priest from the altar and scourge him, while he performed the sacrifice himself, after which he went back to Sparta.

82. Thereupon his enemies brought him up before the Ephors, and made it a charge against him that he had allowed himself to be bribed, and on that account had not taken Argos when he might have captured it easily. To this he answered—whether truly or falsely I cannot say with certainty—but at any rate his answer to the charge was, that " so soon as he discovered the sacred precinct which he had taken to belong to Argos, he directly imagined that the oracle had received its accomplishment; he therefore thought it not good to attempt the town, at the least until he had inquired by sacrifice, and ascertained if the god meant to grant him the place, or was determined to oppose his taking it. So he offered in the temple of Juno, and when the omens were propitious, immediately there flashed forth a flame of fire from the breast of the image; whereby he knew of a surety that he was not to take Argos. For if the flash had come from the head, he would have gained the town, citadel and all; but as it shone from the breast, he had done so much as the god intended." And his words seemed to the Spartans so true and reasonable, that he came clear off from his adversaries.

83. Argos however was left so bare of men, that the slaves managed the state, filled the offices, and administered every-

---

[1] This temple, one of the most famous in antiquity, was near Argos. [Discovered 1831. See Frazer's *Pausanias*, vol. iii. pp. 165-185.—E. H. B.]

thing until the sons of those who were slain by Cleomenes grew up. Then these latter cast out the slaves, and got the city back under their own rule; while the slaves who had been driven out fought a battle and won Tiryns. After this for a time there was peace between the two; but a certain man, a soothsayer, named Cleander, who was by race a Phigalean[1] from Arcadia, joined himself to the slaves, and stirred them up to make a fresh attack upon their lords. Then were they at war with one another by the space of many years; but at length the Argives with much trouble gained the upper hand.

84. The Argives say that Cleomenes lost his senses, and died so miserably, on account of these doings. But his own countrymen declare that his madness proceeded not from any supernatural cause whatever, but only from the habit of drinking wine un-mixed with water, which he learnt of the Scyths. These nomads, from the time that Darius made his inroad into their country, had always had a wish for revenge. They therefore sent ambassadors to Sparta to conclude a league, proposing to endeavour themselves to enter Media by the Phasis, while the Spartans should march inland from Ephesus, and then the two armies should join together in one. When the Scyths came to Sparta on this errand Cleomenes was with them continually; and growing somewhat too familiar, learnt of them to drink his wine without water, a practice which is thought by the Spartans to have caused his madness. From this distance of time the Spartans, according to their own account, have been accustomed, when they want to drink purer wine than common, to give the order to fill "Scythian fashion." The Spartans then speak thus concerning Cleomenes; but for my own part I think his death was a judgment on him for wronging Demaratus.

85. No sooner did the news of Cleomenes' death reach Egina than straightway the Eginetans sent ambassadors to Sparta to complain of the conduct of Leotychides in respect of their hostages, who were still kept at Athens. So they of Lacedæmon assembled a court of justice and gave sentence upon Leotychides, that whereas he had grossly affronted the people of Egina, he should be given up to the ambassadors, to be led away in place of the men whom the Athenians had in their keeping. Then the ambassadors were about to lead him away; but Theasides, the son of Leoprepes, who was a man greatly esteemed in Sparta, interfered, and said to them—

---

[1] Phigalea was an Arcadian town.

" What are ye minded to do, ye men of Egina? To lead away captive the king of the Spartans, whom his countrymen have given into your hands? Though now in their anger they have passed this sentence, yet belike the time will come when they will punish you, if you act thus, by bringing utter destruction upon your country."

The Eginetans, when they heard this, changed their plan, and, instead of leading Leotychides away captive, agreed with him that he should come with them to Athens, and give them back their men.

86. When however he reached that city, and demanded the restoration of his pledge, the Athenians, being unwilling to comply, proceeded to make excuses, saying, " that two kings had come and left the men with them, and they did not think it right to give them back to the one without the other." So when the Athenians refused plainly to restore the men, Leotychides said to them—

" Men of Athens, act which way you choose—give me up the hostages, and be righteous, or keep them, and be the contrary. I wish, however, to tell you what happened once in Sparta about a pledge. The story goes among us that three generations back there lived in Lacedæmon one Glaucus, the son of Epicydes, a man who in every other respect was on a par with the first in the kingdom, and whose character for justice was such as to place him above all the other Spartans. Now to this man at the appointed season the following events happened. A certain Milesian came to Sparta and having desired to speak with him, said,—' I am of Miletus, and I have come hither, Glaucus, in the hope of profiting by thy honesty. For when I heard much talk thereof in Ionia and through all the rest of Greece, and when I observed that whereas Ionia is always insecure, the Peloponnese stands firm and unshaken, and noted likewise how wealth is continually changing hands in our country, I took counsel with myself and resolved to turn one-half of my substance into money, and place it in thy hands, since I am well assured that it will be safe in thy keeping. Here then is the silver—take it—and take likewise these tallies, and be careful of them; remember thou art to give back the money to the person who shall bring you their fellows.' Such were the words of the Milesian stranger; and Glaucus took the deposit on the terms expressed to him. Many years had gone by when the sons of the man by whom the money was left came to Sparta, and had an interview with

Glaucus, whereat they produced the tallies, and asked to have the money returned to them. But Glaucus sought to refuse, and answered them: ' I have no recollection of the matter; nor can I bring to mind any of those particulars whereof ye speak. When I remember, I will certainly do what is just. If I had the money, you have a right to receive it back; but if it was never given to me, I shall put the Greek law in force against you. For the present I give you no answer; but four months hence I will settle the business.' So the Milesians went away sorrowful, considering that their money was utterly lost to them. As for Glaucus, he made a journey to Delphi, and there consulted the oracle. To his question if he should swear,[1] and so make prize of the money, the Pythoness returned for answer these lines following:—

' Best for the present it were, O Glaucus, to do as thou wishest,
Swearing an oath to prevail, and so to make prize of the money.
Swear then—death is the lot e'en of those who never swear falsely.
Yet hath the Oath-God a son who is nameless, footless, and handless;
Mighty in strength he approaches to vengeance, and whelms in destruction
All who belong to the race, or the house of the man who is perjured.
But oath-keeping men leave behind them a flourishing offspring.'

Glaucus when he heard these words earnestly besought the god to pardon his question; but the Pythoness replied that it was as bad to have tempted the god as it would have been to have done the deed. Glaucus, however, sent for the Milesian strangers, and gave them back their money. And now I will tell you, Athenians, what my purpose has been in recounting to you this history. Glaucus at the present time has not a single descendant; nor is there any family known as his—root and branch has he been removed from Sparta. It is a good thing, therefore, when a pledge has been left with one, not even in thought to doubt about restoring it."

Thus spake Leotychides; but, as he found that the Athenians would not hearken to him, he left them and went his way.

87. The Eginetans had never been punished for the wrongs which, to pleasure the Thebans, they had committed upon Athens.[2] Now, however, conceiving that they were themselves wronged, and had a fair ground of complaint against the Athenians, they instantly prepared to revenge themselves. As it

[1] The Greek law allowed an accused person, with the consent of the accuser, to clear himself of a crime imputed to him, by taking an oath that the charge was false.
[2] Vide supra, v. 81, 89.

chanced that the Athenian Theôris,[1] which was a vessel of five banks of oars, lay at Sunium,[2] the Eginetans contrived an ambush, and made themselves masters of the holy vessel, on board of which were a number of Athenians of the highest rank, whom they took and threw into prison.

88. At this outrage the Athenians no longer delayed, but set to work to scheme their worst against the Eginetans; and, as there was in Egina at that time a man of mark, Nicodromus by name, the son of Cnœthus, who was on ill terms with his country-men because on a former occasion they had driven him into banishment, they listened to overtures from this man, who had heard how determined they were to do the Eginetans a mischief, and agreed with him that on a certain day he should be ready to betray the island into their hands, and they would come with a body of troops to his assistance. And Nicodromus, some time after, holding to the agreement, made himself master of what is called the old town.

89. The Athenians, however, did not come to the day; for their own fleet was not of force sufficient to engage the Egine-tans, and while they were begging the Corinthians to lend them some ships, the failure of the enterprise took place. In those days the Corinthians were on the best of terms with the Athe-nians; and accordingly they now yielded to their request, and furnished them with twenty ships; but, as their law did not allow the ships to be given for nothing, they sold them to the Athenians for five drachms a-piece.[3] As soon then as the Athe-nians had obtained this aid, and, by manning also their own ships, had equipped a fleet of seventy sail,[4] they crossed over to Egina, but arrived a day later than the time agreed upon.

90. Meanwhile Nicodromus, when he found the Athenians did not come to the time appointed, took ship and made his escape from the island. The Eginetans who accompanied him were settled by the Athenians at Sunium, whence they were wont to issue forth and plunder the Eginetans of the island. But this took place at a later date.

91. When the wealthier Eginetans had thus obtained the

---

[1] The Athenian *theôris* was the ship which conveyed the sacred messengers (θεωροί) to Delos.

[2] The situation of Sunium was on the extreme southern promontory of Attica.

[3] In this way the letter of the law was satisfied, at an expense to the Athenians of 100 drachms (about £4 of our money).

[4] Thus it appears that Athens at this time maintained a fleet of 50 ships.

victory over the common people who had revolted with Nicodromus,[1] they laid hands on a certain number of them, and led
them out to death.   But here they were guilty of a sacrilege,
which, notwithstanding all their efforts, they were never able to
atone, being driven from the island before they had appeased
the goddess whom they now provoked.   Seven hundred of the
common people had fallen alive into their hands; and they were
all being led out to death, when one of them escaped from his
chains, and flying to the gateway of the temple of Ceres the
Lawgiver,[2] laid hold of the door-handles, and clung to them.
The others sought to drag him from his refuge; but, finding
themselves unable to tear him away, they cut off his hands, and
so took him, leaving the hands still tightly grasping the handles.

92. Such were the doings of the Eginetans among themselves.
When the Athenians arrived, they went out to meet them with
seventy ships; and a battle took place, wherein the Eginetans
suffered a defeat.   Hereupon they had recourse again to their
old allies,[3] the Argives; but these latter refused now to lend
them any aid, being angry because some Eginetan ships, which
Cleomenes had taken by force, accompanied him in his invasion
of Argolis, and joined in the disembarkation.   The same thing
had happened at the same time with certain vessels of the
Sicyonians; and the Argives had laid a fine of a thousand
talents upon the misdoers, five hundred upon each: whereupon
they of Sicyon acknowledged themselves to have sinned, and
agreed with the Argives to pay them a hundred talents,[4] and so
be quit of the debt; but the Eginetans would make no acknowledgment at all, and showed themselves proud and stiff-necked.
For this reason, when they now prayed the Argives for aid, the
state refused to send them a single soldier.   Notwithstanding,
volunteers joined them from Argos to the number of a thousand,
under a captain, Eurybates, a man skilled in the pentathlic
contests.[5]   Of these men the greater part never returned, but

[1] In Egina, as in most Dorian states, the constitution was oligarchical.
The Athenians, it appears, took advantage of this circumstance, and
sought to bring about a revolution, which would have thrown the island,
practically, into their hands.   This is the first instance of *revolutionary*
war in which Athens is known to have engaged.

[2] In whose honour the feast of the Thesmophoria was celebrated in
almost all parts of Greece.

[3] Supra, v. 86.

[4] A sum exceeding £24,000 of our money.

[5] The πένταθλον, or contest of five games, consisted of the five sports of
leaping, running, throwing the quoit or discus, hurling the spear, and
wrestling.

were slain by the Athenians in Egina. Eurybates, their captain, fought a number of single combats, and, after killing three men in this way, was himself slain by the fourth, who was a Decelean,[1] named Sôphanes.

93. Afterwards the Eginetans fell upon the Athenian fleet when it was in some disorder and beat it, capturing four ships with their crews.

94. Thus did war rage between the Eginetans and Athenians. Meantime the Persian pursued his own design, from day to day exhorted by his servant to "remember the Athenians,"[2] and likewise urged continually by the Pisistratidæ, who were ever accusing their countrymen. Moreover it pleased him well to have a pretext for carrying war into Greece, that so he might reduce all those who had refused to give him earth and water. As for Mardonius, since his expedition had succeeded so ill, Darius took the command of the troops from him, and appointed other generals in his stead, who were to lead the host against Eretria and Athens; to wit, Datis, who was by descent a Mede, and Artaphernes, the son of Artaphernes, his own nephew. These men received orders to carry Athens and Eretria away captive, and to bring the prisoners into his presence.

95. So the new commanders took their departure from the court and went down to Cilicia, to the Aleïan plain, having with them a numerous and well-appointed land army. Encamping here, they were joined by the sea force which had been required of the several states, and at the same time by the horse-transports which Darius had, the year before, commanded his tributaries to make ready.[3] Aboard these the horses were embarked; and the troops were received by the ships of war; after which the whole fleet, amounting in all to six hundred triremes, made sail for Ionia. Thence, instead of proceeding with a straight course along the shore to the Hellespont and to Thrace, they loosed from Samos and voyaged across the Icarian sea[4] through the midst of the islands; mainly, as I believe, because they feared the danger of doubling Mount Athos, where the year before they had suffered so grievously on their passage; but a constraining cause also was their former failure to take Naxos.[5]

---

[1] Decelêa was situated on the mountain-range north of Athens (Parnes), within sight of the city.

[2] Supra, v. 105.   [3] Supra, ch. 48.

[4] The Icarian sea received its name from the island of Icaria (now *Nikaria*), which lay between Samos and Myconus.

[5] Supra. v. 34.

96. When the Persians, therefore, approaching from the Icarian sea, cast anchor at Naxos, which, recollecting what there befell them formerly, they had determined to attack before any other state, the Naxians, instead of encountering them, took to flight, and hurried off to the hills. The Persians however succeeded in laying hands on some, and them they carried away captive, while at the same time they burnt all the temples together with the town. This done, they left Naxos, and sailed away to the other islands.

97. While the Persians were thus employed, the Delians likewise quitted Delos, and took refuge in Tenos.[1] And now the expedition drew near, when Datis sailed forward in advance of the other ships; commanding them, instead of anchoring at Delos, to rendezvous at Rhênea, over against Delos, while he himself proceeded to discover whither the Delians had fled; after which he sent a herald to them with this message:—

"Why are ye fled, O holy men? Why have ye judged me so harshly and so wrongfully? I have surely sense enough, even had not the king so ordered, to spare the country which gave birth to the two gods,—to spare, I say, both the country and its inhabitants. Come back therefore to your dwellings; and once more inhabit your island."

Such was the message which Datis sent by his herald to the Delians. He likewise placed upon the altar three hundred talents' weight of frankincense, and offered it.

98. After this he sailed with his whole host against Eretria, taking with him both Ionians and Æolians. When he was departed, Delos (as the Delians told me) was shaken by an earthquake, the first and last shock that has been felt to this day.[2] And truly this was a prodigy whereby the god warned men of the evils that were coming upon them. For in the three following generations of Darius the son of Hystaspes, Xerxes the son of Darius, and Artaxerxes the son of Xerxes, more woes befell Greece than in the twenty generations preceding Darius;—woes caused in part by the Persians, but in part arising from the contentions among their own chief men respecting the supreme power. Wherefore it is not surprising that Delos, though it had never before been shaken, should at that time

---

[1] Tenos (the modern *Tino*) was distant about 13 miles from Delos, in a direction almost due north.

[2] The Delians, whose holy island was believed to be specially exempt from earthquakes, thought it to the credit of their god, that he should mark by such a prodigy the beginning of a great war.

have felt the shock of an earthquake. And indeed there was an oracle, which said of Delos—

" Delos' self will I shake, which never yet has been shaken."

Of the above names Darius may be rendered " Worker," Xerxes " Warrior," and Artaxerxes " Great Warrior." And so might we call these kings in our own language with propriety.

99. The barbarians, after loosing from Delos, proceeded to touch at the other islands, and took troops from each,[1] and likewise carried off a number of the children as hostages. Going thus from one to another, they came at last to Carystus;[2] but here the hostages were refused by the Carystians, who said they would neither give any, nor consent to bear arms against the cities of their neighbours, meaning Athens and Eretria. Hereupon the Persians laid siege to Carystus, and wasted the country round, until at length the inhabitants were brought over and agreed to do what was required of them.

100. Meanwhile the Eretrians, understanding that the Persian armament was coming against them, besought the Athenians for assistance. Nor did the Athenians refuse their aid, but assigned to them as auxiliaries the four thousand landholders to whom they had allotted the estates of the Chalcidean Hippobatæ.[3] At Eretria, however, things were in no healthy state; for though they had called in the aid of the Athenians, yet they were not agreed among themselves how they should act; some of them were minded to leave the city and to take refuge in the heights of Eubœa, while others, who looked to receiving a reward from the Persians, were making ready to betray their country. So when these things came to the ears of Æschines, the son of Nothon, one of the first men in Eretria, he made known the whole state of affairs to the Athenians who were already arrived, and besought them to return home to their own land, and not perish with his countrymen. And the Athenians hearkened to his counsel, and, crossing over to Orôpus, in this way escaped the danger.

101. The Persian fleet now drew near and anchored at Tamynæ, Chœreæ, and Ægilia, three places in the territory of Eretria. Once masters of these posts, they proceeded forthwith to disembark their horses, and made ready to attack the enemy. But the Eretrians were not minded to sally forth and offer

[1] Vide infra, ch. 133.
[2] Carystus was one of the four principal cities of the ancient Eubœa (the *Egripo* of our maps).   [3] Supra, v. 77.

battle; their only care, after it had been resolved not to quit the city, was, if possible, to defend their walls. And now the fortress was assaulted in good earnest, and for six days there fell on both sides vast numbers, but on the seventh day Euphorbus, the son of Alcimachus, and Philagrus, the son of Cyneas, who were both citizens of good repute, betrayed the place to the Persians. These were no sooner entered within the walls than they plundered and burnt all the temples that there were in the town, in revenge for the burning of their own temples at Sardis; moreover, they did according to the orders of Darius, and carried away captive all the inhabitants.

102. The Persians, having thus brought Eretria into subjection after waiting a few days, made sail for Attica, greatly straitening the Athenians as they approached, and thinking to deal with them as they had dealt with the people of Eretria. And, because there was no place in all Attica so convenient for their horse as Marathon, and it lay moreover quite close to Eretria, therefore Hippias, the son of Pisistratus, conducted them thither.

103. When intelligence of this reached the Athenians, they likewise marched their troops to Marathon, and there stood on the defensive, having at their head ten generals,[1] of whom one was Miltiades.

Now this man's father, Cimon, the son of Stesagoras, was banished from Athens by Pisistratus, the son of Hippocrates. In his banishment it was his fortune to win the four-horse chariot-race at Olympia, whereby he gained the very same honour which had before been carried off by Miltiades,[2] his half-brother on the mother's side. At the next Olympiad he won the prize again with the same mares; upon which he caused Pisistratus to be proclaimed the winner, having made an agreement with him that on yielding him this honour he should be allowed to come back to his country. Afterwards, still with the same mares, he won the prize a third time; whereupon he was put to death by the sons of Pisistratus, whose father was no

---

[1] The Ten Generals (Strategi) are a part of the constitution of Clisthenes, who modelled the Athenian army upon the political division of the tribes. Each tribe annually elected its Phylarch to command its contingent of cavalry, its Taxiarch to command its infantry, and its Strategus to direct both. Hence the *ten* Strategi, who seem immediately to have claimed equality with the Polemarch or War-Archon. [Note:—The Strategi were *elected*, unlike the Members of the Senate (Boulé), who were appointed by *lot*.—E. H. B.]

[2] Miltiades, the son of Cypselus, the first king of the Chersonese.

longer living. They set men to lie in wait for him secretly; and these men slew him near the government-house in the night-time. He was buried outside the city, beyond what is called the Valley Road; and right opposite his tomb were buried the mares which had won the three prizes. The same success had likewise been achieved once previously, to wit, by the mares of Evagoras the Lacedæmonian, but never except by them. At the time of Cimon's death Stesagoras, the elder of his two sons, was in the Chersonese, where he lived with Miltiades his uncle; the younger, who was called Miltiades after the founder of the Chersonesite colony, was with his father in Athens.

104. It was this Miltiades who now commanded the Athenians, after escaping from the Chersonese, and twice nearly losing his life. First he was chased as far as Imbrus by the Phœnicians,[1] who had a great desire to take him and carry him up to the king; and when he had avoided this danger, and, having reached his own country, thought himself to be altogether in safety, he found his enemies waiting for him, and was cited by them before a court and impeached for his tyranny in the Chersonese. But he came off victorious here likewise, and was thereupon made general of the Athenians by the free choice of the people.

105. And first, before they left the city, the generals sent off to Sparta a herald, one Pheidippides,[2] who was by birth an Athenian, and by profession and practice a trained runner. This man, according to the account which he gave to the Athenians on his return, when he was near Mount Parthenium, above Tegea, fell in with the god Pan, who called him by his name, and bade him ask the Athenians "wherefore they neglected him so entirely, when he was kindly disposed towards them, and had often helped them in times past, and would do so again in time to come?" The Athenians, entirely believing in the truth of this report, as soon as their affairs were once more in good order, set up a temple to Pan under the Acropolis,[3] and, in return for the message which I have recorded, established in his honour yearly sacrifices and a torch-race.

106. On the occasion of which we speak, when Pheidippides

---

[1] Supra, ch. 41.

[2] [See Browning's poem "Pheidippides" in his Dramatic Idylls.— E. H. B.]

[3] The temple or rather chapel of Pan was contained in a hollow in the rock just below the Propylæa, or entrance to the citadel. The cavern still exists. [Bury, Hist. of Greece, chap. vi.—E. H. B.]

was sent by the Athenian generals, and, according to his own account, saw Pan on his journey, he reached Sparta on the very next day after quitting the city of Athens.[1] Upon his arrival he went before the rulers, and said to them—

" Men of Lacedæmon, the Athenians beseech you to hasten to their aid, and not allow that state, which is the most ancient [2] in all Greece, to be enslaved by the barbarians. Eretria, look you, is already carried away captive; and Greece weakened by the loss of no mean city."

Thus did Pheidippides deliver the message committed to him. And the Spartans wished to help the Athenians, but were unable to give them any present succour, as they did not like to break their established law. It was then the ninth day of the first decade;[3] and they could not march out of Sparta on the ninth, when the moon had not reached the full. So they waited for the full of the moon.

107. The barbarians were conducted to Marathon by Hippias, the son of Pisistratus, who the night before had seen a strange vision in his sleep. He dreamt of lying in his mother's arms, and conjectured the dream to mean that he would be restored to Athens, recover the power which he had lost, and afterwards live to a good old age in his native country. Such was the sense in which he interpreted the vision. He now proceeded to act as guide to the Persians; and, in the first place, he landed the prisoners taken from Eretria upon the island that is called Ægileia,[4] a tract belonging to the Styreans,[5] after which he brought the fleet to anchor off Marathon, and marshalled the bands of the barbarians as they disembarked. As he was thus employed it chanced that he sneezed and at the same time coughed with more violence than was his wont. Now, as he was a man advanced in years, and the greater number of his teeth were loose, it so happened that one of them was driven out with the force of the cough, and fell down into the sand. Hippias took all the pains he could to find it; but the tooth

---

[1] Moderns estimate the direct distance at 135 or 140 miles.

[2] It was the favourite boast of Athens that her inhabitants were αὐτόχ-θονες—sprung from the soil. Hence the adoption of the symbol of the grasshopper.

[3] The Greeks divided their month of 29 or 30 days into three periods:—1 from the 1st day to the 10th inclusively; 2, from the 11th to the 20th; and 3, from the 21st to the end. The ninth day of the first decade is thus the ninth day of the month itself.

[4] Between Eubœa and Attica.

[5] Styra was a town of southern Eubœa.

was nowhere to be seen: whereupon he fetched a deep sigh, and said to the bystanders—

" After all, the land is not ours; and we shall never be able to bring it under. All my share in it is the portion of which my tooth has possession."

So Hippias believed that in this way his dream was out.

108. The Athenians were drawn up in order of battle in a sacred close belonging to Hercules,[1] when they were joined by the Platæans, who came in full force to their aid. Some time before, the Platæans had put themselves under the rule of the Athenians; and these last had already undertaken many labours on their behalf. The occasion of the surrender was the following. The Platæans suffered grievous things at the hands of the men of Thebes; so, as it chanced that Cleomenes, the son of Anaxandridas, and the Lacedæmonians were in their neighbourhood, they first of all offered to surrender themselves to them. But the Lacedæmonians refused to receive them, and said—

" We dwell too far off from you, and ours would be but chill succour. Ye might oftentimes be carried into slavery before one of us heard of it. We counsel you rather to give yourselves up to the Athenians, who are your next neighbours, and well able to shelter you."

This they said, not so much out of good will towards the Platæans as because they wished to involve the Athenians in trouble by engaging them in wars with the Bœotians. The Platæans, however, when the Lacedæmonians gave them this counsel, complied at once; and when the sacrifice to the Twelve Gods was being offered at Athens, they came and sat as suppliants about the altar,[2] and gave themselves up to the Athenians. The Thebans no sooner learnt what the Platæans had done than instantly they marched out against them, while the Athenians sent troops to their aid. As the two armies were about to join battle, the Corinthians, who chanced to be at hand, would not allow them to engage; both sides consented to take them for arbitrators, whereupon they made up the quarrel, and fixed the boundary-line between the two states upon this condition: to wit, that if any of the Bœotians wished no longer to belong to Bœotia, the Thebans should allow them to follow their own inclinations. The Corinthians, when they had thus decreed,

---

[1] Hercules was among the gods specially worshipped at Marathon.

[2] The altar of the Twelve Gods at Athens has been mentioned before (ii. 7). It was in the Agora.

forthwith departed to their homes: the Athenians likewise set off on their return; but the Bœotians fell upon them during the march, and a battle was fought wherein they were worsted by the Athenians. Hereupon these last would not be bound by the line which the Corinthians had fixed, but advanced beyond those limits, and made the Asôpus [1] the boundary-line between the country of the Thebans and that of the Platæans and Hysians. Under such circumstances did the Platæans give themselves up to Athens; and now they were come to Marathon to bear the Athenians aid.

109. The Athenian generals were divided in their opinions; and some advised not to risk a battle, because they were too few to engage such a host as that of the Medes, while others were for fighting at once; and among these last was Miltiades. He therefore, seeing that opinions were thus divided, and that the less worthy counsel appeared likely to prevail, resolved to go to the polemarch, and have a conference with him. For the man on whom the lot fell to be polemarch [2] at Athens was entitled to give his vote with the ten generals, since anciently [3] the Athenians allowed him an equal right of voting with them. The polemarch at this juncture was Callimachus of Aphidnæ; to him therefore Miltiades went, and said:—

" With thee it rests, Callimachus, either to bring Athens to slavery, or, by securing her freedom, to leave behind thee to all future generations a memory beyond even Harmodius and Aristogeiton. For never since the time that the Athenians became a people were they in so great a danger as now. If they bow their necks beneath the yoke of the Medes, the woes which they will have to suffer when given into the power of Hippias are already determined on; if, on the other hand, they fight and overcome, Athens may rise to be the very first city in Greece. How it comes to pass that these things are likely to happen, and how the determining of them in some sort rests with thee, I will now proceed to make clear. We generals are ten in number, and our votes are divided; half of us wish to engage, half to avoid a combat. Now, if we do not fight, I look to see a great disturbance at Athens which will shake men's resolutions, and then I fear they will submit themselves; but if we fight the battle before any unsoundness show itself among our

---

[1] The Asôpus is the modern *Vuriêni*, the great river of southern Bœotia.

[2] The Polemarch, or War-Archon, was the third archon in dignity.

[3] When Herodotus wrote, the polemarch had no military functions at all.

citizens, let the gods but give us fair play, and we are well able
to overcome the enemy. On thee therefore we depend in this
matter, which lies wholly in thine own power. Thou hast only
to add thy vote to my side and thy country will be free, and
not free only, but the first state in Greece. Or, if thou pre-
ferrest to give thy vote to them who would decline the combat,
then the reverse will follow."

110. Miltiades by these words gained Callimachus; and the
addition of the polemarch's vote caused the decision to be in
favour of fighting. Hereupon all those generals who had been
desirous of hazarding a battle, when their turn came to command the army, gave up their right to Miltiades. He however,
though he accepted their offers, nevertheless waited, and would
not fight, until his own day of command arrived in due course.

111. Then at length, when his own turn was come, the Athenian battle was set in array, and this was the order of it. Callimachus the polemarch led the right wing; for it was at that
time a rule with the Athenians to give the right wing to the
polemarch.[1] After this followed the tribes, according as they
were numbered, in an unbroken line; while last of all came the
Platæans, forming the left wing. And ever since that day it
has been a custom with the Athenians, in the sacrifices and
assemblies held each fifth year at Athens,[2] for the Athenian
herald to implore the blessing of the gods on the Platæans conjointly with the Athenians. Now, as they marshalled the host
upon the field of Marathon, in order that the Athenian front
might be of equal length with the Median, the ranks of the
centre were diminished, and it became the weakest part of the
line, while the wings were both made strong with a depth of
many ranks.

112. So when the battle was set in array, and the victims
showed themselves favourable, instantly the Athenians, so soon
as they were let go, charged the barbarians at a run. Now the
distance between the two armies was little short of eight furlongs. The Persians, therefore, when they saw the Greeks
coming on at speed, made ready to receive them, although it
seemed to them that the Athenians were bereft of their senses,

---

[1] The *right* wing was the special post of honour (vide infra, ix. 27). The
Polemarch took the post as representative of the king, whose position it
had been in the ancient times.
[2] The Panathenaic festival is probably intended. It was held every
fifth year (*i.e.* once in every four years, half-way between the Olympic
festivals), and was the great religious assembly of the Athenians.

and bent upon their own destruction; for they saw a mere handful of men coming on at a run without either horsemen or archers. Such was the opinion of the barbarians; but the Athenians in close array fell upon them, and fought in a manner worthy of being recorded. They were the first of the Greeks, so far as I know, who introduced the custom of charging the enemy at a run, and they were likewise the first who dared to look upon the Median garb, and to face men clad in that fashion. Until this time the very name of the Medes had been a terror to the Greeks to hear.

113. The two armies fought together on the plain of Marathon for a length of time; and in the mid battle, where the Persians themselves and the Sacæ had their place, the barbarians were victorious, and broke and pursued the Greeks into the inner country; but on the two wings the Athenians and the Platæans defeated the enemy. Having so done, they suffered the routed barbarians to fly at their ease, and joining the two wings in one, fell upon those who had broken their own centre, and fought and conquered them. These likewise fled, and now the Athenians hung upon the runaways and cut them down, chasing them all the way to the shore, on reaching which they laid hold of the ships and called aloud for fire.

114. It was in the struggle here that Callimachus the polemarch, after greatly distinguishing himself, lost his life; Stesilaüs too, the son of Thrasilaüs, one of the generals, was slain; and Cynægirus, the son of Euphorion, having seized on a vessel of the enemy's by the ornament at the stern,[1] had his hand cut off by the blow of an axe, and so perished; as likewise did many other Athenians of note and name.

115. Nevertheless the Athenians secured in this way seven of the vessels; while with the remainder the barbarians pushed off, and taking aboard their Eretrian prisoners from the island where they had left them, doubled Cape Sunium, hoping to reach Athens before the return of the Athenians. The Alcmæonidæ were accused by their countrymen of suggesting this course to them; they had, it was said, an understanding with the Persians, and made a signal to them, by raising a shield, after they were embarked in their ships.

---

[1] The ornament at the stern consisted of wooden planks curved gracefully in continuance of the sweep by which the stern of the ancient ship rose from the sea. Vessels were ordinarily ranged along a beach with their sterns towards the shore, and thus were liable to be seized by the stern-ornament. [See Rich, *Dict. of Antiquities*.—E. H. B.]

116. The Persians accordingly sailed round Sunium. But the Athenians with all possible speed marched away to the defence of their city, and succeeded in reaching Athens before the appearance of the barbarians: [1] and as their camp at Marathon had been pitched in a precinct of Hercules, so now they encamped in another precinct of the same god at Cynosarges.[2] The barbarian fleet arrived, and lay to off Phalerum, which was at that time the haven of Athens; [3] but after resting awhile upon their oars, they departed and sailed away to Asia.

117. There fell in this battle of Marathon, on the side of the barbarians, about six thousand and four hundred men; on that of the Athenians, one hundred and ninety-two. Such was the number of the slain on the one side and the other. A strange prodigy likewise happened at this fight. Epizêlus, the son of Cuphagoras, an Athenian, was in the thick of the fray, and behaving himself as a brave man should, when suddenly he was stricken with blindness, without blow of sword or dart; and this blindness continued thenceforth during the whole of his after life. The following is the account which he himself, as I have heard, gave of the matter: he said that a gigantic warrior, with a huge beard, which shaded all his shield, stood over against him; but the ghostly semblance passed him by, and slew the man at his side. Such, as I understand, was the tale which Epizêlus told.[4]

118. Datis meanwhile was on his way back to Asia, and had reached Myconus,[5] when he saw in his sleep a vision. What it was is not known; but no sooner was day come than he caused strict search to be made throughout the whole fleet, and finding on board a Phœnician vessel an image of Apollo overlaid with gold, he inquired from whence it had been taken, and learning to what temple it belonged, he took it with him in his own ship to Delos, and placed it in the temple there, enjoining the Delians, who had now come back to their island, to restore the image to the Theban Delium,[6] which lies on the

[1] Marathon is six-and-twenty miles from Athens by the common route.
[2] Supra, v. 63. Cynosarges was situated very near the famous Lycæum, the school of Aristotle.
[3] Supra, v. 63.
[4] According to Plutarch, Theseus was seen by a great number of the Athenians fighting on their side against the Persians.
[5] It lies between Tenos (*Tino*) and Icaria (*Nikaria*).
[6] This temple acquired a special celebrity from the defeat which the Athenians suffered in its neighbourhood in the eighth year of the Peloponnesian war, B.C. 424. The name of Delium is said to have been given to it because it was built after the model of Apollo's temple at Delos.

coast over against Chalcis. Having left these injunctions, he
sailed away; but the Delians failed to restore the statue; and it
was not till twenty years afterwards that the Thebans, warned
by an oracle, themselves brought it back to Delium.

119. As for the Eretrians, whom Datis and Artaphernes had
carried away captive, when the fleet reached Asia, they were
taken up to Susa. Now King Darius, before they were made his
prisoners, nourished a fierce anger against these men for having
injured him without provocation; but now that he saw them
brought into his presence, and become his subjects, he did them
no other harm, but only settled them at one of his own stations
in Cissia—a place called Ardericca—two hundred and ten furlongs distant from Susa, and forty from the well which yields
produce of three different kinds. For from this well they get
bitumen, salt, and oil, procuring it in the way that I will now
describe: They draw with a swipe, and instead of a bucket
make use of the half of a wine-skin; with this the man dips,
and after drawing, pours the liquid into a reservoir, wherefrom
it passes into another, and there takes three different shapes.
The salt and the bitumen forthwith collect and harden, while
the oil is drawn off into casks. It is called by the Persians
" rhadinacé," is black, and has an unpleasant smell. Here then
King Darius established the Eretrians; and here they continued
to my time, and still spoke their old language. So thus it fared
with the Eretrians.

120. After the full of the moon two thousand Lacedæmonians
came to Athens. So eager had they been to arrive in time,
that they took but three days to reach Attica from Sparta.
They came, however, too late for the battle; yet, as they had a
longing to behold the Medes, they continued their march to
Marathon and there viewed the slain. Then, after giving the
Athenians all praise for their achievement, they departed and
returned home.

121. But it fills me with wonderment, and I can in no wise
believe the report, that the Alcmæonidæ had an understanding
with the Persians, and held them up a shield as a signal, wishing
Athens to be brought under the yoke of the barbarians and of
Hippias,—the Alcmæonidæ, who have shown themselves at least
as bitter haters of tyrants as was Callias, the son of Phænippus,
and father of Hipponicus.[1] This Callias was the only person
at Athens who, when the Pisistratidæ were driven out, and their

[1] Vide infra, vii. 151.

goods were exposed for sale by the vote of the people, had the courage to make purchases, and likewise in many other ways to display the strongest hostility.

[122. He was a man very worthy to be had in remembrance by all, on several accounts. For not only did he thus distinguish himself beyond others in the cause of his country's freedom; but likewise, by the honours which he gained at the Olympic games, where he carried off the prize in the horse-race, and was second in the four-horse chariot-race, and by his victory at an earlier period in the Pythian games, he showed himself in the eyes of all the Greeks a man most unsparing in his expenditure. He was remarkable too for his conduct in respect of his daughters, three in number; for when they came to be of marriageable age, he gave to each of them a most ample dowry, and placed it at their own disposal, allowing them to choose their husbands from among all the citizens of Athens,[1] and giving each in marriage to the man of her own choice.[2]]

123. Now the Alcmæonidæ fell not a whit short of this person in their hatred of tyrants, so that I am astonished at the charge made against them, and cannot bring myself to believe that they held up a shield; for they were men who had remained in exile during the whole time that the tyranny lasted, and they even contrived the trick by which the Pisistratidæ were deprived of their throne.[3]   Indeed I look upon them as the persons who in good truth gave Athens her freedom far more than Harmodius and Aristogeiton.[4]   For these last did but exasperate the other Pisistratidæ by slaying Hipparchus,[5] and were far from doing anything towards putting down the tyranny; whereas the Alcmæonidæ were manifestly the actual deliverers of Athens, if at least it be true that the Pythoness was prevailed upon by them to bid the Lacedæmonians set Athens free, as I have already related.

124. But perhaps they were offended with the people of Athens; and therefore betrayed their country.   Nay, but on the

---

[1] In general the Athenian ladies—indeed, the *Greek* ladies without exception—were not even asked to give their consent to the match prepared for them.

[2] This chapter is generally regarded as an interpolation.   It is wanting in several of the best MSS.

[3] Supra, v. 63.

[4] It is plain that Herodotus was of the same opinion as Thucydides (vi. 54-59), that far too much honour was paid to the memory of these persons.

[5] Supra, v. 55, 62.

contrary there were none of the Athenians who were held in such general esteem, or who were so laden with honours. So that it is not even reasonable to suppose that a shield was held up by them on this account. A shield was shown, no doubt; that cannot be gainsaid; but who it was that showed it I cannot any further determine.

125. Now the Alcmæonidæ were, even in days of yore, a family of note at Athens; but from the time of Alcmæon, and again of Megacles, they rose to special eminence. The former of these two personages, to wit, Alcmæon, the son of Megacles, when Crœsus the Lydian sent men from Sardis to consult the Delphic oracle, gave aid gladly to his messengers, and assisted them to accomplish their task. Crœsus, informed of Alcmæon's kindnesses by the Lydians who from time to time conveyed his messages to the god,[1] sent for him to Sardis, and when he arrived, made him a present of as much gold as he should be able to carry at one time about his person. Finding that this was the gift assigned him, Alcmæon took his measures, and prepared himself to receive it in the following way. He clothed himself in a loose tunic, which he made to bag greatly at the waist, and placing upon his feet the widest buskins that he could anywhere find, followed his guides into the treasure-house. Here he fell to upon a heap of gold-dust, and in the first place packed as much as he could inside his buskins, between them and his legs; after which he filled the breast of his tunic quite full of gold, and then sprinkling some among his hair, and taking some likewise in his mouth, he came forth from the treasure-house, scarcely able to drag his legs along, like anything rather than a man, with his mouth crammed full, and his bulk increased every way. On seeing him, Crœsus burst into a laugh, and not only let him have all that he had taken, but gave him presents besides of fully equal worth. Thus this house became one of great wealth; and Alcmæon was able to keep horses for the chariot-race, and won the prize at Olympia.[2]

126. Afterwards, in the generation which followed, Clisthenes, king of Sicyon, raised the family to still greater eminence among the Greeks than even that to which it had attained before. For this Clisthenes, who was the son of Aristonymus, the grandson of Myron, and the great-grandson of Andreas, had a daughter, called Agarista, whom he wished to marry to the

[1] Supra, i. 55.
[2] There are strong reasons for suspecting the whole of this story.

best husband that he could find in the whole of Greece. At
the Olympic games, therefore, having gained the prize in the
chariot-race, he caused public proclamation to be made to the
following effect:—" Whoever among the Greeks deems himself
worthy to become the son-in-law of Clisthenes, let him come,
sixty days hence, or, if he will, sooner, to Sicyon; for within a
year's time, counting from the end of the sixty days, Clisthenes
will decide on the man to whom he shall contract his daughter."
So all the Greeks who were proud of their own merit or of their
country flocked to Sicyon as suitors; and Clisthenes had a foot-
course and a wrestling-ground made ready, to try their powers.

127. From Italy there came Smindyrides, the son of Hippocrates, a native of Sybaris—which city about that time was at
the very height of its prosperity. He was a man who in luxuri-
ousness of living exceeded all other persons. Likewise there
came Damasus, the son of Amyris, surnamed the Wise, a
native of Siris. These two were the only suitors from Italy.
From the Ionian Gulf appeared Amphimnestus, the son of Epis-
trophus, an Epidamnian; from Ætolia Males, the brother of
that Titormus who excelled all the Greeks in strength, and
who wishing to avoid his fellow-men, withdrew himself into the
remotest parts of the Ætolian territory. From the Peloponnese
came several—Leocêdes, son of that Pheidon, king of the
Argives, who established weights and measures throughout the
Peloponnese, and was the most insolent of all the Grecians—the
same who drove out the Elean directors of the games, and himself presided over the contests at Olympia—Leocêdes, I say,
appeared, this Pheidon's son; and likewise Amiantus, son of
Lycurgus, an Arcadian of the city of Trapezus; Laphanes, an
Azenian of Pæus, whose father, Euphorion, as the story goes in
Arcadia, entertained the Dioscuri [1] at his residence, and thenceforth kept open house for all comers; and lastly, Onomastus, the
son of Agæus, a native of Elis. These four came from the
Peloponnese. From Athens there arrived Megacles, the son of
that Alcmæon who visited Crœsus, and Tisander's son, Hippoclides, the wealthiest and handsomest of the Athenians. There
was likewise one Eubœan, Lysanias, who came from Eretria,
then a flourishing city. From Thessaly came Diactorides, a
Cranonian, of the race of the Scopadæ; and Alcon arrived from
the Molossians. This was the list of the suitors.

[1] [Castor and Pollux, " the great twin brethren, to whom the Dorians
pray."—E. H. B.]

128. Now when they were all come, and the day appointed had arrived, Clisthenes first of all inquired of each concerning his country and his family; after which he kept them with him a year, and made trial of their manly bearing, their temper, their accomplishments, and their disposition, sometimes drawing them apart for converse, sometimes bringing them all together. Such as were still youths he took with him from time to time to the gymnasia; but the greatest trial of all was at the banquet-table. During the whole period of their stay he lived with them as I have said; and, further, from first to last he entertained them sumptuously. Somehow or other the suitors who came from Athens pleased him the best of all; and of these Hippoclides, Tisander's son, was specially in favour, partly on account of his manly bearing, and partly also because his ancestors were of kin to the Corinthian Cypselids.

129. When at length the day arrived which had been fixed for the espousals, and Clisthenes had to speak out and declare his choice, he first of all made a sacrifice of a hundred oxen, and held a banquet, whereat he entertained all the suitors and the whole people of Sicyon. After the feast was ended, the suitors vied with each other in music and in speaking on a given subject. Presently, as the drinking advanced, Hippoclides, who quite dumbfoundered the rest, called aloud to the flute-player, and bade him strike up a dance; which the man did, and Hippoclides danced to it. And he fancied that he was dancing excellently well; but Clisthenes, who was observing him, began to misdoubt the whole business. Then Hippoclides, after a pause, told an attendant to bring in a table; and when it was brought, he mounted upon it and danced first of all some Laconian figures, then some Attic ones; after which he stood on his head upon the table, and began to toss his legs about. Clisthenes, notwithstanding that he now loathed Hippoclides for a son-in-law, by reason of his dancing and his shamelessness, still, as he wished to avoid an outbreak, had restrained himself during the first and likewise during the second dance; when, however, he saw him tossing his legs in the air, he could no longer contain himself, but cried out, " Son of Tisander, thou hast danced thy wife away!" " What does Hippoclides care? " was the other's answer. And hence the proverb arose.

130. Then Clisthenes commanded silence, and spake thus before the assembled company:—

" Suitors of my daughter, well pleased am I with you all; and right willingly, if it were possible, would I content you all, and not by making choice of one appear to put a slight upon the rest. But as it is out of my power, seeing that I have but one daughter, to grant to all their wishes, I will present to each of you whom I must needs dismiss a talent of silver, for the honour that you have done me in seeking to ally yourselves with my house, and for your long absence from your homes. But my daughter, Agarista, I betroth to Megacles, the son of Alcmæon, to be his wife, according to the usage and wont of Athens."

Then Megacles expressed his readiness; and Clisthenes had the marriage solemnised.

131. Thus ended the affair of the suitors; and thus the Alcmæonidæ came to be famous throughout the whole of Greece. The issue of this marriage was the Clisthenes—so named after his grandfather the Sicyonian—who made the tribes at Athens, and set up the popular government.[1] Megacles had likewise another son, called Hippocrates, whose children were a Megacles and an Agarista, the latter named after Agarista the daughter of Clisthenes. She married Xanthippus, the son of Ariphron; and when she was with child by him had a dream, wherein she fancied that she was delivered of a lion; after which, within a few days, she bore Xanthippus a son, to wit, Pericles.

132. After the blow struck at Marathon, Miltiades, who was previously held in high esteem by his countrymen, increased yet more in influence. Hence, when he told them that he wanted a fleet of seventy ships,[2] with an armed force, and money, without informing them what country he was going to attack, but only promising to enrich them if they would accompany him, seeing that it was a right wealthy land, where they might easily get as much gold as they cared to have—when he told them this, they were quite carried away, and gave him the whole armament which he required.

133. So Miltiades, having got the armament, sailed against Paros, with the object, as he alleged, of punishing the Parians for having gone to war with Athens, inasmuch as a trireme of theirs had come with the Persian fleet to Marathon. This, however, was a mere pretence; the truth was, that Miltiades owed

[1] Supra, v. 69.
[2] Seventy ships appear to have been the full complement of the Athenian navy, until the time when the number was raised by Themistocles to 200 (vide supra, ch. 89, and infra, vii. 144). Miltiades therefore took the whole Athenian navy on this expedition.

the Parians a grudge, because Lysagoras, the son of Tisias, who was a Parian by birth, had told tales against him to Hydarnes the Persian. Arrived before the place against which his expedition was designed, he drove the Parians within their walls, and forthwith laid siege to the city. At the same time he sent a herald to the inhabitants, and required of them a hundred talents, threatening that, if they refused, he would press the siege, and never give it over till the town was taken. But the Parians, without giving his demand a thought, proceeded to use every means that they could devise for the defence of their city, and even invented new plans for the purpose, one of which was, by working at night to raise such parts of the wall as were likely to be carried by assault to double their former height.

134. Thus far all the Greeks agree in their accounts of this business; what follows is related upon the testimony of the Parians only. Miltiades had come to his wit's end, when one of the prisoners, a woman named Timo, who was by birth a Parian, and had held the office of under-priestess in the temple of the infernal goddesses, came and conferred with him. This woman, they say, being introduced into the presence of Miltiades, advised him, if he set great store by the capture of the place, to do something which she could suggest to him. When therefore she had told him what it was she meant, he betook himself to the hill which lies in front of the city, and there leapt the fence enclosing the precinct of Ceres Thesmophorus,[1] since he was not able to open the door. After leaping into the place he went straight to the sanctuary, intending to do something within it—either to remove some of the holy things which it was not lawful to stir, or to perform some act or other, I cannot say what—and had just reached the door, when suddenly a feeling of horror came upon him,[2] and he returned back the way he had come; but in jumping down from the outer wall, he strained his thigh, or, as some say, struck the ground with his knee.

135. So Miltiades returned home sick, without bringing the Athenians any money, and without conquering Paros, having done no more than to besiege the town for six-and-twenty days, and ravage the remainder of the island. The Parians, however, when it came to their knowledge that Timo, the under-priestess

---

[1] Supra, ch. 16.
[2] He would feel that he was doing an act of great impiety, since the sanctuaries of Ceres were not to be entered by men.

of the goddesses, had advised Miltiades what he should do,
were minded to punish her for her crime; they therefore sent
messengers to Delphi, as soon as the siege was at an end, and
asked the god if they should put the under-priestess to death.
" She had discovered," they said, " to the enemies of her country
how they might bring it into subjection, and had exhibited to
Miltiades mysteries which it was not lawful for a man to
know." But the Pythoness forbade them, and said, " Timo
was not in fault; 'twas decreed that Miltiades should come to
an unhappy end; and she was sent to lure him to his destruction." Such was the answer given to the Parians by the
Pythoness.

136. The Athenians, upon the return of Miltiades from Paros,
had much debate concerning him; and Xanthippus, the son of
Ariphron, who spoke more freely against him than all the rest,
impleaded him before the people, and brought him to trial for his
life, on the charge of having dealt deceitfully with the Athenians.
Miltiades, though he was present in court, did not speak in his
own defence; for his thigh had begun to mortify, and disabled
him from pleading his cause. He was forced to lie on a couch
while his defence was made by his friends, who dwelt at most
length on the fight at Marathon, while they made mention also
of the capture of Lemnos, telling how Miltiades took the island,
and, after executing vengeance on the Pelasgians, gave up his
conquest to Athens. The judgment of the people was in his
favour so far as to spare his life; but for the wrong he had
done them they fined him fifty talents.[1] Soon afterwards his
thigh completely gangrened and mortified: and so Miltiades
died; and the fifty talents were paid by his son Cimon.

137. Now the way in which Miltiades had made himself
master of Lemnos was the following. There were certain Pelasgians whom the Athenians once drove out of Attica; whether
they did it justly or unjustly I cannot say, since I only know
what is reported concerning it, which is the following: Hecatæus, the son of Hegesander, says in his History that it was
unjustly. " The Athenians," according to him, " had given to
the Pelasgi a tract of land at the foot of Hymettus as payment
for the wall with which the Pelasgians had surrounded their
citadel. This land was barren, and little worth at the time;
but the Pelasgians brought it into good condition; whereupon

[1] Fifty talents (above £12,000) is certainly an enormous sum for the
time.

the Athenians begrudged them the tract, and desired to recover
it. And so, without any better excuse, they took arms and
drove out the Pelasgians." But the Athenians maintain that
they were justified in what they did. "The Pelasgians," they
say, "while they lived at the foot of Hymettus, were wont to
sally forth from that region and commit outrages on their
children. For the Athenians used at that time to send their
sons and daughters to draw water at the fountain called 'the
Nine Springs,' inasmuch as neither they nor the other Greeks
had any household slaves in those days; and the maidens, whenever they came, were used rudely and insolently by the Pelasgians. Nor were they even content thus; but at the last they
laid a plot, and were caught by the Athenians in the act of
making an attempt upon their city. Then did the Athenians
give a proof how much better men they were than the Pelasgians; for whereas they might justly have killed them all,
having caught them in the very act of rebelling, they spared
their lives, and only required that they should leave the country.
Hereupon the Pelasgians quitted Attica, and settled in Lemnos
and other places." Such are the accounts respectively of
Hecatæus and the Athenians.

138. These same Pelasgians, after they were settled in Lemnos, conceived the wish to be revenged on the Athenians. So,
as they were well acquainted with the Athenian festivals, they
manned some penteconters, and having laid an ambush to catch
the Athenian women as they kept the festival of Diana at
Brauron,[1] they succeeded in carrying off a large number, whom
they took to Lemnos and there kept as concubines. After a
while the women bore children, whom they taught to speak the
language of Attica and observe the manners of the Athenians.
These boys refused to have any commerce with the sons of the
Pelasgian women; and if a Pelasgian boy struck one of their
number, they all made common cause, and joined in avenging
their comrade; nay, the Greek boys even set up a claim to
exercise lordship over the others, and succeeded in gaining the
upper hand. When these things came to the ears of the Pelas-

---

[1] Brauron, as is sufficiently evident from this place, was one of the
maritime demes of Attica. The Brauronia was a festival held once in
four years, wherein the Attic girls, between the ages of five and ten, went
in procession, dressed in crocus-coloured garments, to the sanctuary, and
there performed a rite wherein they imitated bears. No Attic woman
was allowed to marry till she had gone through this ceremony.

gians, they took counsel together, and, on considering the
matter, they grew frightened, and said one to another, " If
these boys even now are resolved to make common cause against
the sons of our lawful wives, and seek to exercise lordship over
them, what may we expect when they grow up to be men? "
Then it seemed good to the Pelasgians to kill all the sons of the
Attic women; which they did accordingly, and at the same
time slew likewise their mothers. From this deed, and that
former crime of the Lemnian women, when they slew their
husbands in the days of Thoas,[1] it has come to be usual throughout Greece to call wicked actions by the name of " Lemnian
deeds."

139. When the Pelasgians had thus slain their children and
their women, the earth refused to bring forth its fruits for them,
and their wives bore fewer children, and their flocks and herds
increased more slowly than before, till at last, sore pressed by
famine and bereavement, they sent men to Delphi, and begged
the god to tell them how they might obtain deliverance from
their sufferings. The Pythoness answered, that " they must
give the Athenians whatever satisfaction they might demand."
Then the Pelasgians went to Athens and declared their wish to
give the Athenians satisfaction for the wrong which they had
done to them. So the Athenians had a couch prepared in their
townhall, and adorned it with the fairest coverlets, and set by
its side a table laden with all manner of good things, and then
told the Pelasgians they must deliver up their country to them
in a similar condition. The Pelasgians answered and said,
" When a ship comes with a north wind from your country to
ours in a single day, then will we give it up to you." This they
said because they knew that what they required was impossible,
for Attica lies a long way to the south of Lemnos.[2]

140. No more passed at that time. But very many years
afterwards, when the Hellespontian Chersonese had been brought
under the power of Athens, Miltiades, the son of Cimon, sailed,
during the prevalence of the Etesian winds, from Elæus in the

[1] The tale went that the Sintian Lemnians, the original inhabitants of
the island, having become disgusted with their wives, on whom Venus had
sent a curse, married Thracian women from the continent. Hereupon
their wives formed a conspiracy, and murdered their fathers and their
husbands. Hypsipylé alone had compassion on her father Thoas, and
concealed him. Her fraud was afterwards detected; Thoas was killed,
and Hypsipylé sold into slavery.

[2] Lemnos is nearly 140 miles north of Attica.

Chersonese to Lemnos, and called on the Pelasgians to quit their island, reminding them of the prophecy which they had supposed it impossible to fulfil. The people of Hephæstia obeyed the call; but they of Myrina, not acknowledging the Chersonese to be any part of Attica, refused and were besieged and brought over by force. Thus was Lemnos gained by the Athenians and Miltiades.

ADDED NOTE ON THE BATTLE OF MARATHON:
BY THE EDITOR

The importance of the battle of Marathon can hardly be overestimated. The success of the Athenians inspired Greece to gird herself to withstand the later (and greater) invasion of Xerxes. It is one of those victories upon which the destinies of nations have hinged. But, apart from this aspect of the battle, we do well to remember that the great democracy of Athens was baptised, if it was not born, on that immortal field. Rightly did the Athenians regard Marathon as marking a decisive epoch in her history. " It was as if on that day the Gods had said to them: Go on and prosper."

For further information the student is referred to the histories of Thirlwall and of Grote. In Prof. Strachan's edition of the sixth book of Herodotus, a careful account of the battle is given (Appendix i.; see the map). Creasy, in his *Decisive Battles of the World*, supplies a popular description.

What Trafalgar and Waterloo have been to modern Europe, that—and more—Marathon and Salamis proved to the ancient world. Whereas in the former case, the sea-victory preceded the land-victory, in the latter the position is reversed. It is a curious coincidence that, in both these world struggles, a period of just ten years separated the naval and the land battles (B.C. 490 and 480; A.D. 1805, and 1815).

THE SEVENTH BOOK, ENTITLED POLYMNIA

1. Now when tidings of the battle that had been fought at Marathon reached the ears of King Darius, the son of Hystaspes, his anger against the Athenians, which had been already roused by their attack upon Sardis,[1] waxed still fiercer, and he became more than ever eager to lead an army against Greece. Instantly he sent off messengers to make proclamation through the several states, that fresh levies were to be raised, and these at an increased rate; while ships, horses, provisions, and transports were likewise to be furnished. So the men published his commands; and now all Asia was in commotion by the space of three years, while everywhere, as Greece was to be attacked, the best and bravest were enrolled for the service, and had to make their preparations accordingly.

After this, in the fourth year,[2] the Egyptians whom Cambyses had enslaved revolted from the Persians; whereupon Darius was more hot for war than ever,[3] and earnestly desired to march an army against both adversaries.

2. Now, as he was about to lead forth his levies against Egypt and Athens, a fierce contention for the sovereign power arose among his sons; since the law of the Persians was, that a king must not go out with his army, until he has appointed one to succeed him upon the throne.[4] Darius, before he obtained the kingdom, had had three sons born to him from his former wife, who was a daughter of Gobryas; while, since he began to reign, Atossa, the daughter of Cyrus, had borne him four. Artabazanes was the eldest of the first family, and Xerxes of the second. These two, therefore, being the sons of different mothers, were now at variance. Artabazanes claimed the crown as the eldest of all the children, because it was an established custom all over the world for the eldest to have the pre-eminence; while Xerxes, on the other hand, urged that he

[1] Supra, v. 100-102.
[2] B.C. 487. The reckoning is inclusive, as usual.
[3] Probably the revolt of Egypt was attributed to the machinations of the Greeks.
[4] An allusion to this custom is made in the first book (ch. 208), in connection with the expedition of Cyrus against the Massagetæ.

was sprung from Atossa, the daughter of Cyrus, and that it was Cyrus who had won the Persians their freedom.[1]

3. Before Darius had pronounced on the matter, it happened that Demaratus, the son of Ariston, who had been deprived of his crown at Sparta, and had afterwards, of his own accord, gone into banishment, came up to Susa,[2] and there heard of the quarrel of the princes. Hereupon, as report says, he went to Xerxes, and advised him, in addition to all that he had urged before, to plead—that at the time when he was born Darius was already king, and bore rule over the Persians; but when Artabazanes came into the world, he was a mere private person. It would therefore be neither right nor seemly that the crown should go to another in preference to himself. " For at Sparta," said Demaratus, by way of suggestion, " the law is, that if a king has sons before he comes to the throne, and another son is born to him afterwards, the child so born is heir to his father's kingdom." Xerxes followed this counsel, and Darius, persuaded that he had justice on his side, appointed him his successor. For my own part I believe that, even without this, the crown would have gone to Xerxes; for Atossa was all-powerful.[3]

4. Darius, when he had thus appointed Xerxes his heir, was minded to lead forth his armies; but he was prevented by death while his preparations were still proceeding. He died in the year following [4] the revolt of Egypt and the matters here related, after having reigned in all six-and-thirty years, leaving the revolted Egyptians and the Athenians alike unpunished. At his death the kingdom passed to his son Xerxes.

5. Now Xerxes, on first mounting the throne, was coldly disposed towards the Grecian war, and made it his business to collect an army against Egypt. But Mardonius, the son of Gobryas, who was at the court, and had more influence with him than any of the other Persians, being his own cousin, the child of a sister of Darius, plied him with discourses like the following:—

" Master, it is not fitting that they of Athens escape scot-free, after doing the Persians such great injury. Complete the work which thou hast now in hand, and then, when the pride of Egypt

---

[1] This was probably the real *right* on which the claim of Xerxes rested. Xerxes was of the blood of Cyrus; Artabazanes was not.

[2] Supra, vi. 70.

[3] Though Darius had several wives (supra, iii. 88), it is probable that he had but one queen, namely Atossa. This is the rule wherever there is a seraglio, and was clearly the custom of the Persian court.

[4] B.C. 486.

is brought low, lead an army against Athens. So shalt thou
thyself have good report among men, and others shall fear hereafter to attack thy country."

Thus far it was of vengeance that he spoke; but sometimes he
would vary the theme, and observe by the way, " that Europe
was a wondrous beautiful region, rich in all kinds of cultivated
trees, and the soil excellent: no one, save the king, was worthy
to own such a land."

6. All this he said, because he longed for adventures, and
hoped to become satrap of Greece under the king; and after a
while he had his way, and persuaded Xerxes to do according to
his desires. Other things, however, occurring about the same
time, helped his persuasions. For, in the first place, it chanced
that messengers arrived from Thessaly, sent by the Aleuadæ,
Thessalian kings, to invite Xerxes into Greece, and to promise
him all the assistance which it was in their power to give. And
further, the Pisistratidæ, who had come up to Susa, held the
same language as the Aleuadæ, and worked upon him even more
than they, by means of Onomacritus of Athens, an oracle-monger,
and the same who set forth the prophecies of Musæus in their
order.[1] The Pisistratidæ had previously been at enmity with
this man, but made up the quarrel before they removed to Susa.
He was banished from Athens by Hipparchus, the son of Pisistratus, because he foisted into the writings of Musæus a prophecy
that the islands which lie off Lemnos would one day disappear
in the sea. Lasus of Hermioné[2] caught him in the act of so doing.
For this cause Hipparchus banished him, though till then they
had been the closest of friends. Now, however, he went up to
Susa with the sons of Pisistratus, and they talked very grandly
of him to the king; while he, for his part, whenever he was in
the king's company, repeated to him certain of the oracles; and
while he took care to pass over all that spoke of disaster to the
barbarians, brought forward the passages which promised them
the greatest success. " 'Twas fated," he told Xerxes, " that a
Persian should bridge the Hellespont, and march an army from
Asia into Greece." While Onomacritus thus plied Xerxes with

---

[1] Of Musæus, as of Orpheus, with whom his name is commonly joined,
scarcely anything is known. All perhaps that can be said with certainty
is that poems believed to be ancient were current under his name as early
as B.C. 520. [Campbell, Religion in Greek Literature, pp. 245-254.—
E. H. B.]

[2] Lasus of Hermione was a lyric and dithyrambic poet of the highest
repute. He was said to have been the instructor of Pindar.

his oracles, the Pisistratidæ and Aleuadæ did not cease to press on him their advice, till at last the king yielded, and agreed to lead forth an expedition.

7. First, however, in the year following the death of Darius,[1] he marched against those who had revolted from him; and having reduced them, and laid all Egypt under a far harder yoke than ever his father had put upon it, he gave the government to Achæmenes, who was his own brother, and son to Darius. This Achæmenes was afterwards slain in his government by Inarôs, the son of Psammetichus, a Libyan.

8. (§ 1.) After Egypt was subdued, Xerxes, being about to take in hand the expedition against Athens, called together an assembly of the noblest Persians, to learn their opinions, and to lay before them his own designs.[2] So, when the men were met, the king spake thus to them:—

" Persians, I shall not be the first to bring in among you a new custom—I shall but follow one which has come down to us from our forefathers. Never yet, as our old men assure me, has our race reposed itself, since the time when Cyrus overcame Astyages, and so we Persians wrested the sceptre from the Medes. Now in all this God guides us; and we, obeying his guidance, prosper greatly. What need have I to tell you of the deeds of Cyrus and Cambyses, and my own father Darius, how many nations they conquered, and added to our dominions? Ye know right well what great things they achieved. But for myself, I will say that, from the day on which I mounted the throne, I have not ceased to consider by what means I may rival those who have preceded me in this post of honour, and increase the power of Persia as much as any of them. And truly I have pondered upon this, until at last I have found out a way whereby we may at once win glory, and likewise get possession of a land which is as large and as rich as our own—nay, which is even more varied in the fruits it bears—while at the same time we obtain satisfaction and revenge. For this cause I have now called you together, that I may make known to you what I design to do. (§ 2.) My intent is to throw a bridge over the Hellespont and march an army through Europe against Greece,

---

[1] B.C. 485.
[2] These speeches have scarcely any higher historical character than those of the conspirators in the third book. They must be considered however as embodying *Persian* as well as Greek views of the circumstances out of which the war arose, and the feelings of those who engaged in it. Oriental respect for royalty strove to exonerate Xerxes from all blame.

that thereby I may obtain vengeance from the Athenians for the wrongs committed by them against the Persians and against my father.   Your own eyes saw the preparations of Darius against these men; but death came upon him, and balked his hopes of revenge.   In his behalf, therefore, and in behalf of all the Persians, I undertake the war, and pledge myself not to rest till I have taken and burnt Athens, which has dared, unprovoked, to injure me and my father.   Long since they came to Asia with Aristagoras of Miletus, who was one of our slaves, and, entering Sardis, burnt its temples and its sacred groves; [1] again, more lately, when we made a landing upon their coast under Datis and Artaphernes, how roughly they handled us ye do not need to be told.   (§ 3.) For these reasons, therefore, I am bent upon this war; and I see likewise therewith united no few advantages. Once let us subdue this people, and those neighbours of theirs who hold the land of Pelops the Phrygian, and we shall extend the Persian territory as far as God's heaven reaches.   The sun will then shine on no land beyond our borders; for I will pass through Europe from one end to the other, and with your aid make of all the lands which it contains one country.   For thus, if what I hear be true, affairs stand: The nations whereof I have spoken, once swept away, there is no city, no country left in all the world, which will venture so much as to withstand us in arms.   By this course then we shall bring all mankind under our yoke, alike those who are guilty and those who are innocent of doing us wrong.   (§ 4.) For yourselves, if you wish to please me, do as follows: When I announce the time for the army to meet together, hasten to the muster with a good will, every one of you; and know that to the man who brings with him the most gallant array I will give the gifts which our people consider the most honourable.   This then is what ye have to do.   But to show that I am not self-willed in this matter, I lay the business before you, and give you full leave to speak your minds upon it openly."

Xerxes, having so spoken, held his peace.

9. (§ 1.) Whereupon Mardonius took the word, and said—

" Of a truth, my lord, thou dost surpass, not only all living Persians, but likewise those yet unborn.   Most true and right is each word that thou hast now uttered; but best of all thy resolve, not to let the Ionians [2] who live in Europe—a worthless

---

[1] Supra, v. 100-102.

[2] This use of the term " Ionian " for the European Greeks is not casual,

crew—mock us any more. It were indeed a monstrous thing if,
after conquering and enslaving the Sacæ,[1] the Indians, the
Ethiopians, the Assyrians, and many other mighty nations, not
for any wrong that they had done us, but only to increase our
empire, we should then allow the Greeks, who have done us such
wanton injury, to escape our vengeance. What is it that we
fear in them?—not surely their numbers?—not the greatness of
their wealth? We know the manner of their battle—we know
how weak their power is; already have we subdued their
children who dwell in our country, the Ionians, Æolians, and
Dorians. I myself have had experience of these men when I
marched against them by the orders of thy father; and though
I went as far as Macedonia,[2] and came but a little short of
reaching Athens itself, yet not a soul ventured to come out
against me to battle. (§ 2.) And yet, I am told, these very
Greeks are wont to wage wars against one another in the most
foolish way, through sheer perversity and doltishness. For no
sooner is war proclaimed than they search out the smoothest and
fairest plain that is to be found in all the land, and there they
assemble and fight; whence it comes to pass that even the conquerors depart with great loss: I say nothing of the conquered, for they are destroyed altogether. Now surely, as
they are all of one speech, they ought to interchange heralds
and messengers, and make up their differences by any means
rather than battle; or, at the worst, if they must needs fight
one against another, they ought to post themselves as strongly
as possible, and so try their quarrels. But, notwithstanding that
they have so foolish a manner of warfare, yet these Greeks, when
I led my army against them to the very borders of Macedonia,
did not so much as think of offering me battle. (§ 3.) Who
then will dare, O king! to meet thee in arms, when thou comest
with all Asia's warriors at thy back, and with all her ships?
For my part I do not believe the Greek people will be so fool-
hardy. Grant, however, that I am mistaken herein, and that
they are foolish enough to meet us in open fight; in that case
they will learn that there are no such soldiers in the whole world
as we. Nevertheless let us spare no pains; for nothing comes

but characteristic of the Oriental modes of speech, and marks Herodotus
for a keen observer of little peculiarities. Here *two* Ionias are mentioned,
one of which stands clearly for Asiatic, and the other for European Greece.

[1] Apparently Mardonius means the Scythians of Europe, whom he
represents as reduced to slavery by the expedition of Darius.

[2] Supra, vi. 44, 45.

without trouble; but all that men acquire is got by pains-taking."

When Mardonius had in this way softened the harsh speech of Xerxes, he too held his peace.

10. The other Persians were silent; for all feared to raise their voice against the plan proposed to them. But Artabanus, the son of Hystaspes, and uncle of Xerxes, trusting to his relation-ship, was bold to speak:—" O king! " he said, " it is impossible, if no more than one opinion is uttered, to make choice of the best: a man is forced then to follow whatever advice may have been given him; but if opposite speeches are delivered, then choice can be exercised. In like manner pure gold is not recognised by itself; but when we test it along with baser ore, we perceive which is the better. I counselled thy father, Darius, who was my own brother, not to attack the Scyths,[1] a race of people who had no town in their whole land. He thought however to subdue those wandering tribes, and would not listen to me, but marched an army against them, and ere he returned home lost many of his bravest warriors. Thou art about, O king! to attack a people far superior to the Scyths, a people dis-tinguished above others both by land and sea. 'Tis fit there-fore that I should tell thee what danger thou incurrest hereby. (§ 2.) Thou sayest that thou wilt bridge the Hellespont, and lead thy troops through Europe against Greece. Now suppose some disaster befall thee by land or sea, or by both. It may be even so; for the men are reputed valiant. Indeed one may measure their prowess from what they have already done; for when Datis and Artaphernes led their huge army against Attica, the Athenians singly defeated them. But grant they are not suc-cessful on both elements. Still, if they man their ships, and, defeating us by sea, sail to the Hellespont, and there destroy our bridge,—that, sire, were a fearful hazard. (§ 3.) And here 'tis not by my own mother wit alone that I conjecture what will happen; but I remember how narrowly we escaped disaster once, when thy father, after throwing bridges over the Thracian Bosphorus and the Ister, marched against the Scythians, and they tried every sort of prayer to induce the Ionians, who had charge of the bridge over the Ister, to break the passage.[2] On that day, if Histiæus, the king of Miletus, had sided with the other princes, and not set himself to oppose their views, the empire of the Persians would have come to nought. Surely a

[1] Supra, iv. 83.   [2] Supra, iv. 133, 136-139.

dreadful thing is this even to hear said, that the king's fortunes depended wholly on one man.

(§ 4.) "Think then no more of incurring so great a danger when no need presses, but follow the advice I tender. Break up this meeting, and when thou hast well considered the matter with thyself, and settled what thou wilt do, declare to us thy resolve. I know not of aught in the world that so profits a man as taking good counsel with himself; for even if things fall out against one's hopes, still one has counselled well, though fortune has made the counsel of none effect: whereas if a man counsels ill and luck follows, he has gotten a windfall, but his counsel is none the less silly. (§ 5.) Seest thou how God with his lightning smites always the bigger animals, and will not suffer them to wax insolent, while those of a lesser bulk chafe him not? How likewise his bolts fall ever on the highest houses and the tallest trees? So plainly does He love to bring down everything that exalts itself. Thus ofttimes a mighty host is discomfited by a few men, when God in his jealousy sends fear or storm from heaven, and they perish in a way unworthy of them. For God allows no one to have high thoughts but Himself. (§ 6.) Again, hurry always brings about disasters, from which huge sufferings are wont to arise; but in delay lie many advantages, not apparent (it may be) at first sight, but such as in course of time are seen of all. Such then is my counsel to thee, O king!

(§ 7.) "And thou, Mardonius, son of Gobryas, forbear to speak foolishly concerning the Greeks, who are men that ought not to be lightly esteemed by us. For while thou revilest the Greeks, thou dost encourage the king to lead his own troops against them; and this, as it seems to me, is what thou art specially striving to accomplish. Heaven send thou succeed not to thy wish! For slander is of all evils the most terrible. In it two men do wrong, and one man has wrong done to him. The slanderer does wrong, forasmuch as he abuses a man behind his back; and the hearer, forasmuch as he believes what he has not searched into thoroughly. The man slandered in his absence suffers wrong at the hands of both: for one brings against him a false charge; and the other thinks him an evil-doer. (§ 8.) If, however, it must needs be that we go to war with this people, at least allow the king to abide at home in Persia. Then let thee and me both stake our children on the issue, and do thou choose out thy men, and, taking with thee whatever number of troops thou likest, lead forth our armies to battle. If things go well for the king, as thou sayest they will, let me and my children be put to death; but if they fall out as I prophesy, let thy children suffer, and thyself too, if thou shalt come back alive. But shouldest thou refuse this wager, and still resolve to march an army against Greece, sure I am that some of those whom thou leavest behind thee here will one day receive the sad tidings, that Mardonius has brought a great disaster upon the Persian people, and lies a prey to dogs and birds somewhere in the land of the Athenians, or else in that of the Lacedæmonians; unless indeed thou shalt have perished sooner by the way, experiencing in thy own person the might of those men on whom thou wouldest fain induce the king to make war."

11. Thus spake Artabanus. But Xerxes, full of wrath, replied to him—

"Artabanus, thou art my father's brother—that shall save thee from receiving the due meed of thy silly words. One shame however I will lay upon thee, coward and faint-hearted as thou art—thou shalt not come with me to fight these Greeks, but shalt tarry here with the women. Without thy aid I will accomplish all of which I spake. For let me not be thought the child of Darius, the son of Hystaspes, the son of Arsames, the son of Ariaramnes, the son of Teispes, the son of Cyrus,[1] the son of Cambyses, the son of Teispes, the son of Achæmenes, if I take not vengeance on the Athenians. Full well I know that, were we to remain at rest, yet would not they, but would most certainly invade our country, if at least it be right to judge from what they have already done; for, remember, it was they who fired Sardis and attacked Asia. So now retreat is on both sides impossible, and the choice lies between doing and suffering injury; either our empire must pass under the dominion of the Greeks, or their land become the prey of the Persians; for there is no middle course left in this quarrel. It is right then that we, who have in times past received wrong, should now avenge it, and that I should thereby discover what that great

---

[1] The genealogy of himself which Darius caused to be engraved on the rocks of Behistun determines absolutely the number of generations between Xerxes and Achæmenes, *proving* what had been already surmised, that the names of Cyrus and Cambyses do not belong to the stem of Darius, but are thrown by Xerxes into the list of his ancestors in right of his mother Atossa, the daughter of Cyrus.

risk[1] is which I run in marching against these men—men whom
Pelops the Phrygian, a vassal of my forefathers,[2] subdued so
utterly, that to this day both the land, and the people who
dwell therein, alike bear the name of the conqueror!"

12. Thus far did the speaking proceed. Afterwards evening
fell; and Xerxes began to find the advice of Artabanus greatly
disquiet him. So he thought upon it during the night, and concluded at last that it was not for his advantage to lead an army
into Greece. When he had thus made up his mind anew, he
fell asleep. And now he saw in the night, as the Persians
declare, a vision of this nature—he thought a tall and beautiful
man stood over him and said, "Hast thou then changed thy
mind, Persian, and wilt thou not lead forth thy host against the
Greeks, after commanding the Persians to gather together their
levies? Be sure thou doest not well to change; nor is there a
man here who will approve thy conduct. The course that thou
didst determine on during the day, let that be followed." After
thus speaking the man seemed to Xerxes to fly away.

13. Day dawned; and the king made no account of this
dream, but called together the same Persians as before, and
spake to them as follows:—

"Men of Persia, forgive me if I alter the resolve to which I
came so lately. Consider that I have not yet reached to the full
growth of my wisdom, and that they who urge me to engage in
this war leave me not to myself for a moment. When I heard
the advice of Artabanus, my young blood suddenly boiled; and
I spake words against him little befitting his years: now how
ever I confess my fault, and am resolved to follow his counsel.
Understand then that I have changed my intent with respect to
carrying war into Greece, and cease to trouble yourselves."

When they heard these words, the Persians were full of joy,
and, falling down at the feet of Xerxes, made obeisance to him.

14. But when night came, again the same vision stood over
Xerxes as he slept, and said, "Son of Darius, it seems thou hast
openly before all the Persians renounced the expedition, making
light of my words, as though thou hadst not heard them spoken.
Know therefore and be well assured, that unless thou go forth to
the war, this thing shall happen unto thee—as thou art grown

---

[1] Xerxes refers here to the earlier part of the speech of Artabanus, and
the perils there put forward (supra, ch. 10, § 1-3).
[2] Herodotus tells us at the beginning of his History that the Persians
considered Asia and all its nations as their own always.

mighty and puissant in a short space, so likewise shalt thou within a little time be brought low indeed."

15. Then Xerxes, greatly frightened at the vision which he had seen, sprang from his couch, and sent a messenger to call Artabanus, who came at the summons, when Xerxes spoke to him in these words:—

"Artabanus, at the moment I acted foolishly, when I gave thee ill words in return for thy good advice. However it was not long ere I repented, and was convinced that thy counsel was such as I ought to follow. But I may not now act in this way, greatly as I desire to do so. For ever since I repented and changed my mind a dream has haunted me, which disapproves my intentions, and has now just gone from me with threats. Now if this dream is sent to me from God, and if it is indeed his will that our troops should march against Greece, thou too wilt have the same dream come to thee and receive the same commands as myself. And this will be most sure to happen, I think, if thou puttest on the dress which I am wont to wear, and then, after taking thy seat upon my throne, liest down to sleep on my bed."

16. Such were the words of Xerxes. Artabanus would not at first yield to the command of the King; for he deemed himself unworthy to sit upon the royal throne. At the last however he was forced to give way, and did as Xerxes bade him; but first he spake thus to the king:—

"To me, sire, it seems to matter little whether a man is wise himself or willing to hearken to such as give good advice. In thee truly are found both tempers; but the counsels of evil men lead thee astray: they are like the gales of wind which vex the sea—else the most useful thing for man in the whole world—and suffer it not to follow the bent of its own nature. For myself, it irked me not so much to be reproached by thee, as to observe, that when two courses were placed before the Persian people, one of a nature to increase their pride, the other to humble it, by showing them how hurtful it is to allow one's heart always to covet more than one at present possesses, thou madest choice of that which was the worse both for thyself and for the Persians. (§ 2.) Now thou sayest, that from the time when thou didst approve the better course, and give up the thought of warring against Greece, a dream has haunted thee, sent by some god or other, which will not suffer thee to lay aside the expedition. But such things, my son, have of a truth nothing divine in them. The dreams, that wander to and fro among mankind, I will tell thee of what nature they are,—I who have seen so many more years than thou. Whatever a man has been thinking of during the day, is wont to hover round him in the visions of his dreams at night. Now we during these many days past have had our hands full of this enterprise. (§ 3.) If however the matter be not as I suppose, but God has indeed some part therein, thou hast in brief declared the whole that can be said concerning it—let it e'en appear to me as it has to thee, and lay on me the same injunctions. But it ought not to appear to me any the more if I put on thy clothes than if I wear my own, nor if I go to sleep in thy bed than if I do so in mine—supposing, I mean, that it is about to appear at all. For this thing, be it what it may, that visits thee in thy sleep, surely is not so far gone in folly as to see me, and because I am dressed in thy clothes, straightway to mistake me for thee. Now however our business is to see if it will regard me as of small account, and not vouchsafe to appear to me, whether I wear mine own clothes or thine, while it keeps on haunting thee continually. If it does so, and appears often, I should myself say that it was from God. For the rest, if thy mind is fixed, and it is not possible to turn thee from thy design, but I must needs go and sleep in thy bed, well and good, let it be even so; and when I have done as thou wishest, then let the dream appear to me. Till such time, however, I shall keep to my former opinion."

17. Thus spake Artabanus; and when he had so said, thinking to show Xerxes that his words were nought, he did according to his orders. Having put on the garments which Xerxes was wont to wear and taken his seat upon the royal throne, he lay down to sleep upon the king's own bed. As he slept, there appeared to him the very same dream which had been seen by Xerxes; it came and stood over Artabanus, and said—

"Thou art the man, then, who, feigning to be tender of Xerxes, seekest to dissuade him from leading his armies against the Greeks! But thou shalt not escape scathless, either now or in time to come, because thou hast sought to prevent that which is fated to happen. As for Xerxes, it has been plainly told to himself what will befall him, if he refuses to perform my bidding."

18. In such words, as Artabanus thought, the vision threatened him, and then endeavoured to burn out his eyes with red-hot

irons.[1] At this he shrieked, and, leaping from his couch, hurried
to Xerxes, and, sitting down at his side, gave him a full account
of the vision; after which he went on to speak in the words
which follow:—

"I, O King! am a man who have seen many mighty empires
overthrown by weaker ones; and therefore it was that I sought
to hinder thee from being quite carried away by thy youth;
since I knew how evil a thing it is to covet more than one
possesses. I could remember the expedition of Cyrus against
the Massagetæ, and what was the issue of it; I could recollect
the march of Cambyses against the Ethiops; I had taken part
in the attack of Darius upon the Scyths;—bearing therefore all
these things in mind, I thought with myself that if thou shouldst
remain at peace, all men would deem thee fortunate. But as
this impulse has plainly come from above, and a heaven-sent
destruction seems about to overtake the Greeks, behold, I change
to another mind, and alter my thoughts upon the matter. Do
thou therefore make known to the Persians what the god has
declared, and bid them follow the orders which were first given,
and prepare their levies. Be careful to act so that the bounty
of the god may not be hindered by slackness on thy part."

Thus spake these two together; and Xerxes, being in good
heart on account of the vision, when day broke, laid all before
the Persians; while Artabanus, who had formerly been the only
person openly to oppose the expedition, now showed as openly
that he favoured it.

19. After Xerxes had thus determined to go forth to the war,
there appeared to him in his sleep yet a third vision. The
Magi were consulted upon it,[2] and said that its meaning reached
to the whole earth, and that all mankind would become his

---

[1] Putting out the eyes has in all ages been a common Oriental punishment. The earliest instance on record is that of Zedekiah, whose eyes were
put out by Nebuchadnezzar (Jerem. xxix. 7; lii. 11). [But see now a
reference to this hideous form of penalty in the recently discovered "Code
of Khammurâbi," circ. 2500 B.C.—E. H. B.].   Grote sees in this whole
narrative nothing but " religious imagination "—a *mythus* embodying the
deep conviction, alike of Greeks and of Persians, that nothing short of a
direct divine interposition could have brought about the transcendently
great events which were connected with the expedition of Xerxes.   I
incline, with Bishop Thirlwall, to suspect a foundation in *fact* for the stories
that were told. The weak mind of Xerxes may have been imposed upon
by a pretended spectre; and the stronger one of Artabanus may have been
subdued by threats.

[2] Vide supra, i. 108. For the general practice among the Oriental
nations to attend to dreams, and to require an interpretation of them
from their priests, see Gen. xli. 8; and Dan. ii. 2: iv. 6.

servants. Now the vision which the king saw was this: he dreamt that he was crowned with a branch of an olive-tree, and that boughs spread out from the olive-branch and covered the whole earth; then suddenly the garland, as it lay upon his brow, vanished. So when the Magi had thus interpreted the vision, straightway all the Persians who were come together departed to their several governments, where each displayed the greatest zeal, on the faith of the king's offers. For all hoped to obtain for themselves the gifts which had been promised. And so Xerxes gathered together his host, ransacking every corner of the continent.

20. Reckoning from the recovery of Egypt, Xerxes spent four full years[1] in collecting his host, and making ready all things that were needful for his soldiers. It was not till the close of the fifth year that he set forth on his march, accompanied by a mighty multitude. For of all the armaments whereof any mention has reached us, this was by far the greatest; insomuch that no other expedition compared to this seems of any account, neither that which Darius undertook against the Scythians, nor the expedition of the Scythians (which the attack of Darius was designed to avenge), when they, being in pursuit of the Cimmerians, fell upon the Median territory, and subdued and held for a time almost the whole of Upper Asia;[2] nor, again, that of the Atridæ against Troy, of which we hear in story; nor that of the Mysians and Teucrians, which was still earlier, wherein these nations crossed the Bosphorus into Europe, and, after conquering all Thrace, pressed forward till they came to the Ionian sea,[3] while southward they reached as far as the river Peneus.

21. All these expeditions, and others, if such there were, are as nothing compared with this. For was there a nation in all Asia which Xerxes did not bring with him against Greece? Or was there a river, except those of unusual size, which sufficed for his troops to drink? One nation furnished ships; another was arrayed among the foot-soldiers; a third had to supply horses; a fourth, transports for the horse and men likewise for the transport service; a fifth, ships of war towards the bridges; a sixth, ships and provisions.

[1] Various modes have been adopted of explaining the chronology of the period between the battles of Marathon and Salamis. All accounts agree in stating the interval at ten years. The numbers in Herodotus are with difficulty brought within this interval.

[2] Vide supra, i. 103-106; iv. 1, 12.

[3] By the "Ionian Sea" Herodotus means the Adriatic (vide supra, vi. 127; and infra, ix. 92).

22. And in the first place, because the former fleet had met with so great a disaster about Athos,[1] preparations were made, by the space of about three years, in that quarter. A fleet of triremes lay at Elæus in the Chersonese; and from this station detachments were sent by the various nations whereof the army was composed, which relieved one another at intervals, and worked at a trench beneath the lash of taskmasters; while the people dwelling about Athos bore likewise a part in the labour. Two Persians, Bubares, the son of Megabazus, and Artachæes, the son of Artæus, superintended the undertaking.

Athos is a great and famous mountain, inhabited by men, and stretching far out into the sea. Where the mountain ends towards the mainland it forms a peninsula; and in this place there is a neck of land about twelve furlongs across, the whole extent whereof, from the sea of the Acanthians to that over against Torôné, is a level plain, broken only by a few low hills. Here, upon this isthmus where Athos ends, is Sané[2] a Greek city. Inside of Sané, and upon Athos itself, are a number of towns, which Xerxes was now employed in disjoining from the continent: these are, Dium, Olophyxus, Acrothôum, Thyssus, and Cleônæ. Among these cities Athos was divided.

23. Now the manner in which they dug was the following:[3] a line was drawn across by the city of Sané; and along this the various nations parcelled out among themselves the work to be done. When the trench grew deep, the workmen at the bottom continued to dig, while others handed the earth, as it was dug out, to labourers placed higher up upon ladders, and these taking it, passed it on further, till it came at last to those at the top, who carried it off and emptied it away. All the other nations, therefore, except the Phœnicians, had double labour; for the sides of the trench fell in continually, as could not but happen, since they made the width no greater at the top than it was required to be at the bottom. But the Phœnicians showed in this the skill which they are wont to exhibit in all their undertakings. For in the portion of the work which was allotted to them they began by making the trench at the top twice as

---

[1] Supra, vi. 44.

[2] Sané was situated on the southern coast of the isthmus, near the mouth of the canal of Xerxes.

[3] Distinct appearances of the ancient cutting have been discovered almost across its whole extent, only failing where the canal approached the sea, and somewhat indistinctly marked in the alluvial plain north of the hills. The canal forms a line of ponds, from two to eight feet deep and from sixty to ninety broad, nearly from one sea to the other.

wide as the prescribed measure, and then as they dug downwards approached the sides nearer and nearer together, so that when they reached the bottom their part of the work was of the same width as the rest. In a meadow near, there was a place of assembly and a market; and hither great quantities of corn, ready ground, were brought from Asia.

24. It seems to me, when I consider this work, that Xerxes, in making it, was actuated by a feeling of pride, wishing to display the extent of his power, and to leave a memorial behind him to posterity. For notwithstanding that it was open to him, with no trouble at all,[1] to have had his ships drawn across the isthmus, yet he issued orders that a canal should be made through which the sea might flow, and that it should be of such a width as would allow of two triremes passing through it abreast with the oars in action. He likewise gave to the same persons who were set over the digging of the trench, the task of making a bridge across the river Strymon.

25. While these things were in progress, he was having cables prepared for his bridges, some of papyrus and some of white flax, a business which he entrusted to the Phœnicians and the Egyptians. He likewise laid up stores of provisions in divers places, to save the army and the beasts of burthen from suffering want upon their march into Greece. He inquired carefully about all the sites, and had the stores laid up in such as were most convenient, causing them to be brought across from various parts of Asia and in various ways, some in transports and others in merchantmen. The greater portion was carried to Leucé-Acté, upon the Thracian coast; some part, however, was conveyed to Tyrodiza,[2] in the country of the Perinthians, some to Doriscus,[3] some to Eïon[4] upon the Strymon, and some to Macedonia.

26. During the time that all these labours were in progress, the land army which had been collected was marching with Xerxes towards Sardis, having started from Critalla in Cappadocia. At this spot all the host which was about to accompany the king in his passage across the continent had been bidden to assemble. And here I have it not in my power to mention which of the satraps was adjudged to have brought his troops in the most gallant array, and on that account rewarded by the

---

[1] The light ships of the ancients were easily transported in this way across the land.

[2] The exact site cannot be fixed; but it was probably near the Serrhean promontory of Stephen.

[3] Infra, ch. 59. [4] Infra, ch. 113.

king according to his promise; for I do not know whether this matter ever came to a judgment. But it is certain that the host of Xerxes, after crossing the river Halys, marched through Phrygia till it reached the city of Celænæ.[1] Here are the sources of the river Mæander, and likewise of another stream of no less size, which bears the name of Catarrhactes (or the Cataract); the last-named river has its rise in the market-place of Celænæ, and empties itself into the Mæander. Here, too, in this market-place, is hung up to view the skin of the Silênus Marsyas, which Apollo, as the Phrygian story goes, stripped off and placed there.

27. Now there lived in this city a certain Pythius, the son of Atys, a Lydian. This man entertained Xerxes and his whole army in a most magnificent fashion, offering at the same time to give him a sum of money for the war. Xerxes, upon the mention of money, turned to the Persians who stood by, and asked of them, " Who is this Pythius, and what wealth has he, that he should venture on such an offer as this? " They answered him, " This is the man, O king! who gave thy father Darius the golden plane-tree, and likewise the golden vine;[2] and he is still the wealthiest man we know of in all the world, excepting thee."

28. Xerxes marvelled at these last words; and now, addressing Pythius with his own lips, he asked him what the amount of his wealth really was. Pythius answered as follows:—

" O king! I will not hide this matter from thee, nor make pretence that I do not know how rich I am; but as I know perfectly, I will declare all fully before thee. For when thy journey was noised abroad, and I heard thou wert coming down to the Grecian coast, straightway, as I wished to give thee a sum of money for the war, I made count of my stores, and found them to be two thousand talents of silver, and of gold four millions of Daric staters,[3] wanting seven thousand. All this I willingly make over to thee as a gift; and when it is gone, my

---

[1] It is the modern *Deenair* (lat. 38° 3′, long. 30° 20′). This town, which abounds in remains of high antiquity, is situated near the source of the southern or main stream of the Mæander.

[2] The golden vine was even more famous than the plane-tree. The bunches of grapes were imitated by means of the most costly precious stones. It overshadowed the couch on which the kings slept.

[3] The stater was the only gold coin known to the Greeks generally. It was adopted by them from the Asiatics. The stater is equivalent to about £1 3s. The Persian Daric was a gold coin very like the stater and did not greatly differ in value from it.

slaves and my estates in land will be wealth enough for my wants."

29. This speech charmed Xerxes, and he replied, "Dear Lydian, since I left Persia there is no man but thou who has either desired to entertain my army, or come forward of his own free will to offer me a sum of money for the war. Thou hast done both the one and the other, feasting my troops magnificently, and now making offer of a right noble sum. In return, this is what I will bestow on thee. Thou shalt be my sworn friend from this day; and the seven thousand staters which are wanting to make up thy four millions I will supply, so that the full tale may be no longer lacking, and that thou mayest owe the completion of the round sum to me. Continue to enjoy all that thou hast acquired hitherto; and be sure to remain ever such as thou now art. If thou dost, thou wilt not repent of it so long as thy life endures."

30. When Xerxes had so spoken and had made good his promises to Pythius, he pressed forward upon his march; and passing Anaua, a Phrygian city, and a lake from which salt is gathered, he came to Colossæ,[1] a Phrygian city of great size, situated at a spot where the river Lycus plunges into a chasm and disappears. This river, after running under ground a distance of about five furlongs, reappears once more, and empties itself, like the stream above mentioned, into the Mæander. Leaving Colossæ, the army approached the borders of Phrygia where it abuts on Lydia; and here they came to a city called Cydrara,[2] where was a pillar set up by Crœsus, having an inscription on it, showing the boundaries of the two countries.

31. Where it quits Phrygia and enters Lydia the road separates; the way on the left leads into Caria, while that on the right conducts to Sardis. If you follow this route, you must cross the Mæander, and then pass by the city Callatêbus, where the men live who make honey out of wheat and the fruit of the tamarisk.[3] Xerxes, who chose this way, found here a plane-tree [4] so beautiful, that he presented it with golden ornaments, and put it under the care of one of his Immortals.[5] The day after, he entered the Lydian capital.

[1] [A town on the Lycus (*Churuk Su*), a tributary of the Mæander, in that part of the Roman province of Asia called Phrygia by the Greeks. Ramsay, *Hist. Geogr. of Asia Minor*, pp. 36-7; *The Church in the Roman Empire*, p. 466.—E. H. B.]
[2] The hot springs near *Sarai Kieui* seem to mark this site.
[3] The tamarisk still grows here in abundance.
[4] The plane-trees of this district are magnificent.   [5] Infra, ch. 83.

32. Here his first care was to send off heralds into Greece, who were to prefer a demand for earth and water, and to require that preparations should be made everywhere to feast the king. To Athens indeed and to Sparta he sent no such demand;[1] but these cities excepted, his messengers went everywhere. Now the reason why he sent for earth and water to states which had already refused, was this: he thought that although they had refused when Darius made the demand, they would now be too frightened to venture to say him nay. So he sent his heralds, wishing to know for certain how it would be.

33. Xerxes, after this, made preparations to advance to Abydos, where the bridge across the Hellespont from Asia to Europe was lately finished. Midway between Sestos and Madytus[2] in the Hellespontine Chersonese, and right over against Abydos, there is a rocky tongue of land which runs out for some distance into the sea. This is the place where no long time afterwards the Greeks under Xanthippus, the son of Ariphron, took Artaÿctes the Persian, who was at that time governor of Sestos, and nailed him living to a plank.[3] He was the Artaÿctes who brought women into the temple of Protesilaüs at Elæus, and there was guilty of most unholy deeds.

34. Towards this tongue of land then, the men to whom the business was assigned carried out a double bridge from Abydos; and while the Phœnicians constructed one line with cables of white flax, the Egyptians in the other used ropes made of papyrus. Now it is seven furlongs across from Abydos to the opposite coast. When, therefore, the channel had been bridged successfully, it happened that a great storm arising broke the whole work to pieces, and destroyed all that had been done.

35. So when Xerxes heard of it he was full of wrath, and straightway gave orders that the Hellespont should receive three hundred lashes, and that a pair of fetters should be cast into it. Nay, I have even heard it said, that he bade the branders take their irons and therewith brand the Hellespont. It is certain that he commanded those who scourged the waters to utter, as they lashed them, these barbarian and wicked words: " Thou bitter water, thy lord lays on thee this punishment because thou hast wronged him without a cause, having suffered no evil at his hands. Verily King Xerxes will cross thee, whether thou wilt or

---

[1] The reason for this abstinence is given below (ch. 133).
[2] Madytus was one of the less important cities of the Chersonese.
[3] Vide infra, ix. 116-120.

no. Well dost thou deserve that no man should honour thee with sacrifice; for thou art of a truth a treacherous and unsavoury river." [1] While the sea was thus punished by his orders, he likewise commanded that the overseers of the work should lose their heads.

36. Then they, whose business it was, executed the unpleasing task laid upon them; and other master-builders were set over the work, who accomplished it in the way which I will now describe.

They joined together triremes and penteconters, 360 to support the bridge on the side of the Euxine Sea, and 314 to sustain the other; and these they placed at right angles to the sea, and in the direction of the current of the Hellespont, relieving by these means the tension of the shore cables. Having joined the vessels, they moored them with anchors of unusual size, that the vessels of the bridge towards the Euxine might resist the winds which blow from within the straits, and that those of the more western bridge facing the Egean might withstand the winds which set in from the south and from the south-east. A gap was left in the penteconters in no fewer than three places, to afford a passage for such light craft as chose to enter or leave the Euxine. When all this was done, they made the cables taut from the shore by the help of wooden capstans. This time, moreover, instead of using the two materials separately, they assigned to each bridge six cables, two of which were of white flax, while four were of papyrus. Both cables were of the same size and quality; but the flaxen were the heavier, weighing not less than a talent the cubit. When the bridge across the channel was thus complete, trunks of trees were sawn into planks, which were cut to the width of the bridge, and these were laid side by side upon the tightened cables, and then fastened on the top. This done, brushwood was brought, and arranged upon the planks, after which earth was heaped upon the brushwood, and the whole trodden down into a solid mass. Lastly a bulwark was set up on either side of this causeway, of such a height as to prevent the sumpter-beasts and the horses from seeing over it and taking fright at the water.

37. And now when all was prepared—the bridges, and the works at Athos, the breakwaters about the mouths of the cutting, which were made to hinder the surf from blocking up the

---

[1] The remark of Dean Blakesley is just, that "the Hellespont, perfectly land-locked, and with a stream running some three knots an hour, presents to a person who is sailing on it altogether the appearance of a river."

entrances,[1] and the cutting itself; and when the news came to Xerxes that this last was completely finished,—then at length the host, having first wintered at Sardis, began its march towards Abydos, fully equipped, on the first approach of spring. At the moment of departure, the sun suddenly quitted his seat in the heavens, and disappeared, though there were no clouds in sight, but the sky was clear and serene. Day was thus turned into night; whereupon Xerxes, who saw and remarked the prodigy, was seized with alarm, and sending at once for the Magians, inquired of them the meaning of the portent. They replied—" God is foreshowing to the Greeks the destruction of their cities; for the sun foretells for them, and the moon for us." So Xerxes, thus instructed,[2] proceeded on his way with great gladness of heart.

38. The army had begun its march, when Pythius the Lydian, affrighted at the heavenly portent, and emboldened by his gifts, came to Xerxes and said—" Grant me, O my lord! a favour which is to thee a light matter, but to me of vast account." Then Xerxes, who looked for nothing less than such a prayer as Pythius in fact preferred, engaged to grant him whatever he wished, and commanded him to tell his wish freely. So Pythius, full of boldness, went on to say—

" O my lord! thy servant has five sons; and it chances that all are called upon to join thee in this march against Greece. I beseech thee, have compassion upon my years; and let one of my sons, the eldest, remain behind, to be my prop and stay, and the guardian of my wealth. Take with thee the other four; and when thou hast done all that is in thy heart, mayest thou come back in safety."

39. But Xerxes was greatly angered, and replied to him: " Thou wretch! darest thou speak to me of thy son, when I am myself on the march against Greece, with sons, and brothers, and kinsfolk, and friends? Thou, who art my bond-slave, and art in duty bound to follow me with all thy household, not excepting thy wife! Know that man's spirit dwelleth in his ears, and when it hears good things, straightway it fills all his body with delight; but no sooner does it hear the contrary than it heaves and swells with passion. As when thou didst good deeds and madest good offers to me, thou wert not able to boast

---

[1] When these breakwaters were allowed to fall into decay, the two ends of the canal would soon be silted up and disappear.

[2] The anecdote is probably apocryphal.

of having outdone the king in bountifulness, so now when thou art changed and grown impudent, thou shalt not receive all thy deserts, but less. For thyself and four of thy five sons, the entertainment which I had of thee shall gain protection; but as for him to whom thou clingest above the rest, the forfeit of his life shall be thy punishment." Having thus spoken, forthwith he commanded those to whom such tasks were assigned, to seek out the eldest of the sons of Pythius, and having cut his body asunder, to place the two halves, one on the right, the other on the left, of the great road, so that the army might march out between them.[1]

40. Then the king's orders were obeyed; and the army marched out between the two halves of the carcase. First of all went the baggage-bearers, and the sumpter-beasts, and then a vast crowd of many nations mingled together without any intervals,[2] amounting to more than one half of the army. After these troops an empty space was left, to separate between them and the king. In front of the king went first a thousand horsemen, picked men of the Persian nation—then spearmen a thousand, likewise chosen troops, with their spear-heads pointing towards the ground—next ten of the sacred horses called Nisæan, all daintily caparisoned. (Now these horses are called Nisæan, because they come from the Nisæan plain, a vast flat in Media, producing horses of unusual size.) After the ten sacred horses came the holy chariot of Jupiter, drawn by eight milkwhite steeds, with the charioteer on foot behind them holding the reins; for no mortal is ever allowed to mount into the car. Next to this came Xerxes himself, riding in a chariot drawn by Nisæan horses, with his charioteer, Patiramphes, the son of Otanes, a Persian, standing by his side.[3]

41. Thus rode forth Xerxes from Sardis—but he was accustomed every now and then, when the fancy took him, to alight from his chariot and travel in a litter. Immediately behind the king there followed a body of a thousand spearmen, the noblest and bravest of the Persians, holding their lances in the usual

[1] Compare with this the similar story of Œobazus (iv. 84). The tales are important, as indicating the rigour with which personal service was exacted among the Oriental nations, especially when the monarch was himself going to the field.

[2] It is plain from the whole narrative (infra, ch. 60-86, 210; ix. 31), that in the Persian army, as in the Greek, the contingents of the several nations formed distinct and separate corps.

[3] The Persian monarchs fought from chariots down to the era of the Macedonian conquest.

manner [1]—then came a thousand Persian horse, picked men—
then ten thousand, picked also after the rest, and serving on
foot.[2] Of these last one thousand carried spears with golden
pomegranates at their lower end instead of spikes; and these
encircled the other nine thousand, who bore on their spears
pomegranates of silver. The spearmen too who pointed their
lances towards the ground had golden pomegranates; and the
thousand Persians who followed close after Xerxes had golden
apples. Behind the ten thousand footmen came a body of
Persian cavalry, likewise ten thousand; after which there was
again a void space for as much as two furlongs; and then the
rest of the army followed in a confused crowd.

42. The march of the army, after leaving Lydia, was directed
upon the river Caïcus and the land of Mysia. Beyond the Caïcus
the road, leaving Mount Cana upon the left, passed through the
Atarnean plain, to the city of Carina. Quitting this, the troops
advanced across the plain of Thebé,[3] passing Adramyttium,
and Antandrus,[4] the Pelasgic city; then, holding Mount Ida
upon the left hand,[5] it entered the Trojan territory. On this
march the Persians suffered some loss; for as they bivouacked
during the night at the foot of Ida, a storm of thunder and
lightning burst upon them, and killed no small number.

43. On reaching the Scamander, which was the first stream,
of all that they had crossed since they left Sardis, whose water
failed them and did not suffice to satisfy the thirst of men and
cattle,[6] Xerxes ascended into the Pergamus of Priam,[7] since he
had a longing to behold the place. When he had seen everything, and inquired into all particulars, he made an offering of a
thousand oxen to the Trojan Minerva, while the Magians poured
libations to the heroes who were slain at Troy. The night after,
a panic fell upon the camp: but in the morning they set off
with daylight, and skirting on the left hand the towns Rhœteum,

[1] That is, with the point upward.

[2] These were probably the Immortals, who are spoken of in ch. 83, and
are there said to have served on foot.

[3] The plain of Thebé was so called from an ancient town of that name in
the northern part of the plain, at the foot of Mount Ida.

[4] For the situation of Antandrus, vide supra, v. 26.

[5] The true Ida must have been left considerably to the right.

[6] Though the Scamander of Herodotus (the modern *Mendere*) has a bed
from 200 to 300 feet broad, yet the stream in the dry season is reduced to
a slender brook not more than three feet deep.

[7] By the " Pergamus of Priam " is to be understood the acropolis of New
Ilium.

Ophryneum, and Dardanus [1] (which borders on Abydos), on the right the Teucrians of Gergis,[2] so reached Abydos.[3]

44. Arrived here, Xerxes wished to look upon all his host; so as there was a throne of white marble upon a hill near the city, which they of Abydos had prepared beforehand, by the king's bidding, for his especial use, Xerxes took his seat on it, and, gazing thence upon the shore below, beheld at one view all his land forces and all his ships. While thus employed, he felt a desire to behold a sailing-match among his ships, which accordingly took place, and was won by the Phœnicians of Sidon, much to the joy of Xerxes, who was delighted alike with the race and with his army.

45. And now, as he looked and saw the whole Hellespont covered with the vessels of his fleet, and all the shore and every plain about Abydos as full as possible of men, Xerxes congratulated himself on his good fortune; but after a little while he wept.

46. Then Artabanus, the king's uncle (the same who at the first so freely spake his mind to the king, and advised him not to lead his army against Greece), when he heard that Xerxes was in tears, went to him, and said—

" How different, sire, is what thou art now doing, from what thou didst a little while ago! Then thou didst congratulate thyself; and now, behold! thou weepest."

" There came upon me," replied he, " a sudden pity, when I thought of the shortness of man's life, and considered that of all this host, so numerous as it is, not one will be alive when a hundred years are gone by."

" And yet there are sadder things in life than that," returned the other. " Short as our time is, there is no man, whether it be here among this multitude or elsewhere, who is so happy, as not to have felt the wish—I will not say once, but full many a time —that he were dead rather than alive. Calamities fall upon us; sicknesses vex and harass us, and make life, short though it be, to appear long. So death, through the wretchedness of our life, is a most sweet refuge to our race: and God, who gives us the tastes that we enjoy of pleasant times, is seen, in his very gift, to be envious."

47. " True," said Xerxes; " human life is even such as thou

[1] These were all places of small importance on or near the coast.

[2] Supra, v. 122.

[3] The remains of Abydos lie a little north of the upper castle of the Dardanelles [famous in poetry for the loves of Hero and Leander.—E.H.B.]

hast painted it, O Artabanus! But for this very reason let us turn our thoughts from it, and not dwell on what is so sad, when pleasant things are in hand. Tell me rather, if the vision which we saw had not appeared so plainly to thyself, wouldst thou have been still of the same mind as formerly, and have continued to dissuade me from warring against Greece, or wouldst thou at this time think differently? Come now, tell me this honestly."

"O king!" replied the other, "may the dream which hath appeared to us have such issue as we both desire! For my own part, I am still full of fear, and have scarcely power to control myself, when I consider all our dangers, and especially when I see that the two things which are of most consequence are alike opposed to thee."

48. "Thou strange man!" said Xerxes in reply—"what, I pray thee, are the two things thou speakest of? Does my land army seem to thee too small in number, and will the Greeks, thinkest thou, bring into the field a more numerous host? Or is it our fleet which thou deemest weaker than theirs? Or art thou fearful on both accounts? If in thy judgment we fall short in either respect, it were easy to bring together with all speed another armament."

49. "O king!" said Artabanus, "it is not possible that a man of understanding should find fault with the size of thy army or the number of thy ships. The more thou addest to these, the more hostile will those two things, whereof I spake, become. Those two things are the land and the sea. In all the wide sea there is not, I imagine, anywhere a harbour large enough to receive thy vessels, in case a storm arise, and afford them a sure protection. And yet thou wilt want, not one such harbour only, but many in succession, along the entire coast by which thou art about to make thy advance. In default then of such harbours, it is well to bear in mind that chances rule men, and not men chances. Such is the first of the two dangers; and now I will speak to thee of the second. The land will also be thine enemy; for if no one resists thy advance, as thou proceedest further and further, insensibly allured onwards (for who is ever sated with success?), thou wilt find it more and more hostile. I mean this, that, should nothing else withstand thee, yet the mere distance, becoming greater as time goes on, will at last produce a famine. Methinks it is best for men, when they take counsel, to be timorous, and imagine all possible calamities, but when the time for action comes, then to deal boldly."

50. Whereto Xerxes answered—" There is reason, O Arta-banus! in everything which thou hast said; but I pray thee, fear not all things alike, nor count up every risk. For if in each matter that comes before us thou wilt look to all possible chances, never wilt thou achieve anything. Far better is it to have a stout heart always, and suffer one's share of evils, than to be ever fearing what may happen, and never incur a mis-chance. Moreover, if thou wilt oppose whatever is said by others, without thyself showing us the sure course which we ought to take, thou art as likely to lead us into failure as they who advise differently; for thou art but on a par with them. And as for that sure course, how canst thou show it us when thou art but a man? I do not believe thou canst. Success for the most part attends those who act boldly, not those who weigh everything, and are slack to venture. Thou seest to how great a height the power of Persia has now reached—never would it have grown to this point if they who sate upon the throne before me had been like-minded with thee, or even, though not like-minded, had listened to councillors of such a spirit. 'Twas by brave ventures that they extended their sway; for great empires can only be conquered by great risks. We follow then the example of our fathers in making this march; and we set forward at the best season of the year; so, when we have brought Europe under us, we shall return, without suffering from want or experiencing any other calamity. For while on the one hand we carry vast stores of provisions with us, on the other we shall have the grain of all the countries and nations that we attack; since our march is not directed against a pastoral people, but against men who are tillers of the ground."

51. Then said Artabanus—" If, sire, thou art determined that we shall not fear anything, at least hearken to a counsel which I wish to offer; for when the matters in hand are so many, one cannot but have much to say. Thou knowest that Cyrus the son of Cambyses reduced and made tributary to the Persians all the race of the Ionians, except only those of Attica.[1] Now my advice is, that thou on no account lead forth these men against their fathers;[2] since we are well able to overcome them without such aid. Their choice, if we take them with us to the war, lies between showing themselves the most wicked of men

---

[1] This, of course, was not true; but the Persians might not unnaturally be supposed ignorant of all the Ionians of Europe except the Athenians.
[2] Vide infra, viii. 22, where Themistocles makes use of the same argument.

by helping to enslave their fatherland, or the most righteous by joining in the struggle to keep it free. If then they choose the side of injustice, they will do us but scant good; while if they determine to act justly, they may greatly injure our host. Lay thou to heart the old proverb, which says truly, ' The beginning and end of a matter are not always seen at once.' "

52. " Artabanus," answered Xerxes, " there is nothing in all that thou hast said, wherein thou art so wholly wrong as in this, that thou suspectest the faith of the Ionians. Have they not given us the surest proof of their attachment,—a proof which thou didst thyself witness, and likewise all those who fought with Darius against the Scythians? When it lay wholly with them to save or to destroy the entire Persian army, they dealt by us honourably and with good faith, and did us no hurt at all. Besides, they will leave behind them in our country their wives, their children, and their properties—can it then be conceived that they will attempt rebellion? Have no fear, therefore, on this score; but keep a brave heart and uphold my house and empire. To thee, and thee only, do I intrust my sovereignty."

53. After Xerxes had thus spoken, and had sent Artabanus away to return to Susa, he summoned before him all the Persians of most repute, and when they appeared, addressed them in these words:—

" Persians, I have brought you together because I wished to exhort you to behave bravely, and not to sully with disgrace the former achievements of the Persian people, which are very great and famous. Rather let us one and all, singly and jointly, exert ourselves to the uttermost; for the matter wherein we are engaged concerns the common weal. Strain every nerve, then, I beseech you, in this war. Brave warriors are the men we march against, if report says true; and such that, if we conquer them, there is not a people in all the world which will venture thereafter to withstand our arms. And now let us offer prayers to the gods [1] who watch over the welfare of Persia, and then cross the channel."

54. All that day the preparations for the passage continued; and on the morrow they burnt all kinds of spices upon the bridges, and strewed the way with myrtle-boughs, while they waited anxiously for the sun, which they hoped to see as he rose. And now the sun appeared; and Xerxes took a golden goblet

[1] Ormuzd is spoken of throughout the Inscriptions as " the chief of the gods." [See chap. on " Persian Religion," in Menzies' *Hist. of Religion*. —E. H. B.]

and poured from it a libation into the sea, praying the while with his face turned to the sun, " that no misfortune might befall him such as to hinder his conquest of Europe, until he had penetrated to its uttermost boundaries." After he had prayed, he cast the golden cup into the Hellespont, and with it a golden bowl, and a Persian sword of the kind which they call *acinaces*.[1] I cannot say for certain whether it was as an offering to the sun-god that he threw these things into the deep, or whether he had repented of having scourged the Hellespont, and thought by his gifts to make amends to the sea for what he had done.

55. When, however, his offerings were made, the army began to cross; and the foot-soldiers, with the horsemen, passed over by one of the bridges—that (namely) which lay towards the Euxine—while the sumpter-beasts and the camp-followers passed by the other, which looked on the Egean. Foremost went the Ten Thousand Persians, all wearing garlands upon their heads; and after them a mixed multitude of many nations. These crossed upon the first day.

On the next day the horsemen began the passage; and with them went the soldiers who carried their spears with the point downwards, garlanded, like the Ten Thousand;—then came the sacred horses and the sacred chariot; next Xerxes with his lancers and the thousand horse; then the rest of the army. At the same time the ships sailed over to the opposite shore. According, however, to another account which I have heard, the king crossed the last.

56. As soon as Xerxes had reached the European side, he stood to contemplate his army as they crossed under the lash. And the crossing continued during seven days and seven nights, without rest or pause. 'Tis said that here, after Xerxes had made the passage, a Hellespontian exclaimed—

" Why, O Jove, dost thou, in the likeness of a Persian man, and with the name of Xerxes instead of thine own, lead the whole race of mankind to the destruction of Greece? It would have been as easy for thee to destroy it without their aid! "

57. When the whole army had crossed, and the troops were now upon their march, a strange prodigy appeared to them, whereof the king made no account, though its meaning was not difficult to conjecture. Now the prodigy was this:—a mare brought forth a hare. Hereby it was shown plainly enough,

[1] The Persian *acinaces* was a short sword, not a scymitar. It was straight, not curved.

that Xerxes would lead forth his host against Greece with mighty pomp and splendour, but, in order to reach again the spot from which he set out, would have to run for his life. There had also been another portent, while Xerxes was still at Sardis—a mule dropped a foal, neither male nor female; but this likewise was disregarded.

58. So Xerxes, despising the omens, marched forwards; and his land army accompanied him. But the fleet held an opposite course, and, sailing to the mouth of the Hellespont, made its way along the shore. Thus the fleet proceeded westward, making for Cape Sarpêdon,[1] where the orders were that it should await the coming up of the troops; but the land army marched eastward along the Chersonese, leaving on the right the tomb of Hellé, the daughter of Athamas, and on the left the city of Cardia. Having passed through the town which is called Agora, they skirted the shores of the Gulf of Melas, and then crossed the river Melas, whence the gulf takes its name, the waters of which they found too scanty to supply the host. From this point their march was to the west; and after passing Ænos,[2] an Æolian settlement, and likewise Lake Stentoris,[3] they came to Doriscus.

59. The name Doriscus is given to a beach and a vast plain upon the coast of Thrace, through the middle of which flows the strong stream of the Hebrus. Here was the royal fort which is likewise called Doriscus, where Darius had maintained a Persian garrison ever since the time when he attacked the Scythians. This place seemed to Xerxes a convenient spot for reviewing and numbering his soldiers; which things accordingly he proceeded to do. The sea-captains, who had brought the fleet to Doriscus, were ordered to take the vessels to the beach adjoining, where Salé stands, a city of the Samothracians, and Zôné, another city. The beach extends to Serrhêum,[4] the well-known promontory; the whole district in former times was inhabited by the Ciconians.[5] Here then the captains were to bring their

---

[1] The modern Cape *Gremea*.

[2] Ænos retains its name almost unchanged in the modern *Enos* (lat. 40° 45′, long. 26° 4′).

[3] Herodotus appears to intend the vast lake or marsh on the left bank of the Hebrus (*Maritza*), near its mouth, which is one of the most remarkable features of this district.

[4] Serrhêum is undoubtedly Cape *Makri*. It lay east of Mesambria.

[5] The Ciconians were among the most celebrated of the early Thracian tribes. Homer represents them as inhabiting this same tract at the time of the Trojan war (Odyss. ix. 39-59).

ships, and to haul them ashore for refitting, while Xerxes at Doriscus was employed in numbering the soldiers.

60. What the exact number of the troops of each nation was I cannot say with certainty—for it is not mentioned by any one —but the whole land army together was found to amount to one million seven hundred thousand men. The manner in which the numbering took place was the following. A body of ten thousand men was brought to a certain place, and the men were made to stand as close together as possible; after which a circle was drawn around them, and the men were let go: then where the circle had been, a fence was built about the height of a man's middle; and the enclosure was filled continually with fresh troops, till the whole army had in this way been numbered. When the numbering was over, the troops were drawn up according to their several nations.

61. Now these were the nations that took part in this expedition. The Persians, who wore on their heads the soft hat called the tiara, and about their bodies, tunics with sleeves, of divers colours, having iron scales upon them like the scales of a fish. Their legs were protected by trousers; and they bore wicker shields for bucklers; their quivers hanging at their backs, and their arms being a short spear, a bow of uncommon size, and arrows of reed. They had likewise daggers suspended from their girdles along their right thighs. Otanes, the father of Xerxes' wife, Amestris, was their leader. This people was known to the Greeks in ancient times by the name of Cephenians; but they called themselves and were called by their neighbours, Artæans. It was not till Perseus, the son of Jove and Danaë, visited Cepheus the son of Belus, and, marrying his daughter Andromeda, had by her a son called Perses (whom he left behind him in the country because Cepheus had no male offspring), that the nation took from this Perses the name of Persians.[1]

62. The Medes had exactly the same equipment as the Persians; and indeed the dress common to both is not so much Persian as Median.[2] They had for commander Tigranes, of the race of the Achæmenids. These Medes were called anciently by all people Arians; but when Medêa, the Colchian, came to them from Athens, they changed their name. Such is the account which they themselves give.

[1] Vide infra, ch. 150.

[2] Compare Book i. ch. 135, where the adoption by the Persians of the ordinary Median costume is mentioned. It appears by this passage that they likewise adopted their military equipment.

The Cissians were equipped in the Persian fashion, except in one respect:—they wore on their heads, instead of hats, fillets.[1] Anaphes, the son of Otanes, commanded them.

The Hyrcanians were likewise armed in the same way as the Persians. Their leader was Megapanus, the same who was afterwards satrap of Babylon.

63. The Assyrians went to the war with helmets upon their heads made of brass, and plaited in a strange fashion which it is not easy to describe. They carried shields, lances, and daggers very like the Egyptian; but in addition, they had wooden clubs knotted with iron, and linen corselets.[2] This people, whom the Greeks call Syrians, are called Assyrians by the barbarians.[3] The Chaldæans [4] served in their ranks, and they had for commander Otaspes, the son of Artachæus.

64. The Bactrians went to the war wearing a head-dress very like the Median, but armed with bows of cane, after the custom of their country, and with short spears.

The Sacæ, or Scyths, were clad in trousers, and had on their heads tall stiff caps rising to a point. They bore the bow of their country and the dagger; besides which they carried the battle-axe, or *sagaris*. They were in truth Amyrgian [5] Scythians, but the Persians called them Sacæ, since that is the name which they give to all Scythians.[6] The Bactrians and the Sacæ had for leader Hystaspes, the son of Darius and of Atossa, the daughter of Cyrus.

65. The Indians wore cotton dresses, and carried bows of cane, and arrows also of cane with iron at the point. Such was the equipment of the Indians, and they marched under the command of Pharnazathres the son of Artabates.

---

[1] The μίτρα, which was worn also by the Cyprian princes in the fleet of Xerxes (infra, ch. 90), and by the Babylonians as part of their ordinary costume (supra, i. 195), was regarded both by Greeks and Romans as a token of effeminacy. It is generally thought to have been a sort of turban.

[2] This description agrees tolerably, but not quite exactly, with the costume seen in the sculptures. The difference is not surprising, as the latest sculptures are at the least two centuries earlier than the time of Xerxes.

[3] " Syrian " and " Assyrian " are in reality two entirely different words. " Syrian " is nothing but a variant of " Tyrian."

[4] Herodotus seems here to use the word " Chaldæan " in an ethnic sense, and to designate, not the priest-caste of his first Book (chs. 181-183), but the inhabitants of lower Babylonia.

[5] According to Hellanicus, the word " Amyrgian " was strictly a geographical title, *Amyrgium* being the name of the plain in which these Scythians dwelt.

[6] " Saká " is the word used throughout the Persian inscriptions.

66. The Arians carried Median bows, but in other respects were equipped like the Bactrians. Their commander was Sisamnes the son of Hydarnes.

The Parthians and Chorasmians, with the Sogdians, the Gandarians, and the Dadicæ, had the Bactrian equipment in all respects. The Parthians and Chorasmians were commanded by Artabazus the son of Pharnaces, the Sogdians by Azanes the son of Artæus, and the Gandarians and Dadicæ by Artyphius the son of Artabanus.

67. The Caspians were clad in cloaks of skin, and carried the cane bow of their country and the scymitar. So equipped they went to the war; and they had for commander Ariomardus the brother of Artyphius.

The Sarangians had dyed garments which showed brightly, and buskins which reached to the knee: they bore Median bows, and lances. Their leader was Pherendates, the son of Megabazus.

The Pactyans wore cloaks of skin, and carried the bow of their country and the dagger. Their commander was Artyntes, the son of Ithamatres.

68. The Utians, the Mycians, and the Paricanians were all equipped like the Pactyans. They had for leaders, Arsamenes, the son of Darius, who commanded the Utians and Mycians; and Siromitres, the son of Œobazus, who commanded the Paricanians.

69. The Arabians wore the *zeira*,[1] or long cloak, fastened about them with a girdle; and carried at their right side long bows, which when unstrung bent backwards.[2]

The Ethiopians were clothed in the skins of leopards and lions, and had long bows made of the stem of the palm-leaf, not less than four cubits in length. On these they laid short arrows made of reed, and armed at the tip, not with iron, but with a piece of stone,[3] sharpened to a point, of the kind used in engraving seals. They carried likewise spears, the head of which was the sharpened horn of an antelope; and in addition they had knotted clubs. When they went into battle they painted their bodies, half with chalk, and half with vermilion.

---

[1] The flowing dress or petticoat called zeira (zira), supported by a girdle, is very similar to their present costume.

[2] Bows of this kind were not usual among either the Greeks or the oriental nations.

[3] The stone used was an agate.

The Arabians,[1] and the Ethiopians who came from the region above Egypt, were commanded by Arsames, the son of Darius and of Artystônê daughter of Cyrus. This Artystônê was the best-beloved of all the wives of Darius; and it was she whose statue he caused to be made of gold wrought with the hammer. Her son Arsames commanded these two nations.

70. The eastern Ethiopians—for two nations of this name served in the army—were marshalled with the Indians. They differed in nothing from the other Ethiopians, save in their language, and the character of their hair. For the eastern Ethiopians have straight hair, while they of Libya are more woolly-haired than any other people in the world. Their equipment was in most points like that of the Indians; but they wore upon their heads the scalps of horses, with the ears and mane attached; the ears were made to stand upright, and the mane served as a crest. For shields this people made use of the skins of cranes.

71. The Libyans wore a dress of leather, and carried javelins made hard in the fire. They had for commander Massages, the son of Oarizus.

72. The Paphlagonians went to the war with plaited helmets upon their heads, and carrying small shields and spears of no great size. They had also javelins and daggers, and wore on their feet the buskin of their country, which reached half way up the shank. In the same fashion were equipped the Ligyans, the Matienians, the Mariandynians, and the Syrians (or Cappadocians, as they are called by the Persians). The Paphlagonians and Matienians were under the command of Dôtus the son of Megasidrus; while the Mariandynians, the Ligyans, and the Syrians had for leader Gobryas, the son of Darius and Artystônê.

73. The dress of the Phrygians closely resembled the Paphlagonian, only in a very few points differing from it. According to the Macedonian account, the Phrygians, during the time that they had their abode in Europe and dwelt with them in Macedonia, bore the name of Brigians; but on their removal to Asia they changed their designation at the same time with their dwelling-place.[2]

---

[1] The Arabians here spoken of, who served under the same commander as the Ethiopians, were probably those of Africa, who occupied the tract between the valley of the Nile and the Red Sea.

[2] The word "Bryges" in Macedonian would be identical with "Phryges."

The Armenians, who are Phrygian colonists, were armed in the Phrygian fashion. Both nations were under the command of Artochmes, who was married to one of the daughters of Darius.

74. The Lydians were armed very nearly in the Grecian manner. These Lydians in ancient times were called Mæonians, but changed their name, and took their present title from Lydus the son of Atys.

The Mysians wore upon their heads a helmet made after the fashion of their country, and carried a small buckler; they used as javelins staves with one end hardened in the fire. The Mysians are Lydian colonists, and from the mountain-chain of Olympus, are called Olympiêni. Both the Lydians and the Mysians were under the command of Artaphernes, the son of that Artaphernes who, with Datis, made the landing at Marathon.

75. The Thracians went to the war wearing the skins of foxes upon their heads, and about their bodies tunics, over which was thrown a long cloak of many colours.[1] Their legs and feet were clad in buskins made from the skins of fawns; and they had for arms javelins, with light targes, and short dirks. This people, after crossing into Asia, took the name of Bithynians;[2] before, they had been called Strymonians, while they dwelt upon the Strymon; whence, according to their own account, they had been driven out by the Mysians and Teucrians.[3] The commander of these Asiatic Thracians was Bassaces the son of Artabanus.

76. [The Chalybians [4]] had small shields made of the hide of the ox, and carried each of them two spears such as are used in wolf-hunting. Brazen helmets protected their heads; and above these they wore the ears and horns of an ox fashioned in brass. They had also crests on their helms; and their legs were bound round with purple bands. There is an oracle of Mars in the country of this people.

77. The Cabalians, who are Mæonians, but are called Lasonians, had the same equipment as the Cilicians—an equipment which I shall describe when I come in due course to the Cilician contingent.[5]

The Milyans bore short spears, and had their garments fastened with buckles. Some of their number carried Lycian

---

[1] The Thracians of Europe wore exactly the same costume.
[2] Supra, i. 28.   [3] Compare ch. 20 sub fin.
[4] There is a defect here in the text of Herodotus; the name of the nation has been lost.
[5] Infra, ch. 91.

bows.[1] They wore about their heads skull-caps made of leather.
Badres the son of Hystanes led both nations to battle.

78. The Moschians wore helmets made of wood, and carried
shields and spears of a small size: their spear-heads, however,
were long. The Moschian equipment was that likewise of the
Tibarenians, the Macronians, and the Mosynœcians.[2] The
leaders of these nations were the following: the Moschians and
Tibarenians were under the command of Ariomardus, who was
the son of Darius and of Parmys, daughter of Smerdis son of
Cyrus; while the Macronians and Mosynœcians had for leader
Artaÿctes, the son of Cherasmis, the governor of Sestos upon the
Hellespont.

79. The Mares wore on their heads the plaited helmet peculiar
to their country, and used small leathern bucklers, and javelins.

The Colchians wore wooden helmets, and carried small shields
of raw hide, and short spears; besides which they had swords.
Both Mares and Colchians were under the command of Pharandates, the son of Teaspes.

The Alarodians and Saspirians were armed like the Colchians;
their leader was Masistes, the son of Siromitras.

80. The Islanders who came from the Erythræan sea, where
they inhabited the islands to which the king sends those whom
he banishes, wore a dress and arms almost exactly like the
Median. Their leader was Mardontes the son of Bagæus, who
the year after perished in the battle of Mycalé, where he was
one of the captains.

81. Such were the nations who fought upon the dry land, and
made up the infantry of the Persians. And they were commanded by the captains whose names have been above recorded.
The marshalling and numbering of the troops had been committed to them; and by them were appointed the captains over
a thousand, and the captains over ten thousand; but the leaders
of ten men, or a hundred, were named by the captains over
ten thousand. There were other officers also, who gave the
orders to the various ranks and nations; but those whom I
have mentioned above were the commanders.

82. Over these commanders themselves, and over the whole
of the infantry, there were set six generals,—namely, Mardonius,
son of Gobryas; Tritantæchmes, son of the Artabanus who gave

---

[1] That is, bows *of cornel-wood.* Vide infra, ch. 92.
[2] These three nations had become independent of Persia by the time of
Xenophon.

his advice against the war with Greece; Smerdomenes, son of Otanes—these two were the sons of Darius' brothers, and thus were cousins of Xerxes—Masistes, son of Darius and Atossa; Gergis, son of Arizus; and Megabyzus, son of Zopyrus.

83. The whole of the infantry was under the command of these generals, excepting the Ten Thousand. The Ten Thousand, who were all Persians and all picked men, were led by Hydarnes, the son of Hydarnes. They were called " the Immortals," for the following reason. If one of their body failed either by the stroke of death or of disease, forthwith his place was filled up by another man, so that their number was at no time either greater or less than 10,000.

Of all the troops the Persians were adorned with the greatest magnificence, and they were likewise the most valiant. Besides their arms, which have been already described, they glittered all over with gold, vast quantities of which they wore about their persons.[1] They were followed by litters, wherein rode their concubines, and by a numerous train of attendants handsomely dressed. Camels and sumpter-beasts carried their provision, apart from that of the other soldiers.

84. All these various nations fight on horseback; they did not, however, at this time all furnish horsemen, but only the following:—

(i.) The Persians, who were armed in the same way as their own footmen, excepting that some of them wore upon their heads devices fashioned with the hammer in brass or steel.

85. (ii.) The wandering tribe known by the name of Sagartians—a people Persian in language, and in dress half Persian, half Pactyan, who furnished to the army as many as eight thousand horse. It is not the wont of this people to carry arms, either of bronze or steel, except only a dirk; but they use lassoes made of thongs plaited together, and trust to these whenever they go to the wars. Now the manner in which they fight is the following: when they meet their enemy, straightway they discharge their lassoes, which end in a noose; then, whatever the noose encircles, be it man or be it horse, they drag towards them; and the foe, entangled in the toils, is forthwith slain.[2] Such is the manner in which this people fight; and now their horsemen were drawn up with the Persians.

[1] All accounts agree in representing the use of ornaments in pure gold as common among the Persians.

[2] The use of the lasso was common in ancient times to many of the nations of Western Asia. It is seen in the Assyrian sculptures from the palace of Asshur bani-pal.

86. (iii.) The Medes, and Cissians, who had the same equipment as their foot-soldiers.

(iv.) The Indians, equipped as their footmen, but some on horseback and some in chariots,—the chariots drawn either by horses, or by wild asses.

(v.) The Bactrians and Caspians, arrayed as their foot-soldiers.

(vi.) The Libyans, equipped as their foot-soldiers, like the rest; but all riding in chariots.[1]

(vii.) The Caspeirians and Paricanians, equipped as their foot-soldiers.

(viii.) The Arabians, in the same array as their footmen, but all riding on camels, not inferior in fleetness to horses.[2]

87. These nations, and these only, furnished horse to the army: and the number of the horse was eighty thousand, without counting camels or chariots. All were marshalled in squadrons, excepting the Arabians; who were placed last, to avoid frightening the horses, which cannot endure the sight of the camel.[3]

88. The horse was commanded by Armamithras and Tithæus, sons of Datis. The other commander, Pharnuches, who was to have been their colleague, had been left sick at Sardis; since at the moment that he was leaving the city, a sad mischance befell him:—a dog ran under the feet of the horse upon which he was mounted; and the horse, not seeing it coming, was startled, and, rearing bolt upright, threw his rider. After this fall Pharnuches spat blood, and fell into a consumption. As for the horse, he was treated at once as Pharnuches ordered: the attendants took him to the spot where he had thrown his master, and there cut off his four legs at the hough. Thus Pharnuches lost his command.

89. The triremes amounted in all to twelve hundred and seven; and were furnished by the following nations:—

(i.) The Phœnicians, with the Syrians of Palestine, furnished three hundred vessels, the crews of which were thus accoutred:

---

[1] Supra, iv. 170 and 189.
[2] The speed of the dromedary being equal to that of a horse is an error; it scarcely exceeds nine miles an hour. The camel answers to the cart-horse, the dromedary to the saddle-horse. Each has one hump; the Bactrian camel has two. It is singular that the camel is not represented in the Egyptian sculptures. An instance occurs only of late time. But this does not prove its non-existence in Egypt, as it was there in the age of Abraham.
[3] Supra, i. 80.

upon their heads they wore helmets made nearly in the Grecian manner; about their bodies they had breastplates of linen;[1] they carried shields without rims;[2] and were armed with javelins. This nation, according to their own account, dwelt anciently upon the Erythræan sea, but, crossing thence, fixed themselves on the sea-coast of Syria, where they still inhabit. This part of Syria, and all the region extending from hence to Egypt, is known by the name of Palestine.[3]

(ii.) The Egyptians furnished two hundred ships. Their crews had plaited helmets upon their heads, and bore concave shields with rims of unusual size. They were armed with spears suited for a sea-fight, and with huge pole-axes. The greater part of them wore breastplates; and all had long cutlasses.

90. (iii.) The Cyprians furnished a hundred and fifty ships, and were equipped in the following fashion. Their kings had turbans bound about their heads, while the people wore tunics; in other respects they were clad like the Greeks. They are of various races; some are sprung from Athens and Salamis, some from Arcadia, some from Cythnus,[4] some from Phœnicia, and a portion, according to their own account, from Ethiopia.

91. (iv.) The Cilicians furnished a hundred ships. The crews wore upon their heads the helmet of their country, and carried instead of shields light targes made of raw hide; they were clad in woollen tunics, and were each armed with two javelins, and a sword closely resembling the cutlass of the Egyptians. This people bore anciently the name of Hypachæans,[5] but took their present title from Cilix, the son of Agenor, a Phœnician.

(v.) The Pamphylians furnished thirty ships, the crews of which were armed exactly as the Greeks. This nation is descended from those who on the return from Troy were dispersed with Amphilochus and Calchas.

92. (vi.) The Lycians furnished fifty ships. Their crews wore greaves and breastplates, while for arms they had bows of cornel wood, reed arrows without feathers, and javelins. Their outer garment was the skin of a goat, which hung from their shoulders; their head-dress a hat encircled with plumes; and

---

[1] For a description of these corselets, see Book ii. ch. 182.

[2] This was the characteristic of the *pelta*, or light targe. It consisted of a framework of wood or wickerwork, over which was stretched a covering of raw hide or leather.

[3] The name Palestine is beyond a doubt the Greek form of the Hebrew *Philistia*.

[4] Cythnus was one of the Cyclades.

[5] The Cilicians were undoubtedly a kindred race to the Phœnicians.

besides their other weapons they carried daggers and falchions. This people came from Crete, and were once called Termilæ; they got the name which they now bear from Lycus, the son of Pandion, an Athenian.[1]

93. (vii.) The Dorians of Asia furnished thirty ships. They were armed in the Grecian fashion, inasmuch as their forefathers came from the Peloponnese.

(viii.) The Carians furnished seventy ships, and were equipped like the Greeks, but carried, in addition, falchions and daggers. What name the Carians bore anciently was declared in the first part of this History.[2]

94. (ix.) The Ionians furnished a hundred ships, and were armed like the Greeks. Now these Ionians, during the time that they dwelt in the Peloponnese and inhabited the land now called Achæa (which was before the arrival of Danaüs and Xuthus in the Peloponnese), were called, according to the Greek account, Ægialean Pelasgi, or " Pelasgi of the Sea-shore; " [3] but afterwards, from Ion the son of Xuthus, they were called Ionians.

95. The Islanders furnished seventeen ships, and wore arms like the Greeks. They too were a Pelasgian race, who in later times took the name of Ionians for the same reason as those who inhabited the twelve cities founded from Athens.[4]

The Æolians furnished sixty ships, and were equipped in the Grecian fashion. They too were anciently called Pelasgians, as the Greeks declare.

The Hellespontians from the Pontus,[5] who are colonists of the Ionians and Dorians, furnished a hundred ships, the crews of which wore the Grecian armour. This did not include the Abydenians, who stayed in their own country, because the king had assigned them the special duty of guarding the bridges.

96. On board of every ship was a band of soldiers, Persians, Medes, or Sacans. The Phœnician ships were the best sailers in the fleet, and the Sidonian the best among the Phœnicians.

---

[1] Vide supra, i. 173.

[2] Supra, i. 171. We may conclude from this passage that Herodotus regarded his work as divided into certain definite portions; though of course we are not entitled to identify these with the divisions which have come down to us.

[3] See Book i. ch. 145, and Book v. ch. 68. The supposed date of the Ionic migration was about B.C. 1050. Danaüs, Xuthus, and Ion seem to be purely mythological personages.

[4] That is, they received colonies from Athens.

[5] Herodotus includes in this expression the inhabitants of the Greek cities on both sides of the Hellespont, the Propontis, and the Bosphorus.

The contingent of each nation, whether to the fleet or to the land army, had at its head a native leader; but the names of these leaders I shall not mention, as it is not necessary for the course of my History. For the leaders of some nations were not worthy to have their names recorded; and besides, there were in each nation as many leaders as there were cities. And it was not really as commanders that they accompanied the army, but as mere slaves, like the rest of the host. For I have already mentioned the Persian generals who had the actual command, and were at the head of the several nations which composed the army.

97. The fleet was commanded by the following—Ariabignes, the son of Darius, Prêxaspes, the son of Aspathines, Megabazus, the son of Megabates, and Achæmenes, the son of Darius. Ariabignes, who was the child of Darius by a daughter of Gobryas, was leader of the Ionian and Carian ships; Achæmenes, who was own brother to Xerxes, of the Egyptian;[1] the rest of the fleet was commanded by the other two. Besides the triremes, there was an assemblage of thirty-oared and fifty-oared galleys, of cercuri,[2] and transports for conveying horses, amounting in all to three thousand.

98. Next to the commanders, the following were the most renowned of those who sailed aboard the fleet:—Tetramnêstus, the son of Anysus, the Sidonian; Mapên, the son of Sirom,[3] the Tyrian; Merbal,[4] the son of Agbal, the Aradian; Syennesis, the son of Oromedon, the Cilician; Cyberniscus, the son of Sicas, the Lycian; Gorgus, the son of Chersis,[5] and Timônax, the son of Timagoras, the Cyprians; and Histiæus, the son of Timnes,[6] Pigres, the son of Seldômus, and Damasithymus, the son of Candaules, the Carians.

99. Of the other lower officers I shall make no mention, since no necessity is laid on me; but I must speak of a certain leader named Artemisia,[7] whose participation in the attack upon Greece, notwithstanding that she was a woman, moves my special wonder. She had obtained the sovereign power after the death

---

[1] Achæmenes was satrap of Egypt (supra, ch. 7).
[2] Cercuri were light boats of unusual length.
[3] Sirom is probably the same name with Hiram.
[4] Merbal seems to be the Carthaginian Maharbal.
[5] Supra, v. 104.
[6] Histiæus was king of Termera (supra, v. 37).
[7] The special notice taken of Artemisia is undoubtedly due in part to her having been queen of Halicarnassus, the native place of the historian.

of her husband; and, though she had now a son grown up, yet her brave spirit and manly daring sent her forth to the war, when no need required her to adventure. Her name, as I said, was Artemisia, and she was the daughter of Lygdamis; by race she was on his side a Halicarnassian, though by her mother a Cretan. She ruled over the Halicarnassians, the men of Cos, of Nisyrus, and of Calydna; and the five triremes which she furnished to the Persians were, next to the Sidonian, the most famous ships in the fleet. She likewise gave to Xerxes sounder counsel than any of his other allies. Now the cities over which I have mentioned that she bore sway, were one and all Dorian; for the Halicarnassians were colonists from Trœzen,[1] while the remainder were from Epidaurus.[2] Thus much concerning the sea-force.

100. Now when the numbering and marshalling of the host was ended, Xerxes conceived a wish to go himself throughout the forces, and with his own eyes behold everything. Accordingly he traversed the ranks seated in his chariot, and, going from nation to nation, made manifold inquiries, while his scribes wrote down the answers; till at last he had passed from end to end of the whole land army, both the horsemen and likewise the foot. This done, he exchanged his chariot for a Sidonian galley, and, seated beneath a golden awning, sailed along the prows of all his vessels (the vessels having now been hauled down and launched into the sea), while he made inquiries again, as he had done when he reviewed the land-force, and caused the answers to be recorded by his scribes. The captains took their ships to the distance of about four hundred feet from the shore, and there lay to, with their vessels in a single row, the prows facing the land, and with the fighting-men upon the decks accoutred as if for war, while the king sailed along in the open space between the ships and the shore, and so reviewed the fleet.

101. Now after Xerxes had sailed down the whole line and was gone ashore, he sent for Demaratus the son of Ariston, who had accompanied him in his march upon Greece, and bespake him thus:—

"Demaratus, it is my pleasure at this time to ask thee certain things which I wish to know. Thou art a Greek, and, as I hear from the other Greeks with whom I converse, no less than from

---

[1] Trœzen was situated on the eastern coast of the Peloponnese.
[2] Epidaurus was situated on the same coast with Trœzen, but higher up, and close upon the sea-shore.

thine own lips, thou art a native of a city which is not the meanest or the weakest in their land. Tell me, therefore, what thinkest thou? Will the Greeks lift a hand against us? Mine own judgment is, that even if all the Greeks and all the barbarians of the West were gathered together in one place, they would not be able to abide my onset, not being really of one mind. But I would fain know what thou thinkest hereon."

Thus Xerxes questioned; and the other replied in his turn,— " O king! is it thy will that I give thee a true answer, or dost thou wish for a pleasant one? "

Then the king bade him speak the plain truth, and promised that he would not on that account hold him in less favour than heretofore.

102. So Demaratus, when he heard the promise, spake as follows:—

" O king! since thou biddest me at all risks speak the truth, and not say what will one day prove me to have lied to thee, thus I answer. Want has at all times been a fellow-dweller with us in our land, while Valour is an ally whom we have gained by dint of wisdom and strict laws. Her aid enables us to drive out want and escape thraldom. Brave are all the Greeks who dwell in any Dorian land; but what I am about to say does not concern all, but only the Lacedæmonians. First then, come what may, they will never accept thy terms, which would reduce Greece to slavery; and further, they are sure to join battle with thee, though all the rest of the Greeks should submit to thy will. As for their numbers, do not ask how many they are, that their resistance should be a possible thing; for if a thousand of them should take the field, they will meet thee in battle, and so will any number, be it less than this, or be it more."

103. When Xerxes heard this answer of Demaratus, he laughed and answered,—

" What wild words, Demaratus! A thousand men join battle with such an army as this! Come then, wilt thou—who wert once, as thou sayest, their king—engage to fight this very day with ten men? I trow not. And yet, if all thy fellow-citizens be indeed such as thou sayest they are, thou oughtest, as their king, by thine own country's usages,[1] to be ready to fight with twice the number. If then each one of them be a match for ten of my soldiers, I may well call upon thee to be a match for

---

[1] The allusion is apparently to the " double portion " whereto the kings were entitled at banquets.

twenty. So wouldest thou assure the truth of what thou hast
now said. If, however, you Greeks, who vaunt yourselves so
much, are of a truth men like those whom I have seen about
my court, as thyself, Demaratus, and the others with whom I
am wont to converse,—if, I say, you are really men of this sort
and size, how is the speech that thou hast uttered more than a
mere empty boast? For, to go to the very verge of likelihood,
—how could a thousand men, or ten thousand, or even fifty
thousand, particularly if they were all alike free, and not under
one lord,—how could such a force, I say, stand against an army
like mine? Let them be five thousand, and we shall have more
than a thousand men to each one of theirs.[1] If, indeed, like
our troops, they had a single master, their fear of him might
make them courageous beyond their natural bent; or they might
be urged by lashes against an enemy which far outnumbered
them.[2] But left to their own free choice, assuredly they will
act differently. For mine own part, I believe, that if the
Greeks had to contend with the Persians only, and the numbers
were equal on both sides, the Greeks would find it hard to stand
their ground. We too have among us such men as those of
whom thou spakest—not many indeed, but still we possess a
few. For instance, some of my body-guard would be willing to
engage singly with three Greeks. But this thou didst not know;
and therefore it was thou talkedst so foolishly."

104. Demaratus answered him,—" I knew, O king! at the
outset, that if I told thee the truth, my speech would displease
thine ears. But as thou didst require me to answer thee with
all possible truthfulness, I informed thee what the Spartans will
do. And in this I spake not from any love that I bear them—
for none knows better than thou what my love towards them is
likely to be at the present time, when they have robbed me of
my rank and my ancestral honours, and made me a homeless
exile, whom thy father did receive, bestowing on me both shelter
and sustenance. What likelihood is there that a man of understanding should be unthankful for kindness shown him, and not
cherish it in his heart? For mine own self, I pretend not to
cope with ten men, nor with two,—nay, had I the choice, I would
rather not fight even with one. But, if need appeared, or if
there were any great cause urging me on, I would contend with

---

[1] See below, ch. 186, where the entire Persian host is reckoned to exceed
five millions of men!
[2] Supra, vi. 70.

right good will against one of those persons who boast themselves a match for any three Greeks. So likewise the Lacedæmonians, when they fight singly, are as good men as any in the world, and when they fight in a body, are the bravest of all. For though they be freemen, they are not in all respects free; Law is the master whom they own; and this master they fear more than thy subjects fear thee. Whatever he commands they do; and his commandment is always the same: it forbids them to flee in battle, whatever the number of their foes, and requires them to stand firm, and either to conquer or die. If in these words, O king! I seem to thee to speak foolishly, I am content from this time forward evermore to hold my peace. I had not now spoken unless compelled by thee. Certes, I pray that all may turn out according to thy wishes."

105. Such was the answer of Demaratus; and Xerxes was not angry with him at all, but only laughed, and sent him away with words of kindness.

After this interview, and after he had made Mascames the son of Megadostes governor of Doriscus, setting aside the governor appointed by Darius, Xerxes started with his army, and marched upon Greece through Thrace.

106. This man, Mascames, whom he left behind him, was a person of such merit that gifts were sent him yearly by the king as a special favour, because he excelled all the other governors that had been appointed either by Xerxes or by Darius. In like manner, Artaxerxes, the son of Xerxes, sent gifts yearly to the descendants of Mascames. Persian governors had been established in Thrace and about the Hellespont before the march of Xerxes began; but these persons, after the expedition was over, were all driven from their towns by the Greeks, except the governor of Doriscus: no one succeeded in driving out Mascames, though many made the attempt. For this reason the gifts are sent him every year by the king who reigns over the Persians.

107. Of the other governors whom the Greeks drove out, there was not one who, in the judgment of Xerxes, showed himself a brave man, excepting Boges, the governor of Eïon. Him Xerxes never could praise enough; and such of his sons as were left in Persia, and survived their father, he very specially honoured. And of a truth this Boges was worthy of great commendation; for when he was besieged by the Athenians under Cimon, the son of Miltiades, and it was open to him to

retire from the city upon terms, and return to Asia, he refused, because he feared the king might think he had played the coward to save his own life, wherefore, instead of surrendering, he held out to the last extremity. When all the food in the fortress was gone, he raised a vast funeral pile, slew his children, his wife, his concubines, and his household slaves, and cast them all into the flames. Then, collecting whatever gold and silver there was in the place, he flung it from the walls into the Strymon; and, when that was done, to crown all, he himself leaped into the fire. For this action Boges is with reason praised by the Persians even at the present day.

108. Xerxes, as I have said, pursued his march from Doriscus against Greece; and on his way he forced all the nations through which he passed to take part in the expedition. For the whole country as far as the frontiers of Thessaly had been (as I have already shown) enslaved and made tributary to the king by the conquests of Megabazus, and, more lately, of Mardonius.[1] And first, after leaving Doriscus, Xerxes passed the Samothracian fortresses, whereof Mesambria is the furthermost as one goes toward the west. The next city is Strymé, which belongs to Thasos. Midway between it and Mesambria flows the river Lissus, which did not suffice to furnish water for the army, but was drunk up and failed. This region was formerly called Gallaïca; now it bears the name of Briantica; but in strict truth it likewise is really Ciconian.[2]

109. After crossing the dry channel of the Lissus, Xerxes passed the Grecian cities of Marôneia, Dicæa, and Abdêra, and likewise the famous lakes which are in their neighbourhood, Lake Ismaris between Marôneia and Strymé, and Lake Bistonis near Dicæa, which receives the waters of two rivers, the Travus and the Compsatus. Near Abdêra there was no famous lake for him to pass; but he crossed the river Nestus, which there reaches the sea. Proceeding further upon his way, he passed by several continental cities, one of them possessing a lake nearly thirty furlongs in circuit, full of fish, and very salt, of which the sumpter-beasts only drank, and which they drained dry. The name of this city was Pistyrus. All these towns, which were Grecian, and lay upon the coast, Xerxes kept upon his left hand as he passed along.

110. The following are the Thracian tribes through whose country he marched: the Pæti, the Ciconians, the Bistonians,

1 Supra, v. 2-18; vi. 44, 45.   2 See above, ch. 59.

the Sapæans, the Dersæans, the Edonians, and the Satræ. Some of these dwelt by the sea, and furnished ships to the king's fleet; while others lived in the more inland parts, and of these all the tribes which I have mentioned, except the Satræ, were forced to serve on foot.

111. The Satræ, so far as our knowledge goes, have never yet been brought under by any one, but continue to this day a free and unconquered people, unlike the other Thracians. They dwell amid lofty mountains clothed with forests of different trees and capped with snow, and are very valiant in fight. They are the Thracians who have an oracle of Bacchus in their country, which is situated upon their highest mountain-range. The Bessi, a Satrian race, deliver the oracles; but the prophet, as at Delphi, is a woman; and her answers are not harder to read.

112. When Xerxes had passed through the region mentioned above, he came next to the Pierian fortresses, one of which is called Phagres, and another Pergamus.[1] Here his line of march lay close by the walls, with the long high range of Pangæum [2] upon his right, a tract in which there are mines both of gold and silver, some worked by the Pierians and Odomantians, but the greater part by the Satræ.

113. Xerxes then marched through the country of the Pæonian tribes—the Doberians and the Pæoplæ—which lay to the north of Pangæum, and, advancing westward, reached the river Strymon and the city Eïon, whereof Boges, of whom I spoke a short time ago,[3] and who was then still alive, was governor. The tract of land lying about Mount Pangæum, is called Phyllis; on the west it reaches to the river Angites, which flows into the Strymon, and on the south to the Strymon itself, where at this time the Magi were sacrificing white horses to make the stream favourable.[4]

114. After propitiating the stream by these and many other magical ceremonies, the Persians crossed the Strymon, by bridges made before their arrival, at a place called "The Nine Ways,"[5] which was in the territory of the Edonians. And when they learnt that the name of the place was "The Nine Ways," they took nine of the youths of the land and as many of their

[1] The original Pieria was the district between the Haliacmon and the Peneus.
[2] Vide supra, v. 16.   [3] Supra, ch. 107.
[4] *White* horses seem to have been regarded as especially sacred (supra, ch. 40).
[5] Afterwards Amphipolis.

maidens, and buried them alive on the spot. Burying alive is a Persian custom. I have heard that Amestris, the wife of Xerxes, in her old age buried alive seven pairs of Persian youths, sons of illustrious men, as a thank-offering to the god who is supposed to dwell underneath the earth.

115. From the Strymon the army, proceeding westward, came to a strip of shore, on which there stands the Grecian town of Argilus. This shore, and the whole tract above it, is called Bisaltia.[1] Passing this, and keeping on the left hand the Gulf of Posideium, Xerxes crossed the Sylean plain,[2] as it is called, and passing by Stagirus,[3] a Greek city, came to Acanthus. The inhabitants of these parts, as well as those who dwelt about Mount Pangæum, were forced to join the armament, like those others of whom I spoke before; the dwellers along the coast being made to serve in the fleet, while those who lived more inland had to follow with the land forces. The road which the army of Xerxes took remains to this day untouched: the Thracians neither plough nor sow it, but hold it in great honour.

116. On reaching Acanthus, the Persian king, seeing the great zeal of the Acanthians for his service, and hearing what had been done about the cutting, took them into the number of his sworn friends, sent them as a present a Median dress,[4] and besides commended them highly.

117. It was while he remained here that Artachæes, who presided over the canal,[5] a man in high repute with Xerxes, and by birth an Achæmenid, who was moreover the tallest of all the Persians, being only four fingers short of five cubits, royal measure,[6] and who had a stronger voice than any other man in the world, fell sick and died. Xerxes therefore, who was greatly afflicted at the mischance, carried him to the tomb and buried him with all magnificence; while the whole army helped to raise a mound over his grave. The Acanthians, in obedience to an oracle, offer sacrifice to this Artachæes as a hero, invoking him in their prayers by name. But King Xerxes sorrowed greatly over his death.

118. Now the Greeks who had to feed the army, and to entertain Xerxes, were brought thereby to the very extremity of

---

[1] The Bisaltæ were a brave and powerful Thracian people.
[2] By the Sylean plain, which no other writer mentions, is to be understood the flat tract, about a mile in midth, near the mouth of the river which drains the lake of Bolbé (*Besikia*).
[3] Now *Stavros*.
[4] Compare iii. 84.
[5] Supra, ch. 21.
[6] That is, about 8 feet 2 inches.

distress, insomuch that some of them were forced even to forsake house and home. When the Thasians received and feasted the host, on account of their possessions upon the mainland, Antipater, the son of Orges, one of the citizens of best repute, and the man to whom the business was assigned, proved that the cost of the meal was four hundred talents of silver.[1]

119. And estimates almost to the same amount were made by the superintendents in other cities. For the entertainment, which had been ordered long beforehand and was reckoned to be of much consequence, was, in the manner of it, such as I will now describe. No sooner did the heralds who brought the orders [2] give their message, than in every city the inhabitants made a division of their stores of corn, and proceeded to grind flour of wheat and of barley for many months together. Besides this, they purchased the best cattle that they could find, and fattened them; and fed poultry and water-fowl in ponds and buildings, to be in readiness for the army; while they likewise prepared gold and silver vases and drinking-cups, and whatsoever else is needed for the service of the table. These last preparations were made for the king only, and those who sat at meat with him; for the rest of the army nothing was made ready beyond the food for which orders had been given. On the arrival of the Persians, a tent ready pitched for the purpose received Xerxes, who took his rest therein, while the soldiers remained under the open heaven. When the dinner hour came, great was the toil of those who entertained the army; while the guests ate their fill, and then, after passing the night at the place, tore down the royal tent next morning, and seizing its contents, carried them all off, leaving nothing behind.

120. On one of these occasions Megacreon of Abdêra wittily recommended his countrymen " to go to the temples in a body, men and women alike, and there take their station as suppliants, and beseech the gods that they would in future always spare them one-half of the woes which might threaten their peace— thanking them at the same time very warmly for their past goodness in that they had caused Xerxes to be content with one meal in the day." For had the order been to provide breakfast for the king as well as dinner, the Abderites must either have fled before Xerxes came, or, if they awaited his coming, have been brought to absolute ruin. As it was, the nations, though

---

[1] Nearly £100,000 of our money.
[2] Supra, ch. 32.

suffering heavy pressure, complied nevertheless with the directions that had been given.

121. At Acanthus Xerxes separated from his fleet, bidding the captains sail on ahead and await his coming at Therma, on the Thermaic Gulf, the place from which the bay takes its name. Through this town lay, he understood, his shortest road. Previously, his order of march had been the following:—from Doriscus to Acanthus his land force had proceeded in three bodies, one of which took the way along the sea-shore in company with the fleet, and was commanded by Mardonius and Masistes, while another pursued an inland track under Tritantæchmes and Gergis; the third, with which was Xerxes himself, marching midway between the other two, and having for its leaders Smerdomenes and Megabyzus.[1]

122. The fleet, therefore, after leaving the king, sailed through the channel which had been cut for it by Mount Athos, and came into the bay whereon lie the cities of Assa, Pilôrus, Singus, and Sarta; from all which it received contingents. Thence it stood on for the Thermaic Gulf, and rounding Cape Ampelus, the promontory of the Torônæans, passed the Grecian cities Torôné, Galepsus, Sermyla, Mecyberna, and Olynthus, receiving from each a number of ships and men. This region is called Sithonia.[2]

123. From Cape Ampelus the fleet stretched across by a short course to Cape Canastræum,[3] which is the point of the peninsula of Pallêné that runs out furthest into the sea,[4] and gathered fresh supplies of ships and men from Potidæa, Aphytis, Neapolis, Æga, Therambus, Sciôné, Mendé, and Sané.[5] These are the cities of the tract called anciently Phlegra, but now Pallêné.[6] Hence they again followed the coast, still advancing towards the place appointed by the king, and had accessions from all the cities that lie near Pallêné, and border on the Thermaic Gulf, whereof the names are Lipaxus, Cômbreia, Lisæ, Gigônus, Campsa, Smila, and Ænêa. The tract where these towns lie

[1] See above, ch. 82.
[2] The Sithonians were probably an ancient Thracian people.
[3] It is plain from this that only a portion of the ships made the circuit of the bay in order to collect ships and men. The main body of the fleet sailed across the mouth of the bay.
[4] This description sufficiently identifies the Canastræan promontory with the modern Cape *Paliúri*.
[5] The situation and origin of Potidæa are well known from Thucydides i. 56-65).
[6] Pallêné was the name of the peninsula extending from Potidæa to Cape Canastræum.

still retains its old name of Crossæa.¹ After passing Ænêa, the city which I last named, the fleet found itself arrived in the Thermaic Gulf, off the land of Mygdonia. And so at length they reached Therma, the appointed place, and came likewise to Sindus and Chalestra upon the river Axius, which separates Bottiæa from Mygdonia. Bottiæa has a scanty sea-board, which is occupied by the two cities Ichnæ and Pella.²

124. So the fleet anchored off the Axius, and off Therma, and the towns that lay between, waiting the king's coming. Xerxes meanwhile with his land force ³ left Acanthus, and started for Therma, taking his way across the land. This road led him through Pæonia and Crestonia to the river Echeidôrus,⁴ which rising in the country of the Crestonians, flows through Mygdonia, and reaches the sea near the marsh upon the Axius.

125. Upon this march the camels that carried the provisions of the army were set upon by lions, which left their lairs and came down by night, but spared the men and the sumpter-beasts, while they made the camels their prey. I marvel what may have been the cause which compelled the lions to leave the other animals untouched and attack the camels, when they had never seen that beast before, nor had any experience of it.

126. That whole region is full of lions, and wild bulls,⁵ with gigantic horns which are brought into Greece. The lions are confined within the tract lying between the river Nestus (which flows through Abdêra) on the one side, and the Acheloüs (which waters Acarnania) on the other.⁶ No one ever sees a lion in the fore part of Europe east of the Nestus, nor through the entire continent west of the Acheloüs; but in the space between these bounds lions are found.⁷

¹ Now called *Kalamariá*.

² Pella (which became under Philip the capital of Macedonia) was not upon the coast, as we should gather from this passage, but above twenty miles from the sea, on the borders of a lake.

³ The bulk of the land force would undoubtedly have kept the direct road through Apollonia which St. Paul followed (Acts xvii. 1); while Xerxes with his immediate attendants visited Acanthus, to see the canal, and then rejoined the main army by a mountain-path which fell into the main road beyond Apollonia.

⁴ The Echeidôrus is undoubtedly the *Galliko*, which flows from the range of *Karadagh* (Cerciné), and running nearly due south, empties itself into the Gulf of *Saloniki*.

⁵ The bonasus has been thought to be the modern *auroch*; but Sir G. C. Lewis regards it as " a species of wild ox, cognate, but not identical, with the auroch."

⁶ Vide supra, ii. 10.

⁷ Aristotle, a native of this district, makes the same statement as Herodotus; and the elder Pliny follows him.

127. On reaching Therma Xerxes halted his army, which encamped along the coast, beginning at the city of Therma in Mygdonia, and stretching out as far as the rivers Lydias and Haliacmon, two streams which, mingling their waters in one, form the boundary between Bottiæa and Macedonia. Such was the extent of country through which the barbarians encamped. The rivers here mentioned were all of them sufficient to supply the troops, except the Echeidôrus, which was drunk dry.

128. From Therma Xerxes beheld the Thessalian mountains, Olympus and Ossa,[1] which are of a wonderful height. Here, learning that there lay between these mountains a narrow gorge [2] through which the river Peneus ran, and where there was a road that gave an entrance into Thessaly, he formed the wish to go by sea himself, and examine the mouth of the river. His design was to lead his army by the upper road through the country of the inland Macedonians, and so to enter Perrhæbia, and come down by the city of Gonnus;[3] for he was told that that way was the most secure. No sooner therefore had he formed this wish than he acted accordingly. Embarking, as was his wont on all such occasions, aboard a Sidonian vessel,[4] he gave the signal to the rest of the fleet to get under weigh, and quitting his land army, set sail and proceeded to the Peneus. Here the view of the mouth caused him to wonder greatly; and sending for his guides, he asked them whether it were possible to turn the course of the stream, and make it reach the sea at any other point.

129. Now there is a tradition that Thessaly was in ancient times a lake, shut in on every side by huge hills. Ossa and Pelion—ranges which join at the foot [5]—do in fact inclose it upon the east, while Olympus forms a barrier upon the north,[6]

---

[1] In clear weather Olympus and Ossa are in full view from Therma (*Saloniki*), though the latter is more than seventy miles distant.

[2] This description of the pass of Tempé (vide infra, ch. 173), though brief, is remarkably accurate.

[3] Gonnus was at the western extremity of the pass of Tempé, near the modern *Dereli*.

[4] Supra, ch. 100.

[5] Mount Pelium (the modern *Plessidhi*) lies south-east of Ossa at a distance of about 40 miles. The bases of the two mountains nevertheless join, as Herodotus states. The height of Pelium is estimated at 5300 feet. It is richly clothed with wood, nearly to the summit.

[6] The name Olympus is here applied to the entire range.

Pindus upon the west,[1] and Othrys towards the south.[2] The tract contained within these mountains, which is a deep basin, is called Thessaly. Many rivers pour their waters into it; but five of them are of more note than the rest, namely, the Peneus, the Apidanus, the Onochônus, the Enipeus, and the Pamisus. These streams flow down from the mountains which surround Thessaly, and, meeting in the plain, mingle their waters together, and discharge themselves into the sea by a single outlet, which is a gorge of extreme narrowness. After the junction all the other names disappear, and the river is known as the Peneus. It is said that of old the gorge which allows the waters an outlet did not exist; accordingly the rivers, which were then, as well as the Lake Bœbêïs,[3] without names, but flowed with as much water as at present, made Thessaly a sea. The Thessalians tell us that the gorge through which the water escapes was caused by Neptune; and this is likely enough; at least any man who believes that Neptune causes earthquakes, and that chasms so produced are his handiwork, would say, upon seeing this rent, that Neptune did it. For it plainly appeared to me that the hills had been torn asunder by an earthquake.[4]

130. When Xerxes therefore asked the guides if there were any other outlet by which the waters could reach the sea, they, being men well acquainted with the nature of their country, made answer—

"O king! there is no other passage by which this stream can empty itself into the sea save that which thine eye beholds. For Thessaly is girt about with a circlet of hills."

Xerxes is said to have observed upon this—

"Wise men truly are they of Thessaly, and good reason had they to change their minds in time and consult for their own safety. For, to pass by others matters, they must have felt that they lived in a country which may easily be brought under and subdued. Nothing more is needed than to turn the river upon their lands by an embankment which should fill up the gorge and force the stream from its present channel, and lo! all

[1] Mount Pindus, the back-bone of Greece, runs in a direction nearly due north and south.

[2] Othrys, now Mount *Iérako*, is situated due south of Ossa, and south-west of Pelion. Its height is estimated at 5670 feet.

[3] Lake Bœbêïs, so called from a small town Bœbé, at its eastern extremity, is the modern lake of *Karla*, a piece of water which has no outlet to the sea.

[4] Modern science will scarcely quarrel with this description of Thessaly, which shows Herodotus to have had the eye of a physical geographer and the imagination of a geologist.

Thessaly, except the mountains, would at once be laid under water."

The king aimed in this speech at the sons of Aleuas, who were Thessalians, and had been the first of all the Greeks to make submission to him. He thought that they had made their friendly offers in the name of the whole people.[1] So Xerxes, when he had viewed the place, and made the above speech, went back to Therma.

131. The stay of Xerxes in Pieria lasted for several days, during which a third part of his army was employed in cutting down the woods on the Macedonian mountain-range to give his forces free passage into Perrhæbia. At this time the heralds who had been sent into Greece to require earth for the king returned to the camp, some of them empty-handed, others with earth and water.

132. Among the number of those from whom earth and water were brought, were the Thessalians, Dolopians,[2] Enianians,[3] Perrhæbians, Locrians, Magnetians, Malians, Achæans of Phthi-ôtis,[4] Thebans, and Bœotians generally, except those of Platæa and Thespiæ. These are the nations against whom the Greeks that had taken up arms to resist the barbarians swore the oath, which ran thus—" From all those of Greek blood who delivered themselves up to the Persians without necessity, when their affairs were in good condition, we will take a tithe of their goods, and give it to the god at Delphi." So ran the words of the Greek oath.

133. King Xerxes had sent no heralds either to Athens or Sparta to ask earth and water, for a reason which I will now relate. When Darius some time before sent messengers for the same purpose,[5] they were thrown, at Athens, into the pit of punishment,[6] at Sparta into a well, and bidden to take there-from earth and water for themselves, and carry it to their king. On this account Xerxes did not send to ask them. What calamity came upon the Athenians to punish them for their treatment of the heralds I cannot say, unless it were the laying

[1] This was not the case.
[2] The Dolopes inhabited the mountain tract at the base of Pindus.
[3] The Enianes occupied the upper valley of the Spercheius.
[4] The Magnetians, Achæans, and Malians, were the inhabitants of the coast tract between Thessaly and Locris.
[5] Supra, vi. 48.
[6] The barathrum, or " pit of punishment " at Athens, was a deep hole like a well into which criminals were precipitated.

waste of their city and territory; but that I believe was not on account of this crime.

134. On the Lacedæmonians, however, the wrath of Talthybius, Agamemnon's herald, fell with violence. Talthybius has a temple at Sparta; and his descendants, who are called Talthybiadæ, still live there, and have the privilege of being the only persons who discharge the office of herald. When therefore the Spartans had done the deed of which we speak, the victims at their sacrifices failed to give good tokens; and this failure lasted for a very long time. Then the Spartans were troubled; and, regarding what had befallen them as a grievous calamity, they held frequent assemblies of the people, and made proclamation through the town, " Was any Lacedæmonian willing to give his life for Sparta? " Upon this two Spartans, Sperthias, the son of Anêristus, and Bulis, the son of Nicolaüs, both men of noble birth, and among the wealthiest in the place, came forward and freely offered themselves as an atonement to Xerxes for the heralds of Darius slain at Sparta. So the Spartans sent them away to the Medes to undergo death.

135. Nor is the courage which these men hereby displayed alone worthy of wonder; but so likewise are the following speeches which were made by them. On their road to Susa they presented themselves before Hydarnes.[1] This Hydarnes was a Persian by birth, and had the command of all the nations that dwelt along the sea-coast of Asia. He accordingly showed them hospitality, and invited them to a banquet, where, as they feasted, he said to them:—

" Men of Lacedæmon, why will ye not consent to be friends with the king? Ye have but to look at me and my fortune to see that the king knows well how to honour merit. In like manner ye yourselves, were ye to make your submission to him, would receive at his hands, seeing that he deems you men of merit, some government in Greece."

" Hydarnes," they answered, " thou art a one-sided counsellor. Thou hast experience of half the matter; but the other half is beyond thy knowledge. A slave's life thou understandest; but, never having tasted liberty, thou canst not tell whether it be sweet or no. Ah! hadst thou known what freedom is, thou wouldst have bidden us fight for it, not with the spear only, but with the battle-axe."

So they answered Hydarnes.

[1] This Hydarnes seems to be the person alluded to in Book vi. ch. 133.

136. And afterwards, when they were come to Susa into the king's presence, and the guards ordered them to fall down and do obeisance, and went so far as to use force to compel them, they refused, and said they would never do any such thing, even were their heads thrust down to the ground; for it was not their custom to worship men, and they had not come to Persia for that purpose. So they fought off the ceremony; and having done so, addressed the king in words much like the following:—

"O king of the Medes! the Lacedæmonians have sent us hither, in the place of those heralds of thine who were slain in Sparta, to make atonement to thee on their account."

Then Xerxes answered with true greatness of soul "that he would not act like the Lacedæmonians, who, by killing the heralds, had broken the laws which all men hold in common. As he had blamed such conduct in them, he would never be guilty of it himself. And besides, he did not wish, by putting the two men to death, to free the Lacedæmonians from the stain of their former outrage."

137. This conduct on the part of the Spartans caused the anger of Talthybius to cease for a while, notwithstanding that Sperthias and Bulis returned home alive. But many years afterwards it awoke once more, as the Lacedæmonians themselves declare, during the war between the Peloponnesians and the Athenians.

In my judgment this was a case wherein the hand of Heaven was most plainly manifest. That the wrath of Talthybius should have fallen upon ambassadors, and not slacked till it had full vent, so much justice required; but that it should have come upon the sons of the very men who were sent up to the Persian king on its account—upon Nicolaüs, the son of Bulis, and Anêristus, the son of Sperthias (the same who carried off fishermen from Tiryns, when cruising in a well-manned merchant-ship),—this does seem to me to be plainly a supernatural circumstance. Yet certain it is that these two men, having been sent to Asia as ambassadors by the Lacedæmonians, were betrayed by Sitalces, the son of Teres, king of Thrace, and Nymphodôrus, the son of Pythes, a native of Abdêra, and being made prisoners at Bisanthé, upon the Hellespont, were conveyed to Attica, and there put to death by the Athenians, at the same time as Aristeas, the son of Adeimantus,[1]

---

[1] Concerning Adeimantus, see below, viii. 59, 61. 94.

the Corinthian. All this happened, however, very many years after the expedition of Xerxes.[1]

138. To return, however, to my main subject,—the expedition of the Persian king, though it was in name directed against Athens, threatened really the whole of Greece. And of this the Greeks were aware some time before; but they did not all view the matter in the same light. Some of them had given the Persian earth and water, and were bold on this account, deeming themselves thereby secured against suffering hurt from the barbarian army; while others, who had refused compliance, were thrown into extreme alarm. For whereas they considered all the ships in Greece too few to engage the enemy, it was plain that the greater number of states would take no part in the war, but warmly favoured the Medes.

139. And here I feel constrained to deliver an opinion, which most men, I know, will mislike, but which, as it seems to me to be true, I am determined not to withhold. Had the Athenians, from fear of the approaching danger, quitted their country, or had they without quitting it submitted to the power of Xerxes, there would certainly have been no attempt to resist the Persians by sea; in which case the course of events by land would have been the following. Though the Peloponnesians might have carried ever so many breastworks across the Isthmus, yet their allies would have fallen off from the Lacedæmonians, not by voluntary desertion, but because town after town must have been taken by the fleet of the barbarians; and so the Lacedæmonians would at last have stood alone, and, standing alone, would have displayed prodigies of valour, and died nobly. Either they would have done thus, or else, before it came to that extremity, seeing one Greek state after another embrace the cause of the Medes, they would have come to terms with King Xerxes;—and thus, either way Greece would have been brought under Persia. For I cannot understand of what possible use the walls across the Isthmus could have been, if the king had had the mastery of the sea. If then a man should now say that the Athenians were the saviours of Greece, he would not exceed the truth. For they truly held the scales; and whichever side they espoused must have carried the day. They too it was who, when they had determined to maintain the freedom of Greece, roused up that portion of the Greek

[1] The event took place in the year B.C. 430, nearly sixty years after the murder of the Persian envoys.

nation which had not gone over to the Medes; and so, next to the gods, *they* repulsed the invader. Even the terrible oracles which reached them from Delphi, and struck fear into their hearts, failed to persuade them to fly from Greece. They had the courage to remain faithful to their land, and await the coming of the foe.

140. When the Athenians, anxious to consult the oracle, sent their messengers to Delphi, hardly had the envoys completed the customary rites about the sacred precinct, and taken their seats inside the sanctuary of the god, when the Pythoness, Aristonicé by name, thus prophesied—

" Wretches, why sit ye here?   Fly, fly to the ends of creation,
    Quitting your homes, and the crags which your city crowns with her
        circlet.
    Neither the head, nor the body is firm in its place, nor at bottom
    Firm the feet, nor the hands; nor resteth the middle uninjur'd.
    All—all ruined and lost.   Since fire, and impetuous Ares,
    Speeding along in a Syrian chariot,[1] hastes to destroy her.
    Not alone shalt thou suffer; full many the towers he will level,
    Many the shrines of the gods he will give to a fiery destruction.
    Even now they stand with dark sweat horribly dripping,
    Trembling and quaking for fear; and lo! from the high roofs trickleth
    Black blood, sign prophetic of hard distresses impending.
    Get ye away from the temple; and brood on the ills that await ye! "

141. When the Athenian messengers heard this reply, they were filled with the deepest affliction: whereupon Timon, the son of Androbûlus, one of the men of most mark among the Delphians, seeing how utterly cast down they were at the gloomy prophecy, advised them to take an olive-branch, and entering the sanctuary again, consult the oracle as suppliants. The Athenians followed this advice, and going in once more, said—" O king! we pray thee reverence these boughs of suppli-cation which we bear in our hands, and deliver to us something more comforting concerning our country. Else we will not leave thy sanctuary, but will stay here till we die." Upon this the priestess gave them a second answer, which was the following:—

" Pallas has not been able to soften the lord of Olympus,
    Though she has often prayed him, and urged him with excellent counsel.
    Yet once more I address thee in words than adamant firmer.
    When the foe shall have taken whatever the limit of Cecrops [2]
    Holds within it, and all which divine Cithæron shelters,
    Then far-seeing Jove grants this to the prayers of Athenê;
    Safe shall the wooden wall continue for thee and thy children.

---

[1] That is, Assyrian.
[2] By the " limit of Cecrops " the boundaries of Attica are intended.

Wait not the tramp of the horse, nor the footmen mightily moving
Over the land, but turn your back to the foe, and retire ye.
Yet shall a day arrive when ye shall meet him in battle.
Holy Salamis, thou shalt destroy the offspring of women,
When men scatter the seed, or when they gather the harvest."

142. This answer seemed, as indeed it was, gentler than the former one; so the envoys wrote it down, and went back with it to Athens. When, however, upon their arrival, they produced it before the people, and inquiry began to be made into its true meaning, many and various were the interpretations which men put on it; two, more especially, seemed to be directly opposed to one another. Certain of the old men were of opinion that the god meant to tell them the citadel would escape; for this was anciently defended by a palisade; and they supposed that barrier to be the " wooden wall " of the oracle. Others maintained that the fleet was what the god pointed at; and their advice was that nothing should be thought of except the ships, which had best be at once got ready. Still such as said the " wooden wall " meant the fleet, were perplexed by the last two lines of the oracle—

" Holy Salamis, thou shalt destroy the offspring of women,
When men scatter the seed, or when they gather the harvest."

These words caused great disturbance among those who took the wooden wall to be the ships; since the interpreters understood them to mean, that, if they made preparations for a sea-fight, they would suffer a defeat off Salamis.

143. Now there was at Athens a man who had lately made his way into the first rank of citizens: his true name was Themistocles; but he was known more generally as the son of Neocles.[1] This man came forward and said, that the interpreters had not explained the oracle altogether aright—" for if," he argued, " the clause in question had really respected the Athenians, it would not have been expressed so mildly; the phrase used would have been ' Luckless Salamis,' rather than ' Holy Salamis,' had those to whom the island belonged been about to perish in its neighbourhood. Rightly taken, the response of the god threatened the enemy, much more than the Athenians." He therefore counselled his countrymen to make ready to fight on board their ships, since *they* were the wooden wall in which the god told them to trust. When Themistocles had thus cleared the

[1] The practice of addressing persons by their fathers' names was common in Greece.

matter, the Athenians embraced his view, preferring it to that of the interpreters. The advice of these last had been against engaging in a sea-fight; " all the Athenians could do," they said, " was, without lifting a hand in their defence, to quit Attica, and make a settlement in some other country." [1]

144. Themistocles had before this given a counsel which prevailed very seasonably. The Athenians, having a large sum of money in their treasury, the produce of the mines at Laureium,[2] were about to share it among the full-grown citizens, who would have received ten drachmas apiece,[3] when Themistocles persuaded them to forbear the distribution, and build with the money two hundred ships, to help them in their war against the Æginetans. It was the breaking out of the Eginetan war which was at this time the saving of Greece; for hereby were the Athenians forced to become a maritime power. The new ships were not used for the purpose for which they had been built, but became a help to Greece in her hour of need. And the Athenians had not only these vessels ready before the war, but they likewise set to work to build more; while they determined, in a council which was held after the debate upon the oracle, that, according to the advice of the god, they would embark their whole force aboard their ships, and, with such Greeks as chose to join them, give battle to the barbarian invader. Such, then, were the oracles which had been received by the Athenians.

145. The Greeks who were well affected to the Grecian cause, having assembled in one place, and there consulted together, and interchanged pledges with each other, agreed that, before any other step was taken, the feuds and enmities which existed between the different nations should first of all be appeased. Many such there were; but one was of more importance than the rest, namely, the war which was still going on between the Athenians and the Æginetans.[4] When this business was concluded, understanding that Xerxes had reached Sardis with his army, they resolved to despatch spies into Asia to take note of

[1] This plan appears to have been seriously entertained.
[2] Laureium or Laurion was the name of the mountainous country immediately above Cape *Colonna* (Sunium). The silver-mines, with which the whole tract abounded, had been worked from time immemorial.
[3] If the number of citizens at this time was, according to the estimate already made, 30,000 (supra, v. 97), the entire sum which they were about to have shared among them must have been fifty talents, or rather more than £12,000.
[4] Supra, v. 81, 89; vi. 87-93. The council appears to have assembled at the Isthmus (infra, ch. 172).

the king's affairs. At the same time they determined to send
ambassadors to the Argives, and conclude a league with them
against the Persians; while they likewise despatched messengers
to Gelo, the son of Deinomenes, in Sicily, to the people of Cor-
cyra, and to those of Crete, exhorting them to send help to
Greece. Their wish was to unite, if possible, the entire Greek
name in one, and so to bring all to join in the same plan of
defence, inasmuch as the approaching dangers threatened all
alike. Now the power of Gelo was said to be very great, far
greater than that of any single Grecian people.

146. So when these resolutions had been agreed upon, and
the quarrels between the states made up, first of all they sent
into Asia three men as spies. These men reached Sardis, and
took note of the king's forces, but, being discovered, were
examined by order of the generals who commanded the land
army, and, having been condemned to suffer death, were led out
to execution. Xerxes, however, when the news reached him,
disapproving the sentence of the generals, sent some of his
body-guard with instructions, if they found the spies still alive,
to bring them into his presence. The messengers found the
spies alive, and brought them before the king, who, when he
heard the purpose for which they had come, gave orders to his
guards to take them round the camp, and show them all the
footmen and all the horse, letting them gaze at everything to
their hearts' content; then, when they were satisfied, to send
them away unharmed to whatever country they desired.

147. For these orders Xerxes gave afterwards the following
reasons. "Had the spies been put to death," he said, "the
Greeks would have continued ignorant of the vastness of his
army, which surpassed the common report of it; while he would
have done them a very small injury by killing three of their
men. On the other hand, by the return of the spies to Greece,
his power would become known; and the Greeks," he expected,
"would make surrender of their freedom before he began his
march, by which means his troops would be saved all the trouble
of an expedition." This reasoning was like to that which he
used upon another occasion. While he was staying at Abydos,
he saw some corn-ships, which were passing through the Hellespont from the Euxine,[1] on their way to Ægina and the Peloponnese. His attendants, hearing that they were the enemy's,

---

[1] The corn-growing countries upon the Black Sea, in ancient as in modern
times, supplied the commercial nations with their chief article of food.

were ready to capture them, and looked to see when Xerxes would give the signal. He, however, merely asked, " Whither the ships were bound? " and when they answered, " For thy foes, master, with corn on board,"—" We too are bound thither," he rejoined, " laden, among other things, with corn. What harm is it, if they carry our provisions for us? "

So the spies, when they had seen everything, were dismissed, and came back to Europe.

148. The Greeks who had banded themselves together against the Persian king, after despatching the spies into Asia, sent next ambassadors to Argos. The account which the Argives give of their own proceedings is the following. They say that they had information from the very first of the preparations which the barbarians were making against Greece. So, as they expected that the Greeks would come upon them for aid against the assailant, they sent envoys to Delphi to inquire of the god what it would be best for them to do in the matter. They had lost, not long before, six thousand citizens, who had been slain by the Lacedæmonians under Cleomenes the son of Anaxandridas;[1] which was the reason why they now sent to Delphi. When the Pythoness heard their question, she replied—

" Hated of all thy neighbours, beloved of the blessed Immortals,
Sit thou still, with thy lance drawn inward, patiently watching;
Warily guard thine head, and the head will take care of the body."

This prophecy had been given them some time before the envoys came; but still, when they afterwards arrived, it was permitted them to enter the council-house, and there deliver their message. And this answer was returned to their demands—" Argos is ready to do as ye require, if the Lacedæmonians will first make a truce for thirty years, and will further divide with Argos the leadership of the allied army. Although in strict right the whole command should be hers,[2] she will be content to have the leadership divided equally."

149. Such, they say, was the reply made by the council, in spite of the oracle which forbade them to enter into a league with the Greeks. For, while not without fear of disobeying the

[1] We have here an estimate of the Argive loss in the battle and massacre of which an account was given above (see vi. 78-80). If, as is probable, the number of citizens was not greater than at Sparta (about 10,000), the blow was certainly tremendous.

[2] Argos never forgot her claim or relinquished her hopes of the hegemony. It induced her to stand aloof from great struggles—from the Peloponnesian as well as from this—in order to nurse her strength.

oracle, they were greatly desirous of obtaining a thirty years' truce, to give time for their sons to grow to man's estate. They reflected, that if no such truce were concluded, and it should be their lot to suffer a second calamity at the hands of the Persians, it was likely they would fall hopelessly under the power of Sparta. But to the demands of the Argive council the Lacedæmonian envoys made answer—" They would bring before the people the question of concluding a truce. With regard to the leadership, they had received orders what to say, and the reply was, that Sparta had two kings, Argos but one—it was not possible that either of the two Spartans should be stripped of his dignity—but they did not oppose the Argive king having one vote like each of them." The Argives say, that they could not brook this arrogance on the part of Sparta, and rather than yield one jot to it, they preferred to be under the rule of the barbarians. So they told the envoys to be gone, before sunset, from their territory, or they should be treated as enemies.

150. Such is the account which is given of these matters by the Argives themselves. There is another story, which is told generally through Greece, of a different tenor. Xerxes, it is said, before he set forth on his expedition against Greece, sent a herald to Argos, who on his arrival spoke as follows:—

" Men of Argos, King Xerxes speaks thus to you. We Persians deem that the Perses from whom we descend was the child of Perseus the son of Danaë, and of Andromeda the daughter of Cepheus. Hereby it would seem that we come of your stock and lineage. So then it neither befits us to make war upon those from whom we spring; nor can it be right for you to fight, on behalf of others, against us. Your place is to keep quiet and hold yourselves aloof. Only let matters proceed as I wish, and there is no people whom I shall have in higher esteem than you."

This address, says the story, was highly valued by the Argives, who therefore at the first neither gave a promise to the Greeks nor yet put forward a demand. Afterwards, however, when the Greeks called upon them to give their aid, they made the claim which has been mentioned, because they knew well that the Lacedæmonians would never yield it, and so they would have a pretext for taking no part in the war.

151. Some of the Greeks say that this account agrees remarkably with what happened many years afterwards. Callias, the son of Hipponicus, and certain others with him, had gone

up to Susa, the city of Memnon,[1] as ambassadors of the Athenians, upon a business quite distinct from this. While they were there, it happened that the Argives likewise sent ambassadors to Susa, to ask Artaxerxes, the son of Xerxes, "if the friendship which they had formed with his father still continued, or if he looked upon them as his enemies?"—to which King Artaxerxes replied, "Most certainly it continues; and there is no city which I reckon more my friend than Argos."

152. For my own part I cannot positively say whether Xerxes did send the herald to Argos or not; nor whether Argive ambassadors at Susa did really put this question to Artaxerxes about the friendship between them and him; neither do I deliver any opinion hereupon other than that of the Argives themselves. This, however, I know—that if every nation were to bring all its evil deeds to a given place, in order to make an exchange with some other nation, when they had all looked carefully at their neighbours' faults, they would be truly glad to carry their own back again. So, after all, the conduct of the Argives was not perhaps more disgraceful than that of others. For myself, my duty is to report all that is said; but I am not obliged to believe it all alike—a remark which may be understood to apply to my whole History. Some even go so far as to say that the Argives first invited the Persians to invade Greece, because of their ill success in the war with Lacedæmon, since they preferred anything to the smart of their actual sufferings. Thus much concerning the Argives.

153. Other ambassadors, among whom was Syagrus from Lacedæmon, were sent by the allies into Sicily, with instructions to confer with Gelo.

The ancestor of this Gelo, who first settled at Gela, was a native of the isle of Telos, which lies off Triopium.[2] When Gela was colonised by Antiphêmus and the Lindians of Rhodes,[3] he likewise took part in the expedition. In course of time his descendants became the high-priests of the gods who dwell below—an office which they held continually, from the time that Têlines, one of Gelo's ancestors, obtained it in the way which I will now mention. Certain citizens of Gela, worsted in

---

[1] Supra, ii. 106, and v. 53, 54.

[2] Telos, still known by its old name, but more commonly called *Piscopi*, lies due south of the Triopian promontory (near Cape *Crio*, supra, i. 174), at the distance of about twenty miles.

[3] Gela, like most of the Sicilian towns, derived its name from the stream on whose banks it was built.

a sedition, had found a refuge at Mactôrium, a town situated on the heights above Gela. Têlines reinstated these men, without any human help, solely by means of the sacred rites of these deities. From whom he received them, or how he himself acquired them, I cannot say; but certain it is, that relying on their power he brought the exiles back. For this his reward was to be, the office of high-priest of those gods for himself and his seed for ever. It surprises me especially that such a feat should have been performed by Têlines; for I have always looked upon acts of this nature as beyond the abilities of common men, and only to be achieved by such as are of a bold and manly spirit; whereas Têlines is said by those who dwell about Sicily to have been a soft-hearted and womanish person. He however obtained this office in the manner above described.

154. Afterwards, on the death of Cleander the son of Pantares,[1] who was slain by Sabyllus, a citizen of Gela, after he had held the tyranny for seven years, Hippocrates, Cleander's brother, mounted the throne. During his reign, Gelo, a descendant of the high-priest Têlines, served with many others— of whom Ænesidêmus, son of Pataïcus,[2] was one—in the king's bodyguard. Within a little time his merit caused him to be raised to the command of all the horse. For when Hippocrates laid siege to Callipolis,[3] and afterwards to Naxos,[4] to Zanclé,[5] to Leontini,[6] and moreover to Syracuse, and many cities of the barbarians, Gelo in every war distinguished himself above all the combatants. Of the various cities above named, there was none but Syracuse which was not reduced to slavery. The Syracusans were saved from this fate, after they had suffered defeat on the river Elôrus, by the Corinthians and Corcyræans, who made peace between them and Hippocrates, on condition of their ceding Camarina[7] to him; for that city anciently belonged to Syracuse.

155. When, however, Hippocrates, after a reign of the same

[1] Cleander was the first tyrant.
[2] Ænesidêmus was the father of Theron, tyrant of Agrigentum not long afterwards.
[3] Callipolis was a Naxian settlement, and lay at no great distance from Naxos.
[4] Naxos, according to Thucydides (vi. 3), the first of the Greek settlements in Sicily, was founded about the year B.C. 735.
[5] Supra, vi. 23.
[6] Leontini was founded from Naxos, six years after the arrival of the Chalcideans in Sicily.
[7] Camarina was founded from Syracuse about the year B.C. 599.

length as that of Cleander his brother, perished near the city
Hybla, as he was warring with the native Sicilians, then Gelo,
pretending to espouse the cause of the two sons of Hippocrates,
Eucleides and Cleander, defeated the citizens who were seeking
to recover their freedom, and having so done, set aside the
children, and himself took the kingly power. After this piece
of good fortune, Gelo likewise became master of Syracuse, in
the following manner. The Syracusan landholders, as they were
called, had been driven from their city by the common people
assisted by their own slaves, the Cyllyrians, and had fled to
Casmenæ. Gelo brought them back to Syracuse, and so got
possession of the town; for the people surrendered themselves,
and gave up their city on his approach.

156. Being now master of Syracuse, Gelo cared less to govern
Gela, which he therefore entrusted to his brother Hiero, while
he strengthened the defences of his new city, which indeed was
now all in all to him. And Syracuse sprang up rapidly to power
and became a flourishing place. For Gelo razed Camarina to
the ground, and brought all the inhabitants to Syracuse, and
made them citizens; he also brought thither more than half
the citizens of Gela, and gave them the same rights as the
Camarinæans. So likewise with the Megarians of Sicily—after
besieging their town and forcing them to surrender, he took the
rich men, who, having made the war, looked now for nothing
less than death at his hands, and carrying them to Syracuse,
established them there as citizens; while the common people,
who, as they had not taken any share in the struggle, felt
secure that no harm would be done to them, he carried likewise
to Syracuse, where he sold them all as slaves to be conveyed
abroad. He did the like also by the Eubœans of Sicily,[1] making
the same difference. His conduct towards both nations arose
from his belief, that a " people " was a most unpleasant companion. In this way Gelo became a great king.

157. When the Greek envoys reached Syracuse, and were
admitted to an audience, they spoke as follows—

" We have been sent hither by the Lacedæmonians and
Athenians, with their respective allies, to ask thee to join us
against the barbarian. Doubtless thou hast heard of his invasion, and art aware that a Persian is about to throw a bridge
over the Hellespont, and, bringing with him out of Asia all the
forces of the East, to carry war into Greece,—professing indeed

---

[1] Eubœa seems never to have recovered this blow.

that he only seeks to attack Athens, but really bent on bringing all the Greeks into subjection. Do thou therefore, we beseech thee, aid those who would maintain the freedom of Greece, and thyself assist to free her; since the power which thou wieldest is great, and thy portion in Greece, as lord of Sicily, is no small one. For if all Greece join together in one, there will be a mighty host collected, and we shall be a match for our assailants; but if some turn traitors, and others refuse their aid, and only a small part of the whole body remains sound, then there is reason to fear that all Greece may perish. For do not thou cherish a hope that the Persian, when he has conquered our country, will be content and not advance against thee. Rather take thy measures beforehand; and consider that thou defendest thyself when thou givest aid to us. Wise counsels, be sure, for the most part have prosperous issues."

158. Thus spake the envoys; and Gelo replied with vehemence—

"Greeks, ye have had the face to come here with selfish words, and exhort me to join in league with you against the barbarian. Yet when I erewhile asked you to join with me in fighting barbarians, what time the quarrel broke out between me and Carthage;[1] and when I earnestly besought you to revenge on the men of Egesta their murder of Dorieus, the son of Anaxandridas, promising to assist you in setting free the trading-places, from which you receive great profits and advantages, you neither came hither to give me succour, nor yet to revenge Dorieus; but, for any efforts on your part to hinder it, these countries might at this time have been entirely under the barbarians. Now, however, that matters have prospered and gone well with me, while the danger has shifted its ground and at present threatens yourselves, lo! you call Gelo to mind. But though ye slighted me then, I will not imitate you now: I am ready to give you aid, and to furnish as my contribution two hundred triremes, twenty thousand men-at-arms, two thousand cavalry, and an equal number of archers, slingers, and light horsemen, together with corn for the whole Grecian army so long as the war shall last. These services, however, I promise on one condition—that ye appoint me chief captain and commander of the Grecian forces during the war with the barbarian. Unless ye agree to this, I will neither send succours, nor come myself."

[1] No particulars are known of this war.

159. Syagrus, when he heard these words, was unable to contain himself, and exclaimed—

" Surely a groan would burst from Pelops' son, Agamemnon, did he hear that her leadership was snatched from Sparta by Gelo and the men of Syracuse. Speak then no more of any such condition, as that we should yield thee the chief command; but if thou art minded to come to the aid of Greece, prepare to serve under Lacedæmonian generals. Wilt thou not serve under a leader?—then, prithee, withhold thy succours."

160. Hereupon Gelo, seeing the indignation which showed itself in the words of Syagrus, delivered to the envoys his final offer:—" Spartan stranger," he said, " reproaches cast forth against a man are wont to provoke him to anger; but the insults which thou hast uttered in thy speech shall not persuade me to outstep good breeding in my answer. Surely if you maintain so stoutly your right to the command, it is reasonable that I should be still more stiff in maintaining mine, forasmuch as I am at the head of a far larger fleet and army. Since, however, the claim which I have put forward is so displeasing to you, I will yield, and be content with less. Take, if it please you, the command of the land-force, and I will be admiral of the fleet; or assume, if you prefer it, the command by sea, and I will be leader upon the land. Unless you are satisfied with these terms, you must return home by yourselves, and lose this great alliance." Such was the offer which Gelo made.

161. Hereat broke in the Athenian envoy, before the Spartan could answer, and thus addressed Gelo—

" King of the Syracusans! Greece sent us here to thee to ask for an army, and not to ask for a general. Thou, however, dost not promise to send us any army at all, if thou art not made leader of the Greeks; and this command is what alone thou sticklest for. Now when thy request was to have the whole command, we were content to keep silence; for well we knew that we might trust the Spartan envoy to make answer for us both. But since, after failing in thy claim to lead the whole armament, thou hast now put forward a request to have the command of the fleet, know that, even should the Spartan envoy consent to this, we will not consent. The command by sea, if the Lacedæmonians do not wish for it, belongs to us. While they like to keep this command, we shall raise no dispute; but we will not yield our right to it in favour of any one else. Where would be the advantage of our having raised up a naval force greater than that of any other Greek people, if never-theless we should suffer Syracusans to take the command away from us?—from us, I say, who are Athenians, the most ancient nation in Greece, the only Greeks who have never changed their abode—the people who are said by the poet Homer to have sent to Troy the man best able of all the Greeks to array and marshal an army—so that we may be allowed to boast somewhat."

162. Gelo replied—" Athenian stranger, ye have, it seems, no lack of commanders; but ye are likely to lack men to receive their orders. As ye are resolved to yield nothing and claim everything, ye had best make haste back to Greece, and say, that the spring of her year is lost to her." The meaning of this expression was the following: as the spring is manifestly the finest season of the year, so (he meant to say) were his troops the finest of the Greek army—Greece, therefore, deprived of his alliance, would be like a year with the spring taken from it.

163. Then the Greek envoys, without having any further dealings with Gelo, sailed away home. And Gelo, who feared that the Greeks would be too weak to withstand the barbarians, and yet could not any how bring himself to go to the Pelopon-nese, and there, though king of Sicily, serve under the Lacedœ-monians, left off altogether to contemplate that course of action, and betook himself to quite a different plan. As soon as ever tidings reached him of the passage of the Hellespont by the Persians, he sent off three penteconters, under the command of Cadmus, the son of Scythas, a native of Cos, who was to go to Delphi, taking with him a large sum of money and a stock of friendly words: there he was to watch the war, and see what turn it would take: if the barbarians prevailed, he was to give Xerxes the treasure, and with it earth and water for the lands which Gelo ruled—if the Greeks won the day, he was to convey the treasure back.

164. This Cadmus had at an earlier time received from his father the kingly power at Cos in a right good condition, and had of his own free will and without the approach of any danger, from pure love of justice, given up his power into the hands of the people at large, and departed to Sicily; where he assisted in the Samian seizure and settlement of Zanclé,[1] or Messana, as it was afterwards called. Upon this occasion Gelo chose him to send into Greece, because he was acquainted with the proofs of

[1] See above, vi. 23.

honesty which he had given. And now he added to his former
honourable deeds an action which is not the least of his merits.
With a vast sum entrusted to him and completely in his power,
so that he might have kept it for his own use if he had liked,
he did not touch it; but when the Greeks gained the sea-fight
and Xerxes fled away with his army, he brought the whole
treasure back with him to Sicily.

165. They, however, who dwell in Sicily, say that Gelo,
though he knew that he must serve under the Lacedæmonians,
would nevertheless have come to the aid of the Greeks, had not
it been for Têrillus, the son of Crinippus, king of Himera; who,
driven from his city by Thero, the son of Ænesidêmus, king of
Agrigentum,[1] brought into Sicily at this very time an army of
three hundred thousand men, Phœnicians, Libyans, Iberians,
Ligurians, Helisycians, Sardinians, and Corsicans,[2] under the
command of Hamilcar the son of Hanno, king[3] of the Carthaginians. Têrillus prevailed upon Hamilcar, partly as his sworn
friend, but more through the zealous aid of Anaxilaüs the son
of Cretines, king of Rhegium;[4] who, by giving his own sons to
Hamilcar as hostages, induced him to make the expedition.
Anaxilaüs herein served his own father-in-law; for he was
married to a daughter of Têrillus, by name Cydippé. So, as
Gelo could not give the Greeks any aid, he sent (they say) the
sum of money to Delphi.

166. They say too, that the victory of Gelo and Thero in
Sicily over Hamilcar the Carthaginian, fell out upon the very
day that the Greeks defeated the Persians at Salamis. Hamilcar, who was a Carthaginian on his father's side only, but on
his mother's a Syracusan, and who had been raised by his merit
to the throne of Carthage, after the battle and the defeat, as I
am informed, disappeared from sight: Gelo made the strictest
search for him, but he could not be found anywhere, either
dead or alive.

167. The Carthaginians, who take probability for their guide,
give the following account of this matter:—Hamilcar, they say,
during all the time that the battle raged between the Greeks
and the barbarians, which was from early dawn till evening,

---

[1] Agrigentum was founded from Gela, about B.C. 582.
[2] This is the first instance of the mixed mercenary armies of Carthage, by
which her conquests were ordinarily effected.
[3] That is, Suffes. The Greek writers always speak of the Suffetes as
"kings" ($\beta \alpha \sigma \iota \lambda \epsilon \hat{\iota} s$).
[4] Supra, vi. 23.

remained in the camp, sacrificing and seeking favourable omens, while he burned on a huge pyre the entire bodies of the victims which he offered. Here, as he poured libations upon the sacrifices, he saw the rout of his army; whereupon he cast himself headlong into the flames, and so was consumed and disappeared. But whether Hamilcar's disappearance happened, as the Phœnicians tell us, in this way, or, as the Syracusans maintain, in some other, certain it is that the Carthaginians offer him sacrifice, and in all their colonies have monuments erected to his honour, as well as one, which is the grandest of all, at Carthage. Thus much concerning the affairs of Sicily.

168. As for the Corcyræans, whom the envoys that visited Sicily took in their way, and to whom they delivered the same message as to Gelo,—their answers and actions were the following. With great readiness they promised to come and give their help to the Greeks; declaring that " the ruin of Greece was a thing which they could not tamely stand by to see; for should she fall, they must the very next day submit to slavery; so that they were bound to assist her to the very uttermost of their power." But notwithstanding that they answered so smoothly, yet when the time came for the succours to be sent, they were of quite a different mind; and though they manned sixty ships, it was long ere they put to sea with them; and when they had so done, they went no further than the Peloponnese, where they lay to with their fleet, off the Lacedæmonian coast, about Pylos [1] and Tænarum,[2]—like Gelo, watching to see what turn the war would take. For they despaired altogether of the Greeks gaining the day, and expected that the Persian would win a great battle, and then be masters of the whole of Greece. They therefore acted as I have said, in order that they might be able to address Xerxes in words like these: " O king! though the Greeks sought to obtain our aid in their war with thee, and though we had a force of no small size, and could have furnished a greater number of ships than any Greek state except Athens, yet we refused, since we would not fight against thee, nor do aught to cause thee annoyance." The Corcyræans hoped that a speech like this would

---

[1] Pylos, celebrated in poetry as the abode of Nestor (Il. ii. 591-602), and in history as the scene of the first important defeat suffered by the Spartans (Thucyd. iv. 32-40), was situated on the west coast of the Peloponnese, near the site of the modern *Navarino*.

[2] Tænarum was the ancient name of the promontory now called Cape *Matapan*.

gain them better treatment from the Persians than the rest of the Greeks; and it would have done so, in my judgment. At the same time, they had an excuse ready to give their countrymen, which they used when the time came. Reproached by them for sending no succours, they replied, " that they had fitted out a fleet of sixty triremes, but that the Etesian winds did not allow them to double Cape Malea, and this hindered them from reaching Salamis—it was not from any bad motive that they had missed the sea-fight." In this way the Corcyræans eluded the reproaches of the Greeks.

169. The Cretans, when the envoys sent to ask aid from them came and made their request, acted as follows. They despatched messengers in the name of their state to Delphi, and asked the god, whether it would make for their welfare if they should lend succour to Greece. " Fools! " replied the Pythoness, " do ye not still complain of the woes which the assisting of Menelaüs cost you at the hands of angry Minos? How wroth was he, when, in spite of their having lent you no aid towards avenging his death at Camicus, you helped them to avenge the carrying off by a barbarian of a woman from Sparta! " When this answer was brought from Delphi to the Cretans, they thought no more of assisting the Greeks.

170. Minos, according to tradition, went to Sicania, or Sicily, as it is now called, in search of Dædalus, and there perished by a violent death. After a while the Cretans, warned by some god or other, made a great expedition into Sicania, all except the Polichnites and the Præsians, and besieged Camicus (which in my time belonged to Agrigentum) by the space of five years. At last, however, failing in their efforts to take the place, and unable to carry on the siege any longer from the pressure of hunger, they departed and went their way. Voyaging homewards they had reached Iapygia,[1] when a furious storm arose and threw them upon the coast. All their vessels were broken in pieces; and so, as they saw no means of returning to Crete, they founded the town of Hyria, where they took up their abode, changing their name from Cretans to Messapian Iapygians, and at the same time becoming inhabitants of the mainland instead of islanders. From Hyria they afterwards founded those other towns which the Tarentines at a much later period endeavoured to take, but could not, being defeated signally.

[1] Iapygia coincides generally with the *Terra di Otranto* of our maps, extending, however, somewhat further round the Gulf of *Taranto*.

Indeed so dreadful a slaughter of Greeks never happened at any other time, so far as my knowledge extends: nor was it only the Tarentines who suffered; but the men of Rhegium too, who had been forced to go to the aid of the Tarentines by Micythus the son of Chœrus, lost here three thousand of their citizens; while the number of the Tarentines who fell was beyond all count. This Micythus had been a household slave of Anaxilaüs, and was by him left in charge of Rhegium: he is the same man who was afterwards forced to leave Rhegium, when he settled at Tegea in Arcadia, from which place he made his many offerings of statues to the shrine at Olympia.

171. This account of the Rhegians and the Tarentines is a digression from the story which I was relating. To return—the Præsians say that men of various nations now flocked to Crete, which was stript of its inhabitants; but none came in such numbers as the Grecians. Three generations after the death of Minos the Trojan war took place; and the Cretans were not the least distinguished among the helpers of Menelaüs. But on this account, when they came back from Troy, famine and pestilence fell upon them, and destroyed both the men and the cattle. Crete was a second time stript of its inhabitants, a remnant only being left; who form, together with fresh settlers, the third "Cretan" people by whom the island has been inhabited. These were the events of which the Pythoness now reminded the men of Crete; and thereby she prevented them from giving the Greeks aid, though they wished to have gone to their assistance.

172. The Thessalians did not embrace the cause of the Medes until they were forced to do so; for they gave plain proof that the intrigues of the Aleuadæ [1] were not at all to their liking. No sooner did they hear that the Persian was about to cross over into Europe than they despatched envoys to the Greeks who were met to consult together at the Isthmus, whither all the states which were well inclined to the Grecian cause had sent their delegates. These envoys on their arrival thus addressed their countrymen:—

" Men of Greece, it behoves you to guard the pass of Olympus; for thus will Thessaly be placed in safety, as well as the rest of Greece. We for our parts are quite ready to take our share in this work; but you must likewise send us a strong force: otherwise we give you fair warning that we shall make terms

[1] Supra, ch. 6. Compare ch. 140, ad fin.

with the Persians. For we ought not to be left, exposed as we are in front of all the rest of Greece, to die in your defence alone and unassisted. If however you do not choose to send us aid, you cannot force us to resist the enemy; for there is no force so strong as inability. We shall therefore do our best to secure our own safety."

Such was the declaration of the Thessalians.

173. Hereupon the Greeks determined to send a body of foot to Thessaly by sea, which should defend the pass of Olympus. Accordingly a force was collected, which passed up the Euripus, and disembarking at Alus, on the coast of Achæa, left the ships there, and marched by land into Thessaly. Here they occupied the defile of Tempé; which leads from Lower Macedonia into Thessaly along the course of the Peneus, having the range of Olympus on the one hand and Ossa upon the other. In this place the Greek force that had been collected, amounting to about 10,000 heavy-armed men, pitched their camp; and here they were joined by the Thessalian cavalry. The commanders were, on the part of the Lacedæmonians, Evænetus, the son of Carênus, who had been chosen out of the Polemarchs, but did not belong to the blood royal; and on the part of the Athenians, Themistocles, the son of Neocles. They did not however maintain their station for more than a few days; since envoys came from Alexander, the son of Amyntas, the Macedonian, and counselled them to decamp from Tempé, telling them that if they remained in the pass they would be trodden under foot by the invading army, whose numbers they recounted, and likewise the multitude of their ships. So when the envoys thus counselled them, and the counsel seemed to be good, and the Macedonian who sent it friendly, they did even as he advised. In my opinion what chiefly wrought on them was the fear that the Persians might enter by another pass,[1] whereof they now heard, which led from Upper Macedonia [2] into Thessaly through the territory of the Perrhæbi, and by the town of Gonnus,—the pass by which soon afterwards the army of Xerxes actually made its entrance. The Greeks therefore went back to their ships and sailed away to the Isthmus.

174. Such were the circumstances of the expedition into Thessaly; they took place when the king was at Abydos, pre-

[1] Vide supra, ch. 128. The pass intended is probably that which crossed the Olympic range by the town of Petra.

[2] By " Upper Macedonia " Herodotus appears to mean the upper portion of Pieria.

paring to pass from Asia into Europe. The Thessalians, when their allies forsook them, no longer wavered, but warmly espoused the side of the Medes; and afterwards, in the course of the war, they were of the very greatest service to Xerxes.

175. The Greeks, on their return to the Isthmus, took counsel together concerning the words of Alexander, and considered where they should fix the war, and what places they should occupy. The opinion which prevailed was, that they should guard the pass of Thermopylæ; since it was narrower than the Thessalian defile, and at the same time nearer to them. Of the pathway, by which the Greeks who fell at Thermopylæ were intercepted, they had no knowledge, until, on their arrival at Thermopylæ, it was discovered to them by the Trachinians. This pass then it was determined that they should guard, in order to prevent the barbarians from penetrating into Greece through it; and at the same time it was resolved that the fleet should proceed to Artemisium, in the region of Histiæôtis;[1] for, as those places are near to one another, it would be easy for the fleet and army to hold communication. The two places may be thus described.

176. Artemisium is where the sea of Thrace [2] contracts into a narrow channel, running between the isle of Sciathus and the mainland of Magnesia. When this narrow strait is passed you come to the line of coast called Artemisium; which is a portion of Eubœa, and contains a temple of Artemis (Diana). As for the entrance into Greece by Trachis,[3] it is, at its narrowest point, about fifty feet wide. This however is not the place where the passage is most contracted; for it is still narrower a little above and a little below Thermopylæ. At Alpêni,[4] which is lower down than that place, it is only wide enough for a single carriage; and up above, at the river Phœnix, near the town called Anthêla, it is the same. West of Thermopylæ rises a lofty and precipitous hill, impossible to climb, which runs up into the chain of Œta; while to the east the road is shut in by the sea and by marshes. In this place are the warm springs, which the natives call " The Cauldrons; " and above them

---

[1] The northern tract of Eubœa was called Histiæôtis.
[2] The northern portion of the Egean, extending from Magnesia to the Thracian Chersonese.
[3] Trachis was one of the chief cities of the Malians (infra, chs. 198, 199). It afterwards became Heraclea, on being colonised by the Lacedæmonians.
[4] Infra, ch. 216.

stands an altar sacred to Hercules.[1] A wall had once been carried across the opening;[2] and in this there had of old times been a gateway. These works were made by the Phocians, through fear of the Thessalians, at the time when the latter came from Thesprôtia to establish themselves in the land of Æolis, which they still occupy. As the Thessalians strove to reduce Phocis, the Phocians raised the wall to protect themselves, and likewise turned the hot springs upon the pass, that so the ground might be broken up by watercourses, using thus all possible means to hinder the Thessalians from invading their country. The old wall had been built in very remote times; and the greater part of it had gone to decay through age. Now however the Greeks resolved to repair its breaches, and here make their stand against the barbarian. At this point there is a village very nigh the road, Alpêni by name, from which the Greeks reckoned on getting corn for their troops.

177. These places, therefore, seemed to the Greeks fit for their purpose. Weighing well all that was likely to happen, and considering that in this region the barbarians could make no use of their vast numbers, nor of their cavalry, they resolved to await here the invader of Greece. And when news reached them of the Persians being in Pieria, straightway they broke up from the Isthmus, and proceeded, some on foot to Thermopylæ, others by sea to Artemisium.

178. The Greeks now made all speed to reach the two stations;[3] and about the same time the Delphians, alarmed both for themselves and for their country, consulted the god, and received for answer a command to " pray to the winds, for the winds would do Greece good service." So when this answer was given them, forthwith the Delphians sent word of the prophecy to those Greeks who were zealous for freedom, and, cheering them thereby amid the fears which they entertained with respect to the barbarian, earned their everlasting gratitude. This done, they raised an altar to the winds at Thyia (where Thyia, the daughter of Cephissus, from whom the region takes its name, has a precinct), and worshipped them with sacrifices. And even to the present day the Delphians sacrifice to the winds, because of this oracle.

179. The fleet of Xerxes now departed from Therma; and

---

[1] The whole district was regarded as ennobled by the sufferings of Hercules, and as sacred to him.
[2] Vide infra, chs. 208, 223, 225.   [3] Thermopylæ and Artemisium.

ten of the swiftest sailing ships ventured to stretch across direct for Sciathus, at which place there were upon the look-out three vessels belonging to the Greeks, one a ship of Trœzen,[1] another of Egina, and the third from Athens. These vessels no sooner saw from a distance the barbarians approaching than they all hurriedly took to flight.

180. The barbarians at once pursued, and the Trœzenian ship, which was commanded by Prexînus, fell into their hands. Hereupon the Persians took the handsomest of the men-at-arms, and drew him to the prow of the vessel, where they sacrificed him; for they thought the man a good omen to their cause, seeing that he was at once so beautiful, and likewise the first captive they had made. The man who was slain in this way was called Leo; and it may be that the name he bore helped him to his fate in some measure.

181. The Eginetan trireme, under its captain, Asônides, gave the Persians no little trouble, one of the men-at-arms, Pythes, the son of Ischenoüs, distinguishing himself beyond all the others who fought on that day. After the ship was taken this man continued to resist, and did not cease fighting till he fell quite covered with wounds. The Persians who served as men-at-arms in the squadron, finding that he was not dead, but still breathed, and being very anxious to save his life, since he had behaved so valiantly, dressed his wounds with myrrh, and bound them up with bandages of cotton. Then, when they were returned to their own station, they displayed their prisoner admiringly to the whole host, and behaved towards him with much kindness; but all the rest of the ship's crew were treated merely as slaves.

182. Thus did the Persians succeed in taking two of the vessels. The third, a trireme commanded by Phormus of Athens, took to flight and ran aground at the mouth of the river Peneus. The barbarians got possession of the bark, but not of the men. For the Athenians had no sooner run their vessel aground than they leapt out, and made their way through Thessaly back to Athens.

When the Greeks stationed at Artemisium learnt what had happened by fire-signals [2] from Sciathus, so terrified were they, that, quitting their anchorage-ground at Artemisium, and

---

[1] Supra, ch. 99.

[2] The employment of fire-signals among the Greeks was very common. Æschylus represents it as known to them at the time of the Trojan war. [Compare the opening of the *Agamemnon* of Æschylus.—E. H. B.]

leaving scouts to watch the foe on the highlands of Eubœa,
they removed to Chalcis, intending to guard the Euripus.

183. Meantime three of the ten vessels sent forward by the
barbarians advanced as far as the sunken rock between Sciathus
and Magnesia, which is called " The Ant," and there set up a
stone pillar which they had brought with them for that purpose.
After this, their course being now clear, the barbarians set sail
with all their ships from Therma, eleven days from the time that
the king quitted the town. The rock, which lay directly in
their course, had been made known to them by Pammon of
Scyros.[1] A day's voyage without a stop brought them to Sepias
in Magnesia,[2] and to the strip of coast which lies between the
town of Casthanæa and the promontory of Sepias.

184. As far as this point then, and on land, as far as Thermopylæ, the armament of Xerxes had been free from mischance; and the numbers were still, according to my reckoning,
of the following amount. First there was the ancient complement of the twelve hundred and seven vessels which came
with the king from Asia—the contingents of the nations severally
—amounting, if we allow to each ship a crew of two hundred
men,[3] to 241,400. Each of these vessels had on board, besides
native soldiers, thirty fighting men, who were either Persians,
Medes, or Sacans;[4] which gives an addition of 36,210. To these
two numbers I shall further add the crews of the penteconters;
which may be reckoned, one with another, at fourscore men
each. Of such vessels there were (as I said before[5]) three
thousand; and the men on board them accordingly would be
240,000. This was the sea force brought by the king from
Asia; and it amounted in all to 517,610 men. The number of
the foot soldiers was 1,700,000;[6] that of the horsemen 80,000;[7]
to which must be added the Arabs who rode on camels, and the
Libyans who fought in chariots, whom I reckon at 20,000. The
whole number, therefore, of the land and sea forces added
together amounts to 2,317,610 men. Such was the force brought

---

[1] Scyros, still called *Skyro*, lay off the east coast of Eubœa, at the distance of about 23 miles.

[2] The distance is calculated to be about 900 stades or 103 miles.

[3] The crew of a *Greek* trireme seems always to have been 200 (vide infra,
viii. 17).

[4] Vide supra, ch. 96.

[5] Supra, ch. 97. It appears from that passage that in these 3000 vessels
are included, besides penteconters, various other craft of a much smaller
size.

[6] Supra, ch. 60.   [7] See ch. 87.

from Asia, without including the camp followers, or taking any account of the provision-ships and the men whom they had on board.

185. To the amount thus reached we have still to add the forces gathered in Europe, concerning which I can only speak from conjecture. The Greeks dwelling in Thrace, and in the islands off the coast of Thrace, furnished to the fleet one hundred and twenty ships; the crews of which would amount to 24,000 men. Besides these, footmen were furnished by the Thracians, the Pæonians, the Eordians, the Bottiæans, by the Chalcidean tribes, by the Brygians, the Pierians, the Macedonians, the Perrhæbians, the Enianians, the Dolopians, the Magnesians, the Achæans, and by all the dwellers upon the Thracian sea-board; and the forces of these nations amounted, I believe, to three hundred thousand men. These numbers, added to those of the force which came out of Asia, make the sum of the fighting men 2,641,610.

186. Such then being the number of the fighting men, it is my belief that the attendants who followed the camp, together with the crews of the corn-barks, and of the other craft accompanying the army, made up an amount rather above than below that of the fighting men. However I will not reckon them as either fewer or more, but take them at an equal number. We have therefore to add to the sum already reached an exactly equal amount. This will give 5,283,220 as the whole number of men brought by Xerxes, the son of Darius, as far as Sepias and Thermopylæ.[1]

187. Such then was the amount of the entire host of Xerxes. As for the number of the women who ground the corn, of the concubines, and the eunuchs, no one can give any sure account of it; nor can the baggage-horses and other sumpter-beasts, nor the Indian hounds which followed the army, be calculated, by reason of their multitude. Hence I am not at all surprised that the water of the rivers was found too scant for the army in some instances; rather it is a marvel to me how the provisions did not fail, when the numbers were so great. For I find on calculation that if each man consumed no more than a chœnix of corn a-day, there must have been used daily by the army 110,340 medimni,[2] and this without counting what was eaten

---

[1] [These numbers are probably wholly fabulous. Modern historians (e.g. Bury) estimate the land forces at 300,000, and the number of the fleet at about 800 triremes.—E. H. B.]

[2] The medimnus contained about 12 gallons English.

by the women, the eunuchs, the sumpter-beasts, and the hounds. Among all this multitude of men there was not one who, for beauty and stature, deserved more than Xerxes himself to wield so vast a power.

188. The fleet then, as I said, on leaving Therma, sailed to the Magnesian territory, and there occupied the strip of coast between the city of Casthanæa and Cape Sepias. The ships of the first row were moored to the land, while the remainder swung at anchor further off. The beach extended but a very little way, so that they had to anchor off the shore, row upon row, eight deep. In this manner they passed the night. But at dawn of day calm and stillness gave place to a raging sea, and a violent storm, which fell upon them with a strong gale from the east—a wind which the people in those parts call Hellespontias. Such of them as perceived the wind rising, and were so moored as to allow of it, forestalled the tempest by dragging their ships up on the beach, and in this way saved both themselves and their vessels. But the ships which the storm caught out at sea were driven ashore, some of them near the place called Ipni, or "The Ovens," at the foot of Pelion; others on the strand itself; others again about Cape Sepias; while a portion were dashed to pieces near the cities of Melibœa and Casthanæa. There was no resisting the tempest.

189. It is said that the Athenians had called upon Boreas [1] to aid the Greeks, on account of a fresh oracle which had reached them, commanding them to " seek help from their son-in-law." For Boreas, according to the tradition of the Greeks, took to wife a woman of Attica, viz., Orithyia, the daughter of Erechtheus. So the Athenians, as the tale goes, considering that this marriage made Boreas their son-in-law, and perceiving, while they lay with their ships at Chalcis of Eubœa,[2] that the wind was rising, or, it may be, even before it freshened, offered sacrifice both to Boreas and likewise to Orithyia, entreating them to come to their aid and to destroy the ships of the barbarians, as they did once before off Mount Athos. Whether it was owing to this that Boreas fell with violence on the barbarians at their anchorage I cannot say; but the Athenians declare that they had received aid from Boreas before, and that it was he who now caused all these disasters. They therefore,

---

[1] The name Bora is still retained in the Adriatic for the N.E. wind.
[2] Supra, ch. 182.

on their return home, built a temple to this god on the banks of the Ilissus.

190. Such as put the loss of the Persian fleet in this storm at the lowest, say that four hundred of their ships were destroyed, that a countless multitude of men were slain, and a vast treasure engulfed. Ameinocles, the son of Crêtines, a Magnesian, who farmed land near Cape Sepias, found the wreck of these vessels a source of great gain to him; many were the gold and silver drinking-cups, cast up long afterwards by the surf, which he gathered; while treasure-boxes too which had belonged to the Persians, and golden articles of all kinds and beyond count, came into his possession. Ameinocles grew to be a man of great wealth in this way; but in other respects things did not go over well with him: he too, like other men, had his own grief—the calamity of losing his offspring.

191. As for the number of the provision craft and other merchant ships which perished, it was beyond count. Indeed, such was the loss, that the commanders of the sea force, fearing lest in their shattered condition the Thessalians should venture on an attack, raised a lofty barricade around their station out of the wreck of the vessels cast ashore. The storm lasted three days. At length the Magians, by offering victims to the Winds, and charming them with the help of conjurers, while at the same time they sacrificed to Thetis and the Nereids, succeeded in laying the storm four days after it first began; or perhaps it ceased of itself. The reason of their offering sacrifice to Thetis was this: they were told by the Ionians that here was the place whence Peleus carried her off, and that the whole promontory was sacred to her and to her sister Nereids. So the storm lulled upon the fourth day.

192. The scouts left by the Greeks about the highlands of Euboea hastened down from their stations on the day following that whereon the storm began, and acquainted their countrymen with all that had befallen the Persian fleet. These no sooner heard what had happened than straightway they returned thanks to Neptune the Saviour, and poured libations in his honour; after which they hastened back with all speed to Artemisium, expecting to find a very few ships left to oppose them, and arriving there for the second time, took up their station on that strip of coast: nor from that day to the present have they ceased to address Neptune by the name then given him, of "Saviour."

193. The barbarians, when the wind lulled and the sea grew smooth, drew their ships down to the water, and proceeded to coast along the mainland. Having then rounded the extreme point of Magnesia, they sailed straight into the bay that runs up to Pagasæ.[1] There is a place in this bay, belonging to Magnesia, where Hercules is said to have been put ashore to fetch water by Jason and his companions; who then deserted him and went on their way to Æa in Colchis, on board the ship Argo, in quest of the golden fleece. From the circumstance that they intended, after watering their vessel at this place, to quit the shore and launch forth into the deep, it received the name of Aphetæ. Here then it was that the fleet of Xerxes came to an anchor.

194. Fifteen ships, which had lagged greatly behind the rest, happening to catch sight of the Greek fleet at Artemisium, mistook it for their own, and sailing down into the midst of it, fell into the hands of the enemy. The commander of this squadron was Sandôces, the son of Thamasius, governor of Cymé,[2] in Æolis. He was of the number of the royal judges,[3] and had been crucified by Darius some time before, on the charge of taking a bribe to determine a cause wrongly; but while he yet hung on the cross, Darius bethought him that the good deeds of Sandôces towards the king's house were more numerous than his evil deeds; and so, confessing that he had acted with more haste than wisdom, he ordered him to be taken down and set at large. Thus Sandôces escaped destruction at the hands of Darius, and was alive at this time; but he was not fated to come off so cheaply from his second peril; for as soon as the Greeks saw the ships making towards them, they guessed their mistake, and putting to sea, took them without difficulty.

195. Aridôlis, tyrant of Alabanda in Caria, was on board one of the ships, and was made prisoner; as also was the Paphian general, Penthylus, the son of Demonoüs, who was on board another. This person had brought with him twelve ships from Paphos,[4] and, after losing eleven in the storm off Sepias, was taken in the remaining one as he sailed towards Artemisium. The Greeks, after questioning their prisoners as much as they wished concerning the forces of Xerxes, sent them away in chains to the Isthmus of Corinth.

---

[1] The modern Gulf of *Volo*.   [2] Supra, i. 149.   [3] Supra, iii. 31.
[4] Paphos seems to have been one of the earliest Phœnician settlements in Cyprus.

196. The sea force of the barbarians, with the exception of the fifteen ships commanded (as I said) by Sandôces, came safe to Aphetæ. Xerxes meanwhile, with the land army, had proceeded through Thessaly and Achæa, and three days earlier, had entered the territory of the Malians. In Thessaly, he matched his own horses against the Thessalian, which he heard were the best in Greece;[1] but the Greek coursers were left far behind in the race. All the rivers in this region had water enough to supply his army, except only the Onochônus;[2] but in Achæa, the largest of the streams, the Apidanus, barely held out.

197. On his arrival at Alus[3] in Achæa, his guides, wishing to inform him of everything, told him the tale known to the dwellers in those parts concerning the temple of the Laphystian Jupiter[4]—how that Athamas the son of Æolus took counsel with Ino and plotted the death of Phrixus;[5] and how that afterwards the Achæans, warned by an oracle, laid a forfeit upon his posterity, forbidding the eldest of the race ever to enter into the court-house (which they call the people's house), and keeping watch themselves to see the law obeyed. If one comes within the doors, he can never go out again except to be sacrificed. Further, they told him, how that many persons, when on the point of being slain, are seized with such fear that they flee away and take refuge in some other country; and that these, if they come back long afterwards, and are found to be the persons who entered the court-house, are led forth covered with chaplets, and in a grand procession, and are sacrificed. This forfeit is paid by the descendants of Cytissorus the son of Phrixus, because, when the Achæans, in obedience to an oracle, made Athamas the son of Æolus their sin-offering, and were about to slay him, Cytissorus came from Æa in Colchis and rescued Athamas, by which deed he brought the anger of the god upon his own posterity. Xerxes, therefore, having heard this story, when he

---

[1] The excellency of the Thessalian horses was proverbial.
[2] Supra, ch. 129.　　　　　　　[3] Supra, ch. 173.
[4] The most famous temple of Jupiter Laphystius was in Bœotia.
[5] The tale went, that Ino, wishing to destroy the children of Athamas by his first wife Nephelé, produced a dearth by having the seed-corn secretly parched before it was sown, and when Athamas consulted the oracle on the subject, persuaded the messengers to bring back word, that Phrixus must be sacrificed to Jupiter. Athamas was imposed upon, and prepared to offer his son; but Nephelé snatched Phrixus from the altar, and placed him upon a ram with a golden fleece which she had obtained from Mercury, and the ram carried him through the air to Colchis, where it was offered by Phrixus to Jupiter. The fleece he gave to Æetes the Colchian king.

reached the grove of the god, avoided it, and commanded his
army to do the like.   He also paid the same respect to the house
and precinct of the descendants of Athamas.

198. Such were the doing of Xerxes in Thessaly and in
Achæa.   From hence he passed on into Malis, along the shores
of a bay, in which there is an ebb and flow of the tide daily.[1]
By the side of this bay lies a piece of flat land, in one part
broad, but in another very narrow indeed, around which runs
a range of lofty hills, impossible to climb, enclosing all Malis
within them, and called the Trachinian cliffs.   The first city
upon the bay, as you come from Achæa, is Anticyra, near which
the river Spercheius, flowing down from the country of the
Enianians, empties itself into the sea.   About twenty furlongs
from this stream there is a second river, called the Dyras,[2] which
is said to have appeared first to help Hercules when he was
burning.   Again, at the distance of twenty furlongs, there is a
stream called the Melas, near which, within about five furlongs,
stands the city of Trachis.

199. At the point where this city is built, the plain between
the hills and the sea is broader than at any other, for it there
measures 22,000 plethra.[3]   South of Trachis there is a cleft in
the mountain-range which shuts in the territory of Trachinia;
and the river Asôpus [4] issuing from this cleft flows for a while
along the foot of the hills.

200. Further to the south, another river, called the Phœnix,
which has no great body of water, flows from the same hills,
and falls into the Asôpus.   Here is the narrowest place of all;
for in this part there is only a causeway wide enough for a
single carriage.   From the river Phœnix to Thermopylæ is a
distance of fifteen furlongs; and in this space is situate the
village called Anthêla, which the river Asôpus passes ere it
reaches the sea.   The space about Anthêla is of some width,
and contains a temple of Amphictyonian Ceres, as well as the

---

[1] The tides in the Mediterranean seldom rise more than a few feet, in
some places not above 12 or 13 inches.   The flatness of the coast round the
Maliac Gulf would render the rise and fall more perceptible there than
elsewhere.
[2] Colonel Leake has satisfactorily identified this stream as well as the
Melas.
[3] This is certainly an incorrect reading.   Twenty-two thousand plethra
are above 420 miles, whereas the plain is even now, at the utmost, seven
miles across.
[4] The Asôpus is clearly the *Karvunaria*.

seats of the Amphictyonic deputies,[1] and a temple of Amphictyon himself.[2]

201. King Xerxes pitched his camp in the region of Malis called Trachinia, while on their side the Greeks occupied the straits. These straits the Greeks in general call Thermopylæ (the Hot Gates); but the natives, and those who dwell in the neighbourhood, call them Pylæ (the Gates). Here then the two armies took their stand; the one master of all the region lying north of Trachis, the other of the country extending southward of that place to the verge of the continent.

202. The Greeks who at this spot awaited the coming of Xerxes were the following:—From Sparta, three hundred men-at-arms: from Arcadia, a thousand Tegeans and Mantineans, five hundred of each people; a hundred and twenty Orchomenians, from the Arcadian Orchomenus;[3] and a thousand from other cities: from Corinth, four hundred men: from Phlius, two hundred: and from Mycenæ eighty. Such was the number from the Peloponnese. There were also present, from Bœotia, seven hundred Thespians and four hundred Thebans.

203. Besides these troops, the Locrians of Opus and the Phocians had obeyed the call of their countrymen, and sent, the former all the force they had, the latter a thousand men. For envoys had gone from the Greeks at Thermopylæ among the Locrians and Phocians, to call on them for assistance, and to say—" They were themselves but the vanguard of the host, sent to precede the main body, which might every day be expected to follow them. The sea was in good keeping, watched by the Athenians, the Eginetans, and the rest of the fleet. There was no cause why they should fear; for after all the invader was not a god but a man; and there never had been, and never would be, a man who was not liable to misfortunes from the very day of his birth, and those misfortunes greater in proportion to his own greatness. The assailant therefore, being only a mortal, must needs fall from his glory." Thus urged, the Locrians and the Phocians had come with their troops to Trachis.

204. The various nations had each captains of their own

---

[1] Amphictyonies were religious leagues of states possessing a common sanctuary.

[2] Amphictyon would seem to be most clearly an invented name, formed, according to the Greek custom of referring all appellatives to a *heros eponymus*, from the word Amphictyony.

[3] The Arcadian is here distinguished from the Bœotian city of the same name (infra, viii. 34).

under whom they served; but the one to whom all especially
looked up, and who had the command of the entire force, was
the Lacedæmonian, Leonidas. Now Leonidas was the son of
Anaxandridas, who was the son of Leo, who was the son of
Eurycratidas, who was the son of Anaxander, who was the son
of Eurycrates, who was the son of Polydôrus, who was the son of
Alcamenes, who was the son of Têlecles, who was the son of Arche-
laüs, who was the son of Agesilaüs, who was the son of Doryssus,
who was the son of Labôtas, who was the son of Echestratus,
who was the son of Agis, who was the son of Eurysthenes, who
was the son of Aristodêmus, who was the son of Aristomachus,
who was the son of Cleodæus, who was the son of Hyllus, who
was the son of Hercules.

Leonidas had come to be king of Sparta quite unexpectedly.

205. Having two elder brothers, Cleomenes and Dorieus, he
had no thought of ever mounting the throne. However, when
Cleomenes died without male offspring, as Dorieus was likewise
deceased, having perished in Sicily,[1] the crown fell to Leonidas,
who was older than Cleombrotus, the youngest of the sons of
Anaxandridas, and, moreover, was married to the daughter of
Cleomenes. He had now come to Thermopylæ, accompanied
by the three hundred[2] men which the law assigned him, whom
he had himself chosen from among the citizens, and who were
all of them fathers with sons living. On his way he had taken
the troops from Thebes, whose number I have already mentioned, and who were under the command of Leontiades the
son of Eurymachus. The reason why he made a point of taking
troops from Thebes, and Thebes only, was, that the Thebans
were strongly suspected of being well inclined to the Medes.
Leonidas therefore called on them to come with him to the war,
wishing to see whether they would comply with his demand, or
openly refuse, and disclaim the Greek alliance. They, however,
though their wishes leant the other way, nevertheless sent the
men.

206. The force with Leonidas was sent forward by the
Spartans in advance of their main body, that the sight of them
might encourage the allies to fight, and hinder them from going

---

[1] Supra, v. 46.
[2] Leonidas seems to have been fully aware of the desperate nature of the
service which he now undertook. He therefore, instead of taking with him
his ordinary bodyguard of *youths*, selected a bodyguard from among the
men of advanced age, taking none but such as had male offspring living,
in order that no family might altogether perish.

over to the Medes, as it was likely they might have done had they seen that Sparta was backward. They intended presently, when they had celebrated the Carneian festival,[1] which was what now kept them at home, to leave a garrison in Sparta, and hasten in full force to join the army. The rest of the allies also intended to act similarly; for it happened that the Olympic festival fell exactly at this same period.[2] None of them looked to see the contest at Thermopylæ decided so speedily; wherefore they were content to send forward a mere advanced guard. Such accordingly were the intentions of the allies.

207. The Greek forces at Thermopylæ, when the Persian army drew near to the entrance of the pass, were seized with fear; and a council was held to consider about a retreat. It was the wish of the Peloponnesians generally that the army should fall back upon the Peloponnese, and there guard the Isthmus. But Leonidas, who saw with what indignation the Phocians and Locrians heard of this plan, gave his voice for remaining where they were, while they sent envoys to the several cities to ask for help, since they were too few to make a stand against an army like that of the Medes.

208. While this debate was going on, Xerxes sent a mounted spy to observe the Greeks, and note how many they were, and see what they were doing. He had heard, before he came out of Thessaly, that a few men were assembled at this place, and that at their head were certain Lacedæmonians, under Leonidas, a descendant of Hercules. The horseman rode up to the camp, and looked about him, but did not see the whole army; for such as were on the further side of the wall (which had been rebuilt and was now carefully guarded) it was not possible for him to behold; but he observed those on the outside, who were encamped in front of the rampart. It chanced that at this time the Lacedæmonians held the outer guard, and were seen by the spy, some of them engaged in gymnastic exercises, others combing their long hair. At this the spy greatly marvelled, but he counted their number, and when he had taken accurate note of everything, he rode back quietly; for no one pursued after him, nor paid any heed to his visit. So he returned, and told Xerxes all that he had seen.

[1] The Carneian festival fell in the Spartan month Carneius, the Athenian Metageitnion, corresponding nearly to our August. It was held in honour of Apollo Carneius.

[2] Vide infra, viii. 26. The Olympic festival was celebrated at the time of the first full moon after the summer solstice. It therefore ordinarily preceded the Spartan Carneia, falling in the latter end of June or in July.

209. Upon this, Xerxes, who had no means of surmising the truth—namely, that the Spartans were preparing to do or die manfully—but thought it laughable that they should be engaged in such employments, sent and called to his presence Demaratus the son of Ariston, who still remained with the army. When he appeared, Xerxes told him all that he had heard, and questioned him concerning the news, since he was anxious to understand the meaning of such behaviour on the part of the Spartans. Then Demaratus said—

" I spake to thee, O king! concerning these men long since,[1] when we had but just begun our march upon Greece; thou, however, didst only laugh at my words, when I told thee of all this, which I saw would come to pass. Earnestly do I struggle at all times to speak truth to thee, sire; and now listen to it once more. These men have come to dispute the pass with us; and it is for this that they are now making ready. 'Tis their custom, when they are about to hazard their lives, to adorn their heads with care.[2] Be assured, however, that if thou canst subdue the men who are here and the Lacedæmonians who remain in Sparta, there is no other nation in all the world which will venture to lift a hand in their defence. Thou hast now to deal with the first kingdom and town in Greece, and with the bravest men."

Then Xerxes, to whom what Demaratus said seemed altogether to surpass belief, asked further, " how it was possible for so small an army to contend with his? "

" O king! " Demaratus answered, " let me be treated as a liar, if matters fall not out as I say."

210. But Xerxes was not persuaded any the more. Four whole days he suffered to go by, expecting that the Greeks would run away. When, however, he found on the fifth that they were not gone, thinking that their firm stand was mere impudence and recklessness, he grew wroth, and sent against them the Medes and Cissians, with orders to take them alive and bring them into his presence. Then the Medes rushed forward and charged the Greeks, but fell in vast numbers: others however took the places of the slain, and would not be beaten off, though they suffered terrible losses. In this way it became clear to all, and especially to the king, that though he

---

[1] Supra, chs. 101-104.
[2] The Spartan custom of wearing the hair long has been already noticed (supra, i. 82).

had plenty of combatants, he had but very few warriors. The struggle, however, continued during the whole day.

211. Then the Medes, having met so rough a reception, withdrew from the fight; and their place was taken by the band of Persians under Hydarnes, whom the king called his " Immortals:" [1] they, it was thought, would soon finish the business. But when they joined battle with the Greeks, 'twas with no better success than the Median detachment—things went much as before—the two armies fighting in a narrow space, and the barbarians using shorter spears than the Greeks, and having no advantage from their numbers. The Lacedæmonians fought in a way worthy of note, and showed themselves far more skilful in fight than their adversaries, often turning their backs, and making as though they were all flying away, on which the barbarians would rush after them with much noise and shouting, when the Spartans at their approach would wheel round and face their pursuers, in this way destroying vast numbers of the enemy. Some Spartans likewise fell in these encounters, but only a very few. At last the Persians, finding that all their efforts to gain the pass availed nothing, and that, whether they attacked by divisions or in any other way, it was to no purpose, withdrew to their own quarters.

212. During these assaults, it is said that Xerxes, who was watching the battle, thrice leaped from the throne on which he sate, in terror for his army.

Next day the combat was renewed, but with no better success on the part of the barbarians. The Greeks were so few that the barbarians hoped to find them disabled, by reason of their wounds, from offering any further resistance; and so they once more attacked them. But the Greeks were drawn up in detachments according to their cities, and bore the brunt of the battle in turns,—all except the Phocians, who had been stationed on the mountain to guard the pathway. So, when the Persians found no difference between that day and the preceding, they again retired to their quarters.

213. Now, as the king was in a great strait, and knew not how he should deal with the emergency, Ephialtes, the son of Eurydêmus, a man of Malis, came to him and was admitted to a conference. Stirred by the hope of receiving a rich reward at the king's hands, he had come to tell him of the pathway which led across the mountain to Thermopylæ; by which disclosure he

[1] Supra, ch. 83.

brought destruction on the band of Greeks who had there withstood the barbarians. This Ephialtes afterwards, from fear of
the Lacedæmonians, fled into Thessaly; and during his exile, in
an assembly of the Amphictyons held at Pylæ, a price was set
upon his head by the Pylagoræ. When some time had gone
by, he returned from exile, and went to Anticyra, where he was
slain by Athênades, a native of Trachis. Athênades did not
slay him for his treachery, but for another reason, which I shall
mention in a later part of my history: yet still the Lacedæmonians honoured him none the less. Thus then did Ephialtes
perish a long time afterwards.

214. Besides this there is another story told, which I do not
at all believe—to wit, that Onêtas the son of Phanagoras, a
native of Carystus, and Corydallus, a man of Anticyra, were the
persons who spoke on this matter to the king, and took the
Persians across the mountain. One may guess which story is
true, from the fact that the deputies of the Greeks, the Pylagoræ, who must have had the best means of ascertaining the
truth, did not offer the reward for the heads of Onêtas and
Corydallus, but for that of Ephialtes of Trachis; and again from
the flight of Ephialtes, which we know to have been on this
account. Onêtas, I allow, although he was not a Malian, might
have been acquainted with the path, if he had lived much in
that part of the country; but as Ephialtes was the person who
actually led the Persians round the mountain by the pathway,
I leave his name on record as that of the man who did the
deed.

215. Great was the joy of Xerxes on this occasion; and as he
approved highly of the enterprise which Ephialtes undertook
to accomplish, he forthwith sent upon the errand Hydarnes, and
the Persians under him.[1] The troops left the camp about the
time of the lighting of the lamps. The pathway along which
they went was first discovered by the Malians of these parts, who
soon afterwards led the Thessalians by it to attack the Phocians,
at the time when the Phocians fortified the pass with a wall,[2]
and so put themselves under covert from danger. And ever
since, the path has always been put to an ill use by the
Malians.

216. The course which it takes is the following:—Beginning
at the Asôpus, where that stream flows through the cleft in the
hills,[3] it runs along the ridge of the mountain (which is called,

[1] The 10,000 Immortals.   [2] Supra, ch. 176.   [3] Supra, ch. 199.

like the pathway over it, Anopæa), and ends at the city of Alpênus—the first Locrian town as you come from Malis—by the stone called Melampygus and the seats of the Cercopians. Here it is as narrow as at any other point.

217. The Persians took this path, and, crossing the Asôpus, continued their march through the whole of the night, having the mountains of Œta on their right hand, and on their left those of Trachis. At dawn of day they found themselves close to the summit. Now the hill was guarded, as I have already said,[1] by a thousand Phocian men-at-arms, who were placed there to defend the pathway, and at the same time to secure their own country. They had been given the guard of the mountain path, while the other Greeks defended the pass below, because they had volunteered for the service, and had pledged themselves to Leonidas to maintain the post.

218. The ascent of the Persians became known to the Phocians in the following manner:—During all the time that they were making their way up, the Greeks remained unconscious of it, inasmuch as the whole mountain was covered with groves of oak; but it happened that the air was very still, and the leaves which the Persians stirred with their feet made, as it was likely they would, a loud rustling, whereupon the Phocians jumped up and flew to seize their arms. In a moment the barbarians came in sight, and, perceiving men arming themselves, were greatly amazed; for they had fallen in with an enemy when they expected no opposition. Hydarnes, alarmed at the sight, and fearing lest the Phocians might be Lacedæmonians, inquired of Ephialtes to what nation these troops belonged. Ephialtes told him the exact truth, whereupon he arrayed his Persians for battle. The Phocians, galled by the showers of arrows to which they were exposed, and imagining themselves the special object of the Persian attack, fled hastily to the crest of the mountain, and there made ready to meet death; but while their mistake continued, the Persians, with Ephialtes and Hydarnes, not thinking it worth their while to delay on account of Phocians, passed on and descended the mountain with all possible speed.

219. The Greeks at Thermopylæ received the first warning of the destruction which the dawn would bring on them from the seer Megistias,[2] who read their fate in the victims as he was sacrificing. After this deserters came in, and brought the

---

[1] Supra, ch. 212.　　　　　　　　[2] Infra, chs. 221 and 228.

news that the Persians were marching round by the hills: it was still night when these men arrived. Last of all, the scouts came running down from the heights, and brought in the same accounts, when the day was just beginning to break. Then the Greeks held a council to consider what they should do, and here opinions were divided: some were strong against quitting their post, while others contended to the contrary. So when the council had broken up, part of the troops departed and went their ways homeward to their several states; part however resolved to remain, and to stand by Leonidas to the last.

220. It is said that Leonidas himself sent away the troops who departed, because he tendered their safety, but thought it unseemly that either he or his Spartans should quit the post which they had been especially sent to guard. For my own part, I incline to think that Leonidas gave the order, because he perceived the allies to be out of heart and unwilling to encounter the danger to which his own mind was made up. He therefore commanded them to retreat, but said that he himself could not draw back with honour; knowing that, if he stayed, glory awaited him, and that Sparta in that case would not lose her prosperity. For when the Spartans, at the very beginning of the war, sent to consult the oracle concerning it, the answer which they received from the Pythoness was, " that either Sparta must be overthrown by the barbarians, or one of her kings must perish." The prophecy was delivered in hexameter verse, and ran thus:—

" O ye men who dwell in the streets of broad Lacedæmon!
　Either your glorious town shall be sacked by the children of Perseus,
　Or, in exchange, must all through the whole Laconian country
　Mourn for the loss of a king, descendant of great Hêrácles.
　He cannot be withstood by the courage of bulls nor of lions,
　Strive as they may; he is mighty as Jove; there is nought that shall stay
　　him,
　Till he have got for his prey your king, or your glorious city."

The remembrance of this answer, I think, and the wish to secure the whole glory for the Spartans, caused Leonidas to send the allies away. This is more likely than that they quarrelled with him, and took their departure in such unruly fashion.

221. To me it seems no small argument in favour of this view, that the seer also who accompanied the army, Megistias, the Acarnanian,[1]—said to have been of the blood of Melampus,[2] and

---

[1] The celebrity of the Acarnanian seers has been already mentioned (supra, i. 62).

[2] Melampus was placed in the generation before the Trojan war.

the same who was led by the appearance of the victims to warn
the Greeks of the danger which threatened them,—received
orders to retire (as it is certain he did) from Leonidas, that he
might escape the coming destruction.   Megistias, however,
though bidden to depart, refused, and stayed with the army;
but he had an only son present with the expedition, whom he
now sent away.

222. So the allies, when Leonidas ordered them to retire,
obeyed him and forthwith departed.   Only the Thespians and
the Thebans remained with the Spartans; and of these the
Thebans were kept back by Leonidas as hostages, very much
against their will.   The Thespians, on the contrary, stayed
entirely of their own accord, refusing to retreat, and declaring
that they would not forsake Leonidas and his followers.   So
they abode with the Spartans, and died with them.   Their
leader was Demophilus, the son of Diadromes.

223. At sunrise Xerxes made libations, after which he waited
until the time when the forum is wont to fill, and then began
his advance.   Ephialtes had instructed him thus, as the descent
of the mountain is much quicker, and the distance much shorter,
than the way round the hills, and the ascent.   So the barbarians under Xerxes began to draw nigh; and the Greeks under
Leonidas, as they now went forth determined to die, advanced
much further than on previous days, until they reached the
more open portion of the pass.   Hitherto they had held their
station within the wall, and from this had gone forth to fight
at the point where the pass was the narrowest.   Now they
joined battle beyond the defile, and carried slaughter among the
barbarians, who fell in heaps.   Behind them the captains of the
squadrons, armed with whips, urged their men forward with
continual blows.   Many were thrust into the sea, and there
perished; a still greater number were trampled to death by
their own soldiers; no one heeded the dying.   For the Greeks,
reckless of their own safety and desperate, since they knew that,
as the mountain had been crossed, their destruction was nigh at
hand, exerted themselves with the most furious valour against
the barbarians.

224. By this time the spears of the greater number were all
shivered, and with their swords they hewed down the ranks of
the Persians; and here, as they strove, Leonidas fell fighting
bravely, together with many other famous Spartans, whose
names I have taken care to learn on account of their great

worthiness, as indeed I have those of all the three hundred. There fell too at the same time very many famous Persians: among them, two sons of Darius, Abrocomes and Hyperanthes, his children by Phratiguné, the daughter of Artanes. Artanes was brother of King Darius, being a son of Hystaspes, the son of Arsames; and when he gave his daughter to the king, he made him heir likewise of all his substance; for she was his only child.

225. Thus two brothers of Xerxes here fought and fell. And now there arose a fierce struggle between the Persians and the Lacedæmonians over the body of Leonidas, in which the Greeks four times drove back the enemy, and at last by their great bravery succeeded in bearing off the body. This combat was scarcely ended when the Persians with Ephialtes approached; and the Greeks, informed that they drew nigh, made a change in the manner of their fighting. Drawing back into the narrowest part of the pass, and retreating even behind the cross wall, they posted themselves upon a hillock, where they stood all drawn up together in one close body, except only the Thebans. The hillock whereof I speak is at the entrance of the straits, where the stone lion stands which was set up in honour of Leonidas.[1] Here they defended themselves to the last, such as still had swords using them, and the others resisting with their hands and teeth; till the barbarians, who in part had pulled down the wall and attacked them in front, in part had gone round and now encircled them upon every side, overwhelmed and buried the remnant which was left beneath showers of missile weapons.

226. Thus nobly did the whole body of Lacedæmonians and Thespians behave; but nevertheless one man is said to have distinguished himself above all the rest, to wit, Diêneces the Spartan. A speech which he made before the Greeks engaged the Medes, remains on record. One of the Trachinians told him, " Such was the number of the barbarians, that when they shot forth their arrows the sun would be darkened by their multitude." Diêneces, not at all frightened at these words, but making light of the Median numbers, answered, " Our Trachinian friend brings us excellent tidings. If the Medes darken the sun, we shall have our fight in the shade." Other sayings too of a like nature are reported to have been left on record by this same person.

---

[1] The monument seems to have been standing at least as late as the time of Tiberius.

227. Next to him two brothers, Lacedæmonians, are reputed to have made themselves conspicuous: they were named Alpheus and Maro, and were the sons of Orsiphantus. There was also a Thespian who gained greater glory than any of his countrymen: he was a man called Dithyrambus, the son of Harmatidas.

228. The slain were buried where they fell; and in their honour, nor less in honour of those who died before Leonidas sent the allies away, an inscription was set up, which said:—

> " Here did four thousand men from Pelops' land [1]
> Against three hundred myriads bravely stand."

This was in honour of all. Another was for the Spartans alone:—

> " Go, stranger, and to Lacedæmon tell
> That here, obeying her behests, we fell." [2]

This was for the Lacedæmonians. The seer had the following:—

> " The great Megistias' tomb you here may view,
> Whom slew the Medes, fresh from Spercheius' fords.
> Well the wise seer the coming death foreknew,
> Yet scorned he to forsake his Spartan lords."

These inscriptions, and the pillars likewise, were all set up by the Amphictyons, except that in honour of Megistias, which was inscribed to him (on account of their sworn friendship) by Simônides, the son of Leôprepes.[3]

229. Two of the three hundred, it is said, Aristodêmus and Eurytus, having been attacked by a disease of the eyes, had received orders from Leonidas to quit the camp; and both lay at Alpêni in the worst stage of the malady. These two men might, had they been so minded, have agreed together to return alive to Sparta; or if they did not like to return, they might have gone both to the field and fallen with their countrymen. But at this time, when either way was open to them, unhappily they could not agree, but took contrary courses. Eurytus no

---

[1] Herodotus seems to have misconceived this inscription. He regarded it as an epitaph upon the Greeks slain at Thermopylæ. Hence he sets the number of the slain at 4000 (infra, viii. 25). But it plainly appears from the wording to have been an inscription set up in honour of the *Peloponnesians* only, and to have referred to *all who fought*, not merely to those who fell.

[2] This famous inscription Cicero has translated in the Tusculans (i. 42):—
> " Dic, hospes, Spartæ nos te hîc vidisse jacentes,
> Dum sanctis patriæ *legibus* obsequimur."

[3] Simonides was the poet laureate of the time.

sooner heard that the Persians had come round the mountain than straightway he called for his armour, and having buckled it on, bade his Helot [1] lead him to the place where his friends were fighting. The Helot did so, and then turned and fled; but Eurytus plunged into the thick of the battle, and so perished. Aristodêmus, on the other hand, was faint of heart, and remained at Alpêni. It is my belief that if Aristodêmus only had been sick and returned, or if both had come back together, the Spartans would have been content and felt no anger; but when there were two men with the very same excuse, and one of them was chary of his life, while the other freely gave it, they could not but be very wroth with the former.

230. This is the account which some give of the escape of Aristodêmus. Others say that he, with another, had been sent on a message from the army, and, having it in his power to return in time for the battle, purposely loitered on the road, and so survived his comrades; while his fellow-messenger came back in time, and fell in the battle.

231. When Aristodêmus returned to Lacedæmon, reproach and disgrace awaited him; disgrace, inasmuch as no Spartan would give him a light to kindle his fire, or so much as address a word to him; and reproach, since all spoke of him as "the craven." However he wiped away all his shame afterwards at the battle of Platæa. [2]

232. Another of the three hundred is likewise said to have survived the battle, a man named Pantites, whom Leonidas had sent on an embassy into Thessaly. He, they say, on his return to Sparta, found himself in such disesteem that he hanged himself.

233. The Thebans under the command of Leontiades remained with the Greeks, and fought against the barbarians, only so long as necessity compelled them. No sooner did they see victory inclining to the Persians, and the Greeks under Leonidas hurrying with all speed towards the hillock, than they moved away from their companions, and with hands upraised advanced towards the barbarians, exclaiming, as was indeed most true,—"that they for their part wished well to the Medes, and had been among the first to give earth and water to the king; force alone had brought them to Thermopylæ; and so

[1] By the expression "his Helot," we are to understand the special servant ($\theta\epsilon\rho\acute{a}\pi\omega\nu$), whose business it was to attend constantly upon the Spartan warrior.

[2] Vide infra, ix. 71.

they must not be blamed for the slaughter which had befallen the king's army." These words, the truth of which was attested by the Thessalians, sufficed to obtain the Thebans the grant of their lives. However, their good fortune was not without some drawback; for several of them were slain by the barbarians on their first approach; and the rest, who were the greater number, had the royal mark branded upon their bodies by the command of Xerxes,—Leontiades, their captain, being the first to suffer. (This man's son, Eurymachus, was afterwards slain by the Platæans, when he came with a band of 400 Thebans, and seized their city.)

234. Thus fought the Greeks at Thermopylæ. And Xerxes, after the fight was over, called for Demaratus to question him; and began as follows:—

"Demaratus, thou art a worthy man; thy true-speaking proves it. All has happened as thou didst forewarn. Now then, tell me, how many Lacedæmonians are there left, and of those left how many are such brave warriors as these? Or are they all alike?"

"O king!" replied the other, "the whole number of the Lacedæmonians is very great; and many are the cities which they inhabit. But I will tell thee what thou really wishest to learn. There is a town of Lacedæmon called Sparta, which contains within it about eight thousand full-grown men. *They* are, one and all, equal to those who have fought here. The other Lacedæmonians are brave men, but not such warriors as these."

"Tell me now, Demaratus," rejoined Xerxes, "how we may with least trouble subdue these men. Thou must know all the paths of their counsels, as thou wert once their king."

235. Then Demaratus answered—"O king! since thou askest my advice so earnestly, it is fitting that I should inform thee what I consider to be the best course. Detach three hundred vessels from the body of thy fleet, and send them to attack the shores of Laconia. There is an island called Cythera in those parts, not far from the coast, concerning which Chilon, one of our wisest men,[1] made the remark, that Sparta would gain if it were sunk to the bottom of the sea—so constantly did he expect that it would give occasion to some project like that which I

[1] Chilon was included among the seven wise men. The maxims " γνῶθι σεαυτόν " (know thyself) and " μηδὲν ἄγαν " (nothing in excess) were ascribed to him.

now recommend to thee.   I mean not to say that he had a fore-knowledge of thy attack upon Greece; but in truth he feared all armaments.   Send thy ships then to this island, and thence affright the Spartans.   If once they have a war of their own close to their doors, fear not their giving any help to the rest of the Greeks while thy land force is engaged in conquering them. In this way may all Greece be subdued; and then Sparta, left to herself, will be powerless.   But if thou wilt not take this advice, I will tell thee what thou mayest look to see.   When thou comest to the Peloponnese, thou wilt find a narrow neck of land, where all the Peloponnesians who are leagued against thee will be gathered together; and there thou wilt have to fight bloodier battles than any which thou hast yet witnessed.   If, however, thou wilt follow my plan, the Isthmus and the cities of Peloponnese will yield to thee without a battle."

236. Achæmenes, who was present, now took the word, and spoke—he was brother to Xerxes, and, having the command of the fleet, feared lest Xerxes might be prevailed upon to do as Demaratus advised—

"I perceive, O king" (he said), "that thou art listening to the words of a man who is envious of thy good fortune, and seeks to betray thy cause.   This is indeed the common temper of the Grecian people—they envy good fortune, and hate power greater than their own.   If in this posture of our affairs, after we have lost four hundred vessels by shipwreck,[1] three hundred more be sent away to make a voyage round the Peloponnese, our enemies will become a match for us.   But let us keep our whole fleet in one body, and it will be dangerous for them to venture on an attack, as they will certainly be no match for us then.   Besides, while our sea and land forces advance together, the fleet and army can each help the other; but if they be parted, no aid will come either from thee to the fleet, or from the fleet to thee.   Only order thy own matters well, and trouble not thyself to inquire concerning the enemy,—where they will fight, or what they will do, or how many they are.   Surely they can manage their own concerns without us, as we can ours without them.   If the Lacedæmonians come out against the Persians to battle, they will scarce repair the disaster which has befallen them now."

237. Xerxes replied—"Achæmenes, thy counsel pleases me well, and I will do as thou sayest.   But Demaratus advised

[1] Supra, ch. 190.

what he thought best—only his judgment was not so good as thine. Never will I believe that he does not wish well to my cause; for that is disproved both by his former counsels, and also by the circumstances of the case. A citizen does indeed envy any fellow-citizen who is more lucky than himself, and often hates him secretly; if such a man be called on for counsel, he will not give his best thoughts, unless indeed he be a man of very exalted virtue; and such are but rarely found. But a friend of another country delights in the good fortune of his foreign bond-friend, and will give him, when asked, the best advice in his power. Therefore I warn all men to abstain henceforth from speaking ill of Demaratus, who is my bond-friend."

238. When Xerxes had thus spoken, he proceeded to pass through the slain; and finding the body of Leonidas, whom he knew to have been the Lacedæmonian king and captain, he ordered that the head should be struck off, and the trunk fastened to a cross. This proves to me most clearly, what is plain also in many other ways,—namely, that King Xerxes was more angry with Leonidas, while he was still in life, than with any other mortal. Certes, he would not else have used his body so shamefully. For the Persians are wont to honour those who show themselves valiant in fight more highly than any nation that I know. They, however, to whom the orders were given, did according to the commands of the king.

239. I return now to a point in my History, which at the time I left incomplete. The Lacedæmonians were the first of the Greeks to hear of the king's design against their country; and it was at this time that they sent to consult the Delphic oracle, and received the answer of which I spoke a while ago.[1] The discovery was made to them in a very strange way. Demaratus, the son of Ariston, after he took refuge with the Medes, was not, in my judgment, which is supported by probability, a well-wisher to the Lacedæmonians. It may be questioned, therefore, whether he did what I am about to mention from good-will or from insolent triumph. It happened that he was at Susa at the time when Xerxes determined to lead his army into Greece; and in this way becoming acquainted with his design, he resolved to send tidings of it to Sparta. So as there was no other way of effecting his purpose, since the danger of being discovered was great, Demaratus framed the following contrivance. He

[1] Supra, ch. 220.

took a pair of tablets, and, clearing the wax away from them, wrote what the king was purposing to do upon the wood whereof the tablets were made; having done this, he spread the wax once more over the writing, and so sent it.   By these means, the guards placed to watch the roads, observing nothing but a blank tablet, were sure to give no trouble to the bearer.   When the tablet reached Lacedæmon, there was no one, I understand, who could find out the secret, till Gorgo, the daughter of Cleomenes and wife of Leonidas, discovered it, and told the others.   " If they would scrape the wax off the tablet," she said, " they would be sure to find the writing upon the wood."   The Lacedæmonians took her advice, found the writing, and read it; [1] after which they sent it round to the other Greeks.   Such then is the account which is given of this matter.

[1] Here we have one out of many instances of the common practice of writing among the Spartans, so strangely called in question by Grote.

ADDED NOTES BY THE EDITOR

(1.) *The Character of Xerxes.*—Unlike Cyrus, who was a great soldier, or Darius, who was a clear-headed statesman, Xerxes was typical of the Persian character on its weakest side.   He trusted to mere numbers to win the day at Salamis and elsewhere, forgetting that battles (as Herodotus implies) are fought with the head as well as with the hands.   As a ruler, he was arbitrary and unscrupulous; as a man, effeminate, extravagant, and cruel.

(2.) *The Battle of Salamis* (book viii.).   The story of this decisive battle is clear enough in the pages of Herodotus; but we have the good luck to possess the statement of an eye-witness, in the poetical description given us in the *Persæ* of Æschylus (ll. 355-434).   This fine battle-picture should be carefully studied—see the verse rendering in Prof. Lewis Campbell's translation of the plays of Æschylus (Oxford University Press: price 1s.).   Readers will, perhaps, recall Byron's lines (*Don Juan*, canto iii.):—

> " A king sate on the rocky brow
>   That looks o'er sea-born Salamis;
> And ships, by thousands, lay below,
>   And men in nations,—all were his!
> He counted them at break of day—
>   And, when the sun set, where were they? "

Compare book viii. chap. 90.

THE EIGHTH BOOK, ENTITLED URANIA

1. THE Greeks engaged in the sea-service were the following. The Athenians furnished a hundred and twenty-seven vessels to the fleet, which were manned in part by the Platæans, who, though unskilled in such matters, were led by their active and daring spirit to undertake this duty; the Corinthians furnished a contingent of forty vessels; the Megarians sent twenty; the Chalcideans also manned twenty, which had been furnished to them by the Athenians;[1] the Eginetans came with eighteen; the Sicyonians with twelve; the Lacedæmonians with ten; the Epidaurians with eight; the Eretrians with seven; the Trœzenians with five; the Styreans with two; and the Cêans[2] with two triremes and two penteconters. Last of all, the Locrians of Opus came in aid with a squadron of seven penteconters.

2. Such were the nations which furnished vessels to the fleet now at Artemisium; and in mentioning them I have given the number of ships furnished by each. The total number of the ships thus brought together, without counting the penteconters, was two hundred and seventy-one; and the captain, who had the chief command over the whole fleet, was Eurybiades the son of Eurycleides. He was furnished by Sparta, since the allies had said that, " if a Lacedæmonian did not take the command, they would break up the fleet, for never would they serve under the Athenians. "

3. From the first, even earlier than the time when the embassy went to Sicily[3] to solicit alliance, there had been a talk of intrusting the Athenians with the command at sea; but the allies were averse to the plan, wherefore the Athenians did not press it; for there was nothing they had so much at heart as the salvation of Greece, and they knew that, if they quarrelled among themselves about the command, Greece would be brought to ruin.[4] Herein they judged rightly; for internal strife is a thing as much worse than war carried on by a united people,

---

[1] These Chalcideans are beyond a doubt Athenian cleruchs or colonists.
[2] Ceos, one of the Cyclades, now *Tzia* or *Zea*, lies off the promontory of Sunium, at the distance of about 12 miles.
[3] Supra, vii. 153, et seqq.
[4] Athens prudently waived her claim.

215

as war itself is worse than peace. The Athenians therefore, being so persuaded, did not push their claims, but waived them, so long as they were in such great need of aid from the other Greeks. And they afterwards showed their motive; for at the time when the Persians had been driven from Greece, and were now threatened by the Greeks in their own country, they took occasion of the insolence of Pausanias to deprive the Lacedæmonians of their leadership. This, however, happened afterwards.

4. At the present time the Greeks, on their arrival at Artemisium, when they saw the number of the ships which lay at anchor near Aphetæ, and the abundance of troops everywhere, feeling disappointed that matters had gone with the barbarians so far otherwise than they had expected, and full of alarm at what they saw, began to speak of drawing back from Artemisium towards the inner parts of their country. So when the Eubœans heard what was in debate, they went to Eurybiades, and besought him to wait a few days, while they removed their children and their slaves to a place of safety. But, as they found that they prevailed nothing, they left him and went to Themistocles, the Athenian commander, to whom they gave a bribe of thirty talents,[1] on his promise that the fleet should remain and risk a battle in defence of Eubœa.

5. And Themistocles succeeded in detaining the fleet in the way which I will now relate. He made over to Eurybiades five talents out of the thirty paid him, which he gave as if they came from himself; and having in this way gained over the admiral, he addressed himself to Adeimantus, the son of Ocytus, the Corinthian leader, who was the only remonstrant now, and who still threatened to sail away from Artemisium and not wait for the other captains. Addressing himself to this man, Themistocles said with an oath,—" Thou forsake us? By no means! I will pay thee better for remaining than the Mede would for leaving thy friends "—and straightway he sent on board the ship of Adeimantus a present of three talents of silver. So these two captains were won by gifts, and came over to the views of Themistocles, who was thereby enabled to gratify the wishes of the Eubœans. He likewise made his own gain on the occasion; for he kept the rest of the money, and no one knew of it. The commanders who took the gifts thought that the sums were furnished by Athens, and had been sent to be used in this way.

[1] Thirty talents would be above £7000 of our money.

6. Thus it came to pass that the Greeks stayed at Euboea and there gave battle to the enemy.

Now the battle was on this wise. The barbarians reached Aphetæ early in the afternoon, and then saw (as they had previously heard reported) that a fleet of Greek ships, weak in number, lay at Artemisium. At once they were eager to engage, fearing that the Greeks would fly, and hoping to capture them before they should get away. They did not however think it wise to make straight for the Greek station, lest the enemy should see them as they bore down, and betake themselves to flight immediately; in which case night might close in before they came up with the fugitives, and so they might get clean off and make their escape from them; whereas the Persians were minded not to let a single soul slip through their hands.

7. They therefore contrived a plan, which was the following:—They detached two hundred of their ships from the rest, and—to prevent the enemy from seeing them start—sent them round outside the island of Sciathos, to make the circuit of Euboea by Caphareus [1] and Geræstus, [2] and so to reach the Euripus. By this plan they thought to enclose the Greeks on every side; for the ships detached would block up the only way by which they could retreat, while the others would press upon them in front. With these designs therefore they dispatched the two hundred ships, while they themselves waited,—since they did not mean to attack the Greeks upon that day, or until they knew, by signal, of the arrival of the detachment which had been ordered to sail round Euboea. Meanwhile they made a muster of the other ships at Aphetæ.

8. Now the Persians had with them a man named Scyllias, a native of Scioné, who was the most expert diver of his day. At the time of the shipwreck off Mount Pelion he had recovered for the Persians a great part of what they lost; and at the same time he had taken care to obtain for himself a good share of the treasure. He had for some time been wishing to go over to the Greeks; but no good opportunity had offered till now, when the Persians were making the muster of their ships. In what way he contrived to reach the Greeks I am not able to say for certain: I marvel much if the tale that is commonly told be true. 'Tis

---

[1] Caphereus (or Caphareus) was the name of the south-eastern promontory of Euboea, now called *Capo Doro*.

[2] Geræstus was a town and promontory at the extreme southern point of Euboea.

said he dived into the sea at Aphetæ, and did not once come to the surface till he reached Artemisium, a distance of nearly eighty furlongs.[1] Now many things are related of this man which are plainly false; but some of the stories seem to be true. My own opinion is that on this occasion he made the passage to Artemisium in a boat.

However this might be, Scyllias no sooner reached Artemisium than he gave the Greek captains a full account of the damage done by the storm, and likewise told them of the ships sent to make the circuit of Euboea.

9. So the Greeks on receiving these tidings held a council, whereat, after much debate, it was resolved that they should stay quiet for the present where they were, and remain at their moorings, but that after midnight they should put out to sea, and encounter the ships which were on their way round the island. Later in the day, when they found that no one meddled with them, they formed a new plan, which was, to wait till near evening, and then sail out against the main body of the barbarians, for the purpose of trying their mode of fight and skill in manœuvring.

10. When the Persian commanders and crews saw the Greeks thus boldly sailing towards them with their few ships, they thought them possessed with madness,[2] and went out to meet them, expecting (as indeed seemed likely enough) that they would take all their vessels with the greatest ease. The Grᵉek ships were so few, and there own so far outnumbered them, and sailed so much better, that they resolved, seeing their advantage, to encompass their foe on every side. And now such of the Ionians as wished well to the Grecian cause and served in the Persian fleet unwillingly, seeing their countrymen surrounded, were sorely distressed; for they felt sure that not one of them would ever make his escape, so poor an opinion had they of the strength of the Greeks. On the other hand, such as saw with pleasure the attack on Greece, now vied eagerly with each other which should be the first to make prize of an Athenian ship, and thereby to secure himself a rich reward from the king. For through both the hosts none were so much accounted of as the Athenians.

11. The Greeks, at a signal, brought the sterns of their ships together into a small compass, and turned their prows on every

---

[1] The distance across the strait is about 7 miles.
[2] Vide supra, vi. 112.

side towards the barbarians; after which, at a second signal, although inclosed within a narrow space, and closely pressed upon by the foe, yet they fell bravely to work, and captured thirty ships of the barbarians, at the same time taking prisoner Philaon, the son of Chersis, and brother of Gorgus king of Salamis,[1] a man of much repute in the fleet. The first who made prize of a ship of the enemy was Lycomêdes the son of Æschreas, an Athenian, who was afterwards adjudged the meed of valour. Victory however was still doubtful when night came on, and put a stop to the combat. The Greeks sailed back to Artemisium; and the barbarians returned to Aphetæ, much surprised at the result, which was far other than they had looked for. In this battle only one of the Greeks who fought on the side of the king deserted and joined his countrymen. This was Antidôrus of Lemnos, whom the Athenians rewarded for his desertion by the present of a piece of land in Salamis.

12. Evening had barely closed in when a heavy rain—it was about midsummer [2]—began to fall, which continued the whole night, with terrible thunderings and lightnings from Mount Pelion: the bodies of the slain and the broken pieces of the damaged ships were drifted in the direction of Aphetæ, and floated about the prows of the vessels there, disturbing the action of the oars. The barbarians, hearing the storm, were greatly dismayed, expecting certainly to perish, as they had fallen into such a multitude of misfortunes. For before they were well recovered from the tempest and the wreck of their vessels off Mount Pelion, they had been surprised by a sea-fight which had taxed all their strength, and now the sea-fight was scarcely over when they were exposed to floods of rain, and the rush of swollen streams into the sea, and violent thunderings.

13. If, however, they who lay at Aphetæ passed a comfortless night, far worse were the sufferings of those who had been sent to make the circuit of Eubœa; inasmuch as the storm fell on them out at sea, whereby the issue was indeed calamitous. They were sailing along near the Hollows of Eubœa,[3] when the wind began to rise and the rain to pour: overpowered by

[1] Supra, v. 104.
[2] From this passage, and from the fact mentioned above (vii. 206), that the engagements at Thermopylæ and Artemisium coincided with the time of the Olympic games, we may be justified in fixing the battles to the latter part of June or the beginning of July.
[3] " The Hollows " seem to have had at all times a bad name among sailors.

the force of the gale, and driven they knew not whither, at the last they fell upon rocks,—Heaven so contriving, in order that the Persian fleet might not greatly exceed the Greek, but be brought nearly to its level. This squadron, therefore, was entirely lost about the Hollows of Eubœa.

14. The barbarians at Aphetæ were glad when day dawned, and remained in quiet at their station, content if they might enjoy a little peace after so many sufferings. Meanwhile there came to the aid of the Greeks a reinforcement of fifty-three ships from Attica.[1] Their arrival, and the news (which reached Artemisium about the same time) of the complete destruction by the storm of the ships sent to sail round Eubœa, greatly cheered the spirits of the Greek sailors. So they waited again till the same hour as the day before, and, once more putting out to sea, attacked the enemy. This time they fell in with some Cilician vessels, which they sank; when night came on, they withdrew to Artemisium.

15. The third day was now come, and the captains of the barbarians, ashamed that so small a number of ships should harass their fleet, and afraid of the anger of Xerxes, instead of waiting for the others to begin the battle, weighed anchor themselves, and advanced against the Greeks about the hour of noon, with shouts encouraging one another. Now it happened that these sea-fights took place on the very same days with the combats at Thermopylæ; and as the aim of the struggle was in the one case to maintain the pass, so in the other it was to defend the Euripus. While the Greeks, therefore, exhorted one another not to let the barbarians burst in upon Greece, these latter shouted to their fellows to destroy the Grecian fleet, and get possession of the channel.

16. And now the fleet of Xerxes advanced in good order to the attack, while the Greeks on their side remained quite motionless at Artemisium. The Persians therefore spread themselves, and came forward in a half-moon, seeking to encircle the Greeks on all sides, and thereby prevent them from escaping. The Greeks, when they saw this, sailed out to meet their assailants; and the battle forthwith began. In this engagement the two fleets contended with no clear advantage to either,—for the armament of Xerxes injured itself by its own greatness, the vessels falling into disorder, and oft-times running

---

[1] This seems to have been the whole of the Athenian reserve fleet. The policy of Themistocles had raised their navy of 200 vessels.

foul of one another; yet still they did not give way, but made a stout fight, since the crews felt it would indeed be a disgrace to turn and fly from a fleet so inferior in number. The Greeks therefore suffered much, both in ships and men; but the barbarians experienced a far larger loss of each. So the fleets separated after such a combat as I have described.

17. On the side of Xerxes the Egyptians distinguished themselves above all the combatants; for besides performing many other noble deeds, they took five vessels from the Greeks with their crews on board. On the side of the Greeks the Athenians bore off the meed of valour; and among them the most distinguished was Clinias, the son of Alcibiades, who served at his own charge with two hundred men,[1] on board a vessel which he had himself furnished.[2]

18. The two fleets, on separating, hastened very gladly to their anchorage-grounds. The Greeks, indeed, when the battle was over, became masters of the bodies of the slain and the wrecks of the vessels; but they had been so roughly handled, especially the Athenians, one-half of whose vessels had suffered damage, that they determined to break up from their station, and withdraw to the inner parts of their country.

19. Then Themistocles, who thought that if the Ionian and Carian ships could be detached from the barbarian fleet, the Greeks might be well able to defeat the rest, called the captains together. They met upon the sea-shore, where the Eubœans were now assembling their flocks and herds; and here Themistocles told them he thought that he knew of a plan whereby he could detach from the king those who were of most worth among his allies. This was all that he disclosed to them of his plan at that time. Meanwhile, looking to the circumstances in which they were, he advised them to slaughter as many of the Eubœan cattle as they liked—for it was better (he said) that their own troops should enjoy them than the enemy—and to give orders to their men to kindle the fires as usual. With regard to the retreat, he said that he would take upon himself to watch the proper moment, and would manage matters so that they should return to Greece without loss. These words pleased the captains; so they had the fires lighted, and began the slaughter of the cattle.

[1] This was the ordinary crew of a trireme.
[2] The state usually furnished the vessel and its equipment, the trierarch being bound to keep the whole in repair. Trierarchs often went to the expense of equipping their vessels at their own cost.

20. The Eubœans, until now, had made light of the oracle of Bacis, as though it had been void of all significancy, and had neither removed their goods from the island, nor yet taken them into their strong places; as they would most certainly have done if they had believed that war was approaching. By this neglect they had brought their affairs into the very greatest danger. Now the oracle of which I speak ran as follows:—

" When o'er the main shall be thrown a byblus yoke [1] by a stranger,
  Be thou ware, and drive from Eubœa the goats' loud-bleating."

So, as the Eubœans had paid no regard to this oracle when the evils approached and impended, now that they had arrived, the worst was likely to befall them.

21. While the Greeks were employed in the way described above,[2] the scout who had been on the watch at Trachis arrived at Artemisium. For the Greeks had employed two watchers:— Polyas, a native of Anticyra, had been stationed off Artemisium, with a row-boat at his command ready to sail at any moment, his orders being that, if an engagement took place by sea, he should convey the news at once to the Greeks at Thermopylæ; and in like manner Abrônychus, the son of Lysicles, an Athenian, had been stationed with a triaconter near Leonidas, to be ready, in case of disaster befalling the land force, to carry tidings of it to Artemisium. It was this Abrônychus who now arrived with news of what had befallen Leonidas and those who were with him. When the Greeks heard the tidings they no longer delayed to retreat, but withdrew in the order wherein they had been stationed, the Corinthians leading, and the Athenians sailing last of all.

22. And now Themistocles chose out the swiftest sailers from among the Athenian vessels, and, proceeding to the various watering-places along the coast, cut inscriptions on the rocks, which were read by the Ionians the day following, on their arrival at Artemisium. The inscriptions ran thus:—" Men of Ionia, ye do wrong to fight against your own fathers, and to give your help to enslave Greece. We beseech you therefore to come over, if possible, to our side: if you cannot do this, then, we pray you, stand aloof from the contest yourselves, and persuade the Carians to do the like. If neither of these things be possible, and you are hindered, by a force too strong to resist,

[1] [That is, a yoke (or *bridge*) fastened with cords of papyrus.—E. H. B.
[2] Supra, ch. 19, end.

from venturing upon desertion, at least when we come to blows fight backwardly, remembering that you are sprung from us, and that it was through you we first provoked the hatred of the barbarian."[1] Themistocles, in putting up these inscriptions, looked, I believe, to two chances—either Xerxes would not discover them, in which case they might bring over the Ionians to the side of the Greeks; or they would be reported to him and made a ground of accusation against the Ionians, who would thereupon be distrusted, and would not be allowed to take part in the sea-fights.

23. Shortly after the cutting of the inscriptions, a man of Histiæa went in a merchant-ship to Aphetæ, and told the Persians that the Greeks had fled from Artemisium. Disbelieving his report, the Persians kept the man a prisoner, while they sent some of their fastest vessels to see what had happened. These brought back word how matters stood; whereupon at sunrise the whole fleet advanced together in a body, and sailed to Artemisium, where they remained till mid-day; after which they went on to Histiæa.[2] That city fell into their hands immediately; and they shortly overran the various villages upon the coast in the district of Hellopia,[3] which was part of the Histiæan territory.

24. It was while they were at this station that a herald reached them from Xerxes, whom he had sent after making the following dispositions with respect to the bodies of those who fell at Thermopylæ. Of the twenty thousand who had been slain on the Persian side, he left one thousand upon the field while he buried the rest in trenches; and these he carefully filled up with earth, and hid with foliage, that the sailors might not see any signs of them. The herald, on reaching Histiæa, caused the whole force to be collected together, and spake thus to them:

"Comrades, King Xerxes gives permission to all who please, to quit their posts, and see how he fights with the senseless men who think to overthrow his armies."

25. No sooner had these words been uttered, than it became difficult to get a boat, so great was the number of those who desired to see the sight. Such as went crossed the strait, and

[1] Alluding to the assistance given by Athens to the Ionians in the great revolt.

[2] The most important town of northern Eubœa.

[3] The Hellopians, one of the early Pelasgic tribes, seem to have been the original inhabitants of Eubœa, which anciently bore the name of Hellopia.

passing among the heaps of dead, in this way viewed the spec-
tacle. Many Helots were included in the slain,[1] but every one
imagined that the bodies were all either Lacedæmonians or
Thespians. However, no one was deceived by what Xerxes had
done with his own dead. It was indeed most truly a laughable
device—on the one side a thousand men were seen lying about
the field, on the other four thousand crowded together into one
spot. This day then was given up to sight-seeing; on the next
the seamen embarked on board their ships and sailed back to
Histiæa, while Xerxes and his army proceeded upon their march.

26. There came now a few deserters from Arcadia to join the
Persians—poor men who had nothing to live on, and were in
want of employment. The Persians brought them into the
king's presence, and there inquired of them, by a man who
acted as their spokesman, " what the Greeks were doing? "
The Arcadians answered—" They are holding the Olympic
games, seeing the athletic sports and the chariot-races." " And
what," said the man, " is the prize for which they contend? "
" An olive-wreath," returned the others, " which is given to the
man who wins." On hearing this, Tritantæchmes, the son of
Artabanus,[2] uttered a speech which was in truth most noble,
but which caused him to be taxed with cowardice by King
Xerxes. Hearing the men say that the prize was not money
but a wreath of olive, he could not forbear from exclaiming
before them all: " Good heavens! Mardonius, what manner of
men are these against whom thou hast brought us to fight?—men
who contend with one another, not for money, but for honour! "

27. A little before this, and just after the blow had been
struck at Thermopylæ, a herald was sent into Phôcis by the
Thessalians, who had always been on bad terms with the
Phocians, and especially since their last overthrow. For it was
not many years previous to this invasion of Greece by the king,
that the Thessalians, with their allies, entered Phôcis in full
force, but were defeated by the Phocians in an engagement
wherein they were very roughly handled. The Phocians, who
had with them as soothsayer Tellias of Elis, were blocked up in
the mountain of Parnassus, when the following stratagem was
contrived for them by their Elean ally. He took six hundred
of their bravest men, and whitened their bodies and their arms

[1] Herodotus had not directly mentioned these Helots before. If they
bore the proportion, found elsewhere (infra, ix. 10, 28), of seven to each
Spartan, they must have amounted to 2100 men.

[2] Supra, vii. 82.

with chalk; then instructing them to slay every one whom they should meet that was not whitened like themselves, he made a night attack upon the Thessalians. No sooner did the Thessalian sentries, who were the first to see them, behold this strange sight, than, imagining it to be a prodigy, they were all filled with affright. From the sentries the alarm spread to the army, which was seized with such a panic that the Phocians killed four thousand of them, and became masters of their dead bodies and shields. Of the shields one half were sent as an offering to the temple at Abæ,[1] the other half were deposited at Delphi; while from the tenth part of the booty gained in the battle, were made the gigantic figures which stand round the tripod in front of the Delphic shrine, and likewise the figures of the same size and character at Abæ.

28. Besides this slaughter of the Thessalian foot when it was blockading them, the Phocians had dealt a blow to their horse upon its invading their territory, from which they had never recovered. There is a pass near the city of Hyampolis,[2] where the Phocians, having dug a broad trench, filled up the void with empty wine-jars, after which they covered the place with mould, so that the ground all looked alike, and then awaited the coming of the Thessalians. These, thinking to destroy the Phocians at one sweep, rushed rapidly forward, and became entangled in the wine-jars, which broke the legs of their horses.

29. The Thessalians had therefore a double cause of quarrel with the Phocians, when they dispatched the herald above mentioned, who thus delivered his message:—

" At length acknowledge, ye men of Phôcis, that ye may not think to match with us In times past, when it pleased us to hold with the Greeks, we had always the vantage over you; and now our influence is such with the barbarian, that, if we choose it, you will lose your country, and (what is even worse) you will be sold as slaves. However, though we can now do with you exactly as we like, we are willing to forget our wrongs. Quit them with a payment of fifty talents of silver,[3] and we undertake to ward off the evils which threaten your country."

30. Such was the message which the Thessalians sent. The Phocians were the only people in these parts who had not espoused the cause of the Medes; and it is my deliberate opinion

---

[1] For the great celebrity of this temple, see above, i. 46.
[2] Hyampolis lay very near to Abæ.
[3] Rather more than £12,000 of our money.

that the motive which swayed them was none other—neither
more nor less—than their hatred of the Thessalians: for had
the Thessalians declared in favour of the Greeks, I believe that
the men of Phôcis would have joined the Median side. As it
was, when the message arrived, the Phocians made answer, that
" they would not pay anything—it was open to them, equally
with the Thessalians, to make common cause with the Medes,
if they only chose so to do—but they would never of their own
free will become traitors to Greece."

31. On the return of this answer, the Thessalians, full of
wrath against the Phocians, offered themselves as guides to the
barbarian army, and led them forth from Trachinia into Dôris.
In this place there is a narrow tongue of Dorian territory, not
more than thirty furlongs across, interposed between Malis and
Phôcis; it is the tract in ancient times called Dryopis; and the
land, of which it is a part, is the mother-country of the Dorians
in the Peloponnese.[1] This territory the barbarians did not
plunder, for the inhabitants had espoused their side; and
besides, the Thessalians wished that they should be spared.

32. From Dôris they marched forward into Phôcis; but here
the inhabitants did not fall into their power: for some of them
had taken refuge in the high grounds of Parnassus—one summit
of which, called Tithorea, standing quite by itself, not far from
the city of Neon, is well fitted to give shelter to a large body
of men, and had now received a number of the Phocians with
their movables; while the greater portion had fled to the
country of the Ozolian Locrians,[2] and placed their goods in the
city called Amphissa, which lies above the Crissæan plain. The
land of Phôcis, however, was entirely overrun, for the Thessalians led the Persian army through the whole of it; and wherever
they went, the country was wasted with fire and sword, the
cities and even the temples being wilfully set alight by the troops.

33. The march of the army lay along the valley of the
Cephissus;[3] and here they ravaged far and wide, burning the
towns of Drymus, Charadra, Erôchus, Tethrônium, Amphicæa,
Neon, Pedieis, Triteis, Elateia, Hyampolis, Parapotamii, and
Abæ. At the last-named place there was a temple of Apollo,
very rich, and adorned with a vast number of treasures and
offerings. There was likewise an oracle there in those days, as

---

[1] Supra, i. 56.
[2] The Ozolian Locrians dwelt on the shores of the Corinthian Gulf.
[3] The Cephissus rises from the base of Parnassus.

indeed there is at the present time. This temple the Persians plundered and burnt; and here they captured a number of the Phocians before they could reach the hills,[1] and caused the death of some of their women by ill-usage.

34. After passing Parapotamii, the barbarians marched to Panopeis; and now the army separated into two bodies, whereof one, which was the more numerous and the stronger of the two, marched under Xerxes himself, towards Athens, entering Bœotia by the country of the Orchomenians.[2] The Bœotians had one and all embraced the cause of the Medes; and their towns were in the possession of Macedonian garrisons, whom Alexander had sent there, to make it manifest to Xerxes that the Bœotians were on the Median side. Such then was the road followed by one division of the barbarians.

35. The other division took guides, and proceeded towards the temple of Delphi, keeping Mount Parnassus on their right hand. They too laid waste such parts of Phôcis as they passed through, burning the city of the Panopeans, together with those of the Daulians and of the Æolidæ. This body had been detached from the rest of the army, and made to march in this direction, for the purpose of plundering the Delphian temple and conveying to King Xerxes the riches which were there laid up. For Xerxes, as I am informed, was better acquainted with what there was worthy of note at Delphi, than even with what he had left in his own house; so many of those about him were continually describing the treasures—more especially the offerings made by Crœsus the son of Alyattes.[3]

36. Now when the Delphians heard what danger they were in, great fear fell on them. In their terror they consulted the oracle concerning the holy treasures, and inquired if they should bury them in the ground, or carry them away to some other country. The god, in reply, bade them leave the treasures untouched—"He was able," he said, "without help to protect his own." So the Delphians, when they received this answer, began to think about saving themselves. And first of all they sent their women and children across the gulf into Achæa; after which the greater number of them climbed up into the tops of Parnassus,[4] and placed their goods for safety in the Corycian

---

[1] The Persians were determined, however, in true iconoclastic spirit, to destroy, if possible, all the principal Greek fanes.

[2] Orchomenus, the most famous of the Bœotian cities next to Thebes.

[3] Supra, i. 50, 51.

[4] The two peaks rising immediately above Delphi (*Kastri*), are probably intended.

cave;[1] while some effected their escape to Amphissa in Locris.[2] In this way all the Delphians quitted the city, except sixty men, and the Prophet.

37. When the barbarian assailants drew near and were in sight of the place,[3] the Prophet, who was named Acêratus, beheld, in front of the temple, a portion of the sacred armour, which it was not lawful for any mortal hand to touch, lying upon the ground, removed from the inner shrine where it was wont to hang. Then went he and told the prodigy to the Delphians who had remained behind. Meanwhile the enemy pressed forward briskly, and had reached the shrine of Minerva Pronaia, when they were overtaken by other prodigies still more wonderful than the first. Truly it was marvel enough, when warlike harness was seen lying outside the temple, removed there by no power but its own; what followed, however, exceeded in strangeness all prodigies that had ever before been seen. The barbarians had just reached in their advance the chapel of Minerva Pronaia, when a storm of thunder burst suddenly over their heads—at the same time two crags split off from Mount Parnassus, and rolled down upon them with a loud noise, crushing vast numbers beneath their weight—while from the temple of Minerva there went up the war-cry and the shout of victory.

38. All these things together struck terror into the barbarians, who forthwith turned and fled. The Delphians, seeing this, came down from their hiding-places, and smote them with a great slaughter, from which such as escaped fled straight into Bœotia. These men, on their return, declared (as I am told) that besides the marvels mentioned above, they witnessed also other supernatural sights. Two armed warriors, they said, of a stature more than human, pursued after their flying ranks, pressing them close and slaying them.

39. These men, the Delphians maintain, were two Heroes belonging to the place—by name Phylacus and Autonoüs—each of whom has a sacred precinct near the temple; one, that of Phylacus, hard by the road which runs above the temple of Pronaia; the other, that of Autonoüs, near the Castalian spring,[4]

[1] The Corycian cave, sacred to Pan and the Nymphs.
[2] Whither the other Phocians had already fled (supra, ch. 32).
[3] Delphi stood on the side of a rocky hill, in the form of a theatre, to which a succession of terraces gave it a still greater resemblance. The Temple of Apollo was about the centre of the curve.
[4] The Castalian spring may be distinctly recognised in the modern fountain of *Aio Jánni*. It lies at the base of the precipices of Parnassus.

at the foot of the peak called Hyampeia. The blocks of stone which fell from Parnassus might still be seen in my day; they lay in the precinct of Pronaia, where they stopped, after rolling through the host of the barbarians. Thus was this body of men forced to retire from the temple.

40. Meanwhile, the Grecian fleet, which had left Artemisium, proceeded to Salamis, at the request of the Athenians, and there cast anchor. The Athenians had begged them to take up this position, in order that they might convey their women and children out of Attica, and further might deliberate upon the course which it now behoved them to follow. Disappointed in the hopes which they had previously entertained, they were about to hold a council concerning the present posture of their affairs. For they had looked to see the Peloponnesians drawn up in full force to resist the enemy in Bœotia, but found nothing of what they had expected; nay, they learnt that the Greeks of those parts, only concerning themselves about their own safety, were building a wall across the Isthmus, and intended to guard the Peloponnese, and let the rest of Greece take its chance. These tidings caused them to make the request whereof I spoke, that the combined fleet should anchor at Salamis.

41. So while the rest of the fleet lay to off this island, the Athenians cast anchor along their own coast. Immediately upon their arrival, proclamation was made, that every Athenian should save his children and household as he best could; [1] whereupon some sent their families to Egina, some to Salamis, but the greater number to Trœzen. [2] This removal was made with all possible haste, partly from a desire to obey the advice of the oracle, [3] but still more for another reason. The Athenians say that they have in their Acropolis a huge serpent, which lives in the temple, and is the guardian of the whole place. Nor do they only say this, but, as if the serpent really dwelt there, every month they lay out its food, which consists of a honey-cake. Up to this time the honey-cake had always been consumed; but now it remained untouched. So the priestess told the people what had happened; whereupon they left Athens

[For a description of Delphi and its surroundings—so famous in antiquity—see the exhaustive note in Frazer's monumental edition of *Pausanias*, vol. v. pp. 248, sqq.—E. H. B.]

[1] The Athenian who, without such proclamation, left his country at a time of danger, was considered guilty of a capital offence.

[2] The Trœzenians received them with much kindness, and voted them sustenance-money at the rate of two obols (3¼d.) *per diem* for each person.

[3] Supra, vii. 141.

the more readily, since they believed that the goddess had already abandoned the citadel. As soon as all was removed, the Athenians sailed back to their station.

42. And now, the remainder of the Grecian sea-force, hearing that the fleet which had been at Artemisium, was come to Salamis, joined it at that island from Trœzen—orders having been issued previously that the ships should muster at Pôgon, the port of the Trœzenians. The vessels collected were many more in number than those which had fought at Artemisium, and were furnished by more cities. The admiral was the same who had commanded before, to wit, Eurybiades, the son of Eurycleides, who was a Spartan, but not of the family of the kings: the city, however, which sent by far the greatest number of ships, and the best sailers, was Athens.

43. Now these were the nations who composed the Grecian fleet. From the Peloponnese, the following—the Lacedæ-monians with sixteen ships; the Corinthians with the same number as at Artemisium; the Sicyonians with fifteen; the Epidaurians with ten; the Trœzenians with five; and the Her-mionians with three. These were Dorians and Macednians [1] all of them (except those from Hermioné), and had emigrated last from Erineus, Pindus, and Dryopis. The Hermionians were Dryopians, of the race which Hercules and the Malians drove out of the land now called Dôris. Such were the Peloponnesian nations.

44. From the mainland of Greece beyond the Peloponnese, came the Athenians with a hundred and eighty ships, a greater number than that furnished by any other people; and these were now manned wholly by themselves; for the Platæans did not serve aboard the Athenian ships at Salamis, owing to the following reason. When the Greeks, on their withdrawal from Artemisium, arrived off Chalcis, the Platæans disembarked upon the opposite shore of Bœotia, and set to work to remove their households, whereby it happened that they were left behind. (The Athenians, when the region which is now called Greece was held by the Pelasgi, were Pelasgians, and bore the name of Cranaans; but under their king Cecrops, they were called Cecropidæ; when Erechtheus got the sovereignty, they changed their name to Athenians; and when Ion, the son of Xuthus, became their general, they were named after him Ionians.)

45. The Megarians served with the same number of ships as

at Artemisium; the Ambraciots came with seven; the Leucadians (who were Dorians from Corinth) with three.

46. Of the islanders, the Eginetans furnished thirty ships—
they had a larger number equipped; but some were kept back
to guard their own coasts, and only thirty, which however were
their best sailers, took part in the fight at Salamis. (The Eginetans are Dorians from Epidaurus;[1] their island was called
formerly Œnôné). The Chalcideans came next in order; they
furnished the twenty ships with which they had served at Artemisium. The Eretrians likewise furnished their seven. These
races are Ionian. Cêos gave its old number[2]—the Ceans are
Ionians from Attica. Naxos furnished four: this detachment,
like those from the other islands, had been sent by the citizens
at home to join the Medes; but they made light of the orders
given them, and joined the Greeks, at the instigation of Demo-
critus, a citizen of good report, who was at that time captain of
a trireme. The Naxians are Ionians, of the Athenian stock.
The Styreans served with the same ships as before; the Cyth-
nians contributed one, and likewise a penteconter—these two
nations are Dryopians: the Seriphians, Siphnians, and Melians,
also served;[3] they were the only islanders who had not given
earth and water to the barbarian.

47. All these nations dwelt inside the river Acheron and the
country inhabited by the Thesprotians; for that people borders
on the Ambraciots and Leucadians, who are the most remote of
all those by whom the fleet was furnished. From the countries
beyond, there was only one people which gave help to the
Greeks in their danger. This was the people of Crotôna,[4] who
contributed a single ship, under the command of Phayllus, a
man who had thrice carried off the prize at the Pythian games.
The Crotoniats are, by descent, Achæans.

48. Most of the allies came with triremes; but the Melians,
Siphnians, and Seriphians, brought penteconters. The Melians,
who draw their race from Lacedæmon, furnished two; the
Siphnians and Seriphians, who are Ionians of the Athenian
stock, one each. The whole number of the ships, without

[1] Supra, v. 83.
[2] Two triremes and two penteconters (supra, ch. 1).
[3] Seriphus, Siphnus, and Melos—the *Serpho*, *Siphanto*, and *Milo* of the
present day—form, together with Ceos and Cythnus, the western Cyclades,
which were now especially threatened by the advance of the Persian fleet.
Their remoteness from Asia had emboldened them to refuse submission;
their danger now induced them to appear in arms.
[4] Supra, iii. 126.

counting the pentecontars, was three hundred and seventy-eight.[1]

49. When the captains from these various nations were come together at Salamis, a council of war was summoned; and Eurybiades proposed that any one who liked to advise, should say which place seemed to him the fittest, among those still in the possession of the Greeks, to be the scene of a naval combat. Attica, he said, was not to be thought of now; but he desired their counsel as to the remainder. The speakers mostly advised that the fleet should sail away to the Isthmus, and there give battle in defence of the Peloponnese; and they urged as a reason for this, that if they were worsted in a sea-fight at Salamis, they would be shut up in an island where they could get no help; but if they were beaten near the Isthmus, they could escape to their homes.

50. As the captains from the Peloponnese were thus advising, there came an Athenian to the camp, who brought word that the barbarians had entered Attica, and were ravaging and burning everything. For the division of the army under Xerxes was just arrived at Athens from its march through Bœotia, where it had burnt Thespiæ and Platæa—both which cities were forsaken by their inhabitants, who had fled to the Peloponnese—and now it was laying waste all the possessions of the Athenians. Thespiæ and Platæa had been burnt by the Persians, because they knew from the Thebans that neither of those cities had espoused their side.

51. Since the passage of the Hellespont and the commencement of the march upon Greece, a space of four months had gone by; one, while the army made the crossing, and delayed about the region of the Hellespont; and three while they proceeded thence to Attica, which they entered in the archonship of Calliades. They found the city forsaken; a few people only remained in the temple,[2] either keepers of the treasures,[3] or men of the poorer sort. These persons having fortified the citadel [4] with planks and boards, held out against the enemy. It was in some measure their poverty which had prevented them from seeking shelter in Salamis; but there was likewise another

---

[1] The actual number of the Greek ships *engaged* is variously stated. Æschylus, who was one of the combatants, makes them 300, or 310; Thucydides, 400, or according to some MSS., 300.

[2] The temple of Minerva Polias in the Acropolis.

[3] The keepers of the sacred treasures of Minerva were ten in number.

[4] The Athenian citadel, or Acropolis.

reason which in part induced them to remain. They imagined
themselves to have discovered the true meaning of the oracle
uttered by the Pythoness, which promised that " the wooden
wall" should never be taken[1]—the wooden wall, they thought, did
not mean the ships, but the place where they had taken refuge.

52. The Persians encamped upon the hill over against the
citadel, which is called Mars' hill by the Athenians,[2] and began
the siege of the place, attacking the Greeks with arrows whereto
pieces of lighted tow were attached, which they shot at the
barricade. And now those who were within the citadel found
themselves in a most woeful case; for their wooden rampart
betrayed them; still, however, they continued to resist. It was
in vain that the Pisistratidæ came to them and offered terms of
surrender—they stoutly refused all parley, and among their
other modes of defence, rolled down huge masses of stone upon
the barbarians as they were mounting up to the gates: so that
Xerxes was for a long time very greatly perplexed, and could
not contrive any way to take them.

53. At last, however, in the midst of these many difficulties,
the barbarians made discovery of an access. For verily the
oracle had spoken truth; and it was fated that the whole mainland of Attica should fall beneath the sway of the Persians.
Right in front of the citadel, but behind the gates and the
common ascent—where no watch was kept, and no one would
have thought it possible that any foot of man could climb—a
few soldiers mounted from the sanctuary of Aglaurus, Cecrops'
daughter,[3] notwithstanding the steepness of the precipice. As
soon as the Athenians saw them upon the summit, some threw
themselves headlong from the wall, and so perished; while
others fled for refuge to the inner part of the temple. The
Persians rushed to the gates and opened them, after which they
massacred the suppliants. When all were slain, they plundered
the temple, and fired every part of the citadel.[4]

54. Xerxes, thus completely master of Athens, despatched a
horseman to Susa, with a message to Artabanus, informing him

[1] Supra, vii. 141.
[2] Mars' Hill, the seat of the celebrated court of the Areopagus, made still
more famous by the preaching of St. Paul (Acts xvii. 22), is one of the
features of Athenian topography which cannot be mistaken.
[3] Aglaurus, the daughter of Cecrops, was said to have thrown herself
over the precipices of the Acropolis.
[4] The traces of this destruction may still be seen, though the structures
have been rebuilt. [Cf. Gardner, New Chapters in Greek History, chap.
viii.—E. H. B.]

of his success hitherto. The day after, he collected together all the Athenian exiles who had come into Greece in his train, and bade them go up into the citadel, and there offer sacrifice after their own fashion. I know not whether he had had a dream which made him give this order, or whether he felt some remorse on account of having set the temple on fire. However this may have been, the exiles were not slow to obey the command given them.

55. I will now explain why I have made mention of this circumstance: there is a temple of Erechtheus the Earth-born, as he is called, in this citadel, containing within it an olive-tree and a sea.[1] The tale goes among the Athenians, that they were placed there as witnesses by Neptune and Minerva, when they had their contention about the country.[2] Now this olive-tree had been burnt with the rest of the temple when the barbarians took the place. But when the Athenians, whom the king had commanded to offer sacrifice, went up into the temple for the purpose, they found a fresh shoot, as much as a cubit in length, thrown out from the old trunk. Such at least was the account which these persons gave.

56. Meanwhile, at Salamis, the Greeks no sooner heard what had befallen the Athenian citadel, than they fell into such alarm that some of the captains did not even wait for the council to come to a vote, but embarked hastily on board their vessels, and hoisted sail as though they would take to flight immediately. The rest, who stayed at the council board, came to a vote that the fleet should give battle at the Isthmus. Night now drew on; and the captains, dispersing from the meeting, proceeded on board their respective ships.

57. Themistocles, as he entered his own vessel, was met by Mnesiphilus, an Athenian, who asked him what the council had resolved to do. On learning that the resolve was to stand away

---

[1] Pausanias tells us that this " sea " was a well of salt water.

[2] The myth is given more fully by Apollodorus than by any other writer. " The gods," he says, " were minded to choose themselves cities where they should be specially worshipped. Neptune was the first to reach Attica, where he smote with his trident, and made a sea spring up in the midst of the Acropolis, where it remains to this day, and is called the Sea of Erechtheus. Minerva (Athené) followed, and calling Cecrops to be witness that she took the land in possession, planted the olive which still grows in the temple of Pandrosus. Then a strife arose concerning the country: so Jupiter, to reconcile the rivals, appointed judges, who were not Cecrops and Cranaus, as some say, nor yet Erechtheus, but the twelve deities. Their decision adjudged the land to Athené, upon the witness of Cecrops; and so Athens gained its name, being called after the goddess."

for the Isthmus, and there give battle on behalf of the Peloponnese, Mnesiphilus exclaimed—

"If these men sail away from Salamis, thou wilt have no
fight at all for the one fatherland; for they will all scatter
themselves to their own homes; and neither Eurybiades nor
any one else will be able to hinder them, nor to stop the breaking up of the armament. Thus will Greece be brought to ruin
through evil counsels. But haste thee now; and, if there be
any possible way, seek to unsettle these resolves—mayhap
thou mightest persuade Eurybiades to change his mind, and
continue here."

58. The suggestion greatly pleased Themistocles; and without answering a word, he went straight to the vessel of Eurybiades. Arrived there, he let him know that he wanted to
speak with him on a matter touching the public service. So
Eurybiades bade him come on board, and say whatever he
wished. Then Themistocles, seating himself at his side, went
over all the arguments which he had heard from Mnesiphilus,
pretending as if they were his own, and added to them many
new ones besides; until at last he persuaded Eurybiades, by his
importunity, to quit his ship and again collect the captains to
council.

59. As soon as they were come, and before Eurybiades had
opened to them his purpose in assembling them together,
Themistocles, as men are wont to do when they are very
anxious, spoke much to divers of them; whereupon the Corinthian captain, Adeimantus, the son of Ocytus, observed—
"Themistocles, at the games they who start too soon are
scourged" "True," rejoined the other in his excuse, "but they
who wait too late are not crowned."

60. Thus he gave the Corinthian at this time a mild answer;
and towards Eurybiades himself he did not now use any of
those arguments which he had urged before, or say aught of the
allies betaking themselves to flight if once they broke up from
Salamis; it would have been ungraceful for him, when the
confederates were present, to make accusation against any: but
he had recourse to quite a new sort of reasoning, and addressed
him as follows:—

"With thee it rests, O Eurybiades! to save Greece, if thou
wilt only hearken unto me, and give the enemy battle here,
rather than yield to the advice of those among us, who would
have the fleet withdrawn to the Isthmus. Hear now, I beseech

thee, and judge between the two courses. At the Isthmus thou wilt fight in an open sea, which is greatly to our disadvantage, since our ships are heavier and fewer in number than the enemy's; and further, thou wilt in any case lose Salamis, Megara, and Egina, even if all the rest goes well with us. The land and sea force of the Persians will advance together; and thy retreat will but draw them towards the Peloponnese, and so bring all Greece into peril. If, on the other hand, thou doest as I advise, these are the advantages which thou wilt so secure: in the first place, as we shall fight in a narrow sea with few ships against many, if the war follows the common course, we shall gain a great victory; for to fight in a narrow space is favourable to us—in an open sea, to them. Again, Salamis will in this case be preserved, where we have placed our wives and children. Nay, that very point by which ye set most store, is secured as much by this course as by the other; for whether we fight here or at the Isthmus, we shall equally give battle in defence of the Peloponnese. Assuredly ye will not do wisely to draw the Persians upon that region. For if things turn out as I anticipate, and we beat them by sea, then we shall have kept your Isthmus free from the barbarians, and they will have advanced no further than Attica, but from thence have fled back in disorder; and we shall, moreover, have saved Megara, Egina, and Salamis itself, where an oracle has said that we are to overcome our enemies.[1] When men counsel reasonably, reasonable success ensues; but when in their counsels they reject reason, God does not choose to follow the wanderings of human fancies."

61. When Themistocles had thus spoken, Adeimantus the Corinthian again attacked him, and bade him be silent, since he was a man without a city; at the same time he called on Eurybiades not to put the question at the instance of one who had no country, and urged that Themistocles should show of what state he was envoy, before he gave his voice with the rest. This reproach he made, because the city of Athens had been taken, and was in the hands of the barbarians. Hereupon Themistocles spake many bitter things against Adeimantus and the Corinthians generally; and for proof that he had a country, reminded the captains, that with two hundred ships at his command, all fully manned for battle, he had both city and

---

[1] Supra, vii. 141, ad fin.

territory as good as theirs; since there was no Grecian state which could resist his men if they were to make a descent.[1]

62. After this declaration, he turned to Eurybiades, and addressing him with still greater warmth and earnestness—" If thou wilt stay here," he said, " and behave like a brave man, all will be well—if not, thou wilt bring Greece to ruin. For the whole fortune of the war depends on our ships. Be thou persuaded by my words. If not, we will take our families on board, and go, just as we are, to Siris, in Italy, which is ours from of old, and which the prophecies declare we are to colonise some day or other. You then, when you have lost allies like us, will hereafter call to mind what I have now said."

63. At these words of Themistocles, Eurybiades changed his determination; principally, as I believe, because he feared that if he withdrew the fleet to the Isthmus, the Athenians would sail away, and knew that without the Athenians, the rest of their ships could be no match for the fleet of the enemy. He therefore decided to remain, and give battle at Salamis.

64. And now, the different chiefs, notwithstanding their skirmish of words, on learning the decision of Eurybiades, at once made ready for the fight. Morning broke; and, just as the sun rose, the shock of an earthquake was felt both on shore and at sea: whereupon the Greeks resolved to approach the gods with prayer, and likewise to send and invite the Æacids to their aid. And this they did, with as much speed as they had resolved on it. Prayers were offered to all the gods; and Telamon and Ajax were invoked at once from Salamis, while a ship was sent to Egina to fetch Æacus himself, and the other Æacids.

65. The following is a tale which was told by Dicæus, the son of Theocydes, an Athenian, who was at this time an exile, and had gained a good report among the Medes. He declared that after the army of Xerxes had, in the absence of the Athenians, wasted Attica, he chanced to be with Demaratus the Lacedæmonian in the Thriasian plain, and that while there, he saw a cloud of dust advancing from Eleusis, such as a host of thirty thousand men might raise. As he and his companion were wondering who the men, from whom the dust arose, could possibly be, a sound of voices reached his ear, and he thought that he recognised the mystic hymn to Bacchus.[2] Now Dema-

---

[1] Two hundred ships would imply at least 40,000 men, a force greater (probably) than that which any Greek state, except Sparta, could have brought into the field.

[2] The chief details concerning the greater Eleusinia, of which the mystic

ratus was unacquainted with the rites of Eleusis, and so he inquired of Dicæus what the voices were saying. Dicæus made answer—"O Demaratus! beyond a doubt some mighty calamity is about to befall the king's army! For it is manifest, inasmuch as Attica is deserted by its inhabitants, that the sound which we have heard is an unearthly one, and is now upon its way from Eleusis to aid the Athenians and their confederates. If it descends upon the Peloponnese, danger will threaten the king himself and his land army—if it moves towards the ships at Salamis, 'twill go hard but the king's fleet there suffers destruction. Every year the Athenians celebrate this feast to the Mother and the Daughter;[1] and all who wish, whether they be Athenians or any other Greeks, are initiated. The sound thou hearest is the Bacchic song, which is wont to be sung at that festival." "Hush now," rejoined the other; "and see thou tell no man of this matter. For if thy words be brought to the king's ear, thou wilt assuredly lose thy head because of them; neither I nor any man living can then save thee. Hold thy peace therefore. The gods will see to the king's army." Thus Demaratus counselled him; and they looked, and saw the dust, from which the sound arose, become a cloud, and the cloud rise up into the air and sail away to Salamis, making for the station of the Grecian fleet. Then they knew that it was the fleet of Xerxes which would suffer destruction. Such was the tale told by Dicæus the son of Theocýdes; and he appealed for its truth to Demaratus and other eye-witnesses.

66. The men belonging to the fleet of Xerxes, after they had seen the Spartan dead at Thermopylæ,[2] and crossed the channel from Trachis to Histiæa, waited there by the space of three days, and then sailing down through the Euripus,[3] in three more came to Phalêrum. In my judgment, the Persian forces both by land and sea when they invaded Attica were not less numerous than they had been on their arrival at Sêpias and Thermopylæ. For against the Persian loss in the storm and at Thermopylæ, and again in the sea-fights off Artemisium, I set the various nations which had since joined the king—as the

hymn to Bacchus was a part, are carefully collected in Smith's *Dictionary of Antiquities* (ad voc. ELEUSINIA) [and in chap. ix. of Jevons and Gardiner's *Manual of Greek Antiquities.*—E. H. B.].

[1] Ceres [Kore] and Proserpine.

[2] Supra, ch. 25.

[3] The name Euripus applies, strictly speaking, only to the very narrowest part of the channel between Eubœa and the mainland.

Malians, the Dorians, the Locrians, and the Bœotians—each
serving in full force in his army except the last, who did not
number in their ranks either the Thespians or the Platæans;
and together with these, the Carystians, the Andrians, the
Tenians, and the other people of the islands, who all fought on
this side except the five states already mentioned.[1] For as the
Persians penetrated further into Greece, they were joined continually by fresh nations.

67. Reinforced by the contingents of all these various states,
except Paros, the barbarians reached Athens. As for the
Parians, they tarried at Cythnus, waiting to see how the war
would go. The rest of the sea forces came safe to Phalêrum;
where they were visited by Xerxes, who had conceived a desire
to go aboard and learn the wishes of the fleet. So he came and
sate in a seat of honour; and the sovereigns of the nations, and
the captains of the ships, were sent for, to appear before him,
and as they arrived took their seats according to the rank
assigned them by the king. In the first seat sate the king of
Sidon; after him, the king of Tyre;[2] then the rest in their
order. When the whole had taken their places, one after
another, and were set down in orderly array, Xerxes, to try
them, sent Mardonius and questioned each, whether a sea-fight
should be risked or no.

68. Mardonius accordingly went round the entire assemblage,
beginning with the Sidonian monarch, and asked this question;
to which all gave the same answer, advising to engage the
Greeks, except only Artemisia, who spake as follows:—

" Say to the king, Mardonius, that these are my words to
him: I was not the least brave of those who fought at Eubœa,
nor were my achievements there among the meanest; it is my
right, therefore, O my lord, to tell thee plainly what I think to
be most for thy advantage now. This then is my advice.
Spare thy ships, and do not risk a battle; for these people are
as much superior to thy people in seamanship, as men to
women. What so great need is there for thee to incur hazard
at sea? Art thou not master of Athens, for which thou didst
undertake thy expedition?[3] Is not Greece subject to thee?
Not a soul now resists thy advance. They who once resisted,
were handled even as they deserved. (§ 2.) Now learn how I
expect that affairs will go with thy adversaries. If thou art not

---

[1] Naxos, Cythnus, Seriphus, Siphnus, and Melos (vide supra, ch. 46).
[2] Compare vii. 98.   [3] Supra, vii. 8, § 2.

over-hasty to engage with them by sea, but wilt keep thy fleet near the land, then whether thou abidest as thou art, or marchest forward towards the Peloponnese, thou wilt easily accomplish all for which thou art come hither. The Greeks cannot hold out against thee very long; thou wilt soon part them asunder, and scatter them to their several homes. In the island where they lie, I hear they have no food in store; nor is it likely, if thy land force begins its march towards the Peloponnese, that they will remain quietly where they are—at least such as come from that region. Of a surety *they* will not greatly trouble themselves to give battle on behalf of the Athenians. (§ 3.) On the other hand, if thou art hasty to fight, I tremble lest the defeat of thy sea force bring harm likewise to thy land army. This, too, thou shouldst remember, O king; good masters are apt to have bad servants, and bad masters good ones. Now, as thou art the best of men, thy servants must needs be a sorry set. These Egyptians, Cyprians, Cilicians, and Pamphylians, who are counted in the number of thy subject-allies, of how little service are they to thee!"

69. As Artemisia spake, they who wished her well were greatly troubled concerning her words, thinking that she would suffer some hurt at the king's hands, because she exhorted him not to risk a battle; they, on the other hand, who disliked and envied her, favoured as she was by the king above all the rest of the allies, rejoiced at her declaration, expecting that her life would be the forfeit. But Xerxes, when the words of the several speakers were reported to him, was pleased beyond all others with the reply of Artemisia; and whereas, even before this, he had always esteemed her much, he now praised her more than ever. Nevertheless, he gave orders that the advice of the greater number should be followed; for he thought that at Eubœa the fleet had not done its best, because he himself was not there to see—whereas this time he resolved that he would be an eye-witness of the combat.

70. Orders were now given to stand out to sea; and the ships proceeded towards Salamis, and took up the stations to which they were directed, without let or hindrance from the enemy. The day, however, was too far spent for them to begin the battle, since night already approached: so they prepared to engage upon the morrow. The Greeks, meanwhile, were in great distress and alarm, more especially those of the Pelo-ponnese, who were troubled that they had been kept at Salamis

to fight on behalf of the Athenian territory, and feared that, if they should suffer defeat, they would be pent up and besieged in an island, while their own country was left unprotected.

71. The same night the land army of the barbarians began its march towards the Peloponnese, where, however, all that was possible had been done to prevent the enemy from forcing an entrance by land. As soon as ever news reached the Peloponnese of the death of Leonidas and his companions at Thermopylæ, the inhabitants flocked together from the various cities, and encamped at the Isthmus, under the command of Cleombrotus, son of Anaxandridas, and brother of Leonidas. Here their first care was to block up the Scironian Way;[1] after which it was determined in council to build a wall across the Isthmus.[2] As the number assembled amounted to many tens of thousands, and there was not one who did not give himself to the work, it was soon finished. Stones, bricks, timber, baskets filled full of sand, were used in the building; and not a moment was lost by those who gave their aid; for they laboured without ceasing either by night or day.

72. Now the nations who gave their aid, and who had flocked in full force to the Isthmus, were the following: the Lacedæmonians, all the tribes of the Arcadians, the Eleans, the Corinthians, the Sicyonians, the Epidaurians, the Phliasians, the Trœzenians, and the Hermionians. These all gave their aid, being greatly alarmed at the danger which threatened Greece. But the other inhabitants of the Peloponnese took no part in the matter; though the Olympic and Carneian festivals were now over.[3]

73. Seven nations inhabit the Peloponnese. Two of them are aboriginal, and still continue in the regions where they dwelt at the first—to wit, the Arcadians[4] and the Cynurians.[5] A third, that of the Achæans, has never left the Peloponnese, but has been dislodged from its own proper country, and inhabits a district which once belonged to others.[6] The remaining nations,

[1] The Scironian Way led from Megara to Corinth, along the eastern shore of the Isthmus.

[2] The Isthmus is about four miles across at its narrowest point, and nearly five where the wall was built.

[3] Supra, vii. 206.

[4] That the Arcadians were aboriginal inhabitants of the Peloponnese was the unanimous tradition of antiquity.

[5] Cynuria, or Cynosuria, was the border territory between Sparta and Argos upon the coast.

[6] Supra, vii. 94; compare i. 145.

four out of the seven, are all immigrants—namely, the Dorians, the Ætolians, the Dryopians, and the Lemnians. To the Dorians belong several very famous cities;[1] to the Ætolians one only, that is, Elis; to the Dryopians, Hermioné and that Asiné which lies over against Cardamylé in Laconia;[2] to the Lemnians, all the towns of the Paroreats.[3] The aboriginal Cynurians alone seem to be Ionians; even they, however, have, in course of time, grown to be Dorians, under the government of the Argives, whose Orneats and vassals they were. All the cities of these seven nations, except those mentioned above, stood aloof from the war; and by so doing, if I may speak freely, they in fact took part with the Medes.

74. So the Greeks at the Isthmus toiled unceasingly, as though in the greatest peril; since they never imagined that any great success would be gained by the fleet. The Greeks at Salamis, on the other hand, when they heard what the rest were about, felt greatly alarmed; but their fear was not so much for themselves as for the Peloponnese. At first they conversed together in low tones, each man with his fellow, secretly, and marvelled at the folly shown by Eurybiades; but presently the smothered feeling broke out, and another assembly was held; whereat the old subjects provoked much talk from the speakers, one side maintaining that it was best to sail to the Peloponnese and risk battle for that, instead of abiding at Salamis and fighting for a land already taken by the enemy; while the other, which consisted of the Athenians, Eginetans, and Megarians, was urgent to remain and have the battle fought where they were.

75. Then Themistocles, when he saw that the Peloponnesians would carry the vote against him, went out secretly from the council, and, instructing a certain man what he should say, sent him on board a merchant ship to the fleet of the Medes. The man's name was Sicinnus; he was one of Themistocles' household slaves, and acted as tutor to his sons;[4] in after times, when the Thespians were admitting persons to citizenship, Themistocles made him a Thespian, and a rich man to boot. The ship brought Sicinnus to the Persian fleet, and there he delivered his message to the leaders in these words:—

[1] Sparta, Argos, Mycenæ, Trœzen, Epidaurus, Corinth, and Sicyon.
[2] Cardamylé was on the opposite side of the Coronæan Gulf to Asiné. It was an old Achæan settlement, and important enough to be mentioned by Homer (Il. ix. 150).
[3] Supra, iv. 148.   [4] Themistocles is said to have had five sons.

"The Athenian commander has sent me to you privily, without the knowledge of the other Greeks. He is a well-wisher to the king's cause, and would rather success should attend on you than on his countrymen; wherefore he bids me tell you that fear has seized the Greeks and they are meditating a hasty flight. Now then it is open to you to achieve the best work that ever ye wrought, if only ye will hinder their escaping. They no longer agree among themselves, so that they will not now make any resistance—nay, 'tis likely ye may see a fight already begun between such as favour and such as oppose your cause." The messenger, when he had thus expressed himself, departed and was seen no more.

76. Then the captains, believing all that the messenger had said, proceeded to land a large body of Persian troops on the islet of Psyttaleia,[1] which lies between Salamis and the mainland; after which, about the hour of midnight, they advanced their western wing towards Salamis, so as to inclose the Greeks. At the same time the force stationed about Ceos and Cynosura moved forward, and filled the whole strait as far as Munychia with their ships. This advance was made to prevent the Greeks from escaping by flight, and to block them up in Salamis, where it was thought that vengeance might be taken upon them for the battles fought near Artemisium. The Persian troops were landed on the islet of Psyttaleia, because, as soon as the battle began, the men and wrecks were likely to be drifted thither, as the isle lay in the very path of the coming fight,—and they would thus be able to save their own men and destroy those of the enemy. All these movements were made in silence, that the Greeks might have no knowledge of them; and they occupied the whole night, so that the men had no time to get their sleep.

77. I cannot say that there is no truth in prophecies, or feel inclined to call in question those which speak with clearness, when I think of the following:—

"When they shall bridge with their ships to the sacred strand of Diana
 Girt with the golden falchion, and eke to marine Cynosura,[2]
Mad hope swelling their hearts at the downfall of beautiful Athens [3]—
Then shall godlike Right extinguish haughty Presumption,

---

[1] Psyttaleia is the small island now called *Lipsokutáli*, which lies between the Piræus and the eastern extremity of Salamis.

[2] The Marathonian promontory of the name.

[3] "Brilliant" or "fruitful Athens" would be a closer translation. The epithet λιπαραὶ is a favourite one in this connection.

Insult's furious offspring, who thinketh to overthrow all things.
Brass with brass shall mingle, and Mars with blood shall empurple
Ocean's waves.   Then—then shall the day of Grecia's freedom
Come from Victory fair, and Saturn's son all-seeing."

When I look to this, and perceive how clearly Bacis [1] spoke,
I neither venture myself to say anything against prophecies, nor
do I approve of others impugning them.

78. Meanwhile, among the captains at Salamis, the strife of
words grew fierce. As yet they did not know that they were
encompassed, but imagined that the barbarians remained in the
same places where they had seen them the day before.

79. In the midst of their contention, Aristides, the son of
Lysimachus, who had crossed from Egina, arrived in Salamis.
He was an Athenian, and had been ostracised by the commonalty; [2] yet I believe, from what I have heard concerning
his character, that there was not in all Athens a man so worthy
or so just as he. He now came to the council, and, standing
outside, called for Themistocles. Now Themistocles was not his
friend, but his most determined enemy. However, under the
pressure of the great dangers impending, Aristides forgot their
feud, and called Themistocles out of the council, since he wished
to confer with him. He had heard before his arrival of the
impatience of the Peloponnesians to withdraw the fleet to the
Isthmus. As soon therefore as Themistocles came forth,
Aristides addressed him in these words:—

"Our rivalry at all times, and especially at the present
season, ought to be a struggle, which of us shall most advantage
our country. Let me then say to thee, that so far as regards
the departure of the Peloponnesians from this place, much talk
and little will be found precisely alike. I have seen with my
own eyes that which I now report: that, however much the
Corinthians or Eurybiades himself may wish it, they cannot now
retreat; for we are enclosed on every side by the enemy. Go
in to them, and make this known."

80. "Thy advice is excellent," answered the other; "and thy
tidings are also good. That which I earnestly desired to happen,
thine eyes have beheld accomplished. Know that what the
Medes have now done was at my instance; for it was necessary,
as our men would not fight here of their own free will, to make

[1] Supra, ch. 20.
[2] After a long struggle, Aristides had been ostracised through the influence of Themistocles, three years earlier, B.C. 483. The stories told in
connection with his ostracism are well known, and will be found in Plutarch.

them fight whether they would or no. But come now, as thou hast brought the good news, go in and tell it. For if I speak to them, they will think it a feigned tale, and will not believe that the barbarians have inclosed us around. Therefore do thou go to them, and inform them how matters stand. If they believe thee, 'twill be for the best; but if otherwise, it will not harm. For it is impossible that they should now flee away, if we are indeed shut in on all sides, as thou sayest.

81. Then Aristides entered the assembly, and spoke to the captains: he had come, he told them, from Egina, and had but barely escaped the blockading vessels—the Greek fleet was entirely inclosed by the ships of Xerxes—and he advised them to get themselves in readiness to resist the foe. Having said so much, he withdrew. And now another contest arose; for the greater part of the captains would not believe the tidings.

82. But while they still doubted, a Tenian trireme, commanded by Panætius the son of Sôsimenes, deserted from the Persians and joined the Greeks, bringing full intelligence. For this reason the Tenians were inscribed upon the tripod at Delphi among those who overthrew the barbarians. With this ship, which deserted to their side at Salamis, and the Lemnian vessel which came over before at Artemisium,[1] the Greek fleet was brought to the full number of 380 ships; otherwise it fell short by two of that amount.

83. The Greeks now, not doubting what the Tenians told them, made ready for the coming fight. At the dawn of day, all the men-at-arms [2] were assembled together, and speeches were made to them, of which the best was that of Themistocles; who throughout contrasted what was noble with what was base, and bade them, in all that came within the range of man's nature and constitution, *always* to make choice of the nobler part. Having thus wound up his discourse, he told them to go at once on board their ships, which they accordingly did; and about his time the trireme, that had been sent to Egina for the Æacidæ,[3] returned; whereupon the Greeks put to sea with all their fleet.

84. The fleet had scarce left the land when they were attacked

---

[1] Supra, ch. 11. The calculation here made confirms the *total* in ch. 48, ad fin.

[2] The Epibatæ, or armed portion of the crew of a trireme, corresponding to our marines, varied in amount at different periods of Greek history. The greatest number ever found is forty.

[3] Supra, ch. 64

by the barbarians. At once most of the Greeks began to back water, and were about touching the shore, when Ameinias of Pallênê,[1] one of the Athenian captains, darted forth in front of the line, and charged a ship of the enemy. The two vessels became entangled, and could not separate, whereupon the rest of the fleet came up to help Ameinias, and engaged with the Persians. Such is the account which the Athenians give of the way in which the battle began; but the Eginetans maintain that the vessel which had been to Egina for the Æacidæ, was the one that brought on the fight. It is also reported, that a phantom in the form of a woman appeared to the Greeks, and, in a voice that was heard from end to end of the fleet, cheered them on to the fight ; first, however, rebuking them, and saying —" Strange men, how long are ye going to back water? "

85. Against the Athenians, who held the western extremity of the line towards Eleusis, were placed the Phœnicians; against the Lacedæmonians, whose station was eastward towards the Piræus,[2] the Ionians. Of these last a few only followed the advice of Themistocles, to fight backwardly; the greater number did far otherwise. I could mention here the names of many trierarchs who took vessels from the Greeks, but I shall pass over all excepting Theomêstor, the son of Androdamas, and Phylacus, the son of Histiæus, both Samians. I show this preference to them, inasmuch as for this service Theomêstor was made tyrant of Samos by the Persians, which Phylacus was enrolled among the king's benefactors, and presented with a large estate in land. In the Persian tongue the king's benefactors are called *Orosangs*.

86. Far the greater number of the Persian ships engaged in this battle were disabled, either by the Athenians or by the Eginetans. For as the Greeks fought in order and kept their line, while the barbarians were in confusion and had no plan in anything that they did, the issue of the battle could scarce be other than it was. Yet the Persians fought far more bravely here than at Eubœa, and indeed surpassed themselves; each did his utmost through fear of Xerxes, for each thought that the king's eye was upon himself.[3]

87. What part the several nations, whether Greek or barbarian, took in the combat, I am not able to say for certain;

[1] Pallênê was one of the most famous of the Athenian provincial towns.
[2] [The harbour of Athens.—E. H. B.]
[3] Supra, ch. 69, and infra, ch. 90. The anger of Xerxes, as we see in the latter passage, led to very serious consequences.

Artemisia, however, I know, distinguished herself in such a way as raised her even higher than she stood before in the esteem of the king. For after confusion had spread throughout the whole of the king's fleet, and her ship was closely pursued by an Athenian trireme, she, having no way to fly, since in front of her were a number of friendly vessels, and she was nearest of all the Persians to the enemy, resolved on a measure which in fact proved her safety. Pressed by the Athenian pursuer, she bore straight against one of the ships of her own party, a Calyndian, which had Damasithymus, the Calyndian king, himself on board. I cannot say whether she had had any quarrel with the man while the fleet was at the Hellespont, or no—neither can I decide whether she of set purpose attacked his vessel, or whether it merely chanced that the Calyndian ship came in her way— but certain it is that she bore down upon his vessel and sank it, and that thereby she had the good fortune to procure herself a double advantage. For the commander of the Athenian trireme, when he saw her bear down on one of the enemy's fleet, thought immediately that her vessel was a Greek, or else had deserted from the Persians, and was now fighting on the Greek side; he therefore gave up the chase, and turned away to attack others.

88. Thus in the first place she saved her life by the action, and was enabled to get clear off from the battle; while further, it fell out that in the very act of doing the king an injury she raised herself to a greater height than ever in his esteem. For as Xerxes beheld the fight, he remarked (it is said) the destruction of the vessel, whereupon the bystanders observed to him— "Seest thou, master, how well Artemisia fights, and how she has just sunk a ship of the enemy?" Then Xerxes asked if it were really Artemisia's doing; and they answered, "Certainly; for they knew her ensign:" while all made sure that the sunken vessel belonged to the opposite side. Everything, it is said, conspired to prosper the queen—it was especially fortunate for her that not one of those on board the Calyndian ship survived to become her accuser. Xerxes, they say, in reply to the remarks made to him, observed—"My men have behaved like women, my women like men!"

89. There fell in this combat Ariabignes, one of the chief commanders of the fleet, who was son of Darius and brother of Xerxes; and with him perished a vast number of men of high repute, Persians, Medes, and allies. Of the Greeks there died only a few; for, as they were able to swim, all those that were

not slain outright by the enemy escaped from the sinking vessels
and swam across to Salamis. But on the side of the barbarians
more perished by drowning than in any other way, since they
did not know how to swim. The great destruction took place
when the ships which had been first engaged began to fly; for
they who were stationed in the rear, anxious to display their
valour before the eyes of the king, made every effort to force
their way to the front, and thus became entangled with such of
their own vessels as were retreating.

90. In this confusion the following event occurred: Certain
Phœnicians belonging to the ships which had thus perished
made their appearance before the king, and laid the blame of
their loss on the Ionians, declaring that they were traitors, and
had wilfully destroyed the vessels. But the upshot of this
complaint was, that the Ionian captains escaped the death
which threatened them, while their Phœnician accusers received
death as their reward. For it happened that, exactly as they
spoke, a Samothracian vessel bore down on an Athenian and
sank it, but was attacked and crippled immediately by one of
the Eginetan squadron. Now the Samothracians were expert
with the javelin, and aimed their weapons so well, that they
cleared the deck of the vessel which had disabled their own,
after which they sprang on board, and took it. This saved the
Ionians. Xerxes, when he saw the exploit, turned fiercely on
the Phœnicians—(he was ready, in his extreme vexation, to find
fault with any one)—and ordered their heads to be cut off, to
prevent them, he said, from casting the blame of their own
misconduct upon braver men. During the whole time of the
battle Xerxes sate at the base of the hill called Ægaleôs, over
against Salamis; and whenever he saw any of his own captains
perform any worthy exploit he inquired concerning him; and
the man's name was taken down by his scribes,[1] together with
the names of his father and his city. Ariaramnes too, a Persian,[2]
who was a friend of the Ionians, and present at the time whereof
I speak, had a share in bringing about the punishment of the
Phœnicians.

91. When the rout of the barbarians began, and they sought
to make their escape to Phalêrum, the Eginetans, awaiting them
in the channel, performed exploits worthy to be recorded.
Through the whole of the confused struggle the Athenians
employed themselves in destroying such ships as either made

[1] Supra, vii. 100.   [2] He was probably one of the royal house.

resistance or fled to shore, while the Eginetans dealt with those which endeavoured to escape down the strait; so that the Persian vessels were no sooner clear of the Athenians than forthwith they fell into the hands of the Eginetan squadron.

92. It chanced here that there was a meeting between the ship of Themistocles, which was hasting in pursuit of the enemy, and that of Polycritus, son of Crius the Eginetan,[1] which had just charged a Sidonian trireme. The Sidonian vessel was the same that captured the Eginetan guard-ship off Sciathus,[2] which had Pytheas, the son of Ischenoüs, on board—that Pytheas, I mean, who fell covered with wounds, and whom the Sidonians kept on board their ship, from admiration of his gallantry. This man afterwards returned in safety to Egina; for when the Sidonian vessel with its Persian crew fell into the hands of the Greeks, he was still found on board. Polycritus no sooner saw the Athenian trireme than, knowing at once whose vessel it was, as he observed that it bore the ensign of the admiral, he shouted to Themistocles jeeringly, and asked him, in a tone of reproach, if the Eginetans did not show themselves rare friends to the Medes. At the same time, while he thus reproached Themistocles, Polycritus bore straight down on the Sidonian. Such of the barbarian vessels as escaped from the battle fled to Phalêrum, and there sheltered themselves under the protection of the land army.

93. The Greeks who gained the greatest glory of all in the sea-fight off Salamis were the Eginetans, and after them the Athenians. The individuals of most distinction were Polycritus the Eginetan, and two Athenians, Eumenes of Anagyrus,[3] and Ameinias of Pallênê, the latter of whom had pressed Artemisia so hard. And assuredly, if he had known that the vessel carried Artemisia on board, he would never have given over the chase till he had either succeeded in taking her, or else been taken himself. For the Athenian captains had received special orders touching the queen; and moreover a reward of ten thousand drachmas[4] had been proclaimed for any one who should make her prisoner; since there was great indignation felt that a woman should appear in arms against Athens.

[1] Crius had been mentioned as one of the chief men in Egina (supra, vi. 73).
[2] Supra, vii. 181.
[3] Anagyrus was one of the maritime demes [or *parishes*] between the Piraeus and Sunium.
[4] Ten thousand drachmas would be equal to £400 of our money.

However, as I said before, she escaped; and so did some others whose ships survived the engagement; and these were all now assembled at the port of Phalêrum.

94. The Athenians say that Adeimantus, the Corinthian commander, at the moment when the two fleets joined battle, was seized with fear, and being beyond measure alarmed, spread his sails, and hasted to fly away; on which the other Corinthians, seeing their leader's ship in full flight, sailed off likewise. They had reached in their flight that part of the coast of Salamis where stands the temple of Minerva Sciras, when they met a light bark, a very strange apparition: it was never discovered that any one had sent it to them; and till it appeared they were altogether ignorant how the battle was going. That there was something beyond nature in the matter they judged from this—that when the men in the bark drew near to their ships they addressed them, saying—" Adeimantus, while thou playest the traitor's part, by withdrawing all these ships, and flying away from the fight, the Greeks whom thou hast deserted are defeating their foes as completely as they ever wished in their prayers." Adeimantus, however, would not believe what the men said; whereupon they told him, " he might take them with him as hostages, and put them to death if he did not find the Greeks winning." Then Adeimantus put about, both he and those who were with him; and they re-joined the fleet when the victory was already gained. Such is the tale which the Athenians tell concerning them of Corinth; these latter however do not allow its truth.[1] On the contrary, they declare that they were among those who distinguished themselves most in the fight. And the rest of Greece bears witness in their favour.

95. In the midst of the confusion Aristides, the son of Lysimachus, the Athenian, of whom I lately spoke as a man of the greatest excellence, performed the following service. He took a number of the Athenian heavy-armed troops, who had previously been stationed along the shore of Salamis, and, landing with them on the islet of Psyttaleia, slew all the Persians by whom it was occupied.

96. As soon as the sea-fight was ended,[2] the Greeks drew

---

[1] There can be no doubt that the tale was altogether false.

[2] The description of the battle of Salamis in Æschylus (Pers. 359-438), as the account of an eye-witness and combatant, must always hold a primary place among the records of the time. It does not appear to have been known to Herodotus, yet it confirms his account in all the principal features.

together to Salamis all the wrecks that were to be found in that
quarter, and prepared themselves for another engagement,
supposing that the king would renew the fight with the vessels
which still remained to him.   Many of the wrecks had been
carried away by a westerly wind to the coast of Attica, where
they were thrown upon the strip of shore called Côlias.   Thus
not only were the prophecies of Bacis and Musæus [1] concerning
this battle fulfilled completely, but likewise, by the place to
which the wrecks were drifted, the prediction of Lysistratus, an
Athenian soothsayer, uttered many years before these events.
and quite forgotten at the time by all the Greeks, was fully
accomplished.   The words were—

" Then shall the sight of the oars fill Colian dames with amazement."

Now this must have happened as soon as the king was departed.
   97. Xerxes, when he saw the extent of his loss, began to be
afraid lest the Greeks might be counselled by the Ionians, or
without their advice might determine to sail straight to the
Hellespont and break down the bridges there; in which case he
would be blocked up in Europe, and run great risk of perishing.
He therefore made up his mind to fly; but, as he wished to
hide his purpose alike from the Greeks and from his own people,
he set to work to carry a mound across the channel to Salamis,
and at the same time began fastening a number of Phœnician
merchant ships together, to serve at once for a bridge and a
wall.   He likewise made many warlike preparations, as if he
were about to engage the Greeks once more at sea.   Now, when
these things were seen, all grew fully persuaded that the king
was bent on remaining, and intended to push the war in good
earnest.   Mardonius, however, was in no respect deceived; for
long acquaintance enabled him to read all the king's thoughts.
Meanwhile, Xerxes, though engaged in this way, sent off a
messenger to carry intelligence of his misfortune to Persia.
   98. Nothing mortal travels so fast as these Persian messengers.
The entire plan is a Persian invention; and this is the method
of it.   Along the whole line of road there are men (they say)
stationed with horses, in number equal to the number of days
which the journey takes, allowing a man and horse to each
day; and these men will not be hindered from accomplishing
at their best speed the distance which they have to go, either
by snow, or rain, or heat, or by the darkness of night.   The

[1] Concerning these poets, see above, vii. 6, and viii. 20.

first rider delivers his despatch to the second, and the second passes it to the third; and so it is borne from hand to hand along the whole line, like the light in the torch-race, which the Greeks celebrate to Vulcan. The Persians give the riding post in this manner, the name of " Angarum." [1]

99. At Susa, on the arrival of the first message, which said that Xerxes was master of Athens, such was the delight of the Persians who had remained behind, that they forthwith strewed all the streets with myrtle boughs, and burnt incense, and fell to feasting and merriment. In like manner, when the second message reached them, so sore was their dismay, that they all with one accord rent their garments, and cried aloud, and wept and wailed without stint. They laid the blame of the disaster on Mardonius; and their grief on the occasion was less on account of the damage done to their ships, than owing to the alarm which they felt about the safety of the king. Hence their trouble did not cease till Xerxes himself, by his arrival, put an end to their fears.

100. And now Mardonius, perceiving that Xerxes took the defeat of his fleet greatly to heart, and suspecting that he had made up his mind to leave Athens and fly away, began to think of the likelihood of his being visited with punishment for having persuaded the king to undertake the war. He therefore considered that it would be the best thing for him to adventure further, and either become the conqueror of Greece—which was the result he rather expected—or else die gloriously after aspiring to a noble achievement. So with these thoughts in his mind, he said one day to the king—

" Do not grieve, master, or take so greatly to heart thy late loss. Our hopes hang not altogether on the fate of a few planks, but on our brave steeds and horsemen. These fellows, whom thou imaginest to have quite conquered us, will not venture—no, not one of them—to come ashore and contend with our land army; nor will the Greeks who are upon the mainland fight our troops; such as did so have received their punishment. If thou so pleasest, we may at once attack the Peloponnese; if thou wouldst rather wait a while, that too is in our power. Only be not disheartened. For it is not possible that the Greeks can avoid being brought to account, alike for this

---

[1] Probably in the time of Herodotus swift camels were employed in the postal service of the Persian Empire. [For the verb ἀγγαρεύειν see *Matt.* v. 41, and *Esther* viii. 10.—E. H. B.]

and for their former injuries; nor can they anyhow escape being thy slaves. Thou shouldst therefore do as I have said. If, however, thy mind is made up, and thou art resolved to retreat and lead away thy army, listen to the counsel which, in that case, I have to offer. Make not the Persians, O king! a laughing-stock to the Greeks. If thy affairs have succeeded ill, it has not been by their fault; thou canst not say that thy Persians have ever shown themselves cowards. What matters it if Phœnicians and Egyptians, Cyprians and Cilicians, have misbehaved?—their misconduct touches not us. Since then thy Persians are without fault, be advised by me. Depart home, if thou art so minded, and take with thee the bulk of thy army; but first let me choose out 300,000 troops, and let it be my task to bring Greece beneath thy sway."

101. Xerxes, when he heard these words, felt a sense of joy and delight, like a man who is relieved from care. Answering Mardonius, therefore, " that he would consider his counsel, and let him know which course he might prefer," Xerxes proceeded to consult with the chief men among the Persians; and because Artemisia on the former occasion had shown herself the only person who knew what was best to be done, he was pleased to summon her to advise him now. As soon as she arrived, he put forth all the rest, both councillors and body-guards, and said to her:—

" Mardonius wishes me to stay and attack the Peloponnese. My Persians, he says, and my other land forces, are not to blame for the disasters which have befallen our arms; and of this he declares they would very gladly give me the proof. He therefore exhorts me, either to stay and act as I have said, or to let him choose out 300,000 of my troops—wherewith he undertakes to reduce Greece beneath my sway—while I myself retire with the rest of my forces, and withdraw into my own country. Do thou, therefore, as thou didst counsel me so wisely to decline the sea-fight, now also advise me in this matter, and say, which course of the twain I ought to take for my own good."

102. Thus did the king ask Artemisia's counsel; and the following are the words wherewith she answered him:—

" 'Tis a hard thing, O king! to give the best possible advice to one who asks our counsel. Nevertheless, as thy affairs now stand, it seemeth to me that thou wilt do right to return home. As for Mardonius, if he prefers to remain, and undertakes to do as he has said, leave him behind by all means, with the troops which he desires. If his design succeeds, and he subdues the Greeks, as he promises, thine is the conquest, master; for thy slaves will have accomplished it. If, on the other hand, affairs run counter to his wishes, we can suffer no great loss, so long as thou art safe, and thy house is in no danger. The Greeks, too, while thou livest, and thy house flourishes, must be prepared to fight full many a battle for their freedom; whereas if Mardonius fall, it matters nothing—they will have gained but a poor triumph—a victory over one of thy slaves! Remember also, thou goest home having gained the purpose of thy expedition; [1] for thou hast burnt Athens!"

103. The advice of Artemesia pleased Xerxes well; for she had exactly uttered his own thoughts. I, for my part, do not believe that he would have remained had all his counsellors, both men and women, united to urge his stay, so great was the alarm that he felt. As it was, he gave praise to Artemisia, and entrusted certain of his children to her care, ordering her to convey them to Ephesus; for he had been accompanied on the expedition by some of his natural sons.

104. He likewise sent away at this time one of the principal of his eunuchs, [2] a man named Hermotimus, a Pedasian, who was bidden to take charge of these sons. Now the Pedasians inhabit the region above Halicarnassus; and it is related of them, that in their country the following circumstance happens: When a mischance is about to befall any of their neighbours within a certain time, the priestess of Minerva in their city grows a long beard. This has already taken place on two occasions.

105. The Hermotimus of whom I spoke above was, as I said, a Pedasian; and he, of all men whom we know, took the most cruel vengeance on the person who had done him an injury. He had been made a prisoner of war, and when his captors sold him, he was bought by a certain Panionius, a native of Chios, who made his living by a most nefarious traffic. Whenever he could get any boys of unusual beauty, he made them eunuchs, and, carrying them to Sardis or Ephesus, sold them for large sums of money. For the barbarians value eunuchs more than others, since they regard them as more trustworthy. Many were the slaves that Panionius, who made his living by the

---

[1] Vide supra, ch. 68, § 1.
[2] We have here the first instance in authentic Persian history of the influence of the eunuchs, which afterwards became so great an evil.

practice, had thus treated; and among them was this Hermotimus of whom I have here made mention. However, he was not without his share of good fortune; for after a while he was sent from Sardis, together with other gifts, as a present to the king. Nor was it long before he came to be esteemed by Xerxes more highly than all his eunuchs.

106. When the king was on his way to Athens with the Persian army, and abode for a time at Sardis, Hermotimus happened to make a journey upon business into Mysia; and there, in a district which is called Atarneus, but belongs to Chios,[1] he chanced to fall in with Panionius. Recognising him at once, he entered into a long and friendly talk with him, wherein he counted up the numerous blessings he enjoyed through his means, and promised him all manner of favours in return, if he would bring his household to Sardis and live there. Panionius was overjoyed, and, accepting the offer made him, came presently, and brought with him his wife and children. Then Hermotimus, when he had got Panionius and all his family into his power, addressed him in these words:—

" Thou man, who gettest a living by viler deeds than any one else in the whole world, what wrong to thee or thine had I or any of mine done, that thou shouldst have made me the *nothing* that I now am? Ah! surely thou thoughtest that the gods took no note of thy crimes. But they in their justice have delivered thee, the doer of unrighteousness, into my hands; and now thou canst not complain of the vengeance which I am resolved to take on thee."

After these reproaches, Hermotimus commanded the four sons of Panionius to be brought, and forced the father to make them eunuchs with his own hand. Unable to resist, he did as Hermotimus required; and then his sons were made to treat him in the self-same way. So in this way there came to Panionius requital at the hands of Hermotimus.

107. Xerxes, after charging Artemesia to convey his sons safe to Ephesus,[2] sent for Mardonius, and bade him choose from all his army such men as he wished, and see that he made his achievements answer to his promises. During this day he did no more; but no sooner was night come, than he issued his orders, and at once the captains of the ships left Phalêrum, and bore away for the Hellespont, each making all the speed he could, and hasting to guard the bridges against the king's

[1] Vide supra, i. 160; vi. 28, 29.   [2] Supra, ch. 103.

return. On their way, as they sailed by Zôster, where certain narrow points of land project into the sea,[1] they took the cliffs for vessels, and fled far away in alarm. Discovering their mistake, however, after a time, they joined company once more, and proceeded upon their voyage.

108. Next day the Greeks, seeing the land force of the barbarians encamped in the same place, thought that their ships must still be lying at Phalêrum; and, expecting another attack from that quarter, made preparations to defend themselves. Soon however news came that the ships were all departed and gone away; whereupon it was instantly resolved to make sail in pursuit. They went as far as Andros; but, seeing nothing of the Persian fleet, they stopped at that place, and held a council of war. At this council Themistocles advised that the Greeks should follow on through the islands, still pressing the pursuit, and making all haste to the Hellespont, there to break down the bridges. Eurybiades, however, delivered a contrary opinion. " If," he said, " the Greeks should break down the bridges, it would be the worst thing that could possibly happen for Greece. The Persian, supposing that his retreat were cut off, and he compelled to remain in Europe, would be sure never to give them any peace. Inaction on his part would ruin all his affairs, and leave him no chance of ever getting back to Asia—nay, would even cause his army to perish by famine: whereas, if he bestirred himself, and acted vigorously, it was likely that the whole of Europe would in course of time become subject to him; since, by degrees, the various towns and tribes would either fall before his arms, or else agree to terms of submission; and in this way, his troops would find food sufficient for them, since each year the Greek harvest would be theirs. As it was, the Persian, because he had lost the sea-fight, intended evidently to remain no longer in Europe. The Greeks ought to let him depart; and when he was gone from among them, and had returned into his own country, then would be the time for them to contend with him for the possession of *that*."

The other captains of the Peloponnesians declared themselves of the same mind.

109. Whereupon Themistocles, finding that the majority was against him, and that he could not persuade them to push on to the Hellespont, changed round, and addressing himself to the Athenians, who of all the allies were the most nettled at the

---

[1] Cape Zôster is undoubtedly the modern Cape *Lumbardha*.

enemy's escape, and who eagerly desired, if the other Greeks would not stir, to sail on by themselves to the Hellespont and break the bridges, spake as follows:—

"I have often myself witnessed occasions, and I have heard of many more from others, where men who had been conquered by an enemy, having been driven quite to desperation, have renewed the fight, and retrieved their former disasters. We have now had the great good luck to save both ourselves and all Greece by the repulse of this vast cloud of men; let us then be content and not press them too hard, now that they have begun to fly. Be sure we have not done this by our own might. It is the work of gods and heroes, who were jealous [1] that one man should be king at once of Europe and of Asia—more especially a man like this, unholy and presumptuous—a man who esteems alike things sacred and things profane; who has cast down and burnt the very images of the gods themselves; who even caused the sea to be scourged with rods and commanded fetters to be thrown into it.[2] At present all is well with us—let us then abide in Greece, and look to ourselves and to our families. The barbarian is clean gone—we have driven him off—let each now repair his own house, and sow his land diligently. In the spring we will take ship and sail to the Hellespont and to Ionia!"

All this Themistocles said in the hope of establishing a claim upon the king; for he wanted to have a safe retreat in case any mischance should befall him at Athens—which indeed came to pass afterwards.

110. At present, however, he dissembled; and the Athenians were persuaded by his words. For they were ready now to do whatever he advised; since they had always esteemed him a wise man, and he had lately proved himself most truly wise and well-judging. Accordingly, they came in to his views; whereupon he lost no time in sending messengers, on board a light bark, to the king, choosing for this purpose men whom he could trust to keep his instructions secret, even although they should be put to every kind of torture. Among them was the houseslave Sicinnus, the same whom he had made use of previously.[3] When the men reached Attica, all the others stayed with the boat; but Sicinnus went up to the king, and spake to him as follows:—

"I am sent to thee by Themistocles, the son of Neocles, who

---

[1] Supra, vii. 10, § 5. [2] Supra, vii. 35. [3] Supra, ch. 75.

is the leader of the Athenians, and the wisest and bravest man
of all the allies, to bear thee this message: ' Themistocles the
Athenian, anxious to render thee a service, has restrained the
Greeks, who were impatient to pursue thy ships, and to break
up the bridges at the Hellespont. Now, therefore, return home
at thy leisure.' "

The messengers, when they had performed their errand,
sailed back to the fleet.

111. And the Greeks, having resolved that they would
neither proceed further in pursuit of the barbarians, nor push
forward to the Hellespont and destroy the passage, laid siege to
Andros, intending to take the town by storm. For Themistocles had required the Andrians to pay down a sum of money;
and they had refused, being the first of all the islanders who did
so. To his declaration, " that the money must needs be paid, as
the Athenians had brought with him two mighty gods—Per-
suasion and Necessity," they made reply, that " Athens might
well be a great and glorious city, since she was blest with such
excellent gods; but *they* were wretchedly poor, stinted for land,
and cursed with two unprofitable gods, who always dwelt with
them and would never quit their island—to wit, Poverty and
Helplessness. These were the gods of the Andrians, and therefore they would not pay the money. For the power of Athens
could not possibly be stronger than their inability." This
reply, coupled with the refusal to pay the sum required, caused
their city to be besieged by the Greeks.

112. Meanwhile Themistocles, who never ceased his pursuit
of gain,[1] sent threatening messages to the other islanders with
demands for different sums, employing the same messengers
and the same words as he had used towards the Andrians.
" If," he said, " they did not send him the amount required, he
would bring the Greek fleet upon them, and besiege them till
he took their cities." By these means he collected large sums
from the Carystians [2] and the Parians, who, when they heard
that Andros was already besieged, and that Themistocles was
the best esteemed of all the captains, sent the money through
fear. Whether any of the other islanders did the like, I cannot
say for certain; but I think some did besides those I have
mentioned. However, the Carystians, though they complied,
were not spared any the more; but Themistocles was softened
by the Parians' gift, and therefore they received no visit from

[1] Cf. supra, ch. 4.   [2] Supra, vi. 99.

the army. In this way it was that Themistocles, during his stay at Andros, obtained money from the islanders, unbeknown to the other captains.

113. King Xerxes and his army waited but a few days after the sea-fight, and then withdrew into Bœotia by the road which they had followed on their advance. It was the wish of Mardonius to escort the king a part of the way; and as the time of year was no longer suitable for carrying on war, he thought it best to winter in Thessaly, and wait for the spring before he attempted the Peloponnese. After the army was come into Thessaly, Mardonius made choice of the troops that were to stay with him; and, first of all, he took the whole body called the " Immortals," [1] except only their leader, Hydarnes, who refused to quit the person of the king. Next, he chose the Persians who wore breastplates, and the thousand picked horse; [2] likewise the Medes, the Sacans, the Bactrians, and the Indians, foot and horse equally. These nations he took entire: from the rest of the allies he culled a few men, taking either such as were remarkable for their appearance, or else such as had performed, to his knowledge, some valiant deed. The Persians furnished him with the greatest number of troops, men who were adorned with chains and armlets. Next to them were the Medes, who in number equalled the Persians, but in valour fell short of them. The whole army, reckoning the horsemen with the rest, amounted to 300,000 men.

114. At the time when Mardonius was making choice of his troops, and Xerxes still continued in Thessaly, the Lacedæmonians received a message from the Delphic oracle, bidding them seek satisfaction at the hands of Xerxes for the death of Leonidas, and take whatever he chose to give them. So the Spartans sent a herald with all speed into Thessaly, who arrived while the entire Persian army was still there. This man, being brought before the king, spake as follows:—

" King of the Medes, the Lacedæmonians and the Heracleids of Sparta require of thee the satisfaction due for bloodshed, because thou slewest their king, who fell fighting for Greece."

Xerxes laughed, and for a long time spake not a word. At last, however, he pointed to Mardonius, who was standing by him, and said:—" Mardonius here shall give them the satisfac-

---

[1] Supra, vii. 83, 211, 215.
[2] Troops specially attached to the king's person (supra, vii. 40).

tion they deserve to get." And the herald accepted the answer, and forthwith went his way.

115. Xerxes, after this, left Mardonius in Thessaly, and marched away himself, at his best speed, toward the Hellespont. In five-and-forty days he reached the place of passage, where he arrived with scarce a fraction, so to speak, of his former army. All along their line of march, in every country where they chanced to be, his soldiers seized and devoured whatever corn they could find belonging to the inhabitants; while, if no corn was to be found, they gathered the grass that grew in the fields, and stripped the trees, whether cultivated or wild, alike of their bark and of their leaves, and so fed themselves. They left nothing anywhere, so hard were they pressed by hunger. Plague too and dysentery attacked the troops while still upon their march, and greatly thinned their ranks. Many died; others fell sick and were left behind in the different cities that lay upon the route, the inhabitants being strictly charged by Xerxes to tend and feed them. Of these some remained in Thessaly, others in Siris of Pæonia, others again in Macedon. Here [1] Xerxes, on his march into Greece, had left the sacred car and steeds of Jove; which upon his return he was unable to recover; for the Pæonians had disposed of them to the Thracians, and, when Xerxes demanded them back, they said that the Thracian tribes who dwelt about the sources of the Strymon had stolen the mares as they pastured.

116. Here too a Thracian chieftain, king of the Bisaltians and of Crestonia, did a deed which went beyond nature. He had refused to become the willing slave of Xerxes, and had fled before him into the heights of Rhodopé, [2] at the same time forbidding his sons to take part in the expedition against Greece. But they, either because they cared little for his orders, or because they wished greatly to see the war, joined the army of Xerxes. At this time they had all returned home to him—the number of the men was six—quite safe and sound. But their father took them, and punished their offence by plucking out their eyes from the sockets. Such was the treatment which these men received.

117. The Persians, having journeyed through Thrace and reached the passage, entered their ships hastily and crossed the

---

[1] At Siris, not in Macedonia.

[2] Rhodopé proper appears to have been the chain now called *Despoto Dagh.*

Hellespont to Abydos. The bridges were not found stretched across the strait; since a storm had broken and dispersed them. At Abydos the troops halted, and, obtaining more abundant provision than they had yet got upon their march, they fed without stint; from which cause, added to the change in their water, great numbers of those who had hitherto escaped perished. The remainder, together with Xerxes himself, came safe to Sardis.[1]

118. There is likewise another account given of the return of the king. It is said that when Xerxes on his way from Athens arrived at Eïon upon the Strymon, he gave up travelling by land, and, intrusting Hydarnes with the conduct of his forces to the Hellespont, embarked himself on board a Phœnician ship, and so crossed into Asia. On his voyage the ship was assailed by a strong wind blowing from the mouth of the Strymon, which caused the sea to run high. As the storm increased, and the ship laboured heavily, because of the number of the Persians who had come in the king's train, and who now crowded the deck, Xerxes was seized with fear, and called out to the helmsman in a loud voice, asking him, if there were any means whereby they might escape the danger. "No means, master," the helmsman answered, "unless we could be quit of these too numerous passengers." Xerxes, they say, on hearing this, addressed the Persians as follows: "Men of Persia," he said, "now is the time for you to show what love ye bear your king. My safety, as it seems, depends wholly upon you." So spake the king; and the Persians instantly made obeisance, and then leapt over into the sea. Thus was the ship lightened, and Xerxes got safe to Asia. As soon as he had reached the shore, he sent for the helmsman, and gave him a golden crown because he had preserved the life of the king,—but because he had caused the death of a number of Persians, he ordered his head to be struck from his shoulders.

119. Such is the other account which is given of the return of Xerxes; but to me it seems quite unworthy of belief, alike in other respects, and in what relates to the Persians. For had the helmsman made any such speech to Xerxes, I suppose there is not one man in ten thousand who will doubt that this is the course which the king would have followed:—he would have made the men upon the ship's deck,[2] who were not only

[1] Xerxes remained at Sardis the whole of the winter, and during a considerable portion of the next year (infra, ix. 107, ad fin.).

[2] The Epibatæ, or "marines," of which each trireme in the Persian fleet carried thirty (supra, 184).

Persians, but Persians of the very highest rank, quit their place and go down below; and would have cast into the sea an equal number of the rowers, who were Phœnicians. But the truth is, that the king, as I have already said, returned into Asia by the same road as the rest of the army.

120. I will add a strong proof of this. It is certain that Xerxes on his way back from Greece passed through Abdêra, where he made a contract of friendship with the inhabitants, and presented them with a golden scymitar, and a tiara broidered with gold. The Abderites declare — but I put no faith in this part of their story — that from the time of the king's leaving Athens, he never once loosed his girdle till he came to their city, since it was not till then that he felt himself in safety. Now Abdêra is nearer to the Hellespont than Eïon and the Strymon, where Xerxes, according to the other tale, took ship.

121. Meanwhile the Greeks, finding that they could not capture Andros, sailed away to Carystus, and wasted the lands of the Carystians, after which they returned to Salamis. Arrived here, they proceeded, before entering on any other matter, to make choice of the first-fruits which should be set apart as offerings to the gods. These consisted of divers gifts; among them were three Phœnician triremes, one of which was dedicated at the Isthmus, where it continued to my day; another at Sunium; and the third, at Salamis itself, which was devoted to Ajax. This done, they made a division of the booty, and sent away the first-fruits to Delphi. Thereof was made the statue, holding in its hand the beak of a ship, which is twelve cubits high, and which stands in the same place with the golden one of Alexander the Macedonian.

122. After the first-fruits had been sent to Delphi, the Greeks made inquiry of the god, in the name of their whole body, if he had received his full share of the spoils and was satisfied therewith. The god made answer, that all the other Greeks had paid him his full due, except only the Eginetans; on them he had still a claim for the prize of valour which they had gained at Salamis.[1] So the Eginetans, when they heard this, dedicated the three golden stars which stand on the top of a bronze mast in the corner near the bowl offered by Crœsus.[2]

123. When the spoils had been divided, the Greeks sailed to

[1] Supra, ch. 93.
[2] Supra, i. 51. The *silver* bowl of Crœsus is intended, which stood " in the corner of the ante-chapel."

the Isthmus, where a prize of valour was to be awarded to the man who, of all the Greeks, had shown the most merit during the war. When the chiefs were all come, they met at the altar of Neptune, and took the ballots wherewith they were to give their votes for the first and for the second in merit. Then each man gave himself the first vote, since each considered that he was himself the worthiest; but the second votes were given chiefly to Themistocles. In this way, while the others received but one vote apiece, Themistocles had for the second prize a large majority of the suffrages.

124. Envy, however, hindered the chiefs from coming to a decision, and they all sailed away to their homes without making any award. Nevertheless Themistocles was regarded everywhere as by far the wisest man of all the Greeks; and the whole country rang with his fame. As the chiefs who fought at Salamis, notwithstanding that he was really entitled to the prize, had withheld his honour from him, he went without delay to Lacedæmon, in the hope that he would be honoured there. And the Lacedæmonians received him handsomely, and paid him great respect. The prize of valour indeed, which was a crown of olive, they gave to Eurybiades; but Themistocles was given a crown of olive too, as the prize of wisdom and dexterity. He was likewise presented with the most beautiful chariot that could be found in Sparta; and after receiving abundant praises, was, upon his departure, escorted as far as the borders of Tegea, by the three hundred picked Spartans, who are called the Knights. Never was it known, either before or since, that the Spartans escorted a man out of their city.

125. On the return of Themistocles to Athens, Timodëmus of Aphidnæ,[1] who was one of his enemies, but otherwise a man of no repute, became so maddened with envy that he openly railed against him, and, reproaching him with his journey to Sparta, said—" 'Twas not his own merit that had won him honour from the men of Lacedæmon, but the fame of Athens, his country." Then Themistocles, seeing that Timodëmus repeated this phrase unceasingly, replied—

" Thus stands the case, friend. I had never got this honour from the Spartans, had I been a Belbinite [2]—nor thou, hadst thou been an Athenian! "

---

[1] Aphidnæ, or Aphidna, was one of the most ancient of the Attic demi.

[2] An island at the mouth of the Saronic Gulf.

126. Artabazus, the son of Pharnaces,[1] a man whom the Persians had always held in much esteem, but who, after the affair of Platæa, rose still higher in their opinion, escorted King Xerxes as far as the strait, with sixty thousand of the chosen troops of Mardonius. When the king was safe in Asia, Artabazus set out upon his return; and on arriving near Pallênê, and finding that Mardonius had gone into winter-quarters in Thessaly and Macedonia, and was in no hurry for him to join the camp, he thought it his bounden duty, as the Potidæans had just revolted, to occupy himself in reducing them to slavery. For as soon as the king had passed beyond their territory, and the Persian fleet had made its hasty flight from Salamis, the Potidæans revolted from the barbarians openly; as likewise did all the other inhabitants of that peninsula.

127. Artabazus, therefore, laid siege to Potidæa; and having a suspicion that the Olynthians were likely to revolt shortly, he besieged their city also. Now Olynthus was at that time held by the Bottiæans, who had been driven from the parts about the Thermaic Gulf by the Macedonians. Artabazus took the city, and, having so done, led out all the inhabitants to a marsh in the neighbourhood, and there slew them. After this he delivered the place into the hands of the people called Chalcideans, having first appointed Critobûlus of Torônê to be governor. Such was the way in which the Chalcideans got Olynthus.

128. When this town had fallen, Artabazus pressed the siege of Potidæa all the more unremittingly; and was pushing his operations with vigour, when Timoxenus, captain of the Scionæans, entered into a plot to betray the town to him. How the matter was managed at first, I cannot pretend to say, for no account has come down to us: but at the last this is what happened. Whenever Timoxenus wished to send a letter to Artabazus, or Artabazus to send one to Timoxenus, the letter was written on a strip of paper, and rolled round the notched end of an arrow-shaft; the feathers were then put on over the paper, and the arrow thus prepared was shot to some place agreed upon. But after a while the plot of Timoxenus to betray Potidæa was discovered in this way. Artabazus, on one occasion, shot off his arrow, intending to send it to the accustomed place, but, missing his mark, hit one of the Potidæans in the shoulder. A crowd gathered about the wounded man, as

---

[1] Artabazus had previously commanded the Parthians and Chorasmians (supra, vii. 66). His prudent conduct at Platæa is noticed (infra, ix. 66).

commonly happens in war; and when the arrow was pulled out, they noticed the paper, and straightway carried it to the captains who were present from the various cities of the peninsula. The captains read the letter, and, finding who the traitor was, nevertheless resolved, out of regard for the city of Sciônê, that as they did not wish the Scionæans to be thenceforth branded with the name of traitors, they would not bring against him any charge of treachery. Such accordingly was the mode in which this plot was discovered.

129. After Artabazus had continued the siege by the space of three months, it happened that there was an unusual ebb of the tide, which lasted a long while. So when the barbarians saw that what had been sea was now no more than a swamp, they determined to push across it into Pallênê. And now the troops had already made good two-fifths of their passage, and three-fifths still remained before they could reach Pallênê, when the tide came in with a very high flood, higher than had ever been seen before, as the inhabitants of those parts declare, though high floods are by no means uncommon. All who were not able to swim perished immediately; the rest were slain by the Potidæans, who bore down upon them in their sailing vessels. The Potidæans say that what caused this swell and flood, and so brought about the disaster of the Persians which ensued therefrom, was the profanation, by the very men now destroyed in the sea, of the temple and image of Neptune, situated in their suburb. And in this they seem to me to say well. Artabazus afterwards led away the remainder of his army, and joined Mardonius in Thessaly. Thus fared it with the Persians who escorted the king to the strait.

130. As for that part of the fleet of Xerxes which had survived the battle, when it had made good its escape from Salamis to the coast of Asia, and conveyed the king with his army across the strait from the Chersonese to Abydos, it passed the winter at Cymê.[1] On the first approach of spring, there was an early muster of the ships at Samos, where some of them indeed had remained throughout the winter. Most of the men-at-arms who served on board were Persians, or else Medes; and the command of the fleet had been taken by Mardontes, the son of Bagæus, and Artaÿntes, the son of Artachæus; while there was likewise a third commander, Ithamitres, the nephew of Artaÿntes,[2] whom his uncle had advanced to the post. Further west than Samos,

[1] Supra, i. 149.   [2] Infra, ix. 102.

however, they did not venture to proceed; for they remembered
what a defeat they had suffered, and there was no one to compel
them to approach any nearer to Greece. They therefore remained at Samos, and kept watch over Ionia, to hinder it from
breaking into revolt. The whole number of their ships, including those furnished by the Ionians, was three hundred. It did
not enter into their thoughts that the Greeks would proceed
against Ionia; on the contrary, they supposed that the defence
of their own country would content them, more especially as
they had not pursued the Persian fleet when it fled from Salamis,
but had so readily given up the chase. They despaired, however, altogether of gaining any success by sea themselves, though
by land they thought that Mardonius was quite sure of victory.
So they remained at Samos, and took counsel together, if by
any means they might harass the enemy, at the same time
that they waited eagerly to hear how matters would proceed
with Mardonius.

131. The approach of spring, and the knowledge that Mardonius was in Thessaly, roused the Greeks from inaction. Their
land force indeed was not yet come together; but the fleet,
consisting of one hundred and ten ships, proceeded to Egina,
under the command of Leotychides.[1] This Leotychides, who
was both general and admiral, was the son of Menares, the son
of Agesilaüs, the son of Hippocratides, the son of Leotychides,
the son of Anaxilaüs, the son of Archidamus, the son of Anax-
andrides, the son of Theopompus, the son of Nicander, the son
of Charillus, the son of Eunomus, the son of Polydectes, the son
of Prytanis, the son of Euryphon, the son of Procles, the son of
Aristodêmus, the son of Aristomachus, the son of Cleodæus, the
son of Hyllus, the son of Hercules. He belonged to the younger
branch of the royal house.[2] All his ancestors, except the two
next in the above list to himself, had been kings of Sparta.
The Athenian vessels were commanded by Xanthippus, the son
of Ariphron.[3]

132. When the whole fleet was collected together at Egina,
ambassadors from Ionia arrived at the Greek station; they had
but just come from paying a visit to Sparta, where they had
been intreating the Lacedæmonians to undertake the deliverance of their native land. One of these ambassadors was

---

[1] Supra, vi. 71.   [2] Supra, vi. 52.
[3] Supra, vi. 131. That Xanthippus had succeeded Themistocles in the
command of the fleet, does not imply that the latter had ceased to be
a Strategus.

Herodotus, the son of Basileides. Originally they were seven in number; and the whole seven had conspired to slay Strattis the tyrant of Chios; one, however, of those engaged in the plot betrayed the enterprise; and the conspiracy being in this way discovered, Herodotus, and the remaining five, quitted Chios, and went straight to Sparta, whence they had now proceeded to Egina, their object being to beseech the Greeks that they would pass over to Ionia. It was not, however, without difficulty that they were induced to advance even so far as Delos. All beyond that seemed to the Greeks full of danger; the places were quite unknown to them, and to their fancy swarmed with Persian troops; as for Samos, it appeared to them as far off as the Pillars of Hercules.[1] Thus it came to pass, that at the very same time the barbarians were hindered by their fears from venturing any further west than Samos, and the prayers of the Chians failed to induce the Greeks to advance any further east than Delos. Terror guarded the mid region.

133. The Greek fleet was now on its way to Delos; but Mardonius still abode in his winter-quarters in Thessaly. When he was about to leave them, he despatched a man named Mys, a Europian by birth, to go and consult the different oracles, giving him orders to put questions everywhere to all the oracles whereof he found it possible to make trial. What it was that he wanted to know, when he gave Mys these orders, I am not able to say, for no account has reached me of the matter; but for my own part, I suppose that he sent to inquire concerning the business which he had in hand, and not for any other purpose.

134. Mys, it is certain, went to Lebadeia,[2] and, by the payment of a sum of money, induced one of the inhabitants to go down to Trophônius;[3] he likewise visited Abæ of the Phocians, and there consulted the god; while at Thebes, to which place he went first of all, he not only got access to Apollo Ismenius (of whom inquiry is made by means of victims, according to the custom practised also at Olympia), but likewise prevailed on a man, who was not a Theban but a foreigner, to pass the night in the temple of Amphiaraüs.[4] No Theban can lawfully consult

---

[1] Rhetorical exaggeration. The passage from Europe to Asia, through the islands, must have been thoroughly familiar to the Greeks of this period. Even the Spartans were accustomed to make it.

[2] One of the most flourishing towns of Northern Greece.

[3] The cave of Trophonius was situated at a little distance from the city.

[4] Prophetic dreams were supposed to visit those who slept in this temple on the fleece of a ram which they had first offered to the god.

this oracle, for the following reason: Amphiaraüs by an oracle gave the Thebans their choice, to have him for their prophet or for their helper in war; he bade them elect between the two, and forego either one or the other; so they chose rather to have him for their helper. On this account it is unlawful for a Theban to sleep in his temple.

135. One thing which the Thebans declare to have happened at this time is to me very surprising. Mys, the Europian, they say, after he had gone about to all the oracles, came at last to the sacred precinct of Apollo Ptôüs. The place itself bears the name of Ptôüm; it is in the country of the Thebans, and is situate on the mountain side overlooking Lake Copaïs, only a very little way from the town called Acræphia. Here Mys arrived, and entered the temple, followed by three Theban citizens—picked men whom the state had appointed to take down whatever answer the god might give. No sooner was he entered than the prophet delivered him an oracle, but in a foreign tongue; so that his Theban attendants were astonished, hearing a strange language when they expected Greek, and did not know what to do. Mys, however, the Europian, snatched from their hands the tablet which they had brought with them, and wrote down what the prophet uttered. The reply, he told them, was in the Carian dialect. After this, Mys departed and returned to Thessaly.

136. Mardonius, when he had read the answers given by the oracles, sent next an envoy to Athens. This was Alexander, the son of Amyntas, a Macedonian, of whom he made choice for two reasons. Alexander was connected with the Persians by family ties; for Gygæa, who was the daughter of Amyntas, and sister to Alexander himself, was married to Bubares, a Persian, and by him had a son, to wit, Amyntas of Asia; who was named after his mother's father, and enjoyed the revenues of Alabanda, a large city of Phrygia,[1] which had been assigned him by the king. Alexander was likewise (and of this too Mardonius was well aware), both by services which he had rendered, and by formal compact of friendship, connected with Athens. Mardonius therefore thought that, by sending him, he would be most likely to gain over the Athenians to the Persian side. He had heard that they were a numerous and a warlike people, and he knew that the disasters which had befallen the Persians by sea were mainly their work; he therefore expected that, if he

---

[1] Alabanda is said above (vii. 195) to have belonged to Caria.

could form alliance with them, he would easily get the mastery of the sea (as indeed he would have done, beyond a doubt), while by land he believed that he was already greatly superior; and so he thought by this alliance to make sure of overcoming the Greeks. Perhaps, too, the oracles leant this way, and counselled him to make Athens his friend: so that it may have been in obedience to them that he sent the embassy.

137. This Alexander was descended in the seventh degree from Perdiccas, who obtained the sovereignty over the Macedonians in the way which I will now relate. Three brothers, descendants of Têmenus, fled from Argos to the Illyrians; their names were Gauanes, Aëropus, and Perdiccas. From Illyria they went across to Upper Macedonia, where they came to a certain town called Lebæa. There they hired themselves out to serve the king in different employs; one tended the horses; another looked after the cows; while Perdiccas, who was the youngest, took charge of the smaller cattle. In those early times poverty was not confined to the people: kings themselves were poor, and so here it was the king's wife who cooked the victuals. Now, whenever she baked the bread, she always observed that the loaf of the labouring boy Perdiccas swelled to double its natural size. So the queen, finding this never fail, spoke of it to her husband. Directly that it came to his ears, the thought struck him that it was a miracle, and boded something of no small moment. He therefore sent for the three labourers, and told them to begone out of his dominions. They answered, "they had a right to their wages; if he would pay them what was due, they were quite willing to go." Now it happened that the sun was shining down the chimney into the room where they were; and the king, hearing them talk of wages, lost his wits, and said, "There are the wages which you deserve; take that—I give it you!" and pointed, as he spoke, to the sunshine. The two elder brothers, Gauanes and Aëropus, stood aghast at the reply, and did nothing; but the boy, who had a knife in his hand, make a mark with it round the sunshine on the floor of the room, and said, "O king! we accept your payment." Then he received the light of the sun three times into his bosom, and so went away; and his brothers went with him.

138. When they were gone, one of those who sat by told the king what the youngest of the three had done, and hinted that he must have had some meaning in accepting the wages given. Then the king, when he heard what had happened, was angry,

and sent horsemen after the youths to slay them. Now there is a river in Macedonia to which the descendants of these Argives offer sacrifice as their saviour. This stream swelled so much, as soon as the sons of Têmenus were safe across, that the horsemen found it impossible to follow. So the brothers escaped into another part of Macedonia, and took up their abode near the place called " the Gardens of Midas, son of Gordias." In these gardens there are roses which grow of themselves, so sweet that no others can come near them, and with blossoms that have as many as sixty petals apiece. It was here, according to the Macedonians, that Silenus was made a prisoner.[1] Above the gardens stands a mountain called Bermius, which is so cold that none can reach the top. Here the brothers made their abode;[2] and from this place by degrees they conquered all Macedonia.

139. From the Perdiccas of whom we have here spoken, Alexander was descended in the following way:—Alexander was the son of Amyntas, Amyntas of Alcetas; the father of Alcetas was Aëropus; of Aëropus, Philip; of Philip, Argæus; of Argæus, Perdiccas, the first sovereign. Such was the descent of Alexander.

140. (§ 1.) When Alexander reached Athens as the ambassador of Mardonius, he spoke as follows:—

" O men of Athens, these be the words of Mardonius. ' The king has sent a message to me, saying, " All the trespasses which the Athenians have committed against me I freely forgive. Now then, Mardonius, thus shalt thou act towards them. Restore to them their territory; and let them choose for themselves whatever land they like besides, and let them dwell therein as a free people. Build up likewise all their temples which I burned, if on these terms they will consent to enter into a league with me." Such are the orders which I have received, and which I must needs obey, unless there be a hindrance on your part. And now I say unto you,—why are ye so mad as to levy war against the king, whom ye cannot possibly overcome, or even resist for ever? Ye have seen the multitude and the bravery of the host of Xerxes; ye know also how large a power remains with me in your land; suppose then ye should get the better of us, and defeat this army—a thing whereof ye will not, if ye be wise, entertain the least hope—what follows even then

---

[1] The tale went that Midas, one day when he was hunting, caught Silenus, and forced him to answer a number of questions.

[2] Mount Bermius is undoubtedly the range which shuts in the Macedonian maritime plain upon the west.

but a contest with a still greater force? Do not, because you would fain match yourselves with the king, consent to lose your country and live in constant danger of your lives. Rather agree to make peace; which ye can now do without any tarnish to your honour, since the king invites you to it. Continue free, and make an alliance with us, without fraud or deceit.'

(§ 2.) "These are the words, O Athenians! which Mardonius had bid me speak to you. For my own part, I will say nothing of the good will I bear your nation, since ye have not now for the first time to become acquainted with it.[1] But I will add my intreaties also, and beseech you to give ear to Mardonius; for I see clearly that it is impossible for you to go on for ever contending against Xerxes. If that had appeared to me possible, I would not now have come hither the bearer of such a message. But the king's power surpasses that of man, and his arm reaches far. If then ye do not hasten to conclude a peace, when such fair terms are offered you, I tremble to think of what you will have to endure—you, who of all the allies lie most directly in the path of danger, whose land will always be the chief battle-ground of the contending powers, and who will therefore constantly have to suffer alone. Hearken then, I pray you, to Mardonius! Surely it is no small matter that the Great King chooses you out from all the rest of the Greeks, to offer you forgiveness of the wrongs you have done him, and to propose himself as your friend and ally!"

141. Such were the words of Alexander. Now the Lacedæmonians, when tidings reached them that Alexander was gone to Athens to bring about a league between the Athenians and the barbarians, and when at the same time they called to mind the prophecies which declared that the Dorian race should one day be driven from the Peloponnese by the Medes and the Athenians, were exceedingly afraid lest the Athenians might consent to the alliance with Persia. They therefore lost no time in sending envoys to Athens; and it so happened that these envoys were given their audience at the same time with Alexander: for the Athenians had waited and made delays, because they felt sure that the Lacedæmonians would hear that an ambassador was come to them from the Persians, and as soon as they heard it would with all speed send an embassy. They contrived matters therefore of set purpose, so that the Lacedæmonians might hear them deliver their sentiments on the occasion.

[1] Supra, vii. 173.

142. As soon as Alexander had finished speaking, the ambassadors from Sparta took the word and said,—

"We are sent here by the Lacedæmonians to entreat of you that ye will not do a new thing in Greece, nor agree to the terms which are offered you by the barbarian. Such conduct on the part of any of the Greeks were alike unjust and dishonourable; but in you 'twould be worse than in others, for divers reasons. 'Twas by you that this war was kindled at the first among us—our wishes were in no way considered; the contest began by your seeking to extend your empire—now the fate of Greece is involved in it. Besides it were surely an intolerable thing that the Athenians, who have always hitherto been known as a nation to which many men owed their freedom, should now become the means of bringing all other Greeks into slavery. We feel, however, for the heavy calamities which press on you—the loss of your harvest these two years, and the ruin in which your homes have lain for so long a time. We offer you, therefore, on the part of the Lacedæmonians and the allies, sustenance for your women and for the unwarlike portion of your households, so long as the war endures. Be ye not seduced by Alexander the Macedonian, who softens down the rough words of Mardonius. He does as is natural for him to do —a tyrant himself, he helps forward a tyrant's cause.[1] But ye, Athenians, should do differently, at least if ye be truly wise; for ye should know that with barbarians there is neither faith nor truth."

143. Thus spake the envoys. After which the Athenians returned this answer to Alexander:—

"We know, as well as thou dost, that the power of the Mede is many times greater than our own: we did not need to have *that* cast in our teeth. Nevertheless we cling so to freedom that we shall offer what resistance we may. Seek not to persuade us into making terms with the barbarian—say what thou wilt, thou wilt never gain our assent. Return rather at once, and tell Mardonius that our answer to him is this:—'So long as the sun keeps his present course, we will never join alliance with Xerxes. Nay, we shall oppose him unceasingly, trusting in the aid of those gods and heroes whom he has lightly esteemed, whose houses and whose images he has burnt with fire.' And come not thou again to us with words like these; nor, thinking to do us a service, persuade us to unholy actions. Thou art the

---

[1] Alexander was not a tyrant (τύραννος) in any proper acceptation of the word. He was a king (βασιλεύς) as truly as Xerxes or Leonidas.

guest and friend of our nation—we would not that thou shouldst receive hurt at our hands."

144. Such was the answer which the Athenians gave to Alexander. To the Spartan envoys they said,—

" 'Twas natural no doubt that the Lacedæmonians should be afraid we might make terms with the barbarian; but nevertheless 'twas a base fear in men who knew so well of what temper and spirit we are. Not all the gold that the whole earth contains—not the fairest and most fertile of all lands—would bribe us to take part with the Medes and help them to enslave our countrymen. Even could we anyhow have brought ourselves to such a thing, there are many very powerful motives which would now make it impossible. The first and chief of these is the burning and destruction of our temples and the images of our gods, which forces us to make no terms with their destroyer, but rather to pursue him with our resentment to the uttermost. Again, there is our common brotherhood with the Greeks: our common language, the altars and the sacrifices of which we all partake, the common character which we bear— did the Athenians betray all these, of a truth it would not be well. Know then now, if ye have not known it before, that while one Athenian remains alive, we will never join alliance with Xerxes. We thank you, however, for your forethought on our behalf, and for your wish to give our families sustenance, now that ruin has fallen on us—the kindness is complete on your part; but for ourselves, we will endure as we may, and not be burdensome to you. Such then is our resolve. Be it your care with all speed to lead out your troops; for if we surmise aright, the barbarian will not wait long ere he invade our territory, but will set out so soon as he learns our answer to be, that we will do none of those things which he requires of us. Now then is the time for us, before he enters Attica, to go forth ourselves into Bœotia, and give him battle."

When the Athenians had thus spoken, the ambassadors from Sparta departed, and returned back to their own country.

ADDED NOTE BY THE EDITOR

The great historical drama is now drawing to its close. The opposing forces of East and West, of Barbarism and Hellenism, have met at Salamis, in one of the most decisive sea-battles ever fought; Platæa is yet to decide their fortunes by land; at Mykale the Greeks are no longer in the position of those who act merely on the defensive; they are to begin a system of retaliation on the foe. This system is to reach its climax 150 years later in the great victories of Alexander.

THE NINTH BOOK, ENTITLED CALLIOPÉ

1. MARDONIUS, when Alexander upon his return made known to him the answer of the Athenians, forthwith broke up from Thessaly,[1] and led his army with all speed against Athens; forcing the several nations through whose land he passed to furnish him with additional troops. The chief men of Thessaly, far from repenting of the part which they had taken in the war hitherto, urged on the Persians to the attack more earnestly than ever. Thorax of Larissa in particular, who had helped to escort Xerxes on his flight to Asia, now openly encouraged Mardonius in his march upon Greece.

2. When the army reached Bœotia, the Thebans sought to induce Mardonius to make a halt: " He would not," they told him, " find anywhere a more convenient place in which to pitch his camp; and their advice to him was, that he should go no further, but fix himself there, and thence take measures to subdue all Greece without striking a blow. If the Greeks, who had held together hitherto, still continued united among themselves, it would be difficult for the whole world to overcome them by force of arms. But if thou wilt do as we advise," they went on to say, " thou mayest easily obtain the direction of all their counsels. Send presents to the men of most weight in the several states, and by so doing thou wilt sow division among them. After that, it will be a light task, with the help of such as side with thee, to bring under all thy adversaries."

3. Such was the advice of the Thebans: but Mardonius did not follow it. A strong desire of taking Athens a second time possessed him, in part arising from his inborn stubbornness, in part from a wish to inform the king at Sardis, by fire-signals along the islands, that he was master of the place. However, he did not on his arrival in Attica find the Athenians in their country—they had again withdrawn, some to their ships, but

---

[1] Mardonius wintered his army in Thessaly *and Macedonia* (supra, viii. 126). The difficulty of procuring supplies, after the exhaustion caused by the presence of the immense host of Xerxes, made it necessary to fall back upon those rich and fertile countries, the chief granaries of Greece. The same cause compelled the wide dispersion of his troops, indicated by their occupation of both regions.

the greater part to Salamis—and he only gained possession of a deserted town. It was ten months after the taking of the city by the king that Mardonius came against it for the second time.

4. Mardonius, being now in Athens, sent an envoy to Salamis, one Murychides, a Hellespontine Greek, to offer the Athenians once more the same terms which had been conveyed to them by Alexander. The reason for his sending a second time, though he knew beforehand their unfriendly feelings towards him, was,—that he hoped, when they saw the whole land of Attica conquered and in his power, their stubbornness would begin to give way. On this account, therefore, he dispatched Murychides to Salamis.

5. Now, when Murychides came before the council, and delivered his message, one of the councillors, named Lycidas, gave it as his opinion—" that the best course would be, to admit the proposals brought by Murychides, and lay them before the assembly of the people." This he stated to be his opinion, perhaps because he had been bribed by Mardonius, or it may be because that course really appeared to him the most expedient. However, the Athenians—both those in the council, and those who stood without, when they heard of the advice—were full of wrath, and forthwith surrounded Lycidas, and stoned him to death. As for Murychides, the Hellespontine Greek, him they sent away unharmed. Now there was a stir in the island about Lycidas, and the Athenian women learnt what had happened. Then each exhorted her fellow, and one brought another to take part in the deed; and they all flocked of their own accord to the house of Lycidas, and stoned to death his wife and his children.

6. The circumstances under which the Athenians had sought refuge in Salamis were the following. So long as any hope remained that a Peloponnesian army would come to give them aid, they abode still in Attica; but when it appeared that the allies were slack and slow to move, while the invader was reported to be pressing forward and to have already entered Bœotia, then they proceeded to remove their goods and chattels from the mainland, and themselves again crossed the strait to Salamis. At the same time they sent ambassadors to Lacedæmon, who were to reproach the Lacedæmonians for having allowed the barbarian to advance into Attica, instead of joining them and going out to meet him in Bœotia. They were likewise to remind the Lacedæmonians of the offers by which the Persian

had sought to win Athens over to his side,[1] and to warn them, that if no aid came from Sparta, the Athenians must consult for their own safety.

7. The truth was, the Lacedæmonians were keeping holiday at that time; for it was the feast of the Hyacinthia,[2] and they thought nothing of so much moment as to perform the service of the god. They were also engaged in building their wall across the Isthmus, which was now so far advanced that the battlements had begun to be placed upon it.

When the envoys of the Athenians, accompanied by ambassadors from Megara and Platæa, reached Lacedæmon, they came before the Ephors, and spoke as follows:—

" The Athenians have sent us to you to say,—the king of the Medes offers to give us back our country, and wishes to conclude an alliance with us on fair and equal terms, without fraud or deceit. He is willing likewise to bestow on us another country besides our own, and bids us choose any land that we like. But we, because we reverenced Hellenic Jupiter, and thought it a shameful act to betray Greece, instead of consenting to these terms, refused them; notwithstanding that we have been wronged and deserted by the other Greeks, and are fully aware that it is far more for our advantage to make peace with the Persian than to prolong the war with him. Still we shall not, of our own free will, consent to any terms of peace. Thus do we, in all our dealings with the Greeks, avoid what is base and counterfeit: while contrariwise, ye, who were but now so full of fear least we should make terms with the enemy,[3] having learnt of what temper we are, and assured yourselves that we shall not prove traitors to our country—having brought moreover your wall across the Isthmus to an advanced state—cease altogether to have any care for us. Ye covenanted with us to go out and meet the Persian in Bœotia; but when the time came, ye were false to your word, and looked on while the barbarian host advanced into Attica. At this time, therefore, the Athenians are angered with you; and justly,—for ye have not done what was right. They bid you, however, make haste to send forth

[1] Supra, viii. 140, § 1.
[2] Held annually at midsummer. Hyacinthus, the beautiful youth slain accidentally by Apollo, was the chief object of the worship. He took his name from the flower, which was an emblem of death; and the original feast seems to have been altogether a mournful ceremony,—a lamentation over the destruction of the flowers of spring by the summer heat, passing on to a more general lament over death itself.
[3] Supra, viii. 142.

your army, that we may even yet meet Mardonius in Attica. Now that Bœotia is lost to us, the best place for the fight within our country, will be the plain of Thria."

8. The Ephors, when they had heard this speech, delayed their answer till the morrow; and when the morrow came, till the day following. And thus they acted for ten days, continually putting off the ambassadors from one day to the next. Meanwhile the Peloponnesians generally were labouring with great zeal at the wall, and the work nearly approached completion. I can give no other reason for the conduct of the Lacedæmonians in showing themselves so anxious, at the time when Alexander came, that the Athenians should not join the Medes, and now being quite careless about it, except that at the former time the wall across the Isthmus was not complete, and they worked at it in great fear of the Persians, whereas now the bulwark had been raised, and so they imagined that they had no further need of the Athenians.

9. At last the ambassadors got an answer, and the troops marched forth from Sparta, under the following circumstances. The last audience had been fixed for the ambassadors, when, the very day before it was to be given, a certain Tegean, named Chileüs, a man who had more influence at Sparta than any other foreigner, learning from the Ephors exactly what the Athenians had said, addressed these words to them—" The case stands thus, O ye Ephors! If the Athenians are not our friends, but league themselves with the barbarians, however strong our wall across the Isthmus may be, there will be doors enough, and wide enough open too, by which the Persian may gain entrance to the Peloponnese.[1] Grant their request then, before they make any fresh resolve, which may bring Greece to ruin."

10. Such was the counsel which Chileüs gave: and the Ephors, taking the advice into consideration, determined forthwith, without speaking a word to the ambassadors from the three cities, to despatch to the Isthmus a body of five thousand Spartans; and accordingly they sent them forth the same night, appointing to each Spartan a retinue of seven Helots, and giving the command of the expedition to Pausanias the son of Cleombrotus. The chief power belonged of right at this time to Pleistarchus, the son of Leonidas; but as he was still a child,

---

[1] That is, the naval power of Athens would lay the whole coast of the Peloponnese open to the Persians.

Pausanias, his cousin, was regent in his room. For the father of Pausanias, Cleombrotus, the son of Anaxandridas, no longer lived; he had died a short time after bringing back from the Isthmus the troops who had been employed in building the wall. A prodigy had caused him to bring his army home; for while he was offering sacrifice to know if he should march out against the Persian, the sun was suddenly darkened in mid sky. Pausanias took with him, as joint-leader of the army, Euryanax, the son of Dorieus, a member of his own family.

11. The army accordingly had marched out from Sparta with Pausanias: while the ambassadors, when day came, appeared before the Ephors, knowing nothing of the march of the troops, and purposing themselves to leave Sparta forthwith, and return each man to his own country. They therefore addressed the Ephors in these words:—" Lacedæmonians, as you do not stir from home, but keep the Hyacinthian festival, and amuse yourselves, deserting the cause of your confederates, the Athenians, whom your behaviour wrongs, and who have no other allies, will make such terms with the Persians as they shall find possible. Now when terms are once made, it is plain that, having become the king's allies, we shall march with the barbarians whithersoever they choose to lead. Then at length you will perceive what the consequences will be to yourselves." When the envoys had spoken, the Ephors declared to them with an oath:—" Our troops must be at Orestêum [1] by this time, on their march against the strangers." (The Spartans say " strangers " for " barbarians.") At this the ambassadors, quite ignorant of what had happened, questioned them concerning their meaning; and when, by much questioning, they had discovered the truth, they were greatly astonished thereat, and forthwith set off, at their best speed, to overtake the Spartan army. At the same time a body of five thousand Lacedæmonian Periœci, all picked men and fully armed, set forth from Sparta, in the company of the ambassadors.

12. So these troops marched in haste towards the Isthmus. Meanwhile the Argives, who had promised Mardonius that they would stop the Spartans from crossing their borders, as soon as they learnt that Pausanias with his army had started from Sparta, took the swiftest courier they could find, and sent him off to Attica. The message which he delivered, on his arrival

---

[1] Orestêum, or Orestasium, was a small town in the district of Arcadia called Mænalia.

at Athens, was the following: "Mardonius," he said, "the Argives have sent me to tell thee that the Lacedæmonian youth are gone forth from their city, and that the Argives are too weak to hinder them. Take good heed therefore to thyself at this time." After thus speaking, without a word more, he returned home.

13. When Mardonius learnt that the Spartans were on their march, he no longer cared to remain in Attica. Hitherto he had kept quiet, wishing to see what the Athenians would do, and had neither ravaged their territory, nor done it any the least harm; for till now he had cherished the hope that the Athenians would come to terms with him. As, however, he found that his persuasions were of no avail, and as their whole policy was now clear to him, he determined to withdraw from Attica before Pausanias with his army reached the Isthmus; first, however, he resolved to burn Athens, and to cast down and level with the ground whatever remained standing of the walls, temples, and other buildings. His reason for retreating was, that Attica was not a country where horse could act with advantage; and further, that if he suffered defeat in a battle, no way of escape was open to him, except through defiles,[1] where a handful of troops might stop all his army. So he determined to withdraw to Thebes, and give the Greeks battle in the neighbourhood of a friendly city, and on ground well suited for cavalry.

14. After he had quitted Attica and was already upon his march, news reached him that a body of a thousand Lacedæmonians, distinct from the army of Pausanias, and sent on in advance, had arrived in the Megarid. When he heard it, wishing, if possible, to destroy this detachment first, Mardonius considered with himself how he might compass their ruin. With a sudden change of march he made for Megara, while the horse, pushing on in advance, entered and ravaged the Megarid. (Here was the furthest point in Europe towards the setting sun to which this Persian army ever penetrated.)

15. After this, Mardonius received another message, whereby he learnt that the forces of the Greeks were collected together at the Isthmus; which tidings caused him to draw back, and leave Attica by the way of Deceleia. The Bœotarchs[2] had sent

[1] Three roads only connected Attica with Bœotia. The one, which Mardonius now followed, led from Athens into the Tanagræa by the fortress of Deceleia. This is comparatively an easy route.

[2] On the Bœotarchs, or chief magistrates of the Bœotians.

for some of the neighbours of the Asopians; [1] and these persons
served as guides to the army, and led them first to Sphendalé,
and from thence to Tanagra, [2] where Mardonius rested a night;
after which, upon the morrow, he bent his course to Scôlus,
which brought him into the territory of the Thebans. And
now, although the Thebans had espoused the cause of the Medes,
yet Mardonius cut down all the trees in these parts; not however from any enmity towards the Thebans, but on account of
his own urgent needs; for he wanted a rampart to protect his
army from attack, and he likewise desired to have a place of
refuge, whither his troops might flee, in case the battle should
go contrary to his wishes. His army at this time lay on the
Asôpus, and stretched from Erythræ, along by Hysiæ, to the
territory of the Platæans. The wall, however, was not made to
extend so far, but formed a square of about ten furlongs each
way.

While the barbarians were employed in this work, a certain
citizen of Thebes, Attagînus by name, the son of Phrynon,
having made great preparations, gave a banquet, and invited
Mardonius thereto, together with fifty of the noblest Persians.
Now the banquet was held at Thebes; and all the guests who
were invited came to it.

16. What follows was recounted to me by Thersander, a
native of Orchomenus, [3] a man of the first rank in that city.
Thersander told me that he was himself among those invited to
the feast, and that besides the Persians fifty Thebans were
asked; [4] and the two nations were not arranged separately, but
a Persian and a Theban were set side by side upon each couch.
After the feast was ended, and the drinking had begun, the
Persian who shared Thersander's couch addressed him in the
Greek tongue, and inquired of him from what city he came.
He answered, that he was of Orchomenus; whereupon the
other said—

" Since thou hast eaten with me at one table, and poured
libation from one cup, I would fain leave with thee a memorial
of the belief I hold—the rather that thou mayest have timely
warning thyself, and so be able to provide for thy own safety.
Seest thou these Persians here feasting, and the army which we

---

[1] The Asopians are the inhabitants of the rich valley of the Asôpus,
which ay immediately beyond the Attic frontier.
[2] Tanagra was situated on the left or northern bank of the Asôpus.
[3] Vide supra, viii. 34.
[4] By Thebans we must understand here Bœotians.

left encamped yonder by the river-side? Yet a little while, and of all this number thou wilt behold but a few surviving!"

As he spake, the Persian let fall a flood of tears: whereon Thersander, who was astonished at his words, replied—"Surely thou shouldest say all this to Mardonius, and the Persians who are next him in honour"—but the other rejoined—"Dear friend, it is not possible for man to avert that which God has decreed shall happen. No one believes warnings, however true. Many of us Persians know our danger, but we are constrained by necessity to do as our leader bids us. Verily 'tis the sorest of all human ills, to abound in knowledge and yet have no power over action." All this I heard myself from Thersander the Orchomenian; who told me further, that he mentioned what had happened to divers persons, before the battle was fought at Platæa.

17. When Mardonius formerly held his camp in Bœotia, all the Greeks of those parts who were friendly to the Medes sent troops to join his army, and these troops accompanied him in his attack upon Athens. The Phocians alone abstained, and took no part in the invasion; for, though they had espoused the Median cause warmly, it was very much against their will, and only because they were compelled so to do.[1] However, a few days after the arrival of the Persian army at Thebes, a thousand of their heavy-armed soldiers came up, under the command of Harmocŷdes, one of their most distinguished citizens. No sooner had these troops reached Thebes, than some horsemen came to them from Mardonius, with orders that they should take up a position upon the plain, away from the rest of the army. The Phocians did so, and forthwith the entire Persian cavalry drew nigh to them: whereupon there went a rumour through the whole of the Greek force encamped with the Medes, that Mardonius was about to destroy the Phocians with missiles. The same conviction ran through the Phocian troops themselves; and Harmocŷdes, their leader, addressed them thus with words of encouragement—"Phocians," said he, "'tis plain that these men have resolved beforehand to take our lives, because of the accusations of the Thessalians, as I imagine. Now, then, is the time for you all to show yourselves brave men. 'Tis better to die fighting and defending our lives, than tamely to allow them to slay us in this shameful fashion. Let them

[1] Supra, viii. 30-33.

learn that they are barbarians, and that the men whose death they have plotted are Greeks!"

18. Thus spake Harmocŷdes; and the Persian horse, having encircled the Phocians, charged towards them, as if about to deal out death, with bows bent, and arrows ready to be let fly; nay, here and there some did even discharge their weapons. But the Phocians stood firm, keeping close one to another, and serrying their ranks as much as possible: whereupon the horse suddenly wheeled round and rode off. I cannot say with certainty whether they came, at the prayer of the Thessalians, to destroy the Phocians, but seeing them prepared to stand on their defence, and fearing to suffer damage at their hands, on that account beat a retreat, having orders from Mardonius so to act; or whether his sole intent was to try the temper of the Phocians and see whether they had any courage or no. However this may have been, when the horsemen retired, Mardonius sent a herald to the Phocians, saying—"Fear not, Phocians—ye have shown yourselves valiant men—much unlike the report I had heard of you. Now therefore be forward in the coming war. Ye will not readily outdo either the king or myself in services." Thus ended the affair of the Phocians.

19. The Lacedæmonians, when they reached the Isthmus, pitched their camp there; and the other Peloponnesians who had embraced the good side, hearing or else seeing that they were upon the march, thought it not right to remain behind when the Spartans were going forth to the war. So the Peloponnesians went out in one body from the Isthmus, the victims being favourable for setting forth; and marched as far as Eleusis, where again they offered sacrifices, and, finding the omens still encouraging, advanced further. At Eleusis they were joined by the Athenians, who had come across from Salamis, and now accompanied the main army. On reaching Erythræ [1] in Bœotia, they learnt that the barbarians were encamped upon the Asôpus; wherefore they themselves, after considering how they should act, disposed their forces opposite to the enemy upon the slopes of Mount Cithæron.

20. Mardonius, when he saw that the Greeks would not come down into the plain, sent all his cavalry, under Masistius (or Macistius, as the Greeks call him), to attack them where they were. Now Masistius was a man of much repute among the Persians, and rode a Nisæan charger with a golden bit, and

¹ Supra, ch. 15.

otherwise magnificently caparisoned. So the horse advanced against the Greeks, and made attacks upon them in divisions, doing them great damage at each charge, and insulting them by calling them women.

21. It chanced that the Megarians were drawn up in the position most open to attack, and where the ground offered the best approach to the cavalry. Finding themselves therefore hard pressed by the assaults upon their ranks, they sent a herald to the Greek leaders, who came and said to them, " This is the message of the Megarians—We cannot, brothers-in-arms, continue to resist the Persian horse in that post which we have occupied from the first, if we are left without succours. Hitherto, although hard pressed, we have held out against them firmly and courageously. Now, however, if you do not send others to take our place, we warn you that we shall quit our post." Such were the words of the herald. Pausanias, when he heard them, inquired among his troops if there were any who would volunteer to take the post, and so relieve the Megarians. Of the rest none were willing to go, whereupon the Athenians offered themselves; and a body of picked men, three hundred in number, commanded by Olympiodôrus, the son of Lampo, undertook the service.

22. Selecting, to accompany them, the whole body of archers, these men relieved the Megarians, and occupied a post which all the other Greeks collected at Erythræ had shrunk from holding. After the struggle had continued for a while, it came to an end on this wise. As the barbarians continued charging in divisions, the horse of Masistius, which was in front of the others, received an arrow in his flank, the pain of which caused him to rear and throw his rider. Immediately the Athenians rushed upon Masistius as he lay, caught his horse, and when he himself made resistance, slew him. At first, however, they were not able to take his life; for his armour hindered them. He had on a breastplate formed of golden scales,[1] with a scarlet tunic covering it. Thus the blows, all falling upon his breast-plate, took no effect, till one of the soldiers, perceiving the reason, drove his weapon into his eye and so slew him. All this took place without any of the other horsemen seeing it: they had neither observed their leader fall from his horse, nor beheld him slain; for he fell as they wheeled round and prepared for another charge, so that they were quite ignorant of

[1] Vide supra, vii. 6, and viii. 113.

what had happened. When, however, they halted, and found that there was no one to marshal their line, Masistius was missed; and instantly his soldiers, understanding what must have befallen him, with loud cheers charged the enemy in one mass, hoping to recover the dead body.

23. So when the Athenians saw that, instead of coming up in squadrons, the whole mass of the horse was about to charge them at once, they called out to the other troops to make haste to their aid. While the rest of the infantry, however, was moving to their assistance, the contest waxed fierce about the dead body of Masistius. The three hundred, so long as they fought by themselves, had greatly the worse of the encounter, and were forced to retire and yield up the body to the enemy; but when the other troops approached, the Persian horse could no longer hold their ground, but fled without carrying off the body, having incurred in the attempt a further loss of several of their number. They therefore retired about two furlongs, and consulted with each other what was best to be done. Being without a leader, it seemed to them the fittest course to return to Mardonius.

24. When the horse reached the camp, Mardonius and all the Persian army made great lamentation for Masistius. They shaved off all the hair from their own heads, and cut the manes from their war-horses and their sumpter-beasts, while they vented their grief in such loud cries that all Bœotia resounded with the clamour,[1] because they had lost the man who, next to Mardonius, was held in the greatest esteem, both by the king and by the Persians generally. So the barbarians, after their own fashion, paid honours to the dead Masistius.

25. The Greeks, on the other hand, were greatly emboldened by what had happened, seeing that they had not only stood their ground against the attacks of the horse, but had even compelled them to beat a retreat. They therefore placed the dead body of Masistius upon a cart, and paraded it along the ranks of the army. Now the body was a sight which well deserved to be gazed upon, being remarkable both for stature and for beauty; and it was to stop the soldiers from leaving their ranks to look at it, that they resolved to carry it round. After this the Greeks determined to quit the high ground and go nearer Platæa, as the land there seemed far more suitable for an encampment than the country about Erythræ, particularly

[1] Such free indulgence of grief is characteristic of the Oriental temper.

because it was better supplied with water. To this place therefore, and more especially to a spring-head which was called Gargaphia, they considered that it would be best for them to remove, after which they might once more encamp in their order. So they took their arms, and proceeded along the slopes of Cithæron, past Hysiæ, to the territory of the Platæans; and here they drew themselves up, nation by nation, close by the fountain Gargaphia, and the sacred precinct of the Hero Androcrates, partly along some hillocks of no great height, and partly upon the level of the plain.

26. Here, in the marshalling of the nations, a fierce battle of words arose between the Athenians and the Tegeans, both of whom claimed to have one of the wings assigned to them. On each side were brought forward the deeds which they had done, whether in earlier or in later times; and first the Tegeans urged their claim as follows:—

"This post has been always considered our right, and not the right of any of the other allies, in all the expeditions which have been entered into conjointly by the Peloponnesians, both anciently and in later times. Ever since the Heraclidæ made their attempt, after the death of Eurystheus, to return by force of arms into the Peloponnese, this custom has been observed. It was then that the right became ours, and this was the way in which we gained it:—When, in company with the Achæans and Ionians who then dwelt in the Peloponnese,[1] we marched out to the Isthmus, and pitched our camp over against the invaders, then, as the tale goes, that Hyllus made proclamation, saying— 'It needs not to imperil two armies in a general battle; rather let one be chosen from the Peloponnesian ranks, whomseover they deem the bravest, and let him engage with me in single combat, on such terms as shall be agreed upon.' The saying pleased the Peloponnesians, and oaths were sworn to the effect following:—'If Hyllus conquer the Peloponnesian champion, the Heraclidæ shall return to their inheritance; if, on the other hand, he be conquered, the Heraclidæ shall withdraw, lead back their army, and engage for the next hundred years to make no further endeavours to force their return." Hereupon

---

[1] Before the Dorian immigration the entire Peloponnese was occupied, with trifling exceptions, by three races:—the Arcadians, the Achæans, and the Ionians. The Ionians occupied the country along the Corinthian Gulf, which in later times became Achæa (supra, i. 145); the Arcadians held the strong central position in which they always maintained themselves; the Achæans were masters of the remainder.

Echemus, the son of Aëropus and grandson of Phêgeus, who was our leader and king, offered himself, and was preferred before all his brothers-in-arms as champion, engaged in single combat with Hyllus, and slew him upon the spot. For this exploit we were rewarded by the Peloponnesians of that day with many goodly privileges, which we have ever since enjoyed; and, among the rest, we obtained the right of holding the leading post in one wing, whenever a joint expedition goes forth beyond our borders. With you then, O Lacedæmonians, we do not claim to compete; choose you which wing ye please; we yield and grant you the preference: but we maintain that the command of the other wing belongs of right to us, now no less than formerly. Moreover, set aside this exploit which we have related, and still our title to the chief post is better than that of the Athenians: witness the many glorious fights in which we have been engaged against yourselves, O Spartans! as well as those which we have maintained with others. We have therefore more right to this place than they; for they have performed no exploits to be compared to ours, whether we look to earlier or to later times."

27. Thus spake the Tegeans; and the Athenians made reply as follows:—" We are not ignorant that our forces were gathered here, not for the purpose of speech-making, but for battle against the barbarian. Yet as the Tegeans have been pleased to bring into debate the exploits performed by our two nations, alike in earlier and in later times, we have no choice but to set before you the grounds on which we claim it as our heritage, deserved by our unchanging bravery, to be preferred above Arcadians. In the first place, then, those very Heraclidæ, whose leader they boast to have slain at the Isthmus, and whom the other Greeks would not receive when they asked a refuge from the bondage wherewith they were threatened by the people of Mycênæ, were given a shelter by us; and we brought down the insolence of Eurystheus, and helped to gain the victory over those who were at that time lords of the Peloponnese. Again, when the Argives led their troops with Polynices against Thebes, and were slain and refused burial, it is our boast that we went out against the Cadmeians, recovered the bodies, and buried them at Eleusis in our own territory. Another noble deed of ours was that against the Amazons, when they came from their seats upon the Thermôdon, and poured their hosts into Attica; and in the Trojan war too we were not a whit

behind any of the Greeks.   But what boots it to speak of these
ancient matters?   A nation which was brave in those days
might have grown cowardly since, and a nation of cowards then
might now be valiant.   Enough therefore of our ancient achievements.   Had we performed no other exploit than that at Marathon—though in truth we have performed exploits as many and
as noble as any of the Greeks—yet had we performed no other,
we should deserve this privilege, and many a one beside.   There
we stood alone, and singly fought with the Persians; nay, and
venturing on so dangerous a cast, we overcame the enemy, and
conquered on that day forty and six nations!   Does not this one
achievement suffice to make good our title to the post we claim?
Nevertheless, Lacedæmonians, as to strive concerning place at
such a time as this is not right, we are ready to do as ye command, and to take our station at whatever part of the line, and
face whatever nation ye think most expedient.   Wheresoever
ye place us, 'twill be our endeavour to behave as brave men.
Only declare your will, and we shall at once obey you." [1]

28. Such was the reply of the Athenians; and forthwith all
the Lacedæmonian troops cried out with one voice, that the
Athenians were worthier to have the left wing than the
Arcadians.   In this way were the Tegeans overcome; and the
post was assigned to the Athenians.

When this matter had been arranged, the Greek army, which
was in part composed of those who came at the first, in part of
such as had flocked in from day to day, drew up in the following
order:—Ten thousand Lacedæmonian troops held the right
wing, five thousand of whom were Spartans; and these five
thousand were attended by a body of thirty five thousand
Helots, who were only lightly armed—seven Helots to each
Spartan. [2]   The place next to themselves the Spartans gave to
the Tegeans, on account of their courage and of the esteem in
which they held them.   They were all fully armed, and
numbered fifteen hundred men.   Next in order came the Corinthians, five thousand strong; and with them Pausanias had
placed, at their request, [3] the band of three hundred which had
come from Potidæa in Pallêné.   The Arcadians of Orchomenus,
in number six hundred, came next; then the Sicyonians, three
thousand; then the Epidaurians, eight hundred; then the

---

[1] [See *n.* on p. 328 infra.—E. H. B.]   [2] Vide supra, ch. 10.
[3] The Corinthians naturally desired to have *their colonists* under their
immediate protection.

Trœzenians, one thousand; then the Lepreats, two hundred; the Mycenæans and Tirynthians,[1] four hundred; the Phliasians, one thousand; the Hermionians, three hundred; the Eretrians and Styreans, six hundred; the Chalcideans,[2] four hundred; and the Ambraciots, five hundred. After these came the Leucadians and Anactorians,[3] who numbered eight hundred; the Paleans of Cephallênia, two hundred; the Eginetans, five hundred; the Megarians, three thousand; and the Platæans, six hundred. Last of all, but first at their extremity of the line, were the Athenians, who, to the number of eight thousand, occupied the left wing, under the command of Aristides, the son of Lysimachus.

29. All these, except the Helots—seven of whom, as I said, attended each Spartan—were heavy-armed troops; and they amounted to thirty-eight thousand seven hundred men. This was the number of Hoplites, or heavy-armed soldiers, which was brought together against the barbarian. The light-armed troops consisted of the thirty-five thousand ranged with the Spartans, seven in attendance upon each, who were all well equipped for war; and of thirty-four thousand five hundred others, belonging to the Lacedæmonians and the rest of the Greeks, at the rate (nearly) of one light to one heavy armed. Thus the entire number of the light-armed was sixty-nine thousand five hundred.

30. The Greek army, therefore, which mustered at Platæa, counting light-armed as well as heavy-armed, was but eighteen hundred men short of one hundred and ten thousand; and this amount was exactly made up by the Thespians who were present in the camp; for eighteen hundred Thespians, being the whole number left,[4] were likewise with the army; but these men were without arms. Such was the array of the Greek troops when they took post on the Asôpus.

31. The barbarians under Mardonius, when the mourning for Masistius was at an end, and they learnt that the Greeks were in the Platæan territory, moved likewise towards the river Asôpus, which flows in those parts. On their arrival Mardonius marshalled them against the Greeks in the following order:—

---

[1] For the site of Tiryns, vide supra, vi. 76.

[2] Not the Chalcideans of Thrace, but those of Eubœa.

[3] Anactorium was a Corinthian, or perhaps a joint Corinthian and Corcyræan colony situated at the mouth of the Ambracian gulf.

[4] That is, the whole number left after the destruction of the 700 at Thermopylæ (supra, vii. 222-225).

Against the Lacedæmonians he posted his Persians; and as the Persians were far more numerous, he drew them up with their ranks deeper than common, and also extended their front so that part faced the Tegeans; and here he took care to choose out the best troops to face the Lacedæmonians, whilst against the Tegeans he arrayed those on whom he could not so much depend. This was done at the suggestion and by the advice of the Thebans. Next to the Persians he placed the Medes, facing the Corinthians, Potidæans, Orchomenians, and Sicyonians; then the Bactrians, facing the Epidaurians, Trœzenians, Lepreats, Tirynthians, Mycenæans, and Phliasians; after them the Indians, facing the Hermionians, Eretrians, Styreans, and Chalcidians; then the Sacans, facing the Ambraciots, Anactorians, Leucadians, Paleans, and Eginetans; last of all, facing the Athenians, the Platæans, and the Megarians, he placed the troops of the Bœotians, Locrians, Malians, and Thessalians, and also the thousand Phocians.[1] The whole nation of the Phocians had not joined the Medes; on the contrary, there were some who had gathered themselves into bands about Parnassus, and made expeditions from thence, whereby they distressed Mardonius and the Greeks who sided with him, and so did good service to the Grecian cause. Besides those mentioned above, Mardonius likewise arrayed against the Athenians the Macedonians and the tribes dwelling about Thessaly.

32. I have named here the greatest of the nations which were marshalled by Mardonius on this occasion, to wit, all those of most renown and account. Mixed with these, however, were men of divers other peoples,[2] as Phrygians, Thracians, Mysians, Pæonians, and the like; Ethiopians again, and Egyptians, both of the Hermotybian and Calasirian races,[3] whose weapon is the sword, and who are the only fighting men in that country. These persons had formerly served on board the fleet of Xerxes, but Mardonius disembarked them before he left Phalerum; in the land force which Xerxes brought to Athens there were no Egyptians. The number of the barbarians, as I have already mentioned,[4] was three hundred thousand; that of the Greeks who had made alliance with Mardonius is known to none, for

---

[1] That is, the thousand Phocians who had been previously mentioned (supra, chs. 17, 18).
[2] See above, viii. 113, ad fin.
[3] The whole of the former amounted to 160,000 men. The Calisiries to 250,000. (Bk. ii. chs. 164, 165, 166.)
[4] Supra, viii. 113, end.

they were never counted: I should guess that they mustered near fifty thousand strong. The troops thus marshalled were all foot soldiers. As for the horse, it was drawn up by itself.

33. When the marshalling of Mardonius' troops by nations and by maniples was ended, the two armies proceeded on the next day to offer sacrifice. The Grecian sacrifice was offered by Tisamenus, the son of Antiochus, who accompanied the army as soothsayer: he was an Elean, and belonged to the Clytiad branch of the Iamidæ, but had been admitted among their own citizens by the Lacedæmonians. Now his admission among them was on this wise:—Tisamenus had gone to Delphi to consult the god concerning his lack of offspring, when it was declared to him by the Pythoness that he would win five very glorious combats.[1] Misunderstanding the oracle, and imagining that he was to win combats in the games, Tisamenus at once applied himself to the practice of gymnastics. He trained himself for the Pentathlum,[2] and, on contending at Olympia, came within a little of winning it; for he was successful in everything, except the wrestling-match, which was carried off by Hieronymus the Andrian. Hereon the Lacedæmonians perceived that the combats of which the oracle spoke were not combats in the games, but battles: they therefore sought to induce Tisamenus to hire out his services to them, in order that they might join him with their Heracleid kings in the conduct of their wars. He however, when he saw that they set great store by his friendship, forthwith raised his price, and told them, " If they would receive him among their citizens, and give him equal rights with the rest, he was willing to do as they desired, but on no other terms would they ever gain his consent." The Spartans, when they heard this, at first thought it monstrous, and ceased to implore his aid. Afterwards, however, when the fearful danger of the Persian war hung over their heads, they sent for him and agreed to his terms; but Tisamenus now, perceiving them so changed, declared, " He could no longer be content with what he had asked before: they must likewise make his brother Hagias[3] a Spartan, with the same rights as himself."

34. In acting thus he did but follow the example once set by

[1] On the habit of the Pythoness to disregard the question asked, and to answer on an entirely different subject, see above, iv. 151 and 155; v. 63.

[2] For the nature of the Pentathlum, vide supra, vi. 92.

[3] Hagias the *brother* must be distinguished from Hagias the *grandson* of Tisamenus.

Melampus, at least if kingship may be compared with citizen-ship. For when the women of Argos were seized with madness, and the Argives would have hired Melampus to come from Pylos and heal them of their disease, he demanded as his reward one-half of the kingdom; but as the Argives disdained to stoop to this, they left him and went their way. Afterwards, however, when many more of their women were seized, they brought themselves to agree to his terms; and accordingly they went again to him, and said they were content to give what he required. Hereon Melampus, seeing them so changed, raised his demand, and told them, " Except they would give his brother Bias one-third of the kingdom likewise, he would not do as they wished." So, as the Argives were in a strait, they consented even to this.

35. In like manner the Spartans, as they were in great need of Tisamenus, yielded everything: and Tisamenus the Elean, having in this way become a Spartan citizen, afterwards, in the capacity of soothsayer, helped the Spartans to gain five very glorious combats. He and his brother were the only men whom the Spartans ever admitted to citizenship.[1] The five combats were these following:—The first was the combat at Platæa; the second, that near Tegea, against the Tegeans and the Argives; the third, that at Dipæeis, against all the Arcadians excepting those of Mantinea; the fourth, that at the Isthmus, against the Messenians; and the fifth, that at Tanagra, against the Athenians and the Argives. The battle here fought was the last of all the five.

36. The Spartans had now brought Tisamenus with them to the Platæan territory, where he acted as soothsayer for the Greeks. He found the victims favourable, if the Greeks stood on the defensive, but not if they began the battle or crossed the river Asôpus.

37. With Mardonius also, who was very eager to begin the battle, the victims were not favourable for so doing; but he likewise found them bode him well, if he was content to stand on his defence. He too had made use of the Grecian rites; for Hêgêsistratus, an Elean, and the most renowned of the Telliads, was his soothsayer. This man had once been taken captive by the Spartans, who, considering that he had done them many grievous injuries, laid him in bonds, with the intent to put him

[1] Herodotus must be supposed to mean the only *foreigners ;* otherwise his statement will be very incorrect.

to death. Thereupon Hêgêsistratus, finding himself in so sore a case, since not only was his life in danger, but he knew that he would have to suffer torments of many kinds before his death,—Hêgêsistratus, I say, did a deed for which no words suffice. He had been set with one foot in the stocks, which were of wood but bound with iron bands; and in this condition received from without an iron implement, wherewith he contrived to accomplish the most courageous deed upon record. Calculating how much of his foot he would be able to draw through the hole, he cut off the front portion with his own hand; and then, as he was guarded by watchmen, forced a way through the wall of his prison, and made his escape to Tegea, travelling during the night, but in the daytime stealing into the woods, and staying there. In this way, though the Lacedæmonians went out in full force to search for him, he nevertheless escaped, and arrived the third evening at Tegea. So the Spartans were amazed at the man's endurance, when they saw on the ground the piece which he had cut off his foot, and yet for all their seeking could not find him anywhere. Hêgêsistratus, having thus escaped the Lacedæmonians, took refuge in Tegea; for the Tegeans at that time were ill friends with the Lacedæmonians. When his wound was healed, he procured himself a wooden foot, and became an open enemy to Sparta. At the last, however, this enmity brought him to trouble; for the Spartans took him captive as he was exercising his office in Zacynthus, and forthwith put him to death. But these things happened some while after the fight at Platæa. At present he was serving Mardonius on the Asôpus, having been hired at no inconsiderable price; and here he offered sacrifice with a right good will, in part from his hatred of the Lacedæmonians, in part for lucre's sake.

38. So when the victims did not allow either the Persians or their Greek allies to begin the battle—these Greeks had their own soothsayer in the person of Hippomachus, a Leucadian—and when soldiers continued to pour into the opposite camp and the numbers on the Greek side to increase continually, Timagenidas, the son of Herpys, a Theban, advised Mardonius to keep a watch on the passes of Cithæron, telling him how supplies of men kept flocking in day after day, and assuring him that he might cut off large numbers.

39. It was eight days after the two armies first encamped opposite to one another when this advice was given by Tima-

genidas. Mardonius, seeing it to be good, as soon as evening
came, sent his cavalry to that pass of Mount Cithæron which
opens out upon Platæa, a pass called by the Bœotians the
"Three Heads," but called the "Oak-Heads" by the
Athenians.[1] The horse sent on this errand did not make the
movement in vain. They came upon a body of five hundred
sumpter-beasts which were just entering the plain, bringing
provisions to the Greek camp from the Peloponnese, with a
number of men driving them. Seeing this prey in their power,
the Persians set upon them and slaughtered them, sparing none,
neither man nor beast; till at last, when they had had enough
of slaying, they secured such as were left, and bore them off to
the camp to Mardonius.

40. After this they waited again for two days more, neither
army wishing to begin the fight. The barbarians indeed
advanced as far as the Asôpus, and endeavoured to tempt the
Greeks to cross; but neither side actually passed the stream.
Still the cavalry of Mardonius harassed and annoyed the
Greeks incessantly; for the Thebans, who were zealous in the
cause of the Medes, pressed the war forward with all eagerness,
and often led the charge till the lines met, when the Medes and
Persians took their place, and displayed, many of them, uncommon valour.

41. For ten days nothing was done more than this; but on
the eleventh day from the time when the two hosts first took
station, one over against the other, near Platæa—the number of
the Greeks being now much greater than it was at the first, and
Mardonius being impatient of the delay—there was a conference
held between Mardonius, son of Gobryas, and Artabazus, son of
Pharnaces,[2] a man who was esteemed by Xerxes more than
almost any of the Persians. At this consultation the following
were the opinions delivered:—Artabazus thought it would be
best for them to break up from their quarters as soon as possible,
and withdraw the whole army to the fortified town of Thebes,
where they had abundant stores of corn for themselves, and of
fodder for the sumpter-beasts. There, he said, they had only to
sit quiet, and the war might be brought to an end on this
wise:—Coined gold was plentiful in the camp, and uncoined
gold too; they had silver moreover in great abundance, and

---

[1] The name "Oak-Heads" (Dryos-Cephalæ) seems to have belonged
to the entire dip in the mountain range through which passed both the
roads above mentioned.

[2] Supra, viii. 126-129.

drinking-cups. Let them not spare to take of these, and distribute them among the Greeks, especially among the leaders in the several cities; 'twould not be long before the Greeks gave up their liberty, without risking another battle for it. Thus the opinion of Artabazus agreed with that of the Thebans;[1] for he too had more foresight than some. Mardonius, on the other hand, expressed himself with more fierceness and obstinacy, and was utterly disinclined to yield. "Their army," he said, "was vastly superior to that of the Greeks; and they had best engage at once, and not wait till greater numbers were gathered against them. As for Hêgêsistratus and his victims, they should let them pass unheeded, not seeking to force them to be favourable, but, according to the old Persian custom, hasting to join battle."

42. When Mardonius had thus declared his sentiments, no one ventured to say him nay; and accordingly his opinion prevailed, for it was to him, and not to Artabazus, that the king had given the command of the army.

Mardonius now sent for the captains of the squadrons, and the leaders of the Greeks in his service, and questioned them:— "Did they know of any prophecy which said that the Persians were to be destroyed in Greece?" All were silent; some because they did not know the prophecies, but others, who knew them full well, because they did not think it safe to speak out. So Mardonius, when none answered, said, "Since ye know of no such oracle, or do not dare to speak of it, I, who know it well, will myself declare it to you. There is an oracle which says that the Persians shall come into Greece, sack the temple at Delphi, and when they have so done, perish one and all. Now we, as we are aware of the prediction, will neither go against the temple nor make any attempt to sack it: we therefore shall not perish for this trespass. Rejoice then thus far, all ye who are well-wishers to the Persians, and doubt not we shall get the better of the Greeks." When he had so spoken, he further ordered them to prepare themselves, and to put all in readiness for a battle upon the morrow.

43. As for the oracle of which Mardonius spoke, and which he referred to the Persians, it did not, I am well assured, mean them, but the Illyrians and the Enchelean host. There are, however, some verses of Bacis which did speak of this battle:—

[1] Supra, ch. 2.

" By Thermôdon's stream, and the grass-clad banks of Asôpus,
　See where gather the Grecians, and hark to the foreigners' war-shout—
There in death shall lie, ere fate or Lachesis doomed him,
Many a bow-bearing Mede, when the day of calamity cometh."

These verses, and some others like them which Musæus wrote,
referred, I well know, to the Persians. The river Thermôdon
flows between Tanagra and Glisas.[1]

44. After Mardonius had put his question about the prophecies, and spoken the above words of encouragement, night
drew on apace, and on both sides the watches were set. As
soon then as there was silence throughout the camp,—the night
being now well advanced, and the men seeming to be in their
deepest sleep,—Alexander, the son of Amyntas, king and leader
of the Macedonians, rode up on horseback to the Athenian out-
posts, and desired to speak with the generals. Hereupon, while
the greater part continued on guard, some of the watch ran to
the chiefs, and told them, " There had come a horseman from
the Median camp who would not say a word, except that he
wished to speak with the generals, of whom he mentioned the
names."

45. They at once, hearing this, made haste to the outpost,
where they found Alexander, who addressed them as follows:—
" Men of Athens, that which I am about to say I trust to
your honour; and I charge you to keep it secret from all excepting Pausanias, if you would not bring me to destruction. Had
I not greatly at heart the common welfare of Greece, I should
not have come to tell you; but I am myself a Greek by descent,[2] and I would not willingly see Greece exchange freedom
for slavery. Know then that Mardonius and his army cannot
obtain favourable omens; had it not been for this, they would
have fought with you long ago. Now, however, they have
determined to let the victims pass unheeded, and, as soon as
day dawns, to engage in battle. Mardonius, I imagine, is afraid
that, if he delays, you will increase in number. Make ready
then to receive him. Should he however still defer the combat,
do you abide where you are; for his provisions will not hold out
many more days.[3] If ye prosper in this war, forget not to do
something for my freedom; consider the risk I have run, out of
zeal for the Greek cause, to acquaint you with what Mardonius

[1] Glisas was one of the most ancient of the Bœotian towns. It is
mentioned by Homer.
[2] Supra, v. 22; viii. 137, 138.
[3] It seems very unlikely that this could be true.

intends, and to save you from being surprised by the barbarians. I am Alexander of Macedon."

As soon as he had said this, Alexander rode back to the camp, and returned to the station assigned him.

46. Meanwhile the Athenian generals hastened to the right wing, and told Pausanias all that they had learnt from Alexander. Hereupon Pausanias, who no sooner heard the intention of the Persians than he was struck with fear, addressed the generals, and said,—

" Since the battle is to come with to-morrow's dawn, it were well that you Athenians should stand opposed to the Persians, and we Spartans to the Bœotians and the other Greeks; for ye know the Medes and their manner of fight, since ye have already fought with them once at Marathon, but we are quite ignorant and without any experience of their warfare. While, however, there is not a Spartan here present who has ever fought against a Mede, of the Bœotians and Thessalians we have had experience. Take then your arms, and march over to our post upon the right, while we supply your place in the left wing."

Hereto the Athenians replied—" We, too, long ago, when we saw that the Persians were drawn up to face you, were minded to suggest to you the very course which you have now been the first to bring forward. We feared, however, that perhaps our words might not be pleasing to you. But, as you have now spoken of these things yourselves, we gladly give our consent, and are ready to do as ye have said."

47. Both sides agreeing hereto, at the dawn of day the Spartans and Athenians changed places. But the movement was perceived by the Bœotians, and they gave notice of it to Mardonius; who at once, on hearing what had been done, made a change in the disposition of his own forces, and brought the Persians to face the Lacedæmonians. Then Pausanias, finding that his design was discovered, led back his Spartans to the right wing; and Mardonius, seeing this, replaced his Persians upon the left of his army.

48. When the troops again occupied their former posts, Mardonius sent a herald to the Spartans, who spoke as follows:—

" Lacedæmonians, in these parts the men say that you are the bravest of mankind, and admire you because you never turn your backs in flight nor quit your ranks, but always stand firm, and either die at your posts or else destroy your adversaries.[1]

[1] Vide supra, vii. 209.

But in all this which they say concerning you there is not one word of truth; for now have we seen you, before battle was joined or our two hosts had come to blows, flying and leaving your posts, wishing the Athenians to make the first trial of our arms, and taking your own station against our slaves.   Surely these are not the deeds of brave men.   Much do we find ourselves deceived in you; for we believed the reports of you that reached our ears, and expected that you would send a herald with a challenge to us, proposing to fight by yourselves against our division of native Persians.   We for our part were ready to have agreed to this; but ye have made us no such offer—nay! ye seem rather to shrink from meeting us.   However, as no challenge of this kind comes from you to us, lo! we send a challenge to you.   Why should not you on the part of the Greeks, as you are thought to be the bravest of all, and we on the part of the barbarians, fight a battle with equal numbers on both sides?   Then, if it seems good to the others to fight likewise, let them engage afterwards — but if not,—if they are content that we should fight on behalf of all, let us so do—and whichever side wins the battle, let them win it for their whole army."

49. When the herald had thus spoken, he waited a while, but, as no one made him any answer, he went back, and told Mardonius what had happened.   Mardonius was full of joy thereat, and so puffed up by the empty victory, that he at once gave orders to his horse to charge the Greek line.   Then the horsemen drew near, and with their javelins and their arrows— for though horsemen they used the bow [1]—sorely distressed the Greek troops, which could not bring them to close combat. The fountain of Gargaphia,[2] whence the whole Greek army drew its water, they at this time choked up and spoiled.   The Lacedæmonians were the only troops who had their station near this fountain; the other Greeks were more or less distant from it, according to their place in the line; they however were not far from the Asôpus.   Still, as the Persian horse with their missile weapons did not allow them to approach, and so they could not get their water from the river, these Greeks, no less than the Lacedæmonians, resorted at this time to the fountain.

50. When the fountain was choked, the Grecian captains,

---

[1] Supra, vii. 84 (compare vii. 61).   The custom is noticed by several writers.
[2] Supra, ch. 25.

seeing that the army had no longer a watering-place, and observing moreover that the cavalry greatly harassed them, held a meeting on these and other matters at the head-quarters of Pausanias upon the right. For besides the above-named difficulties, which were great enough, other circumstances added to their distress. All the provisions that they had brought with them were gone; and the attendants who had been sent to fetch supplies from the Peloponnese, were prevented from returning to camp by the Persian horse, which had now closed the passage.

51. The captains therefore held a council, whereat it was agreed, that if the Persians did not give battle that day, the Greeks should move to the Island—a tract of ground which lies in front of Platæa, at the distance of ten furlongs from the Asôpus and fount Gargaphia, where the army was encamped at that time. This tract was a sort of island in the continent: for there is a river which, dividing near its source, runs down from Mount Cithæron into the plain below in two streams, flowing in channels about three furlongs apart, which after a while unite and become one. The name of this river is Oëroë, and the dwellers in those parts call it, the daughter of the Asôpus. This was the place to which the Greeks resolved to remove; and they chose it, first because they would there have no lack of water, and secondly, because the horse could not harass them as when it was drawn up right in their front. They thought it best to begin their march at the second watch of the night, lest the Persians should see them as they left their station, and should follow and harass them with their cavalry. It was agreed likewise, that after they had reached the place, which the Asôpus-born Oëroë surrounds, as it flows down from Cithæron, they should despatch, the very same night, one half of their army towards that mountain-range, to relieve those whom they had sent to procure provisions, and who were now blocked up in that region.

52. Having made these resolves, they continued during that whole day to suffer beyond measure from the attacks of the enemy's horse. At length when towards dusk the attacks of the horse ceased, and, night having closed in, the hour arrived at which the army was to commence its retreat, the greater number struck their tents and began the march towards the rear. They were not minded, however, to make for the place agreed upon; but in their anxiety to escape from the Persian horse, no sooner had they begun to move than they fled straight

to Platæa; where they took post at the temple of Juno, which lies outside the city, at the distance of about twenty furlongs from Gargaphia; and here they pitched their camp in front of the sacred building.

53. As soon as Pausanias saw a portion of the troops in motion, he issued orders to the Lacedæmonians to strike their tents and follow those who had been the first to depart, supposing that they were on their march to the place agreed upon. All the captains but one were ready to obey his orders: Amompharetus, however, the son of Poliadas, who was leader of the Pitanate cohort, refused to move, saying, " He for one would not fly from the strangers,[1] or of his own will bring disgrace upon Sparta." It had happened that he was absent from the former conference of the captains;[2] and so what was now taking place astonished him. Pausanias and Euryanax[3] thought it a monstrous thing that Amompharetus would not hearken to them; but considered that it would be yet more monstrous, if, when he was so minded, they were to leave the Pitanates to their fate; seeing that, if they forsook them to keep their agreement with the other Greeks, Amompharetus and those with him might perish. On this account, therefore, they kept the Lacedæmonian force in its place, and made every endeavour to persuade Amompharetus that he was wrong to act as he was doing.

54. While the Spartans were engaged in these efforts to turn Amompharetus—the only man unwilling to retreat either in their own army or in that of the Tegeans—the Athenians on their side did as follows. Knowing that it was the Spartan temper to say one thing and do another,[4] they remained quiet in their station until the army began to retreat, when they despatched a horseman to see whether the Spartans really meant to set forth, or whether after all they had no intention of moving. The horseman was also to ask Pausanias what he wished the Athenians to do.

55. The herald on his arrival found the Lacedæmonians drawn up in their old position, and their leaders quarrelling with one another. Pausanias and Euryanax had gone on urging Amompharetus not to endanger the lives of his men by staying

[1] Vide supra, ch. 11, and infra, ch. 55.
[2] Vide supra, ch. 51.
[3] Euryanax had been mentioned as having some share in the command, supra, ch. 10.
[4] Vide supra, chs. 6 and 8.

behind while the others drew off, but without succeeding in persuading him; until at last the dispute had waxed hot between them just at the moment when the Athenian herald arrived. At this point Amompharetus, who was still disputing, took up with both his hands a vast rock, and placed it at the feet of Pausanias, saying—" With this pebble I give my vote not to run away from the strangers." (By " strangers " he meant barbarians.[1]) Pausanias, in reply, called him a fool and a madman, and, turning to the Athenian herald, who had made the inquiries with which he was charged, bade him tell his countrymen how he was occupied, and ask them to approach nearer, and retreat or not according to the movements of the Spartans.

56. So the herald went back to the Athenians; and the Spartans continued to dispute till morning began to dawn upon them. Then Pausanias, who as yet had not moved, gave the signal for retreat—expecting (and rightly, as the event proved) that Amompharetus, when he saw the rest of the Lacedæmonians in motion, would be unwilling to be left behind. No sooner was the signal given, than all the army except the Pitanates began their march, and retreated along the line of the hills; the Tegeans accompanying them. The Athenians likewise set off in good order, but proceeded by a different way from the Lacedæmonians. For while the latter clung to the hilly ground and the skirts of Mount Cithæron, on account of the fear which they entertained of the enemy's horse, the former betook themselves to the low country and marched through the plain.

57. As for Amompharetus, at first he did not believe that Pausanias would really dare to leave him behind; he therefore remained firm in his resolve to keep his men at their post; when, however, Pausanias and his troops were now some way off, Amompharetus, thinking himself forsaken in good earnest, ordered his band to take their arms, and led them at a walk towards the main army. Now the army was waiting for them at a distance of about ten furlongs, having halted upon the river Moloeis at a place called Argiopius, where stands a temple dedicated to Eleusinian Ceres. They had stopped here, that, in case Amompharetus and his band should refuse to quit the spot where they were drawn up, and should really not stir from it, they might have it in their power to move back and lend them assistance. Amompharetus, however, and his companions

[1] Vide supra, ch. 11.

rejoined the main body; and at the same time the whole mass
of the barbarian cavalry arrived and began to press hard upon
them. The horsemen had followed their usual practice and
ridden up to the Greek camp, when they discovered that the
place where the Greeks had been posted hitherto was deserted.
Hereupon they pushed forward without stopping, and, as soon
as they overtook the enemy, pressed heavily on them.

58. Mardonius, when he heard that the Greeks had retired
under cover of the night, and beheld the place, where they had
been stationed, empty, called to him Thorax of Larissa,[1] and his
brethren, Eurypylus and Thrasideius, and said—

" O sons of Aleuas! what will ye say now, when ye see yonder
place empty? Why, you, who dwell in their neighbourhood,
told me the Lacedæmonians never fled from battle, but were
brave beyond all the rest of mankind. Lately, however, you
yourselves beheld them change their place in the line;[2] and
here, as all may see, they have run away during the night.
Verily, when their turn came to fight with those who are of a
truth the bravest warriors in all the world, they showed plainly
enough that they are men of no worth, who have distinguished
themselves among *Greeks*—men likewise of no worth at all.
However, I can readily excuse you, who, knowing nothing of the
Persians, praised these men from your acquaintance with certain
exploits of theirs; but I marvel all the more at Artabazus, that
he should have been afraid of the Lacedæmonians, and have
therefore given us so dastardly a counsel,—bidding us, as he
did, break up our camp, and remove to Thebes, and there allow
ourselves to be besieged by the Greeks [3]—advice whereof I shall
take care to inform the king. But of this hereafter. Now we
must not allow them to escape us, but must pursue after them
till we overtake them; and then we must exact vengeance for
all the wrongs which have been suffered at their hands by the
Persians."

59. When he had so spoken, he crossed the Asôpus, and led
the Persians forward at a run directly upon the track of the
Greeks, whom he believed to be in actual flight. He could not
see the Athenians; for, as they had taken the way of the plain,
they were hidden from his sight by the hills; he therefore led
on his troops against the Lacedæmonians and the Tegeans only.
When the commanders of the other divisions of the barbarians
saw the Persians pursuing the Greeks so hastily, they all forth-

[1] Supra, ch. 1.   [2] Supra, ch. 47.   [3] Supra, ch. 41.

with seized their standards, and hurried after at their best speed in great disorder and disarray. On they went with loud shouts and in a wild rout, thinking to swallow up the runaways.

60. Meanwhile Pausanias had sent a horseman to the Athenians, at the time when the cavalry first fell upon him, with this message:—

" Men of Athens! now that the great struggle has come, which is to decide the freedom or the slavery of Greece, we twain, Lacedæmonians and Athenians, are deserted by all the other allies, who have fled away from us during the past night. Nevertheless, we are resolved what to do—we must endeavour, as best we may, to defend ourselves and to succour one another. Now, had the horse fallen upon you first, we ourselves with the Tegeans (who remain faithful to the Greek cause) would have been bound to render you assistance against them. As, however, the entire body has advanced upon us, 'tis your place to come to our aid, sore pressed as we are by the enemy. Should you yourselves be so straitened that you cannot come, at least send us your archers, and be sure you will earn our gratitude. We acknowledge that throughout this whole war there has been no zeal to be compared to yours—we therefore doubt not that you will do us this service."

61. The Athenians, as soon as they received this message, were anxious to go to the aid of the Spartans, and to help them to the uttermost of their power; but, as they were upon the march, the Greeks on the king's side, whose place in the line had been opposite theirs, fell upon them, and so harassed them by their attacks that it was not possible for them to give the succour they desired. Accordingly the Lacedæmonians, and the Tegeans—whom nothing could induce to quit their side—were left alone to resist the Persians. Including the light-armed, the number of the former was 50,000; while that of the Tegeans was 3000. Now, therefore, as they were about to engage with Mardonius and the troops under him, they made ready to offer sacrifice. The victims, however, for some time were not favourable; and, during the delay, many fell on the Spartan side, and a still greater number were wounded. For the Persians had made a rampart of their wicker shields,[1] and shot from behind them such clouds of arrows, that the Spartans were sorely distressed. The victims continued unpropitious; till at last

[1] The wicker shield used by the Persians seems to have been adopted from the Assyrians

Pausanias raised his eyes to the Heræum of the Platæans, and calling the goddess to his aid, besought her not to disappoint the hopes of the Greeks.

62. As he offered his prayer, the Tegeans, advancing before the rest, rushed forward against the enemy; and the Lacedæmonians, who had obtained favourable omens the moment that Pausanias prayed, at length, after their long delay, advanced to the attack; while the Persians, on their side, left shooting, and prepared to meet them. And first the combat was at the wicker shields. Afterwards, when these were swept down, a fierce contest took place by the side of the temple of Ceres, which lasted long, and ended in a hand-to-hand struggle. The barbarians many times seized hold of the Greek spears and brake them; for in boldness and warlike spirit the Persians were not a whit inferior to the Greeks; but they were without bucklers,[1] untrained, and far below the enemy in respect of skill in arms. Sometimes singly, sometimes in bodies of ten, now fewer and now more in number, they dashed forward upon the Spartan ranks, and so perished.

63. The fight went most against the Greeks, where Mardonius, mounted upon a white horse, and surrounded by the bravest of all the Persians, the thousand picked men,[2] fought in person. So long as Mardonius was alive, this body resisted all attacks, and, while they defended their own lives, struck down no small number of Spartans; but after Mardonius fell, and the troops with him, which were the main strength of the army, perished, the remainder yielded to the Lacedæmonians, and took to flight. Their light clothing, and want of bucklers, were of the greatest hurt to them; for they had to contend against men heavily armed, while they themselves were without any such defence.

64. Then was the warning of the oracle fulfilled; and the vengeance which was due to the Spartans for the slaughter of Leonidas was paid them by Mardonius—then too did Pausanias, the son of Cleombrotus, and grandson of Anaxandridas (I omit to recount his other ancestors, since they are the same with those of Leonidas), win a victory exceeding in glory all those to which our knowledge extends. Mardonius was slain by Aeimnêstus, a man famous in Sparta—the same who in the Messenian war, which came after the struggle against the

---

[1] The wicker shields of the Persians were useless for close combat.
[2] Supra, vii. 40 and viii. 113.

Medes, fought a battle near Stenyclêrus with but three hundred men against the whole force of the Messenians, and himself perished, and the three hundred with him.

65. The Persians, as soon as they were put to flight by the Lacedæmonians, ran hastily away, without preserving any order, and took refuge in their own camp, within the wooden defence which they had raised in the Theban territory.[1] It is a marvel to me how it came to pass, that although the battle was fought quite close to the grove of Ceres, yet not a single Persian appears to have died on the sacred soil, nor even to have set foot upon it, while round about the precinct, in the unconsecrated ground, great numbers perished. I imagine—if it is lawful, in matters which concern the gods, to imagine anything —that the goddess herself kept them out, because they had burnt her dwelling at Eleusis. Such, then, was the issue of this battle.

66. Artabazus, the son of Pharnaces, who had disapproved from the first of the king's leaving Mardonius behind him, and had made great endeavours, but all in vain, to dissuade Mardonius from risking a battle,[2] when he found that the latter was bent on acting otherwise than he wished, did as follows. He had a force under his orders which was far from inconsiderable, amounting, as it did, to near forty thousand men. Being well aware, therefore, how the battle was likely to go, as soon as the two armies began to fight, he led his soldiers forward in an orderly array, bidding them one and all proceed at the same pace, and follow him with such celerity as they should observe him to use. Having issued these commands, he pretended to lead them to the battle. But when, advancing before his army, he saw that the Persians were already in flight, instead of keeping the same order, he wheeled his troops suddenly round, and beat a retreat; nor did he even seek shelter within the palisade or behind the walls of Thebes, but hurried on into Phocis, wishing to make his way to the Hellespont with all possible speed. Such accordingly was the course which these Persians took.

67. As for the Greeks upon the king's side, while most of them played the coward purposely, the Bœotians, on the contrary, had a long struggle with the Athenians. Those of the Thebans who were attached to the Medes, displayed especially no little zeal; far from playing the coward, they fought with

[1] Supra, ch. 15. [2] Supra, ch. 41.

such fury that three hundred of the best and bravest among them were slain by the Athenians in this passage of arms. But at last they too were routed, and fled away—not, however, in the same direction as the Persians and the crowd of allies, who, having taken no part in the battle, ran off without striking a blow—but to the city of Thebes.

68. To me it shows very clearly how completely the rest of the barbarians were dependent upon the Persian troops, that here they all fled at once, without ever coming to blows with the enemy, merely because they saw the Persians running away. And so it came to pass that the whole army took to flight, except only the horse, both Persian and Bœotian. These did good service to the flying foot-men, by advancing close to the enemy, and separating between the Greeks and their own fugitives.

69. The victors however pressed on, pursuing and slaying the remnant of the king's army.

Meantime, while the flight continued, tidings reached the Greeks who were drawn up round the Heræum,[1] and so were absent from the battle, that the fight was begun, and that Pausanias was gaining the victory. Hearing this, they rushed forward without any order, the Corinthians taking the upper road across the skirts of Cithæron and the hills, which led straight to the temple of Ceres; while the Megarians and Phliasians followed the level route through the plain. These last had almost reached the enemy, when the Theban horse espied them, and, observing their disarray, despatched against them the squadron of which Asôpodôrus, the son of Timander, was captain. Asôpodôrus charged them with such effect that he left six hundred of their number dead upon the plain, and, pursuing the rest, compelled them to seek shelter in Cithæron. So these men perished without honour.

70. The Persians, and the multitude with them, who fled to the wooden fortress, were able to ascend into the towers before the Lacedæmonians came up. Thus placed, they proceeded to strengthen the defences as well as they could; and when the Lacedæmonians arrived, a sharp fight took place at the rampart. So long as the Athenians were away, the barbarians kept off their assailants, and had much the best of the combat, since the Lacedæmonians were unskilled in the attack of walled places:[2]

[1] Supra, ch. 52.
[2] The inability to conduct sieges is one of the most striking features of the Spartan military character. The Athenian skill contrasted remarkably with the Spartan inefficiency.

but on the arrival of the Athenians, a more violent assault was made, and the wall was for a long time attacked with fury. In the end the valour of the Athenians and their perseverance prevailed—they gained the top of the wall, and, breaking a breach through it, enabled the Greeks to pour in. The first to enter here were the Tegeans, and they it was who plundered the tent of Mardonius; where among other booty they found the manger from which his horses ate, all made of solid brass, and well worth looking at. This manger was given by the Tegeans to the temple of Minerva Alea, while the remainder of their booty was brought into the common stock of the Greeks. As soon as the wall was broken down, the barbarians no longer kept together in any array, nor was there one among them who thought of making further resistance—in good truth, they were all half dead with fright, huddled as so many thousands were into so narrow and confined a space. With such tameness did they submit to be slaughtered by the Greeks, that of the 300,000 men who composed the army—omitting the 40,000 by whom Artabazus was accompanied in his flight—no more than 3000 outlived the battle. Of the Lacedæmonians from Sparta there perished in this combat ninety-one; of the Tegeans, sixteen; of the Athenians, fifty-two.

71. On the side of the barbarians, the greatest courage was manifested, among the foot-soldiers, by the Persians; among the horse, by the Sacæ; while Mardonius himself, as a man, bore off the palm from the rest. Among the Greeks, the Athenians and the Tegeans fought well; but the prowess shown by the Lacedæmonians was beyond either. Of this I have but one proof to offer—since all the three nations overthrew the force opposed to them—and that is, that the Lacedæmonians fought and conquered the best troops. The bravest man by far on that day was, in my judgment, Aristodêmus—the same who alone escaped from the slaughter of the three hundred at Thermopylæ, and who on that account had endured disgrace and reproach: [1] next to him were Posidônius, Philocyon, and Amompharetus the Spartan. The Spartans, however, who took part in the fight, when the question of "who had distinguished himself most," came to be talked over among them, decided—"that Aristodêmus, who, on account of the blame which attached to him, had manifestly courted death, and had therefore left his place in the line and behaved like a madman, had done of a truth very

[1] Supra, vii. 229-231.

notable deeds; but that Posidônius, who, with no such desire to lose his life, had quitted himself no less gallantly, was by so much a braver man than he." Perchance, however, it was envy that made them speak after this sort. Of those whom I have named above as slain in this battle, all, save and except Aristodêmus, received public honours: Aristodêmus alone had no honours, because he courted death for the reason which I have mentioned.

72. These then were the most distinguished of those who fought at Platæa. As for Callicrates,—the most beautiful man, not among the Spartans only, but in the whole Greek camp,— he was not killed in the battle; for it was while Pausanias was still consulting the victims, that as he sat in his proper place in the line, an arrow struck him on the side. While his comrades advanced to the fight, he was borne out of the ranks, very loath to die, as he showed by the words which he addressed to Arimnestus, one of the Platæans;—" I grieve," said he, " not because I have to die for my country, but because I have not lifted my arm against the enemy, nor done any deed worthy of me, much as I have desired to achieve something."

73. The Athenian who is said to have distinguished himself the most was Sôphanes, the son of Eutychides, of the Deceleian canton. The men of this canton, once upon a time, did a deed, which (as the Athenians themselves confess) has ever since been serviceable to them. When the Tyndaridæ, in days of yore, invaded Attica with a mighty army to recover Helen,[1] and, not being able to find out whither she had been carried, desolated the cantons,—at this time, they say, the Deceleians (or Decelus himself, according to some), displeased at the rudeness of Theseus, and fearing that the whole territory would suffer, discovered everything to the enemy, and even showed them the way to Aphidnæ, which Titacus, a native of the place, betrayed into their hands. As a reward for this action, Sparta has always,

---

[1] Pirithoüs and Theseus resolved to wed daughters of Jove, and to help one another. They had heard of the beauty of Helen, though she was no more than seven years old, and went to Sparta to carry her off. There they found her dancing in the temple of Diana Orthia. Having seized her and borne her away, they cast lots whose she should be, and Theseus was the winner. So he brought Helen to Attica, and secreted her at Aphidnæ, giving her in charge to his friend Aphidnus, and his mother Æthra. Theseus then accompanied Pirithoüs into Thesprotia, to obtain Persephoné for him. Meanwhile the Dioscûri had collected a vast host, and invaded Attica, where they sought everywhere for their sister. At length her hiding-place was pointed out to them; and they laid siege to Aphidnæ, and having taken it, recovered Helen, and made Æthra prisoner.

from that time to the present, allowed the Deceleians to be free from all dues, and to have seats of honour at their festivals; and hence too, in the war which took place many years after these events between the Peloponnesians and the Athenians, the Lacedæmonians, while they laid waste all the rest of Attica, spared the lands of the Deceleians.

74. Of this canton was Sôphanes, the Athenian, who most distinguished himself in the battle. Two stories are told concerning him: according to the one, he wore an iron anchor, fastened to the belt which secured his breastplate by a brazen chain; and this, when he came near the enemy, he threw out; to the intent that, when they made their charge, it might be impossible for him to be driven from his post: as soon, however, as the enemy fled, his wont was to take up his anchor and join the pursuit. Such, then, is one of the said stories. The other, which is contradictory to the first, relates that Sôphanes, instead of having an iron anchor fastened to his breastplate, bore the device of an anchor upon his shield,[1] which he never allowed to rest, but made to run round continually.

75. Another glorious deed was likewise performed by this same Sôphanes. At the time when the Athenians were laying siege to Egina, he took up the challenge of Eurybates the Argive, a winner of the Pentathlum, and slew him.[2] The fate of Sôphanes in after times was the following: he was leader of an Athenian army in conjunction with Leagrus, the son of Glaucon, and in a battle with the Edonians near Datum,[3] about the gold-mines there, he was slain, after displaying uncommon bravery.

76. As soon as the Greeks at Platæa had overthrown the barbarians, a woman came over to them from the enemy. She was one of the concubines of Pharandates, the son of Teäspes, a Persian; and when she heard that the Persians were all slain and that the Greeks had carried the day, forthwith she adorned herself and her maids with many golden ornaments, and with the bravest of the apparel that she had brought with her, and, alighting from her litter, came forward to the Lacedæmonians, ere the work of slaughter was well over. When she saw that

---

[1] Devices upon shields were in use among the Greeks from very early times.

[2] Supra, vi. 92.

[3] The battle here mentioned was fought about the year B.C. 465, on occasion of the first attempt which the Athenians made to colonise Amphipolis.

all the orders were given by Pausanias, with whose name and country she was well acquainted, as she had oftentimes heard tell of them, she knew who he must be; wherefore she embraced his knees, and said—

"O king of Sparta! save thy suppliant from the slavery that awaits the captive. Already I am beholden to thee for one service—the slaughter of these men, wretches who had no regard either for gods or angels. I am by birth a Coan, the daughter of Hêgêtoridas, son of Antagoras. The Persian seized me by force in Cos, and kept me against my will."

"Lady," answered Pausanias, "fear nothing: as a suppliant thou art safe—and still more, if thou hast spoken truth, and Hêgêtoridas of Cos is thy father—for he is bound to me by closer ties of friendship than any other man in those regions."

When he had thus spoken, Pausanias placed the woman in the charge of some of the Ephors who were present, and afterwards sent her to Egina, whither she had a desire to go.

77. About the time of this woman's coming, the Mantineans arrived upon the field, and found that all was over, and that it was too late to take any part in the battle. Greatly distressed hereat, they declared themselves to deserve a fine, as laggarts; after which, learning that a portion of the Medes had fled away under Artabazus, they were anxious to go after them as far as Thessaly. The Lacedæmonians however would not suffer the pursuit; so they returned again to their own land, and sent the leaders of their army into banishment. Soon after the Mantineans, the Eleans likewise arrived, and showed the same sorrow; after which they too returned home, and banished their leaders. But enough concerning these nations.

78. There was a man at Platæa among the troops of the Eginetans, whose name was Lampon; he was the son of Pytheas, and a person of the first rank among his countrymen. Now this Lampon went about this same time to Pausanias, and counselled him to do a deed of exceeding wickedness. "Son of Cleombrotus," he said very earnestly, "what thou hast already done is passing great and glorious. By the favour of Heaven thou hast saved Greece, and gained a renown beyond all the Greeks of whom we have any knowledge. Now then so finish thy work, that thine own fame may be increased thereby, and that henceforth barbarians may fear to commit outrages on the Grecians. When Leonidas was slain at Thermopylæ, Xerxes and Mardonius commanded that he should be beheaded and

crucified.[1] Do thou the like at this time by Mardonius, and thou wilt have glory in Sparta, and likewise through the whole of Greece. For, by hanging him upon a cross, thou wilt avenge Leonidas, who was thy father's brother."

79. Thus spake Lampon, thinking to please Pausanias; but Pausanias answered him—" My Eginetan friend, for thy foresight and thy friendliness I am much beholden to thee: but the counsel which thou hast offered is not good. First hast thou lifted me up to the skies, by thy praise of my country and my achievement; and then thou hast cast me down to the ground, by bidding me maltreat the dead, and saying that thus I shall raise myself in men's esteem. Such doings befit barbarians rather than Greeks; and even in barbarians we detest them. On such terms then I could not wish to please the Eginetans, nor those who think as they think—enough for me to gain the approval of my own countrymen, by righteous deeds as well as by righteous words. Leonidas, whom thou wouldst have me avenge, is, I maintain, abundantly avenged already. Surely the countless lives here taken are enough to avenge not him only, but all those who fell at Thermopylæ. Come not thou before me again with such a speech, nor with such counsel; and thank my forbearance that thou art not now punished." Then Lampon, having received this answer, departed, and went his way.

80. After this Pausanias caused proclamation to be made, that no one should lay hands on the booty, but that the Helots should collect it and bring it all to one place. So the Helots went and spread themselves through the camp, wherein were found many tents richly adorned with furniture of gold and silver, many couches covered with plates of the same, and many golden bowls, goblets, and other drinking-vessels. On the carriages were bags containing silver and golden kettles; and the bodies of the slain furnished bracelets and chains, and scymitars with golden ornaments—not to mention embroidered apparel, of which no one made any account. The Helots at this time stole many things of much value, which they sold in after times to the Eginetans; however, they brought in likewise no small quantity, chiefly such things as it was not possible for them to hide. And this was the beginning of the great wealth of the Eginetans, who bought the gold of the Helots as if it had been mere brass.[2]

[1] Supra, vii. 238.
[2] This ignorance of the helots has been well compared to that of the

81. When all the booty had been brought together, a tenth of the whole was set apart for the Delphian god; and hence was made the golden tripod which stands on the bronze serpent with the three heads, quite close to the altar.[1] Portions were also set apart for the gods of Olympia, and of the Isthmus; from which were made, in the one case, a bronze Jupiter ten cubits high; and in the other, a bronze Neptune of seven cubits. After this, the rest of the spoil was divided among the soldiers, each of whom received less or more according to his deserts; and in this way was a distribution made of the Persian concubines, of the gold, the silver, the beasts of burthen, and all the other valuables. What special gifts were presented to those who had most distinguished themselves in the battle, I do not find mentioned by any one;[2] but I should suppose that they must have had some gifts beyond the others. As for Pausanias, the portion which was set apart for him consisted of ten specimens of each kind of thing—women, horses, talents, camels, or whatever else there was in the spoil.

82. It is said that the following circumstance happened likewise at this time. Xerxes, when he fled away out of Greece, left his war-tent with Mardonius:[3] when Pausanias, therefore, saw the tent with its adornments of gold and silver, and its hangings of divers colours, he gave commandment to the bakers and the cooks to make him ready a banquet in such fashion as was their wont for Mardonius. Then they made ready as they were bidden; and Pausanias, beholding the couches of gold and silver daintily decked out with their rich covertures, and the tables of gold and silver laid, and the feast itself prepared with all magnificence, was astonished at the good things which were set before him, and, being in a pleasant mood, gave commandment to his own followers to make ready a Spartan supper. When the suppers were both served, and it was apparent how

Swiss after the battle of Granson, when, according to Philippe de Comines they " ne connurent les biens qu'ils eurent en leurs mains . . . il y en eut qui vendirent grande quantité de plats et d'escuelles d'argent, pour deux grands blancs la pièce, *cuidans que ce fust estaing* " (Mémoires, v. 2).

[1] Upon this tripod Pausanias placed the inscription which was one of the first indications of his ambitious aims:—

" Pausanias, Grecia's chief, the Mede o'erthrew,
And gave Apollo that which here ye view."

[2] This is one of the very few passages of his History in which Herodotus seems to imply that he consulted *authors* in compiling it. For the most part he derives his materials from personal observation and inquiry.

[3] The capture of this tent was commemorated at Athens by the erection of a building in imitation of it. This was the Odeum.

vast a difference lay between the two, Pausanias laughed, and sent his servants to call to him the Greek generals. On their coming, he pointed to the two boards, and said:—

" I sent for you, O Greeks, to show you the folly of this Median captain, who, when he enjoyed such fare as this, must needs come here to rob us of our penury."

Such, it is said, were the words of Pausanias to the Grecian generals.

83. During many years afterwards, the Platæans used often to find upon the field of battle concealed treasures of gold, and silver, and other valuables. More recently they likewise made discovery of the following: the flesh having all fallen away from the bodies of the dead, and their bones having been gathered together into one place, the Platæans found a skull without any seam, made entirely of a single bone; likewise a jaw, both the upper bone and the under, wherein all the teeth, front and back, were joined together and made of one bone; also, the skeleton of a man not less than five cubits in height.

84. The body of Mardonius disappeared the day after the battle; but who it was that stole it away I cannot say with certainty. I have heard tell of a number of persons, and those too of many different nations, who are said to have given him burial; and I know that many have received large sums on this score from Artontes the son of Mardonius: but I cannot discover with any certainty which of them it was who really took the body away, and buried it. Among others, Dionysophanes, an Ephesian, is rumoured to have been the actual person.

85. The Greeks, after sharing the booty upon the field of Platæa, proceeded to bury their own dead, each nation apart from the rest. The Lacedæmonians made three graves; in one they buried their youths, among whom were Posidônius, Amompharetus, Philocyon, and Callicrates;—in another, the rest of the Spartans; and in the third, the Helots. Such was their mode of burial. The Tegeans buried all their dead in a single grave; as likewise did the Athenians theirs, and the Megarians and Phliasians those who were slain by the horse. These graves, then, had bodies buried in them: as for the other tombs which are to be seen at Platæa, they were raised, as I understand, by the Greeks whose troops took no part in the battle; and who, being ashamed of themselves, erected empty barrows upon the field, to obtain credit with those who should come after them. Among others, the Eginetans have a grave there,

which goes by their name; but which, as I learn, was made ten years later by Cleades, the son of Autodicus, a Platæan, at the request of the Eginetans, whose agent he was.

86. After the Greeks had buried their dead at Platæa, they presently held a council, whereat it was resolved to make war upon Thebes, and to require that those who had joined the Medes should be delivered into their hands. Two men, who had been the chief leaders on the occasion, were especially named—to wit, Timagenidas and Attagînus.[1] If the Thebans should refuse to give these men up, it was determined to lay siege to their city, and never stir from before it till it should surrender. After this resolve, the army marched upon Thebes; and having demanded the men, and been refused, began the siege, laying waste the country all around, and making assaults upon the wall in divers places.

87. When twenty days were gone by, and the violence of the Greeks did not slacken, Timagenidas thus bespake his countrymen—

"Ye men of Thebes, since the Greeks have so decreed, that they will never desist from the siege till either they take Thebes or we are delivered to them, we would not that the land of Bœotia should suffer any longer on our behalf. If it be money that they in truth desire, and their demand of us be no more than a pretext, let money from the treasury of the state be given them; for the state, and not we alone, embraced the cause of the Medes. If, however, they really want our persons, and on that account press this siege, we are ready to be delivered to them and to stand our trial."

The Thebans thought this offer very right and seasonable; wherefore they despatched a herald without any delay to Pausanias, and told him they were willing to deliver up the men.

88. As soon as an agreement had been concluded upon these terms, Attagînus made his escape from the city; his sons, however, were surrendered in his place; but Pausanias refused to hold them guilty, since children (he said) could have had no part in such an offence. The rest of those whom the Thebans gave up had expected to obtain a trial, and in that case their trust was to escape by means of bribery; but Pausanias, afraid of this, dismissed at once the whole army of allies, and took the men with him to Corinth, where he slew them all. Such were the events which happened at Platæa and at Thebes.

[1] Supra, chs. 15 and 38.

89. Artabazus, the son of Pharnaces, who fled away from Platæa, was soon far sped on his journey. When he reached Thessaly, the inhabitants received him hospitably, and made inquiries of him concerning the rest of the army, since they were still altogether ignorant of what had taken place at Platæa: whereupon the Persian, knowing well that, if he told them the truth, he would run great risk of perishing himself, together with his whole army—for if the facts were once blazoned abroad, all who learnt them would be sure to fall upon him—the Persian, I say, considering this, as he had before kept all secret from the Phocians, so now answered the Thessalians after the following fashion:—

" I myself, Thessalians, am hastening, as ye see, into Thrace; and I am fain to use all possible despatch, as I am sent with this force on special business from the main army. Mardonius and his host are close behind me, and may be looked for shortly. When he comes, receive him as ye have received me, and show him every kindness. Be sure ye will never hereafter regret it, if ye so do."

With these words he took his departure, and marched his troops at their best speed through Thessaly and Macedon straight upon Thrace, following the inland route, which was the shortest, and, in good truth, using all possible despatch. He himself succeeded in reaching Byzantium; but a great part of his army perished upon the road—many being cut to pieces by the Thracians, and others dying from hunger and excess of toil. From Byzantium Artabazus set sail, and crossed the strait; returning into Asia in the manner which has been here described.

90. On the same day that the blow was struck at Platæa, another defeat befell the Persians at Mycalé in Ionia. While the Greek fleet under Leotychides the Lacedæmonian was still lying inactive at Delos, there arrived at that place an embassy from Samos, consisting of three men, Lampon the son of Thrasycles, Athenagoras the son of Archestratidas, and Hêgêsistratus the son of Aristagoras. The Samians had sent them secretly, concealing their departure both from the Persians and from their own tyrant Theomestor, the son of Androdamas, whom the Persians had made ruler of Samos.[1] When the ambassadors came before the Greek captains Hêgêsistratus took the word, and urged them with many and various arguments, saying, " that the Ionians only needed to see them arrive in

[1] The reason of this was given, viii. 85.

order to revolt from the Persians; and that the Persians would never abide their coming; or if they did, 'twould be to offer them the finest booty that they could anywhere expect to gain;" while at the same time he made appeal to the gods of their common worship, and besought them to deliver from bondage a Grecian race, and withal to drive back the barbarians. "This," he said, "might very easily be done, for the Persian ships were bad sailers, and far from a match for theirs;" adding, moreover, "that if there was any suspicion lest the Samians intended to deal treacherously, they were themselves ready to become hostages, and to return on board the ships of their allies to Asia."

91. When the Samian stranger continued importunately beseeching him, Leotychides, either because he wanted an omen, or by a mere chance, as God guided him, asked the man— "Samian stranger! prithee, tell me thy name?" "Hêgêsistratus (army-leader)," answered the other, and might have said more, but Leotychides stopped him by exclaiming—"I accept, O Samian! the omen which thy name affords. Only, before thou goest back, swear to us, thyself and thy brother-envoys, that the Samians will indeed be our warm friends and allies."

92. No sooner had he thus spoken than he proceeded to hurry forward the business. The Samians pledged their faith upon the spot; and oaths of alliance were exchanged between them and the Greeks. This done, two of the ambassadors forthwith sailed away; as for Hêgêsistratus, Leotychides kept him to accompany his own fleet, for he considered his name to be a good omen. The Greeks abode where they were that day, and on the morrow sacrificed, and found the victims favourable. Their soothsayer was Deïphonus, the son of Evênius, a man of Apollonia—I mean the Apollonia which lies upon the Ionian Gulf.

93. A strange thing happened to this man's father, Evênius. The Apolloniats have a flock of sheep sacred to the sun. During the day-time these sheep graze along the banks of the river which flows from Mount Lacmon through their territory and empties itself into the sea by the port of Oricus;[1] while at night they are guarded by the richest and noblest of the citizens, who are chosen to serve the office, and who keep the watch each for one year. Now the Apolloniats set great store by these sheep, on account of an oracle which they received concerning them.

[1] The geography of Herodotus is here somewhat at fault.

The place where they are folded at night is a cavern, a long way from the town. Here it happened that Evênius, when he was chosen to keep the watch, by some accident fell asleep upon his guard; and while he slept, the cave was entered by wolves, which destroyed some sixty of the flock under his care. Evênius, when he woke and found what had occurred, kept silence about it and told no one; for he thought to buy other sheep and put them in the place of the slain. But the matter came to the ears of the Apolloniats, who forthwith brought Evênius to trial, and condemned him to lose his eyes, because he had gone to sleep upon his post. Now when Evênius was blinded, straightway the sheep had no young, and the land ceased to bear its wonted harvests. Then the Apolloniats sent to Dodôna, and to Delphi, and asked the prophets, what had caused the woes which so afflicted them. The answer which they received was this—" The woes were come for Evênius, the guardian of the sacred sheep, whom the Apolloniats had wrongfully deprived of sight. They (the gods) had themselves sent the wolves; nor would they ever cease to exact vengeance for Evênius, till the Apolloniats made him whatever atonement he liked to ask. When this was paid, *they* would likewise give him a gift, which would make many men call him blessed."

94. Such was the tenor of the prophecies. The Apolloniats kept them close, but charged some of their citizens to go and make terms with Evênius; and these men managed the business for them in the way which I will now describe. They found Evênius sitting upon a bench, and, approaching him, they sat down by his side, and began to talk: at first they spoke of quite other matters, but in the end they mentioned his misfortune, and offered him their condolence. Having thus beguiled him, at last they put the question—" What atonement would he desire, if the Apolloniats were willing to make him satisfaction for the wrong which they had done to him?" Hereupon Evênius, who had not heard of the oracle, made answer—" If I were given the lands of this man and that—" (here he named the two men whom he knew to have the finest farms in Apollonia), " and likewise the house of this other "—(and here he mentioned the house which he knew to be the handsomest in the town), " I would, when master of these, be quite content, and my wrath would cease altogether." As soon as Evênius had thus spoken, the men who sat by him rejoined—" Evênius, the Apolloniats give thee the atonement which thou hast desired, according to

the bidding of the oracles." Then Evênius understood the whole matter, and was enraged that they had deceived him so; but the Apolloniats bought the farms from their owners, and gave Evênius what he had chosen. After this was done, straightway Evênius had the gift of prophecy, insomuch that he became a famous man in Greece.

95. Deïphonus, the son of this Evênius, had accompanied the Corinthians, and was soothsayer, as I said before, to the Greek armament. One account, however, which I have heard, declares that he was not really the son of this man, but only took the name, and then went about Greece and let out his services for hire.

96. The Greeks, as soon as the victims were favourable, put to sea, and sailed across from Delos to Samos. Arriving off Calami, a place upon the Samian coast, they brought the fleet to an anchor near the temple of Juno which stands there,[1] and prepared to engage the Persians by sea. These latter, however, no sooner heard of the approach of the Greeks, than, dismissing the Phœnician ships, they sailed away with the remainder to the mainland. For it had been resolved in council not to risk a battle, since the Persian fleet was thought to be no match for that of the enemy. They fled, therefore, to the main, to be under the protection of their land army, which now lay at Mycalé,[2] and consisted of the troops left behind by Xerxes to keep guard over Ionia. This was an army of sixty thousand men, under the command of Tigranes, a Persian of more than common beauty and stature. The captains resolved therefore to betake themselves to these troops for defence, to drag their ships ashore, and to build a rampart around them, which might at once protect the fleet, and serve likewise as a place of refuge for themselves.

97. Having so resolved, the commanders put out to sea; and passing the temple of the Eumenides, arrived at Gæson and Scolopoeis, which are in the territory of Mycalé. Here is a temple of Eleusinian Ceres, built by Philistus the son of Pasicles who came to Asia with Neileus the son of Codrus,[3] what time he founded Miletus. At this place they drew the ships up on the beach, and surrounded them with a rampart made of stones and

---

[1] Supra, iii. 60. I understand by this the *great* temple of Juno near the town of Samos.

[2] Supra, i. 148. Mycalé is the modern *Cape St. Mary*, the promontory which runs out towards Samos.

[3] Supra, i. 147.

trunks of trees, cutting down for this purpose all the fruit-trees which grew near, and defending the barrier by means of stakes firmly planted in the ground. Here they were prepared either to win a battle, or undergo a siege—their thoughts embracing both chances.

98. The Greeks, when they understood that the barbarians had fled to the mainland, were sorely vexed at their escape: nor could they determine at first what they should do, whether they should return home, or proceed to the Hellespont. In the end, however, they resolved to do neither, but to make sail for the continent. So they made themselves ready for a sea-fight by the preparation of boarding-bridges, and what else was necessary; provided with which they sailed to Mycalé. Now when they came to the place where the camp was, they found no one venture out to meet them, but observed the ships all dragged ashore within the barrier, and a strong land-force drawn up in battle array upon the beach; Leotychides therefore sailed along the shore in his ship, keeping as close hauled to the land as possible, and by the voice of a herald thus addressed the Ionians:—

"Men of Ionia—ye who can hear me speak—do ye take heed to what I say; for the Persians will not understand a word that I utter. When we join battle with them, before aught else, remember Freedom—and next, recollect our watchword, which is Hêbé. If there be any who hear me not, let those who hear me report my words to the others."

In all this Leotychides had the very same design which Themistocles entertained at Artemisium.[1] Either the barbarians would not know what he had said, and the Ionians would be persuaded to revolt from them; or if his words were reported to the former, they would mistrust their Greek soldiers.

99. After Leotychides had made this address, the Greeks brought their ships to the land, and, having disembarked, arrayed themselves for the battle. When the Persians saw them marshalling their array, and bethought themselves of the advice which had been offered to the Ionians, their first act was to disarm the Samians, whom they suspected of complicity with the enemy. For it had happened lately that a number of the Athenians who lingered in Attica, having been made prisoners by the troops of Xerxes, were brought to Asia on board the barbarian fleet; and these men had been ransomed, one and all,

[1] Supra, viii. 22, end.

by the Samians, who sent them back to Athens, well furnished
with provisions for the way.   On this account, as much as on
any other, the Samians were suspected, as men who had paid
the ransom of five hundred of the king's enemies.   After dis-
arming them, the Persians next despatched the Milesians to
guard the paths which lead up into the heights of Mycalé,
because (they said) the Milesians were well acquainted with
that region: their true object, however, was to remove them to
a distance from the camp.   In this way the Persians sought to
secure themselves against such of the Ionians as they thought
likely, if occasion offered, to make rebellion.   They then joined
shield to shield, and so made themselves a breastwork against
the enemy.[1]

100. The Greeks now, having finished their preparations,
began to move towards the barbarians; when, lo! as they
advanced, a rumour flew through the host from one end to the
other—that the Greeks had fought and conquered the army of
Mardonius in Bœotia.   At the same time a herald's wand was
observed lying upon the beach.   Many things prove to me that
the gods take part in the affairs of man.   How else, when the
battles of Mycalé and Platæa were about to happen on the self
same day, should such a rumour have reached the Greeks in
that region, greatly cheering the whole army, and making them
more eager than before to risk their lives.

101. A strange coincidence too it was, that both the battles
should have been fought near a precinct of Eleusinian Ceres.
The fight at Platæa took place, as I said before, quite close
to one of Ceres' temples; and now the battle at Mycalé was
to be fought hard by another.   Rightly, too, did the rumour
run, that the Greeks with Pausanias *had gained* their victory;
for the fight at Platæa fell early in the day, whereas that at
Mycalé was towards evening.   That the two battles were really
fought on the same day of the same month became apparent
when inquiries were made a short time afterwards.   Before the
rumour reached them, the Greeks were full of fear, not so much
on their own account, as for their countrymen, and for Greece
herself, lest she should be worsted in her struggle with Mardonius.   But when the voice fell on them, their fear vanished,
and they charged more vigorously and at a quicker pace.   So
the Greeks and the barbarians rushed with like eagerness to the
fray; for the Hellespont and the Islands formed the prize for
which they were about to fight.

[1] See above, chapters 61 and 62.

102. The Athenians, and the force drawn up with them, who formed one half of the army, marched along the shore, where the country was low and level; but the way for the Lacedæmonians, and the troops with them, lay across hills and a torrent-course. Hence, while the Lacedæmonians were effecting their passage round, the Athenians on the other wing had already closed with the enemy. So long as the wicker bucklers of the Persians continued standing, they made a stout defence, and had not even the worst of the battle; but when the Athenians, and the allies with them, wishing to make the victory their own, and not share it with the Lacedæmonians, cheered each other on with shouts, and attacked them with the utmost fierceness, then at last the face of things became changed. For, bursting through the line of shields, and rushing forwards in a body, the Greeks fell upon the Persians; who, though they bore the charge and for a long time maintained their ground, yet at length took refuge in their intrenchment. Here the Athenians themselves, together with those who followed them in the line of battle, the Corinthians, the Sicyonians, and the Trœzenians, pressed so closely on the steps of their flying foes, that they entered along with them into the fortress. And now, when even their fortress was taken, the barbarians no longer offered resistance, but fled hastily away, all save only the Persians. *They* still continued to fight in knots of a few men against the Greeks, who kept pouring into the intrenchment. And here, while two of the Persian commanders fled, two fell upon the field: Artaÿntes and Ithamitres, who were leaders of the fleet,[1] escaped; Mardontes, and the commander of the land force, Tigranes, died fighting.

103. The Persians still held out, when the Lacedæmonians, and their part of the army, reached the camp, and joined in the remainder of the battle. The number of Greeks who fell in the struggle here was not small; the Sicyonians especially lost many, and, among the rest, Perilaüs their general.

The Samians, who served with the Medes, and who, although disarmed, still remained in the camp, seeing from the very beginning of the fight that the victory was doubtful, did all that lay in their power to render help to the Greeks. And the other Ionians likewise, beholding their example, revolted and attacked the Persians.

104. As for the Milesians, who had been ordered, for the

[1] Supra, viii. 130.

better security of the Persians, to guard the mountain-paths,—
that, in case any accident befell them such as had now happened,
they might not lack guides to conduct them into the high tracts
of Mycalé,—and who had also been removed to hinder them
from making an outbreak in the Persian camp; they, instead of
obeying their orders, broke them in every respect. For they
guided the flying Persians by wrong roads, which brought them
into the presence of the enemy; and at last they set upon them
with their own hands, and showed themselves the hottest of
their adversaries. Ionia, therefore, on this day revolted a
second time from the Persians.

105. In this battle the Greeks who behaved with the greatest
bravery were the Athenians; and among them the palm was
borne off by Hermolycus, the son of Euthynus, a man accomplished in the Pancratium.[1] This Hermolycus was afterwards
slain in the war between the Athenians and Carystians. He
fell in the fight near Cyrnus in the Carystian territory, and was
buried in the neighbourhood of Geræstus. After the Athenians,
the most distinguished on the Greek side were the Corinthians,
the Trœzenians, and the Sicyonians.

106. The Greeks, when they had slaughtered the greater portion of the barbarians, either in the battle or in the rout, set
fire to their ships and burnt them, together with the bulwark
which had been raised for their defence, first however removing
therefrom all the booty, and carrying it down to the beach.
Besides other plunder, they found here many caskets of money.
When they had burnt the rampart and the vessels, the Greeks
sailed away to Samos, and there took counsel together concerning the Ionians, whom they thought of removing out of
Asia. Ionia they proposed to abandon to the barbarians; and
their doubt was, in what part of their own possessions in Greece
they should settle its inhabitants. For it seemed to them a
thing impossible that they should be ever on the watch to guard
and protect Ionia; and yet otherwise there could be no hope
that the Ionians would escape the vengeance of the Persians.
Hereupon the Peloponnesian leaders proposed, that the seaport
towns of such Greeks as had sided with the Medes should be
taken away from them, and made over to the Ionians. The
Athenians, on the other hand, were very unwilling that any
removal at all should take place, and misliked the Pelopon-

[1] The Pancratium was a contest in which wrestling and boxing were
united.

nesians holding councils concerning their colonists. So, as they set themselves against the change, the Peloponnesians yielded with a good will. Hereupon the Samians, Chians, Lesbians, and other islanders, who had helped the Greeks at this time, were received into the league of the allies; and took the oaths, binding themselves to be faithful, and not desert the common cause. Then the Greeks sailed away to the Hellespont, where they meant to break down the bridges, which they supposed to be still extended across the strait.

107. The barbarians who escaped from the battle—a scanty remnant—took refuge in the heights of Mycalé, whence they made good their retreat to Sardis. During the march, Masistes, the son of Darius, who had been present at the disaster, had words with Artaÿntes, the general, on whom he showered many reproaches. He called him, among other things, " worse than a woman," for the way in which he had exercised his command, and said there was no punishment which he did not deserve to suffer for doing the king's house such grievous hurt. Now with the Persians there is no greater insult than to call a man " worse than a woman." [1] So when Artaÿntes had borne the reproaches for some while, at last he fell in a rage, and drew his scymitar upon Masistes, being fain to kill him. But a certain Halicarnassian, Xenagoras by name, the son of Praxilaüs, who stood behind Artaÿntes at the time, seeing him in the act of rushing forward, seized him suddenly round the waist, and, lifting him from his feet, dashed him down upon the ground; which gave time for the spearmen who guarded Masistes to come to his aid. By his conduct here Xenagoras gained the favour, not of Masistes only, but likewise of Xerxes himself, whose brother he had preserved from death; and the king rewarded his action by setting him over the whole land of Cilicia.[2] Except this, nothing happened upon the road; and the men continued their march and came all safe to Sardis. At Sardis they found the king, who had been there ever since he lost the sea-fight and fled from Athens to Asia.

108. During the time that Xerxes abode at this place, he fell in love with the wife of Masistes, who was likewise staying in the city. He therefore sent her messages, but failed to win her consent; and he could not dare to use violence, out of regard to Masistes, his brother. This the woman knew well enough,

---

[1] Supra, viii. 88, and ix. 20.
[2] Probably this is an overstatement, natural in one jealous for the honour of a countryman.

and hence it was that she had the boldness to resist him. So Xerxes, finding no other way open, devised a marriage between his own son Darius and a daughter of this woman and Masistes —thinking that he might better obtain his ends if he effected this union. Accordingly he betrothed these two persons to one another, and, after the usual ceremonies were completed, took his departure for Susa. When he was come there, and had received the woman into his palace as his son's bride, a change came over him, and, losing all love for the wife of Masistes, he conceived a passion for his son's bride, Masistes' daughter. And Artaÿnta—for so was she called—very soon returned his love.

109. After a while the thing was discovered in the way which I will now relate. Amestris, the wife of Xerxes, had woven with her own hands a long robe, of many colours, and very curious, which she presented to her husband as a gift. Xerxes, who was greatly pleased with it, forthwith put it on; and went in it to visit Artaÿnta, who happened likewise on this day to please him greatly. He therefore bade her ask him whatever boon she liked, and promised that, whatever it was, he would assuredly grant her request. Then Artaÿnta, who was doomed to suffer calamity together with her whole house, said to him— " Wilt thou indeed give me whatever I like to ask? " So the king, suspecting nothing less than that her choice would fall where it did, pledged his word, and swore to her. She then, as soon as she heard his oath, asked boldly for the robe. Hereupon Xerxes tried all possible means to avoid the gift; not that he grudged to give it, but because he dreaded Amestris, who already suspected, and would now, he feared, detect his love. So he offered her cities instead, and heaps of gold, and an army which should obey no other leader. (The last of these is a thoroughly Persian gift.) But, as nothing could prevail on Artaÿnta to change her mind, at the last he gave her the robe. Then Artaÿnta was very greatly rejoiced, and she often wore the garment and was proud of it. And so it came to the ears of Amestris that the robe had been given to her.

110. Now when Amestris learnt the whole matter, she felt no anger against Artaÿnta; but, looking upon her mother, the wife of Masistes, as the cause of all the mischief, she determined to compass her death. She waited, therefore, till her husband gave the great royal banquet, a feast which takes place once every year, in celebration of the king's birthday [1]—" Tykta "

---

[1] The custom of celebrating birthdays by a feast was universal in Persia. Even the poorest are said to have conformed to it.

the feast is called in the Persian tongue, which in our language may be rendered " perfect "—and this is the only day in all the year on which the king soaps his head, and distributes gifts to the Persians. Amestris waited, accordingly, for this day, and then made request of Xerxes, that he would please to give her, as her present, the wife of Masistes. But he refused; for it seemed to him shocking and monstrous to give into the power of another a woman who was not only his brother's wife, but was likewise wholly guiltless of what had happened—the more especially as he knew well enough with what intent Amestris had preferred her request.

111. At length, however, wearied by her importunity, and constrained moreover by the law of the feast, which required that no one who asked a boon that day at the king's board should be denied his request, he yielded, but with a very ill will, and gave the woman into her power.[1] Having so done, and told Amestris she might deal with her as she chose, the king called his brother into his presence, and said—

" Masistes, thou art my brother, the son of my father Darius; and, what is more, thou art a good man. I pray thee, live no longer with the wife whom thou now hast. Behold, I will give thee instead my own daughter in marriage; take her to live with thee. But part first with the wife thou now hast—I like not that thou keep to her."

To this Masistes, greatly astonished, answered—

" My lord and master, how strange a speech hast thou uttered! Thou biddest me put away my wife, who has borne me three goodly youths, and daughters besides, whereof thou hast taken one and espoused her to a son of thine own—thou biddest me put away this wife, notwithstanding that she pleases me greatly, and marry a daughter of thine! In truth, O king! that I am accounted worthy to wed thy daughter, is an honour which I mightily esteem; but yet to do as thou sayest am I in no wise willing. I pray thee, use not force to compel me to yield to thy prayer. Be sure thy daughter will find a husband to the full as worthy as myself. Suffer me then to live on with my own wife."

Thus did Masistes answer; and Xerxes, in wrath, replied—

" I will tell thee, Masistes, what thou hast gained by these words. I will not give thee my daughter; nor shalt thou live

[1] Few readers can fail to be struck by the resemblance between this scene and that described by St. Matthew, ch. xiv. 6-9, and St. Mark, vi. 21-26. In the East kings celebrated their birthdays by holding feasts and granting graces from very early times (see Gen. ch. xl. 20, 21).

any longer with thy own wife. So mayest thou learn, in time
to come, to take what is offered thee." Masistes, when he heard
this, withdrew, only saying—"Master, thou hast not yet taken
my life."

112. While these things were passing between Xerxes and
his brother Masistes, Amestris sent for the spearmen of the
royal body-guard, and caused the wife of Masistes to be mutilated
in a horrible fashion. Her two breasts, her nose, ears, and lips
were cut off and thrown to the dogs; her tongue was torn out
by the roots, and thus disfigured she was sent back to her home.

113. Masistes, who knew nothing of what had happened, but
was fearful that some calamity had befallen him, ran hastily to
his house. There, finding his wife so savagely used, he forthwith took counsel with his sons, and, accompanied by them and
certain others also, set forth on his way to Bactria, intending to
stir up revolt in that province, and hoping to do great hurt to
Xerxes: all which, I believe, he would have accomplished, if
he had once reached the Bactrian and Sacan people; for he was
greatly beloved by them both, and was moreover satrap of
Bactria. But Xerxes, hearing of his designs, sent an armed
force upon his track, and slew him while he was still upon the
road, with his sons and his whole army. Such is the tale of
King Xerxes' love and of the death of his brother Masistes.

114. Meanwhile the Greeks, who had left Mycalé, and sailed
for the Hellespont, were forced by contrary winds to anchor
near Lectum;[1] from which place they afterwards sailed on to
Abydos. On arriving here, they discovered that the bridges,
which they had thought to find standing, and which had been
the chief cause of their proceeding to the Hellespont, were
already broken up and destroyed. Upon this discovery, Leotychides, and the Peloponnesians under him, were anxious to
sail back to Greece; but the Athenians, with Xanthippus their
captain, thought good to remain, and resolved to make an
attempt upon the Chersonese. So, while the Peloponnesians
sailed away to their homes, the Athenians crossed over from
Abydos to the Chersonese, and there laid siege to Sestos.

115. Now, as Sestos was the strongest fortress in all that
region, the rumour had no sooner gone forth that the Greeks
were arrived at the Hellespont, than great numbers flocked
thither from all the towns in the neighbourhood. Among the
rest there came a certain Œobazus, a Persian, from the city of

---

[1] Lectum is the modern *Cape Baba*, the extreme point of the Troas
towards the south-west. It is mentioned by Homer.

Cardia, where he had laid up the shore-cables which had been used in the construction of the bridges. The town was guarded by its own Æolian inhabitants, but contained also some Persians, and a great multitude of their allies.

116. The whole district was under the rule of Artaÿctes, one of the king's satraps; who was a Persian, but a wicked and cruel man. At the time when Xerxes was marching against Athens, he had craftily possessed himself of the treasures belonging to Protesilaüs the son of Iphiclus,[1] which were at Elæûs in the Chersonese. For at this place is the tomb of Protesilaüs, surrounded by a sacred precinct; and here there was great store of wealth, vases of gold and silver, works in brass, garments, and other offerings, all which Artaÿctes made his prey, having got the king's consent by thus cunningly addressing him—

" Master, there is in this region the house of a Greek, who, when he attacked thy territory, met his due reward, and perished. Give me his house, I pray thee, that hereafter men may fear to carry arms against *thy* land."

By these words he easily persuaded Xerxes to give him the man's house; for there was no suspicion of his design in the king's mind. And he could say in a certain sense that Protesilaüs had borne arms against the land of the king; because the Persians consider all Asia to belong to them, and to their king for the time being. So when Xerxes allowed his request, he brought all the treasures from Elæûs to Sestos, and made the sacred land into cornfields and pasture grounds; nay, more, whenever he paid a visit to Elæûs, he polluted the shrine itself by vile uses. It was this Artaÿctes who was now besieged by the Athenians—and he was but ill prepared for defence; since the Greeks had fallen upon him quite unawares, nor had he in the least expected their coming.

117. When it was now late in the autumn, and the siege still continued, the Athenians began to murmur that they were kept abroad so long; and, seeing that they were not able to take the place, besought their captains to lead them back to their own country. But the captains refused to move, till either the city had fallen, or the Athenian people ordered them to return home. So the soldiers patiently bore up against their sufferings.

118. Meanwhile those within the walls were reduced to the last straits, and forced even to boil the very thongs of their beds

---

[1] Protesilaüs, the son of Iphiclus, was one of the Trojan heroes. He led the Thessalians of Phthiôtis, and was the first Greek who fell on the disembarkation of the army (Hom. Il. ii. 695-702).

for food. At last, when these too failed them, Artaÿctes and
Œobazus, with the native Persians, fled away from the place by
night, having let themselves down from the wall at the back of
the town, where the blockading force was scantiest. As soon as
day dawned, they of the Chersonese made signals to the Greeks
from the walls, and let them know what had happened, at the
same time throwing open the gates of their city. Hereupon,
while some of the Greeks entered the town, others, and those
the more numerous body, set out in pursuit of the enemy.

119. Œobazus fled into Thrace; but there the Apsinthian
Thracians seized him, and offered him, after their wonted
fashion, to Pleistôrus, one of the gods of their country. His
companions they likewise put to death, but in a different
manner. As for Artaÿctes and the troops with him, who had
been the last to leave the town, they were overtaken by the
Greeks, not far from Ægos-potami,[1] and defended themselves
stoutly for a time, but were at last either killed or taken prisoners.
Those whom they made prisoners the Greeks bound with chains,
and brought with them to Sestos. Artaÿctes and his son were
among the number.

120. Now the Chersonesites relate that the following prodigy
befell one of the Greeks who guarded the captives. He was
broiling upon a fire some salted fish, when of a sudden they
began to leap and quiver, as if they had been only just caught.
Hereat, the rest of the guards hurried round to look, and were
greatly amazed at the sight. Artaÿctes, however, beholding
the prodigy, called the man to him, and said—

"Fear not, Athenian stranger, because of this marvel. It has
not appeared on thy account, but on mine. Protesilaüs of
Elæûs has sent it to show me, that albeit he is dead and embalmed with salt, he has power from the gods to chastise his
injurer. Now then I would fain acquit my debt to him thus.
For the riches which I took from his temple, I will fix my fine
at one hundred talents—while for myself and this boy of mine,
I will give the Athenians two hundred talents,[2] on condition
that they will spare our lives."

Such were the promises of Artaÿctes; but they failed to
persuade Xanthippus. For the men of Elæûs, who wished to
avenge Protesilaüs, entreated that he might be put to death;
and Xanthippus himself was of the same mind. So they led

---

[1] Celebrated for the final defeat of the Athenians in the Peloponnesian
war. [See Thirlwall, *History of Greece*, vol. iv. chap. xxx.—E. H. B.]

[2] Two hundred talents would be nearly £50,000 of our money.

Artaÿctes to the tongue of land where the bridges of Xerxes
had been fixed [1]—or, according to others, to the knoll above the
town of Madytus; and, having nailed him to a board, they left
him hanging thereupon. As for the son of Artaÿctes, him they
stoned to death before his eyes.

121. This done, they sailed back to Greece, carrying with
them, besides other treasures, the shore cables from the bridges
of Xerxes, which they wished to dedicate in their temples.
And this was all that took place that year.

122. It was the grandfather of this Artaÿctes, one Artembares
by name, who suggested to the Persians a proposal which they
readily embraced, and thus urged upon Cyrus:—" Since Jove,"
they said, " has overthrown Astyages, and given the rule to
the Persians, and to thee chiefly, O Cyrus! come now, let us
quit this land wherein we dwell—for it is a scant land and a
rugged—and let us choose ourselves some other better country.
Many such lie around us, some nearer, some further off: if we
take one of these, men will admire us far more than they do
now. Who that had the power would not so act? And when
shall we have a fairer time than now, when we are lords of so
many nations, and rule all Asia?" Then Cyrus, who did not
greatly esteem the counsel, told them,—" they might do so, if
they liked—but he warned them not to expect in that case to
continue rulers, but to prepare for being ruled by others—soft
countries gave birth to soft men—there was no region which
produced very delightful fruits, and at the same time men of a
warlike spirit." So the Persians departed with altered minds,
confessing that Cyrus was wiser than they; and chose rather to
dwell in a churlish land, and exercise lordship, than to cultivate
plains, and be the slaves of others.[2]

[1] Supra, vii. 33.

[2] The work of Herodotus, though not finished throughout, is *concluded*.
This is, I think, the case both historically and artistically. Historically,
the action ends with the victorious return of the Athenian fleet from
the cruise in which they had destroyed the last remnant of the invading
host, and recovered the key of their continent, which was still held, after
all his defeats, by the invader. Artistically,—by this last chapter—the
end is brought back into a connection with the beginning—the tail of the
snake is curved round into his mouth; while at the same time the key-note
of the whole narrative is struck, its moral suggested—that victory is to
the hardy dwellers in rough and mountainous countries, who lay aside old warlike habits and sink into
inhabitants of fertile plains, who lay aside old warlike habits and sink into
sloth and luxury.

[Note the phil-Athenian feelings of Herodotus, and his anti-Ionian pre-
judices all through the latter books of his history. For the former cf. vii.
161, ix. 27. The claim of Athens to a hegemony of the Greeks at the time
of the Persian war is an anachronism. At that time Sparta was the leader.
Cf. Bury, *Ancient Greek Historians*, p. 63.—E. H. B.]

INDEX

Roman numerals refer to the two volumes of the present work

Index

Bactrians, in Xerxes' army, their equipment for war, ii. 146, 152

Barca, in Libya, Greeks settle at, i. 350; Arcesilaus, king of Cyrênê, killed by the Barcæans, 352; Pheretina, his mother, at the head of the government, 352; besieged by Persians from Egypt on her behalf, 364-365; their mines discovered by means of a shield, 365; city taken by fraud, 365; cruelty of Pheretina to the inhabitants, 365, 366; the enslaved Barcæans are given a village in Bactria, and name it Barca, 366

Barcæans, submit to Cambyses, i. 215

Battus, leader of the Greek colony in Platea, i. 347, 348; founds another colony on the mainland of Libya, 349

Battus, grandson of above, king of the Cyrenæans, i. 349, 350; deprived of his power by Demônax, 351

Beavers, i. 330

Bees, in country north of the Ister, ii. 3

Bias of Priênê, his advice to the Ionians, i. 86

Bœotians, give help to the Lacedæmonians, ii. 33; defeated by the Athenians, 34; their struggle with the Athenians at Platæa, ii. 304

Boges, governor of Eïon, his valiant conduct, ii. 159-160

Boryes, animals found in Africa, i. 362

Borysthenes (Dnieper), the, i. 294; description of its beauties, fish, pleasant taste, etc., 308, 309

Borysthenites, the, or Scythian husbandmen, i. 294, 318

Bosphorus, the, i. 321, 322; pillars erected on its shores by Darius, 322; bridge thrown across for him 322; memorial of, left by its architect, 322, 323

Branchidæ, temple of Apollo at, i. 197; treasures given to by Crœsus, ii. 15, 16

Bubares, son of Megabazus, is bribed by Alexander of Macedon to hush up the death of the Persia ambassadors, ii. 8

Bubastis (Diana), goddess of the Egyptians, her temple, i. 185, 196

Budini, the, i. 295; colour of their eyes and hair, 329; their build-

ings entirely of wood, 329; their worship of Bacchus, 329; their language, 329; they feed on lice, 329; agree to help the Scythians, 333

Bulis, story of, and Sperthias, ii. 169-171

Busiris, i. 144

Buto, oracle of Latona at, i. 143, 144, 193, 195

Byblus (Papyrus), i. 158

Cabalians, the, African tribe, i. 354; in Xerxes' army, their equipment for war, ii. 149

Cabiri, the Phœnician gods, i. 140, 229

Cadmeian characters engraved on tripods, ii. 25, 26

Cadmus, ii. 24, 25

Cadmus, native of Cos, sent by Gelo to watch the war between Greeks and Persians, ii. 183, 184

Calantian Indians, i. 258

Calascirians, warrior class in Egypt, i. 200, 201

Callatians, their custom of eating their fathers, i. 229

Callatêbus, manufacture of honey by inhabitants of, ii. 133

Callimachus, polemarch at Athens, is persuaded by Miltiades to vote for war, ii. 101, 102; leads the right wing at Marathon, 102; is killed, 103

Callicrates, his beauty and death, ii. 307

Callisté, Cadmus at, i. 344; arrival of Theras and the Lacedæmonians at, 347. See Thera

Cambyses, marries daughter of king of the Medes, i. 57; ascends the Persian throne, 110; cause of his expedition against Egypt, 210, 211; obtains safe-conduct through the Syrian Desert, 213; conquers Egypt, 214, 215; takes Memphis, 215; his treatment of Psammenitus, 216, 217; insults and burns the body of Amasis, 217, 218; plans expeditions against the Carthaginians, Ammonians, and Ethiopians, 218; sends spies into Ethiopia, 219, 220; proceeds on his expedition against, 222; his men lack food and turn cannibals, 222; forced to give up the expedition, 222; slays the priests of Apis, 223, 224;

CONTENTS OF VOLUME ONE

THE FIRST BOOK, ENTITLED CLIO

THE SECOND BOOK, ENTITLED EUTERPÉ

Contents

THE THIRD BOOK, ENTITLED THALIA

Contents

THE FOURTH BOOK, ENTITLED MELPOMENE

Contents